# BEST
# TIPS
# & PROJECTS
# 2014

# THE FAMILY
# Handyman®

# BEST
# TIPS
# & PROJECTS
# 2014

by The Editors of *The Family Handyman* magazine

**THE FAMILY HANDYMAN BEST TIPS & PROJECTS 2014**
(See page 288 for complete staff listing.)
Editor in Chief: Ken Collier
Project Editor: Teresa Marrone
Contributing Designers: Joel Anderson, Teresa Marrone
Contributing Copy Editors: Donna Bierbach, Peggy Parker
Indexing: Stephanie Reymann

Vice President, Group Publisher: Russell S. Ellis

The Reader's Digest Association, Inc.
President & Chief Executive Officer: Robert E. Guth

ISBN 978-1-62145-181-5

Address any comments about *The Family Handyman Best Tips & Projects 2014* to:
Editor, Best Tips & Projects 2014
2915 Commers Drive, Suite 700
Eagan, MN 55121

To order additional copies of *The Family Handyman Best Tips & Projects 2014,* call 1-800-344-2560.

For more Reader's Digest products and information, visit our Web site at rd.com.
For more about *The Family Handyman* magazine, visit familyhandyman.com.

Printed in the United States of America.
1  3  5  7  9  10  8  6  4  2

# SAFETY FIRST–ALWAYS!

Tackling home improvement projects and repairs can be endlessly rewarding. But as most of us know, with the rewards come risks. DIYers use chain saws, climb ladders and tear into walls that can contain big and hazardous surprises.

The good news is, armed with the right knowledge, tools and procedures, homeowners can minimize risk. As you go about your projects and repairs, stay alert for these hazards:

## Aluminum wiring

Aluminum wiring, installed in about 7 million homes between 1965 and 1973, requires special techniques and materials to make safe connections. This wiring is dull gray, not the dull orange characteristic of copper. Hire a licensed electrician certified to work with it. For more information go to cpsc.gov and search for "aluminum wiring."

## Spontaneous combustion

Rags saturated with oil finishes like Danish oil and linseed oil, and oil-based paints and stains can spontaneously combust if left bunched up. Always dry them outdoors, spread out loosely. When the oil has thoroughly dried, you can safely throw them in the trash.

## Vision and hearing protection

Safety glasses or goggles should be worn whenever you're working on DIY projects that involve chemicals, dust and anything that could shatter or chip off and hit your eye. Sounds louder than 80 decibels (dB) are considered potentially dangerous. Sound levels from a lawn mower can be 90 dB, and shop tools and chain saws can be 90 to 100 dB.

## Lead paint

If your home was built before 1979, it may contain lead paint, which is a serious health hazard, especially for children six and under. Take precautions when you scrape or remove it. Contact your public health department for detailed safety information or call (800) 424-LEAD (5323) to receive an information pamphlet. Or visit epa.gov/lead.

## Buried utilities

A few days before you dig in your yard, have your underground water, gas and electrical lines marked. Just call 811 or go to call811.com.

## Smoke and carbon monoxide (CO) alarms

Almost two-thirds of home fire deaths from 2003 to 2006 resulted from fires in homes with missing or nonworking smoke alarms. Test your smoke alarms every month, replace batteries as necessary and replace units that are more than 10 years old. As you make your home more energy-efficient and airtight, existing ducts and chimneys can't always successfully vent combustion gases, including potentially deadly carbon monoxide (CO). Install a UL-listed CO detector, and test your CO and smoke alarms at the same time.

## Five-gallon buckets and window covering cords

Since 1984, more than 275 children have drowned in 5-gallon buckets. Always store them upside down and store ones containing liquid with the covers securely snapped.

According to Parents for Window Blind Safety, over 500 children have been seriously injured or killed in the United States in the past few decades after becoming entangled in looped window treatment cords. For more information, visit pfwbs.org or cpsc.gov.

## Working up high

If you have to get up on your roof to do a repair or installation, always install roof brackets and wear a roof harness.

## Asbestos

Texture sprayed on ceilings before 1978, adhesives and tiles for vinyl and asphalt floors before 1980, and vermiculite insulation (with gray granules) all may contain asbestos. Other building materials, made between 1940 and 1980, could also contain asbestos. If you suspect that materials you're removing or working around contain asbestos, contact your health department or visit epa.gov/asbestos for information.

For additional information about home safety, visit mysafehome.org. This site offers helpful information about dozens of home safety issues.

# Contents

# 5 EXTERIOR REPAIRS & IMPROVEMENTS

# 6 OUTDOOR STRUCTURES, LANDSCAPING & GARDENING

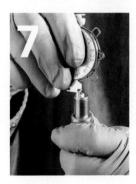

# 7 VEHICLES & GARAGES

# 1 Interior Projects, Repairs & Remodeling

## IN THIS CHAPTER

## CHEATER'S CHAIR FIX

I know this isn't the proper way to repair furniture, but I had this ugly, rickety kitchen chair that was almost worthless. There was no way I was going to spend hours disassembling and regluing it. So I just drilled pilot holes and drove trim head screws through the bottom of the rungs and into the legs.

I didn't expect this crude fix to last long, but 15 years later, that chair is still in my kitchen, still rock solid and still ugly. If you want to cheat at a chair repair, be sure to use screws that are long enough to run through the rungs and well into the legs.

Jeff Gorton,
Associate
Editor

## ANCHORING TO CONCRETE BLOCK

**SLEEVE ANCHOR**

Fastening heavy items to concrete block is simple if you use the right tools and fasteners. Where most people mess up is in thinking they can use plastic anchors. Uh, no. At the very least you should use a lag shield, but even then, you can use that type of anchor only when mounting to one of the three solid sections of the block.

Sleeve anchors are a better option because they work in the solid and hollow sections of the block, as well as the mortar joints. Here are two important tips when you're installing sleeve anchors.

**1** **Get rid of the dust in the hole.** Leaving drilling dust in the hole will reduce the fastener's holding power. So remove it with a vacuum or blower. A baby's ear syringe (about $5 at any drugstore) works great for this (keep one in your toolbox). Just shove it into the hole and puff out the dust.

**2** **Protect the threads while you pound the bolt.** Protect the bolt threads by unscrewing the nut until it extends slightly past the bolt threads. Then drive it home with light hammer blows.

## MOLDY CRAWL SPACE INSULATION

*I have a crawl space with insulation attached to the floor joists. I recently discovered mold growing on the insulation's paper backing. What kind of vapor barrier should I install?*

Some homeowners use poly sheeting; others add more outside venting. Unfortunately, the fix isn't that simple. A vapor barrier may prevent hot, humid air from condensing on the insulation in the summer. But then it would trap moisture inside the insulation in the winter. And adding venting can make the problem even worse.

Instead of venting, some building professionals now recommend "conditioning" the crawl space. For a complete description of this approach and the logic behind it, go to buildingscience.com, click on "information" and download research paper RR-0401. Then consult a few local contractors to see if they've used this approach in your area.

## LUBE A STICKING VINYL WINDOW OR DOOR

When vinyl windows and doors don't operate smoothly, it's usually because gunk has built up in the channels. But sometimes even clean

windows and doors can bind. Try spraying dry lubricant on the contact points and wiping it off with a rag. Don't use oil lubricants; they can attract dirt, and some can damage the vinyl. Pella recommends Teflon Dry Lubricant. Our daughter was getting quotes to replace her 10-year-old patio door when this "one-minute fix" saved her a lot of money.

Alena Gust, Field Editor

DRY LUBRICANT

## TOP 7 WINDOW CLEANING TIPS FROM A PRO

Brad Bolt is a Field Editor and a pro window cleaner. Here are some of his favorite DIY tips.

Brad Bolt, Owner of Clearly Professional Window Cleaning, Maricopa, AZ

**1** Use two different scrubbers– one for inside and one for outside— so you don't carry pollutants and bird excrement inside.

**2** Any kitchen dish liquid cleans dirt and grease and leaves the glass slippery so your squeegee glides well. A 100 percent biodegradable soap will protect sensitive plants outside. Inside, it will protect toddlers and pets who put their mouth on the windows or sills.

**3** A 12- to 14-in. squeegee is a good size for most situations. Put in a new rubber blade after each cleaning to prevent streaks.

**4** Mr. Clean Magic Eraser removes silicone caulk and water drips.

**5** Carry two detailing rags—one for dirty jobs like sills and the other for detailing the edges of the glass.

**6** A paint can opener is perfect for popping out window screens.

**7** A razor blade removes paint overspray and gunk. Keep the glass wet and use a new blade each time. Microscopic rust particles on the blade can scratch the glass.

# HomeCare & Repair

## STUCK-ON RUBBER COASTERS

*I have hardwood floors and made the mistake of using rubber coasters under my sofa. Now they're stuck to the floor. What's the best way to remove them and prevent this from happening again?*

Without knowing how the floors were finished, it's pretty hard to give you a definitive answer. Some people have had luck with WD-40 or adhesive solvents like Goo Gone. But test either product in a hidden spot first. Even then, clean up the petroleum residue ASAP to avoid damaging the finish. When you shop for new coasters, look for the words "non-staining" or "approved for use on hardwood floors" on the package. These coasters use a specially formulated O-ring material that's safe for hardwood and laminate flooring. Slipstick is one brand, available in various sizes at amazon.com.

O-RING

## SILICONE REPAIR TAPE

This tape is unique. It has no adhesive; it's just pure silicone. When you wrap it around something, the silicone essentially welds to itself to form a single flexible unit. No gaps, no slipping and no end to come undone.

Silicone tape is amazing stuff: It's an electrical insulator and it resists just about everything (oil, solvents, acids, salt water). It's heat-proof to 500 degrees F and flexible at arctic temperatures. I've personally used it to fix electrical cords, wrap cables on my trailer and make a heat-proof grip for a frying pan. I've heard stories of people using it to make gaskets, repair high-pressure hoses, even make an emergency fan belt by wrapping the tape around rope. In short, it's a miracle worker.

It has only one drawback: It ain't cheap. A 12-ft. roll, 1 in. wide, is about 10 bucks. The brand I use is called Rescue Tape, and I buy it online. Expensive or not, it's got a permanent place in my toolbox.

Ken Collier,
Editor in Chief

DRAWER BOX FRONT

POLYURETHANE GLUE

DRAWER FRONT

QUARTER-ROUND

## REINFORCE A DRAWER FRONT

My most recent quick fix was to a drawer front that one of my kids pulled off. I cut a couple of lengths of quarter-round the same height as the drawer sides. I held them in place while I drilled a couple of holes through the sides and front of the drawer box. I dabbed some polyurethane glue (wood glue doesn't stick well to finished surfaces) on the pieces of quarter-round before screwing them into place. Once the drawer front was screwed back on, all that was left was to wait for my kids to break something else... I didn't wait long.

Melanie Ternes,
Field Editor

# REBUILD AN OFFICE CHAIR

SPRING CLIP

GAS CYLINDER SHAFT

**1** **Remove the clip and pedestal.** Jam a needle-nose pliers into the spring clip and pull it off. Then lift the pedestal off the chair.

If the lift mechanism in your office chair is shot but the upholstery portion is still in good shape, don't toss the chair. Fix it! You can replace the gas cylinder yourself for about $40 (search online for "office chair parts").

Rebuilding the lift mechanism is a two-part process. First you have to disassemble the lift mechanism so you can measure the size of the gas cylinder and order the new part. You'll need a needle-nose pliers, a pipe wrench with a long handle, and a helper. Disassembly takes about a half hour. Then you just reassemble when the part arrives. That only takes 15 minutes, and you can do it without a helper.

Start by flipping the chair upside down on your workbench. Then remove the spring retaining clip on the bottom of the pedestal (**Photo 1**). Next, lift the entire pedestal and column off the chair. Lift off the bearing, washers and rubber bumper and keep the parts together for reuse. Remove the telescoping trim bezel (**Photo 2**).

Then grab your pipe wrench and helper and remove the cylinder (**Photo 3**). If it won't budge, soak it with rust penetrant and tap with a hammer to set up vibrations. Then try the wrench again.

Measure the length of the gas cylinder from the bottom of the taper to the top. Don't include the piston rod in the measurement. Then measure the cylinder width at the widest part. Order the replacement from a chair parts Web site.

To reassemble, just push the tapered end of the cylinder into the chair seat and install the telescoping trim bezel. Slide on the rubber bumper. Then lubricate the bearing with grease and install it back on the piston rod with the original washers. Next, slide the pedestal base and column over the rod and secure the piston rod with the washer and spring clip. Finish the job by turning the chair right side up and bouncing on it a few times. Your weight will drive the tapered gas cylinder into the seat retainer. Then raise the lift mechanism to the proper height and get back to work.

TRIM BEZEL

**2** **Remove the trim bezel.** Grab the smallest portion of the telescoping trim bezel and twist it while you pull the entire trim assembly off the gas cylinder. It's just a friction fit.

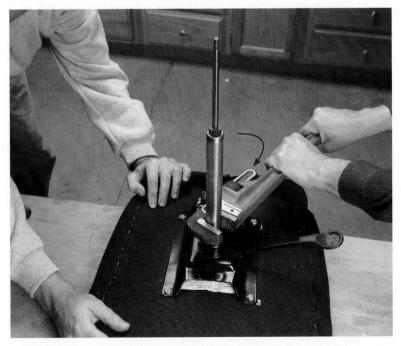

**3** **Twist the gas cylinder.** Use a pipe wrench to loosen the press-fit gas cylinder (there are no threads). Then lift the cylinder out of the tilt mechanism.

# SMART REMODELING

*Work smarter, not harder*

by **Mark Petersen, Contributing Editor**

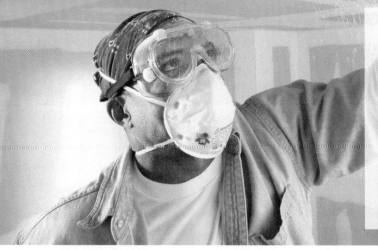

The key to a smart remodeling project is efficiency. And in order to be efficient, you need to work fast, safe and clean. You have to contain the mess in the areas you're working in, and protect those areas you're not. You also need to think ahead and organize the job materials, both the new and the old. These tips will help your next project run smoother, save you time and money, and prove to your customer that you're a true pro.

## Protect finished flooring with hardboard

Rosin paper, cardboard and dropcloths are all legit ways to protect a floor—that is, until you knock your trim gun off the top of a 6-ft. ladder. If you really want to ensure that a floor stays dent- and scratch-free, cover it with 1/8-in. hardboard. It's pretty cheap (less than $10 a sheet at home centers), and as the name suggests, it's pretty hard. Cut the sheets with a circular saw or jigsaw, and to prevent scratches, make sure both the floor and the hardboard are perfectly clean before you lay the hardboard down. Tape the seams with masking tape to keep the dirt and debris from slipping through the cracks. When the job is done, pull up the sheets and save them for the next job.

## Blow the dust outside

Set a box fan in a window and blow the dust out of your work area. Wedge the fan into place with scrap pieces of foam and a few rags. For the best results, open windows beyond the dusty area or on the opposite side of the room to help keep the air moving in the right direction.

## Know when to have it delivered

Before you load those 80 sheets of drywall onto your trailer and shear the axle on the freeway, ask about your delivery options. Most suppliers charge a fee, but you need to weigh that fee against your time, your gas and your back. Maneuvering 8-ft. sheets of drywall up a narrow stairway doesn't make sense if a crane truck can deliver 12-ft. sheets right up to a second-story window. And humping 60 bundles of shingles up a ladder is just plain silly when you can have them hoisted right onto the roof.

## Make big pieces

Tearing out drywall can be frustrating because it always seems to crumble into little pieces, and it takes a long time to demo a wall one handful at time. Take a little extra time to find the seams between the sheets, and cut them open with a utility knife. Then bust out a couple of holes for your hands to fit through. Instead of pulling super-hard right away, tug and wiggle the drywall away from the studs until the screw heads break through.

## Faster concrete fastening

A concrete screw installation tool allows you to use one tool without having to switch between a masonry bit and a screw-driving bit. Just drill the hole and slip the driver shaft over the masonry bit and then sink the screw. If you have a bunch of concrete fasteners to install, it's definitely worth the money (about $30 at home centers). The Tapcon version shown here is one of several brands.

## Separate your lumber

When you unload lumber, set the studs, top plates and bottom plates in different piles. That way, every time you start a new wall section, you won't have to move 20 studs to grab the top plate buried at the bottom of the pile. Also, moving lumber from one side of the room to the other is not an efficient use of time, so make sure your pile is located in a close but out-of-the-way location.

## Pull those nails

A good rule of thumb: "Never let a chunk of lumber leave your hand until you've dealt with the nails." If you're going to reuse lumber from a demo job, make sure you pull the nails right away. If you aren't going to reuse the wood, just bend the nails over. Stepping on a nail is a bad way to remember that it's been 10 years since your last tetanus shot.

## Be a smart packer

Renting a trash bin isn't cheap, so take advantage of every square inch of it by strategically placing the debris in the container instead of tossing it in willy-nilly. Long boards should always run the length of the container. Set in large, hollow items like bathtubs or sinks open side up so you can fill them in instead of creating a void.

Use small pieces to fill in and around large ones. Think of the debris as puzzle pieces, each with its own proper spot. If your trash bin has a door, don't park the bin so close to the house that you can't open it. Walking in heavy items is a lot easier than lifting them over the side. Also, make sure you order the proper size. If you explain your project to the sanitation company, the staff should be able to suggest a bin size that's right for your project.

## Make a plastic passage

Hanging sheets of plastic from the ceiling is a good way to isolate a room that's being remodeled. But instead of hanging one continuous sheet to keep the dust in, hang two and overlap them 4 ft. or so. That way you'll have a handy door to walk through, which beats having to duck under the plastic every time you come and go. Lay a scrap piece of lumber on the bottom of the plastic to keep it in place.

## Cover the return air vents

A furnace is an extremely efficient tool to spread dust from a room under construction to all the other rooms in the house. Sure, an expensive furnace filter may catch most of the dust, but it'll also get clogged in hours, instead of weeks, and running a furnace with a clogged filter could result in costly furnace repairs.

Avoid these problems by covering the return air vents in, or near, the area where you're working. If you're kicking up a dust storm, shut the furnace down until that phase of the job is done, and replace the furnace filter once the whole job is done.

## Knock it off from the back side

Who says you have to *pull* drywall from the wall? If the drywall on one side of a wall has already been removed, pound off the other side from the back with a sledgehammer. You should be able to remove several large chunks at a time if you keep the blows close to studs and don't pound too hard.

## Save those buckets

Buckets are a remodeler's best friend. They work great for mixing, hauling heavy debris, storing water, dragging tools in and out, organizing fasteners, setting stuff on, bailing water, sitting on. There's a reason why home centers sell empty ones. Never, ever throw away a usable bucket!

## Lay down a protective path

It's impossible to demo a wall or bust up a floor without making a mess, but that doesn't mean you need to track that mess all over the rest of the house. The next time you have to tear out some carpet, cut several long strips, and use them as pathways to protect the flooring in other areas of the house. Make sure to flip the carpet upside down so the abrasive backing won't scratch the finish on wood floors. Canvas drop cloths are still the best method for protecting stair treads. A 4-ft. x 15-ft. drop cloth costs about $18 at home centers.

DROP CLOTH

SALVAGED CARPET

## Organize tools by the job

Knowing exactly which tools you'll need for every job is next to impossible. Organize your toolboxes and storage bins according to the work that needs to be done. A box for plumbing tools, electrical, drywall, etc. No doubt this will lead to owning more than one of the same tool. But you won't believe how much time you'll save having all the proper tools on hand.

## Clean up every day

It's tempting to leave the mess at the end of the day, knowing you're just going to mess up the site again the next day, but a true professional leaves a job site clean. You may be the best at what you do, but your customers won't be able to recognize your craftsmanship through all that filth, especially if it gets tracked around the house while you're gone. Also, showing up at a pigsty is just not a positive way to start your workday.

## Throw together a junk station

As soon as the major demo is completed, make yourself a junk station. Bring extra sawhorses, and throw a couple of boards or a piece of plywood on them. It's smart to have a central location for your tools, fasteners, batteries and chargers, radio, beverages and whatever else it takes to get the job done. Having items scattered all over the job site floor makes cleanup harder, and wandering around looking for the stuff you need is a waste of time.

# MODERN TRICKS FOR MODERN TILE

*New techniques and tips for this updated favorite*

by **Jeff Gorton, Associate Editor**

Tile just keeps getting bigger and bigger—in popularity and in size. The materials have changed too: Ceramic is still around, but porcelain and glass are now almost as common. Our tile guru, Dean, has had to change how he works. Here are some of his tips.

**MEET AN EXPERT**

Dean Sorem has been setting tile for more than three decades and prides himself on keeping up with the latest products, tools and techniques.

# 1 Pick a large-notched trowel for big tile

Tiles up to 2 ft. square have become more popular, and they require a deep layer of thin-set to allow for adjustments. To get the right amount of thin-set, use a 1/2 x 1/2-in. notched trowel for tiles up to 16 in. square, and a 3/4 x 3/4-in. notched trowel for larger tiles. Don't forget: Using large notched trowels means you'll need a lot more thin-set. As a general rule, a 50-lb. bag of thin-set will cover about 40 to 50 sq. ft. using a 1/2 x 1/2-in. notched trowel, and about 30 to 40 sq. ft. using a 3/4 x 3/4-in. notched trowel. When using large notched trowels, buy thin-set labeled "medium bed," "large tile" or "large format."

3/4" x 3/4" NOTCHED TROWEL

1/2" x 1/2" NOTCHED TROWEL

MEDIUM-BED THIN-SET

CARDBOARD SHIMS

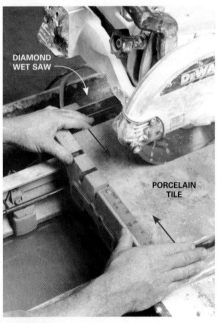

DIAMOND WET SAW

PORCELAIN TILE

# 2 Cut without cracking the tile

You'll need a diamond wet saw to cut large porcelain tiles. Dean recommends renting a contractor-quality saw for about $60 per day rather than buying a cheapie. But even with a saw like this, tiles larger than about 8 in. square have a tendency to crack before you finish the cut, often ruining the tile. You can help prevent this by pressing the two pieces together as you near completion of the cut. Holding the tile like this stabilizes it and dampens vibration, resulting in a cleaner cut.

GROUT HAZE

# 3 Upgrade your grout sponge

It's hard to get the last bit of grout haze off using a grout sponge. After the grout dries, you usually have to polish off the remaining cloudy layer with a rag. But if you finish your grout cleanup with a micro-fiber sponge, you'll end up with a job so clean you may not have to do anything more.

Start your cleanup with the plain side of the sponge after the grout firms up. If you need more information on this process, go to familyhandyman.com and search for "tile grout." Then when the joints are nicely shaped and most of the grout is off the face of the tile, switch to the microfiber side of the sponge. You'll find microfiber sponges for about $3 at home centers and tile shops.

MICROFIBER SPONGE

# 4 Flatten the framing

Old-school tile setters made up for wavy walls by installing wire lath and floating a layer of mortar over it. But modern tile backer boards simply follow along the crooked wall, and if you don't fix the wall, you'll have a wavy tile job.

The best solution is to straighten the walls before you install the backer board. Lay a straightedge against the walls to find high and low spots. In most cases, you can fix problems by adding shims to the face of the studs until the faces all line up. But if you have just one protruding stud, then it may be quicker to plane it down with a power planer or replace it if you can.

Dean prefers thin paper shims as shown (available in the drywall section of some home centers) because they provide precise control over shim thickness and can be offset to create a tapered shim. You can make your own thin shims from heavy felt paper or thin cardboard. Staple the shims in place.

## 5 Back-butter large tiles

The increased surface area of tiles larger than about 8 x 8 in. makes it critical that you butter the back to ensure a strong bond. It takes only a few extra seconds per tile to spread a thin layer of thin-set on the back of the tile with the flat side of the trowel. Then when you set the tile, this thin layer bonds easily with the layer you've troweled onto the floor or wall and creates a strong connection.

Dean also butters the back of larger transparent glass tiles to provide a consistent color. Otherwise you'll see air bubbles and other imperfections in the thin-set through the transparent glass.

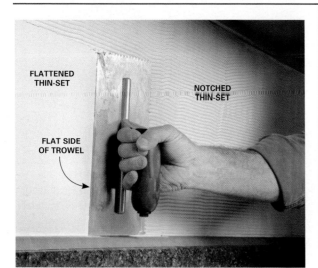

## 6 Flatten thin-set before installing mosaic tile

Mosaic tile is typically thin, and it has a lot of grout joints. If you simply apply thin-set with a notched trowel and embed the sheets of mosaic in it, the ridges of thin-set will squeeze out of all those grout joints and you'll have a real mess to clean up.

The way to avoid this is to flatten the ridges with the flat side of the trowel before you set the mosaic tiles in it. Use the notched side of a 1/4 x 1/4-in. V-notched trowel first to apply the right amount of thin-set. Then flip the trowel over to the flat side and, holding the trowel fairly flat to the surface and using medium pressure, flatten the ridges. Now you can safely embed the sheets of mosaic tile without worrying about thin-set filling the grout joints.

## 7 Level mosaic tile with a block

Mosaic tiles are so small and numerous that getting their faces flush using just your fingers is nearly impossible. But tamping them with a flat block of wood creates a perfectly aligned surface in no time. Make a tamping block out of any flat scrap of wood. An 8-in. length of hardwood 1x6 or a 6 x 8-in. rectangle of plywood is perfect. After you set several square feet of mosaic tile, pat the tile into the thin-set with the tamping block. Hold the block in place and bump it with your fist to flatten the mosaic. Repeat the tamping process on each new section of tile you install.

## 8 Clean grout joints with a toothbrush

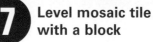

No matter how careful you are, you're bound to end up with some thin-set in the joints between tiles. And if you allow it to harden, it'll interfere with your grout job. A toothbrush works great to clean excess thin-set from grout joints, especially for the skinny joints between mosaic tiles. Let the thin-set get firm, but not hard, before you start the cleanup process. If you try to clean up thin-set too soon, you risk disturbing the tiles.

 **9** **Make a custom trowel**

Dean has discovered that inexpensive auto-body filler spatulas, available at home centers and auto parts stores, are perfect for making custom trowels for special circumstances. One way Dean uses a custommade trowel is for insetting thinner tiles into a field of thicker tiles. After finishing the field tile installation, he cuts notches on each edge of the spatula with a utility knife to create a mini screed. He cuts the notches about 1/16 in. deeper than the thickness of the decorative tile to allow for thin-set. Then he uses this trowel to add a layer of thin-set that acts as a shim when it hardens (top photo). After this layer hardens, he cuts 3/16-in.-deep teeth in the spatula to make a notched trowel and uses it to apply thin-set (middle photo). Now when he sets the decorative tile, it's perfectly flush with the field tile (bottom photo).

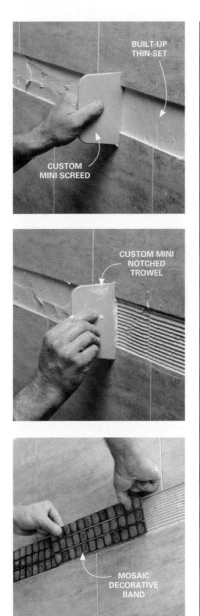

BUILT-UP THIN-SET

CUSTOM MINI SCREED

CUSTOM MINI NOTCHED TROWEL

MOSAIC DECORATIVE BAND

**10** **Finish your job with premium grout**

There's been a revolution in grout technology over the past several years, and all of the big-name grout producers have modern grout that's easier to apply, denser, more stain resistant and more colorfast than standard grout. These new grouts also cure faster and are resistant to mold and mildew.

You no longer have to mix in latex additives, worry about uneven or blotchy grout joints or decide between sanded and unsanded grout. Power Grout, Custom Building Products' Prism and Fusion Pro grouts, and Laticrete's PermaColor are a few examples of premium grout. You may have to visit a specialty tile store to find them, though. The formulas vary, but all of these will outperform standard grout. And some, like Power Grout and Fusion Pro, don't even require sealing, saving you time and money.

Premium grouts are more expensive, of course, and might add $20 to $50 to the total cost of your project. But considering all the other costs (and all your hard work), premium grout is a bargain.

## CAULK PROBLEMS IN A TILE SHOWER

*I have a ceramic tile shower that's 15 years old. I have to caulk it at least twice a year because the caulk develops mildew and comes loose. I scrape off the old caulk and clean the tile with mineral spirits, denatured alcohol and, lately, even vinegar and water. Then I let it dry for 24 hours before applying a latex kitchen/bath caulk that's supposed to resist mold. What am I doing wrong?*

You either have residue from a previous application of silicone caulk or a problem with water seepage behind the tile. If anyone has ever used silicone caulk on the tile and the residue was not properly removed, that'll cause bonding problems for the new caulk. Silicone residue must be removed with silicone remover before you apply any new caulk, even new silicone. Find silicone remover products in the paint department at any home center or at any paint store.

Rather than reinstall a latex caulk, you may want to try one of the newer "advanced polymer sealants" (DAP 3.0 is one brand). They seal better and resist mildew better than many latex formulas. And seal the grout, too. If the caulk still comes loose, you probably have water penetration behind the tile. That would be the time to throw in the towel and call a tile pro.

# LUXURY VINYL

*A kinder, gentler tile*

by **Mark Petersen,
Contributing Editor**

**W**e wanted to find out what was behind all the buzz about luxury vinyl tile (LVT). Why are people opting for vinyl when they can get ceramic tile for about the same price?

So we tracked down Andy and Nate from Distinctive Flooring in Burnsville, MN. They've been installing LVT floors for several years now and told us that it's the fastest grow-ing portion of their business.

Nate and Andy

Andy says, "Our customers love it because it feels good under their feet and because there are hundreds of colors and patterns to choose from, and we love it because it's easy to work with." LVT is definitely a DIY project, espe-cially with these tips from the pros.

## What the heck is LVT?

Luxury vinyl tile (LVT) has been installed in commercial buildings for years, but now it's finding its way into more and more homes. It looks like tile and is priced similarly, and both are waterproof and groutable, but there are big differences.

LVT is softer and feels warmer underfoot, which is especially nice in bathrooms. Ceramic is harder to scratch, but LVT won't crack if you drop your cast iron skillet. If a piece of LVT does get damaged, it's much easier to replace. LVT has a lower profile, which makes it easier to work with around cabinets, existing door openings and transitions. LVT can be installed over some existing floor-ing and is far more DIY-friendly.

## Prep the floor

LVT can be glued down directly to plywood subfloors as long as the wood is smooth, flat and structurally sound, but not over wafer board, particleboard or oriented strand board (OSB).

Most floors aren't perfect, so find high and low spots with a straightedge. Sand down the high spots with a belt sander using a 40- or 60-grit belt. This is a dusty job, so turn off your furnace to avoid spreading dust all over the house, and wear a dust mask.

Fill the low spots (1/4-in. dip in 3 ft.), gaps and seams in the plywood with floor patch (**Photo 1**). If the plywood is in pretty rough shape, the pros will skim-coat the whole

floor with floor patch. This seems like a big job but takes only a few minutes. Andy prefers Ardex Feather Finish but says the products sold at home centers will work too. Buy a Portland cement–based product—the gypsum-based patches crack easier. Henry and SimplePrep are two other brands.

LVT can be installed directly over concrete, but the concrete must be at least six weeks old, proven to be dry, and free of powder and flaking. It also needs to be free of solvent, wax, grease, oil, paint and any other sealing com-pounds. Large cracks and expansion joints should be filled and troweled smooth. The same floor patch you would use on wood floors should also work for concrete.

PLYWOOD SEAM

6" TAPER'S KNIFE

**1** **Fill gaps and seams.** LVT will follow the profile of the existing subfloor, so make sure you fill in seams, low spots and large gaps with floor patch.

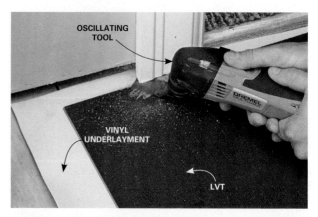

OSCILLATING TOOL

VINYL UNDERLAYMENT

LVT

**2** **Trim jambs and casing.** Undercut door trim so you can slip tiles underneath. Use a tile and underlayment as a guide. If you don't have an oscillating saw, a handsaw will work just fine.

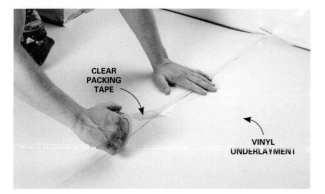

**3** **Install underlayment.** Roll out the underlayment and tape the seams. If your existing floor is in good shape, you might be able to skip this step and glue the tile directly to the floor.

**4** **Mark the first tile location.** Once you have your layout figured out, use a tile to mark the location of the first tile. Make sure it's by the door, where you'll have to start tiling.

## Dealing with trim

Your installation will be easier and you'll end up with a cleaner look if you remove the base trim before you install the new floor. However, if the new LVT floor will be lower than the floor you removed, you may want to leave the base on. If the base trim is removed and reinstalled lower, there will be a noticeable gap on the wall, which may require painting. If you don't want to mess with painting, install base shoe molding at the bottom of the trim.

There's no reason to pull off door trim, unless the new floor is going to be significantly lower and you need to install longer casing or rehang the door. You'll have to trim off a bit of the casing if the new floor will be higher. An oscillating tool works great to accomplish this task. An upside-down tile and whatever underlayment you plan on using are the perfect height for a guide (**Photo 2**).

## Underlayment options

If your wooden subfloor is in really rough shape, install 1/4-in. plywood underlayment over it.

Another option is to install a vinyl underlayment. This will allow you to lay LVT over all sorts of surfaces: plywood, particleboard, OSB, ceramic tile, sheet vinyl or painted cement. Buy the product recommended by the tile manufacturer.

One thing to consider when using a vinyl underlayment: The tile is adhered to the vinyl, but the vinyl is not attached to anything else, so the floor will "float" above the surface. The only drawback to a floating floor is that it expands and contracts more than a permanently fastened floor. This means you'll have to leave a 1/4-in. gap around the perimeter of the room and all floor vents to allow for expansion. And avoid setting more than one extremely heavy object (pool table, piano, large bookcase) in a room with a floating floor—pinning the flooring down in two or more locations won't allow it to expand between those points, which may cause the flooring to buckle.

Vinyl underlayment is easy to install. Just lay it down, cut it with a knife or heavy-duty scissors, and tape the seams with packing tape (**Photo 3**). We used Mannington underlayment, which costs 40¢ per sq. ft.

**5** **Spread the adhesive.** Spread the adhesive with a small notched trowel. Cover every inch, and don't leave puddles. Start at the end of the room and work your way toward the door.

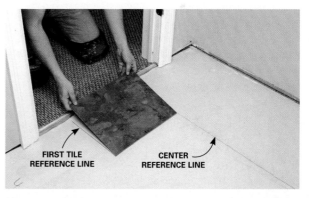

**6** **Lay the first tile carefully.** Position the first tile perfectly, because all the other tiles in the room will line up with that one.

## What it takes:

**Materials cost:** $2 to $6 per sq. ft. (not including base shoe, floor patch or underlayment)
**Skill:** Beginner to intermediate
**Time:** One day for a bathroom
**Tools:** Tape measure, utility knife, oscillating tool, heat gun, chalk line, rigid rubber trowel, notched trowel

## Figure A   Bad tile layout

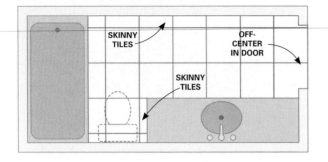

SKINNY TILES

OFF-CENTER IN DOOR

SKINNY TILES

## Figure B   Good tile layout

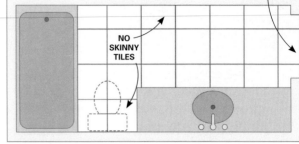

TILE CENTERED IN DOOR

NO SKINNY TILES

Whichever underlayment you choose, you'll still have to knock down ridges and fill in the severe dips in the subfloor. And underlayment is not a solution to a rotten or structurally unsound subfloor.

### Lay out the pattern

Balance is the key to any good layout. Try to avoid ending with a row of narrow tiles along any wall (**Figure A**). And if at all possible, center either a grout line or a full tile in the middle of the doorway (**Figure B**). Nate starts by snapping two centerlines dividing the room into four equal quarters. He measures from those lines to determine the layout. If math isn't your strong suit, just lay a few tiles next to those lines at several places in the room to see how it will all work. Don't forget to figure in the grout lines.

A room rarely works out perfectly, so expect to make compromises. In this case, Nate opted to start with full tiles near the door, which left almost full ones on the opposite side of the room. He also chose to center a tile in the door opening even though that left smaller tiles along the walls next to the tub. Nate was able to use the first centerline he snapped, but that's rare. You'll likely have to measure from that centerline to find the location for your first tile.

Once you've decided on your layout, mark a set of guidelines for the first tile to be installed. Make these

marks close to the door; that's where you need to start. Nate uses a tile to mark the location (**Photo 4**).

### Glue your way out

Start spreading the adhesive in the area of the room farthest from the door. If you don't, you'll literally glue yourself into a corner. Buy the adhesive recommended by your flooring manufacturer, and spread it with a trowel that has the recommended tooth size and spacing (usually 1/16 in. to 1/32 in.; **Photo 5**). Avoid creating puddles, and make sure every inch of the floor gets covered.

The drying time for the product Nate used was 15 to 45 minutes. Temperature and humidity greatly affect drying times. When the adhesive is ready for installing the tile, it will change to a lighter color. And if you press your finger into the glue, the floor should feel sticky, but no adhesive should stick to your finger when you pull it away. The adhesive should dry clear enough so that you can see your lines. Wet glue can be cleaned up with water, but you'll need mineral spirits to clean it up once it's dry.

### Tile your way in

Since all the other tiles rely on the position of the first one, it's critical that you set the first tile straight (**Photo 6**). Unlike ceramic tile, LVT tiles stay put, so you can work your way into the room without waiting. When slid-

**7** **Slide tiles under trim.** Once a tile is laid flat on the glue, it's stuck. In order to set a tile under jambs and casing trim, hold the back side of a tile just barely off the floor and slide it into place.

SPACERS

**8** **Position tiles with spacers.** Set in tile spacers the same way you would for ceramic tile. The spacers will stick to the floor adhesive, so you'll have to pry them out with a small screwdriver.

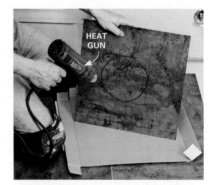

HEAT GUN

**9** **Heat tile to cut curves.** If you have to make a cut other than a straight line, heat the tile with a heat gun and you'll be able to cut right through it. Straight lines don't require heat—just score and snap. Protect the floor with cardboard and a spare tile.

ing tiles under doorjambs and door trim, lift up on the back of the tile and carefully slide it into place (**Photo 7**). You'll only have a little wiggle room once you drop the tile flat.

Regular tile spacers work fine, but keep the grout lines smaller than 1/4 in. (**Photo 8**). Nate likes to pull out his spacers as he goes so he doesn't need to use as many. The spacers will get stuck in the glue, so you'll have to pry them out with a small screwdriver. Lay down all your full tiles first, and come back to finish the ones that need cutting.

Be sure the tiles are the same temperature as the room you're putting them in, and check to see that the lot numbers on the containers are the same so you don't get noticeable color variations. Mix tiles from different containers as you go. Also, there are arrows on the bottom of each tile. Some manufacturers have you keep the arrows all the same direction; others have you rotate every other tile a quarter turn. This is to ensure a varied pattern.

The best thing about installing LVT is how easy it is to cut. All you have to do is score it with a utility knife and break it in two: no wet-saw mess, no grinder dust, no trips to a cut station, and no broken tiles! If you have to cut a hole or a curve, heat the tile with a heat gun first (**Photo 9**). Protect the floor as you cut (**Photo 10**).

The last step before grouting is to press the tiles flat with a 100-lb. roller (**Photo 11**). Most tile manufacturers require this step; don't skip it or cheat with a rolling pin or laminate roller. You can rent a roller for less than $20 at a rental center.

## Grout the tiles

Buy the grout the manufacturer recommends. Never use cement-based grout; it's too brittle and it will crack. Pack the joints with a rigid rubber float. Remove the excess at a 45-degree angle. To reduce the area that will have to be cleaned, don't plow the grout all over the tile as you would with ceramic tile—use the narrow end of the trowel and cover only the gaps between tiles (**Photo 12**). Do a 15- to 20-sq.-ft. section at a time. Wait a few minutes before you clean the tiles with water and sponges.

When you clean up the grout, don't use too much water. That can cause the grout to pull away from the tile. Just mist the tile with a spray bottle. Go back and wipe it with a thoroughly wrung-out sponge. Wipe gently—you don't want to pull the grout right out of the joints.

Start in a closet or other inconspicuous area. If any tiles are still a little hazy the next day, clean them with mineral spirits or ammonia. Stay off the floor for 24 hours, keep pets off it and avoid washing it for a few days. You can either caulk or grout between the tile and showers, tubs and cabinets. Caulk all gaps larger than 1/4 in. Reinstall the trim and your toilet.

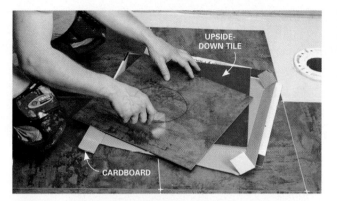

**10** **Cut with a utility knife.** You can cut LVT with just a utility knife. That means you don't have to run back and forth to a saw every time you need to make a cut. An upside-down tile and a little cardboard make an excellent cutting station.

**11** **Set the tiles with a roller.** A 100-lb. roller provides consistent pressure to permanently set the tiles in place. Roll each tile from at least two directions.

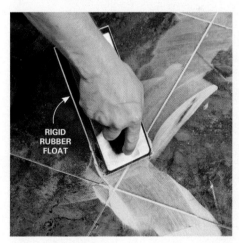

**12** **Spread the grout.** To lessen the mess, use the narrow end of a rigid rubber float to work the grout into the joints. Scrape off the excess in a 45-degree motion.

### Easy transition

There are a thousand and one ways to transition from one floor surface to another. Probably the easiest and cheapest is to install a carpet bar ($7). A hammer and a hacksaw are all you need to install it.

# HOW TO INSTALL
# AN INTERIOR DOOR

*Attention to detail
pays off with a
smooth-operating door*

by **Mark Petersen,
Contributing Editor**

Nobody pays much atten-
tion to doors that work
the way they should.
They open—they close. But
doors that were improperly
installed can bind, swing open
by themselves or rattle in the
breeze when they're closed.

We asked longtime trim
carpenter Jerome
Worm to show us his
best door-hanging
tricks. Whether you've
hung a hundred doors
or you're installing your
first, we're confident that
Jerome has a tip or two
that will result in your door
operating properly and
standing the test of time
(and the occasional slam
from an emotional teenager).

## MEET AN EXPERT

Jerome Worm has installed thousands
of interior doors, but he no longer hangs
them the same way he did when he started
out. He uses a system that has evolved
over his 30-year trim carpentry career.

## Check the rough opening

Make sure your door is going to fit into the opening. Measure the height of the opening, and then measure the width at both the top and the bottom. Next, check each side with a level. The sides don't have to be perfectly plumb (they rarely are), but they do have to be close enough to allow adequate room for your door.

If your rough opening is 1/2 in. bigger than your door but the sides of the opening are each 1/2 in. out of plumb, that opening is not big enough to hang your door properly. Finally, check to see if the walls are plumb.

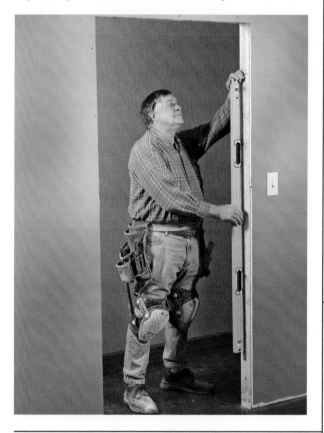

## Use blocks to level jamb bottoms

If you're installing a door on an unfinished floor and need space under the jambs for carpet, just rest the jambs on temporary blocks while you're hanging the door. Adjust the size of the blocks so the bottoms of the jambs are on a level plane. Jerome leaves a space under his jambs of anywhere from 3/8 in. to 5/8 in., depending on the thickness of the carpet and pad.

## Check the plug

Make sure the plug that holds the door slab in place is the type that can be removed *after* the door is installed. If it's not, sometimes you can cut off the plastic strap and insert the plug back in through the doorknob hole. It's difficult to move the door when the slab is flopping all over the place, but it's worse to install a door that won't open.

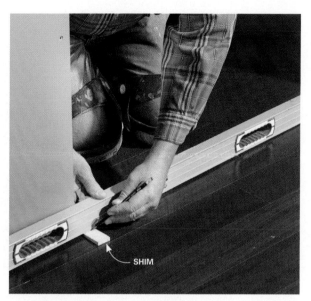

SHIM

## Level the floor

For Jerome, the most critical step of any door installation is making sure the bottom of each doorjamb is at the proper height. If you're installing a door on a finished floor and the floor isn't level, you'll have to cut a little off the bottom of one of the jambs.

Use a level to check the floor. Rest a level across the opening and level it with one or more shims. Mark the shim at the thickest point, and measure the thickness of the shim at the mark. That's exactly how much you'll need to cut off the jamb at the opposite side of the opening.

## Cut down the high side of the jamb

Jerome prefers a circular saw to cut down jambs when they need it. He installs an 80-tooth blade in his saw to prevent tearing out the wood veneer. It's easy to cut off the wrong jamb, so make sure you cut the jamb that rests on the high side of the floor. It's the one on the opposite side of the opening where you marked your shim. A rafter square works great as a saw guide.

## Attach temporary blocks to the jamb

To hold the doorjamb flush with the drywall before permanently fastening it, Jerome attaches temporary blocks to both sides of the jamb. He uses scrap lumber to make five 4-in. to 5-in. blocks. He attaches each with 2-in. 18-gauge brads. He nails three blocks on the latch side and two on the hinge side (the door slab keeps the middle of the hinge side rigid). Keep the blocks away from the hinges so they won't interfere with shimming. The casing will cover up the nail holes when the blocks are removed.

## Nail the blocks to the wall

Set the door in the center of the opening. Make sure you have a consistent gap between the door slab and all three sides of the jamb. If the bottoms of the jambs were properly cut beforehand, the gaps will be consistent, the top jamb will be level and the sides will be plumb.

Double-check the hinge side for plumb before nailing the blocks to the wall with a couple of 2-in., 15-gauge finish nails. Nail the hinge side first, and then recheck the gap around the door slab before fastening the blocks on the latch side. The blocks will allow enough wiggle room for fine-tuning before the jamb is shimmed and nailed to the framing.

## Check gap at door stops

Before installing any shims, remove the plug that holds the door slab in place, and make sure the door opens and closes properly. The door should come in contact with the door stop evenly the whole length of the stop. If one side of the door hits the stop first, you'll have to adjust the jambs by moving either the top side or the bottom side of the jamb in or out, depending on which part of the door hits first.

## Shim behind hinges

Remove the center screw from all three hinges, and slide shims behind the empty screw hole, starting with the top hinge. Fill the whole gap evenly between the jamb and the framing or you'll pull the door out of alignment when you drive in the screw.

If the framing on the rough opening seems to be twisted one way or the other, position your shims so the jamb stays perpendicular to the wall. Once the shims are in place, make sure the jambs are still flush with the drywall (if your walls are plumb).

Recheck the gap between the slab and the jambs. Recheck the gap between the door slab and the door stop. If this gap is more than 3/8 in., it's best to split this adjustment between the hinge-side and the latch-side jambs; adjust the jamb so it's only halfway corrected. And finally, nail the shims into place using three 2-in., 15-gauge nails.

## Shim the top jamb

It's not always necessary to use shims on the top doorjamb—the casing will hold it in place. And on new homes and additions, walls can compress as they settle and push down on the top shims, causing the jamb to bow down. Jerome only shims the top jamb if he's working with a 3-ft.-wide door, and the top jamb arrives bowed from the factory.

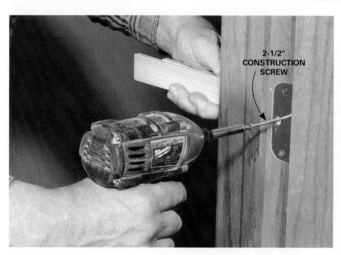

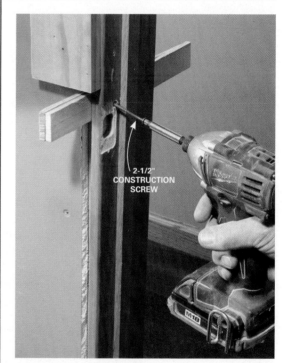

## Install longer screws in each hinge

Replace one factory screw in each hinge with a longer screw. Drive the screw in very slowly the last few turns, and pay close attention to the jamb. You don't want to suck the jamb in and throw off the alignment of the door. Check all the gaps, and open and close the door after you install each screw.

Make sure the screws penetrate the framing a minimum of 1 in. The gap between the framing and this doorjamb was about 1/2 in., so Jerome installed 2-1/2-in. screws. Don't use drywall screws—they're brittle and won't hold up to years of abuse. Buy construction screws instead, and try to find one that's close to the same color as your hinges.

## Secure the latch side

Insert and secure shims 4 in. down from the top of the door and 4 in. up from the floor. Nail the shims the same way that you did on the hinge side.

Jerome has repaired doors that were slammed shut so violently from the wind that the jamb on the latch side was knocked several inches out of place. To prevent this problem, he installs a long construction screw behind the latch plate. He predrills and countersinks a hole in the corner of the latch plate space so it won't interfere with the latch plate screws. He doesn't use longer screws in the latch plate holes because they're too close to the edge and can split the framing lumber.

# INSTANT
# STORAGE

*These 10 creative DIY ideas will instantly provide more storage*

by **TFH Editors**

 **Kitchen window plant perch**

Do you like having fresh herbs at your fingertips? Keeping them on your counter takes up valuable space and doesn't expose them to enough light. Instead, install a wire shelf between the upper cabinets flanking your kitchen window. You can set your plants where they'll get plenty of light without blocking the view. This also makes watering easy and keeps them readily available for snipping. Make sure to install the shelf high enough so you don't bump into it when you're working at the sink.

—Elisa Bernick

**2** **Under-sink storage bins**

What's hiding under your kitchen sink? If the space under your sink is anything like ours, it's an overcrowded jumble of cleaning supplies, sponges and plastic bags. I came up with a great way to store these items right on the door of the sink cabinet. I cut a plastic storage tub in half with a utility knife and screwed it to the inside of the cabinet door through the plastic lip at the top of the tub. Just make sure you position it so you can shut the cabinet door when all your bags and other supplies are in the bin.

—Alexy E. Pagan, Field Editor

 **3  Above-the-door shelves**

The space above a doorway is an overlooked storage bonanza! It's the perfect spot for a cookbook cubby in the kitchen or a towel shelf in the bathroom. Consider adding a shelf or cubby over the doorways in your home office, laundry room and bedrooms too. You'll be surprised how many books, knickknacks and other items you can find room for in these valuable unused spaces.

—Elisa Bernick

**4  Instant laundry room cubbies**

We don't have cabinets or shelves in our tiny laundry room, so I bought inexpensive plastic crates at a discount store ($5 each) and created my own wall of cubbies. I just screwed them to the wall studs using a fender washer in the upper corner of each crate for extra strength. The crates hold a lot of supplies, and they keep tippy things like my iron from falling over.

—Angie Copeland, Field Editor

## 6 Cabinet-end fruit basket

Oh, sure, you can just set your fruit bowl anywhere on your countertop. But you'll free up valuable counter space if you put your fruit in a basket on the end of an upper cabinet near your kitchen sink. The fruits and veggies will ripen nicely, and they'll look beautiful too. Wire baskets work well because they allow light and air to circulate for even ripening. You'll find them at discount, office supply and organization stores starting at $4 and up. The basket shown costs $5 at Target.

—Elisa Bernick

## 7 Clothes hanger holder

If you have shelves or cabinets above your washer or dryer, you've got the perfect spot to store clothes hangers. Just mount a towel bar to the bottom of the cabinets. This puts hangers at your fingertips so you can hang up shirts and slacks fresh from the dryer.

—Jeff Gorton, Associate Editor

## 5 Toilet paper shelf

I have to credit my wife with this idea. She bought a deep "shadow box" picture frame at a craft store for $12 and asked me to make a bathroom shelf. I slapped a couple of coats of white enamel paint on the frame and hung it around our toilet paper holder. It gives us two convenient shelves for small items in our very small bathroom.

—Ron Vanover, Field Editor

## 8 Pullout towel rack

Pullout towel racks are typically meant for kitchens, but they're also perfect for cramped bathrooms. They keep damp hand towels and washcloths off the counter so they can dry out of the way. You can find pullout towel racks for $15 to $40 at discount stores and online retailers.

—Travis Larson, Senior Editor

## 10 Charger and cord pockets

We got tired of rummaging through drawers and boxes trying to find the right cords and chargers for all of our electronic gadgets. Our solution was to use a clear vinyl over-the-door shoe organizer. We made labels for each pocket and put every item in its new home. Now we can find everything we need without getting frustrated.

—Peggy Kolar, Field Editor

READER PHOTO

## 9 Add a spice shelf

Spices are a pain to store. They get easily lost in your cabinets, so you end up buying duplicates when you can't find what you need. Here's a simple solution. Pick up a bag of adjustable shelf supports and a 1x4 board at a home center ($6 altogether). Just measure the height of your tallest spices, measure down from your shelf, drill holes and mount your spice shelf on shelf supports. You'll put an end to buying three tins of poultry seasoning and more bay leaves than you'll use in a lifetime.

—Gary Wentz, Senior Editor

INSTANT STORAGE **33**

# HandyHints®

## EASIER CEILING TILE HANGING

Lori Peterson

If you've ever replaced a damaged ceiling tile, you know how hard it is to get it seated in the grid work because you can't access the top of the tile to push it down. Since you can't grab the tile's edges either, the sides always get hung up. Here's a great shortcut—use a vacuum cleaner wand to "suck" the tile corners and edges into place. Works like a charm!

## STAY-TIGHT BOLTS

If you have a loose bolt and you're out of thread sealant (Loctite is one brand), here's a quick solution. Coat the bolt threads with fingernail polish and screw the bolt into place. The bolt will stay tight.

—Suzan L. Wiener

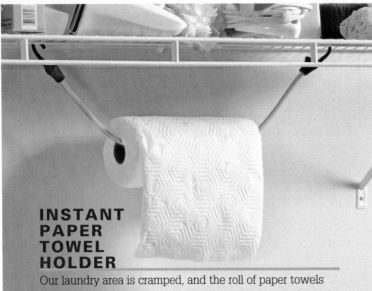

## INSTANT PAPER TOWEL HOLDER

Our laundry area is cramped, and the roll of paper towels we keep on the shelf near the sink kept falling into the sink. I solved the problem by slipping a bungee cord through the roll and hanging it from the wire shelving. Works great!

—Robert Stambaugh

## NO-SPILL GROCERY BAGS

It's a pain to crawl deep into the trunk to get all the groceries that spill out of your bags on the way home from the store. Here's a simple solution: Run a long bungee cord through the bag handles and hook the ends to the sides of the trunk. Keep the bungee cord in the trunk so it's there when you need it.

—Vern McMeans

## WOOD SCRATCH REMOVER

Doug Wainwright

Are there scratches on your wood door or cabinet? Try using a brown dry-erase marker to make them disappear. Just draw over the scratch and immediately wipe off the excess ink. The worst of the scratch will be covered. Just make sure the shade of brown isn't too dark for your cabinet.

## HOT GLUE IS HOT STUFF

For years, I had a snobby attitude toward hot glue. I've been a builder and wood-worker for decades, and I thought glue guns were something kids and old ladies used to make holiday decorations and craft projects. Then I got one as a gift—and I used it once, then again—and again.

I fix my wife's knickknacks, use it in my shop (it's great for temporary clamping!), and use it for countless other quick fixes. It's wonderful. Dab on a bit, hold the part for a few seconds to let it cool, and you're ready to go! It sticks to just about anything, and you can actually take stuff apart with some prying or heat (if you have to). Now I love hot glue. I also love old ladies and kids, by the way.

—Travis Larson, Senior Editor

STAIN

PLASTIC

BLEACH AND WATER MIXTURE

## DOG-PROOF FLOORING

After living with dogs for 30 years, I've learned it's important to take your pets into account when you remodel. For years I had beautiful oak hardwood floors, and there was an obvious path through the house where the dogs' feet had worn away the finish. So when I decided to install new flooring, I did my research first.

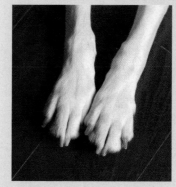

I got a bunch of samples and tried to scratch them with the pointed end of a can opener to simulate 25 years of dog claws. Some of the samples were ruined instantly, some showed slight damage and one was unscratch-able. My Pergo floor is several years old now and it looks exactly like it did the day I bought it!

—Anne Wimsey, Field Editor

## BLEACH AWAY A WATER STAIN

Scott Pauly, Field Editor

As a professional drywall finisher for 25 years, I get tons of calls from customers wanting me to fix a water stain on their ceiling. Before I go see it, I tell them to spray it with bleach and water solution (10 percent bleach), and wait a day or two. If it's an old stain, I recommend Tilex Mold & Mildew Remover. You'd be surprised how often I get a call back saying, "Problem solved." It works on both flat and textured ceilings.

Wear safety goggles, and make sure you protect the walls and floors with plastic. I hate giving away work, but guess who they call back for their bigger projects.

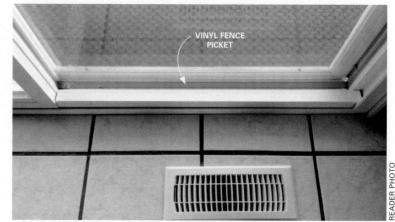

VINYL FENCE PICKET

READER PHOTO

## SLIDING DOOR SECURITY

Ron Dippel

I used to secure my patio door by putting a wooden stick in the track, but it wasn't very attractive because it didn't match the white vinyl. I was at a home center and noticed that a vinyl fence picket matched my door perfectly and was the exact size I needed. You could easily cut it to fit a smaller door.

# HandyHints®

## QUICK-SETTING MUD FOR SPEEDY REPAIRS

I like to keep a bag of this 20-minute setting-type joint compound around for patching and repairs. It's great for small jobs because it sets up fast enough for you to apply two or three coats in a few hours.

Unlike regular joint compound, which has to dry to harden, this stuff hardens by a chemical reaction that starts when you add the water. And within 15 or 20 minutes, it's hard enough to shape with a rasp or coarse sandpaper, and recoat. It's also handy for filling holes that are too deep to fill with regular joint compound. You'll find 20-minute joint compound at home centers and drywall suppliers.

—Jeff Gorton,
Associate Editor

## FIX A WALLPAPER SEAM

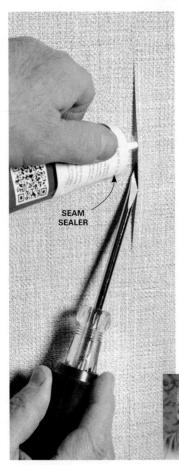

SEAM SEALER

If you have a seam that's coming apart, reactivate the paste around the gap with a rag soaked in warm water. Hold the rag over the area for a minute or two, and then carefully open the gap a little larger so you'll have more room for the sealer. Squeeze seam sealer (Elmer's Glue works in a pinch) into the gap, and press the paper to the wall with a roller. Clean off the excess sealer with a sponge.

Bob Rowland,
Field Editor

STRIKE

MAGNETIC CATCH

## KEEP CABINET DOORS CLOSED

Mark Petersen,
Contributing Editor

There's a cabinet door in my kitchen that wouldn't stay shut. It's on the cabinet where we keep the junk food (it probably broke from overuse), and it didn't take long for our new puppy to discover this easily accessible new source of food.

My 10-minute fix was to install a magnetic door catch. I bought a magnetic catch because it's easier to line up the catch with the strike than with a roller-style one. No more midnight snacks for Roxy. Now I need to figure out how to stop her from eating our books and my shoes.

HOLE

SMOKE DETECTOR BASE

## HIDE A HOLE WITH A SMOKE DETECTOR

Kevin Lind,
Field Editor

I'm a professional handyman, and some of my customers don't have a lot of money for home repairs. Recently, an elderly lady had me remove a hanging planter, which left a large hole in her ceiling. She was shocked when I told her how much it would cost to repair the hole and repaint the ceiling.

Luckily I had just come from a job installing smoke detectors, which gave me the idea of covering the hole with the spare detector I had in my van. She was thrilled, especially since she didn't already have a smoke detector in that area.

**SCREW EXTRACTOR**

## STRIPPED SCREWS, NO PROBLEM

A stripped screw can turn a 10-minute fix into a two-hour nightmare. One of the best investments I've made is the screw extraction kit I bought last summer. It came with three different size bits and cost me about $20. I've already used it several times. One side of the extractor bit reams a hole into the screw, and the other side has reverse threads that dig into the screw as you turn it out.

**REAMING END**

**REMOVER END**

Dana Blouin,
Field Editor

## DRYWALL INSPECTION LIGHT

Here's a handy way to find and fix imperfections while sanding drywall. Wear a hiker's headlamp and peer down the wall for divots and bulges. The headlamp is better than a trouble light or flashlight because it keeps your hands free. Headlamps cost about $12 at camping and discount stores.

Vince Russo,
Field Editor

## A FIX FOR CLICKING CEILING FANS

We use our ceiling fan year-round, and the bead chains had been tapping against the light fixture and driving us nuts! I finally figured out how to silence them. I unhooked the chains, slipped them through clear 1/4-in. tubing ($2 for 10 ft. at home centers) and reattached them. No more chattering chains to contend with.

Roy Edwards

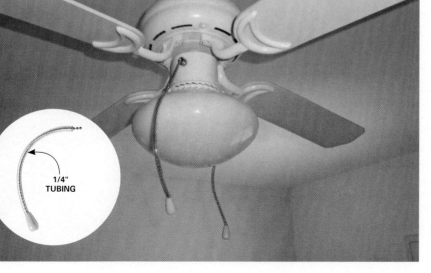

**1/4" TUBING**

# HANGING SHELVES

*Easy tips for perfect shelf alignment and positioning*

by **Jeff Gorton, Associate Editor**

From leveling to anchoring, here are 10 tips to make sure your next shelf-hanging project is quick, easy and strong. We'll show you tips for hanging and installing everything from store-bought display shelves to DIY closet shelves. And even if you don't have any shelf projects in the near future, you'll find leveling and anchoring tips here that you can use on other building projects.

 **Mark the tape, not the wall**

The first step in any shelf-hanging project is to locate the studs so you can anchor the shelf to the studs if possible. Here's a tip that allows you to make marks that are clearly visible without the need to repaint the wall.

Use a level and draw a very light pencil line where you want the top of the shelf to be. The shelf will hide the line. Apply a strip of masking tape above the line. Use "delicate surface" masking tape to avoid any possibility of messing up the paint. Locate the studs and mark the centers on the tape. Electronic stud finders are the go-to tool for this task. Now you can plan your shelf-mounting project to hit as many studs as possible and use the tape as a guide for leveling and attaching the shelf.

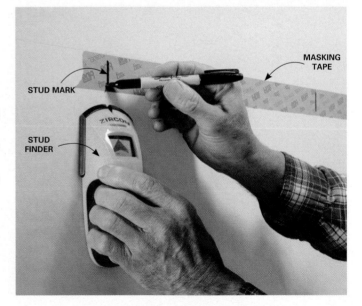

## 2 Figure-eights simplify the job

These nifty little fasteners are actually designed to attach table and desktops to aprons (the vertical skirt around the perimeter), but they're also a handy solution for hanging shelves. You can buy a pack of eight for about $6 at woodworking stores or online.

The only caveat is that the top of the figure-eight shows above the surface of the shelf, so it may be visible if you hang the shelf low. Try to position the figure-eights where there are studs if possible. You can use good-quality hollow-wall anchors if the studs don't line up with the figure-eights.

**Drill a recess for the figure-eight.** Use a spade bit or Forstner bit to drill a slight recess in the back of the shelf to accommodate the thickness of the figure-eight. Then chisel out the remaining wood until the figure-eight sits flush to the shelf. Attach the figure-eight with a screw.

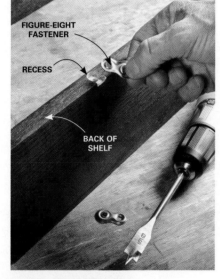

FIGURE-EIGHT FASTENER

RECESS

BACK OF SHELF

**Simply screw it on.** Mount the shelf by driving screws through the figure-eights either into hollow-wall anchors or into studs.

SHELF LEVEL

LASER LINE

SELF-LEVELING LASER

## 3 Dead-on leveling with a laser

Got a lot of shelves to level? A laser level is the perfect tool. We're using a self-leveling laser, but any laser that projects a horizontal level line will work. The tip is that you don't have to mess with getting the laser line at the height of your shelf. Just project it anywhere on the wall, and use it as a reference by measuring up from the line. This is especially handy if you're mounting several shelves at different heights, since you never need to reposition the laser. You can pick up a self-leveling laser for as little as $30 and use it for many other interior leveling tasks.

## 4 Super-sturdy closet shelves

Here's a fast, strong and easy way to install closet shelves. Paint a 1x4 to match your shelf. Then draw a level line and locate the studs or use our masking tape trick (p. 38). Nail the 1x4 to the studs with 8d finish nails. Run the strip across the back and ends of the closet. Then put blocks in the locations where you want brackets. Now you have solid wood to attach the brackets and the closet pole sockets to. And the back of the shelf is fully supported to prevent sagging.

HOOK STRIP

## 5 Ditch those old-school toggle bolts

**TOGGLE BOLT**

Of course it's always best to fasten heavy shelves to studs, but if you can't, there's an anchor that's almost as good. If you've used standard toggle bolts, you know they hold well. But they're a hassle to work with, and they leave an oversize hole that may show. And if you ever need to take the shelf down to paint, the toggle falls into the wall and you have to repeat the whole tedious process when you reinstall the shelf.

**SNAP-TOGGLE ANCHOR**

Snaptoggle anchors by Toggler solve these problems. After installing the toggle according to the instructions, you'll have a threaded opening in the wall ready to receive the included bolt. You can simply screw the shelf to the captured toggle. And you can remove the bolt and the toggle will stay put, ready for you to reinstall the shelf. You'll find Snaptoggle anchors in hardware stores and home centers alongside the other wall anchors. Go to toggler.com to see a video showing how to install them.

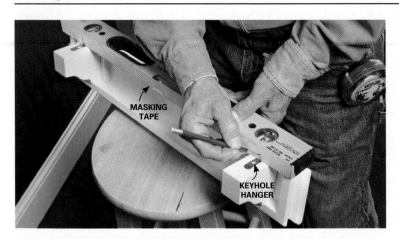

**MASKING TAPE**

**KEYHOLE HANGER**

**Mark; don't measure.** Place a strip of masking tape on one edge of your level and mark the center of each keyhole on the tape.

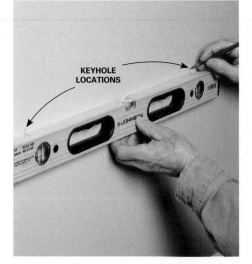

**KEYHOLE LOCATIONS**

**Transfer to the wall.** Hold the level against the wall at the height you want the shelf. Remember that the top of the shelf will be above your marks. Adjust the level until the bubble is centered, and mark the keyhole locations on the wall. Then install anchors or drive the screws into the studs and hang the shelf.

## 7 The key to keyholes

Keyhole slots on the back of shelves are a common way to hang shelves or brackets on hidden screws, but you have to get the screws perfectly aligned or you'll have all kinds of trouble.

Here's one foolproof method for transferring a pair of keyhole locations to the wall for perfect screw placement. If you're lucky, you may be able to line up the screw locations with studs. Otherwise, use this method to mark the center of the hollow-wall anchors you'll need.

## 6 Build in a hanging rail

Whether you're building a shelf or modifying a store-bought unit, including a hanging rail is a great way to add strength and allow for more flexible positioning while anchoring to studs. The rail strengthens the shelf and lets you anchor the shelf by driving screws anywhere along the length of the rail.

If the shelf isn't too heavy, you can hang it with finish-head screws that are easy to hide with wood putty. For heavier shelves, drill recesses for wood plugs to hide the screws.

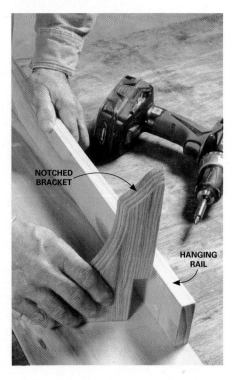

**NOTCHED BRACKET**

**HANGING RAIL**

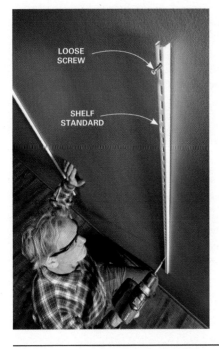

LOOSE SCREW

SHELF STANDARD

## 8 Self-plumbing standards

The next time you install metal shelf standards, remember this tip. Rather than use a level to plumb the standards before you attach them, simply hang them loosely from the top with one of the screws and let gravity do the work. The standard will hang plumb, and all you have to do is press it to the wall and drive in the remaining screws. If you're using hollow-wall anchors, hang the standard from the top screw and use an awl to mark the screw locations. Then take the standard down and install the anchors.

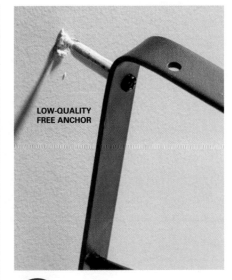

LOW-QUALITY FREE ANCHOR

## 9 Throw away the free anchors

Most of the hollow-wall anchors included with shelves or shelf brackets aren't worth using. If you can't attach your shelf to studs and must use hollow-wall anchors, make sure to choose one that will support your shelf in the long run.

For light-duty shelves, we like the type of anchor shown here. You'll find them at any hardware store or home center. Make sure you know how thick your drywall or plaster is before you head to the store, though. Then match the anchor to the wall thickness.

To install the anchors, check the instructions and drill the right size hole. Then fold the wings so the anchor will fit and press it into the hole. You may have to tap it with a hammer until it's fully seated. Finish by pressing the included red tool through the hole to expand the wings behind the drywall or plaster. And make sure to use the screws included with the anchors, or ones that are the same diameter.

SHELF CLEAT

WALL CLEAT

## 10 French cleats for fast, solid hanging

Pairs of beveled strips that interlock to support shelves, cabinets or pictures are called French cleats. They're great for hanging any shelf or cabinet and have a few advantages in certain situations.

First, the cleats work well for heavy cabinets because you can easily mount the wall cleat and then simply lift the cabinet and "hook" it on. There's no need to support a heavy cabinet temporarily while you drive screws to anchor it.

Another common use for French cleats is to create a flexible system of shelves or cabinets. You can screw one or more lengths of wall cleats across the entire wall, and then easily relocate shelves, or add more shelves at a later date. Make cleats by ripping strips of 3/4-in. plywood with a 45-degree bevel on one edge. Screw one strip to the wall and the other to the back of the shelf or cabinet.

BETTER HOLLOW-WALL ANCHOR

# HANGING WALLPAPER

*Tricks of the trade from an expert*

by **Mark Petersen, Contributing Editor**

Anyone can hang wallpaper, but it takes a little know-how to hang it straight and with tight, nearly invisible seams. We asked professional paperhanger Bob Rowland to give us some insight into what it takes to get the job done right. He told us that every quality job starts with careful planning and proper preparation.

## Prep the walls

Start by removing plate covers, heat registers and light fixtures. Fill any holes with a *nonshrinking* joint compound so you don't have to wait until it dries and apply another layer. Scrape the walls with a drywall knife or sand them with 50-grit sandpaper to remove smaller imperfections.

Finally, cover the whole wall with "wall size," a primer/sizing product. Bob uses Shieldz made by Zinsser. Don't skip this step! Using wall size will help the paper adhere to the wall and reduce the chance that the paper will shrink. It also makes it easier to remove the paper when the time comes. One gallon costs $20 at a home center. And never, hang wallpaper over unfinished drywall—it won't ever come off if you do. Make sure all the walls have at least one coat of primer.

# Map out the room

## A. Use a roll to lay out the wall

Use a full roll of paper as a guide to lay out the room. Butt a roll into the corner where you plan to start, and make a pencil mark on the wall at the edge of the roll. Slide the roll down to that mark, and make another pencil mark at the other edge of the roll. Keep doing this until you know where every seam is going to fall. You may have to cut down the first panel to avoid hanging small strips (3 in. or less) near doors and corners.

## B. Work away from the door you enter

Wallpaper seams on straight walls are butted, not overlapped, but seams are less visible if you place them at the point farthest from where the first panel was installed. Minimize the visibility of seams by starting in the area opposite the most-used entrance to the room.

## C. Start with a plumb line

Don't assume the corner you're starting in is plumb. Use a level and draw a straight plumb line about 1/4 in. past where you want the first panel of paper to end. Take into account that inside corner seams need to be overlapped at least 1/8 in. For more information, see "Seam Inside Corners" on p. 43.

## D. Hide the last seam

If you're hanging paper that has a repeatable pattern, the pattern on the last seam is not going to line up, so try to hide it in a low-visibility area. The corner just above the entry is usually the best spot.

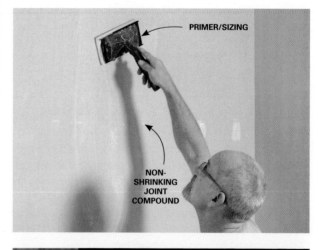

PRIMER/SIZING

NON-SHRINKING JOINT COMPOUND

**MEET AN EXPERT**

Bob Rowland has been hanging wallpaper for more than 44 years. He's covered hundreds of acres of commercial walls and has worked on everything from modest starter homes up to the governor's mansion in St. Paul, MN.

## Order enough paper

When measuring a room, you need to take into account the pattern of the paper. Sometimes the pattern on one panel needs to line up horizontally with the pattern on the panel next to it. If you're measuring a room with 8-ft. walls and the paper you're hanging has a pink poodle that repeats every 54 in., only two poodles will fit on each length of panel. If you cut off the first panel so the two poodles are centered on the wall, you'll have to cut about 1 ft. off the roll to make the poodle on the next panel line up with the first one. This means you'll be using 9 ft. of paper for every 8 ft. of wall. So in this case, you would multiply the linear feet of the room by 9 ft. instead of 8 ft.

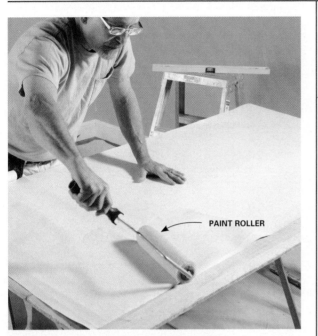

PAINT ROLLER

## Roll on the paste—don't dunk!

Use a high-quality 1/2-in.-nap paint roller cover to apply paste—the cheap ones will leave fuzz balls all over the paper. When working with prepasted products, Bob prefers to use a paint roller to roll the water on the paper. Submerging paper in a tray is messy and doesn't guarantee uniform coverage. He even adds a little paste to the water (2 cups per gallon) to encourage stronger adhesion.

## Gently smooth out the paper

Once the paper is on the wall, be sure to run your smoother over every square inch of the paper. But don't push too hard on your smoother or you'll squeeze out the paste and stretch the paper. This is especially important when you're working with prepasted paper. Stretched-out paper with too little paste behind it is guaranteed to shrink when it dries. Shrinking causes gaps in the seams—gaps are bad.

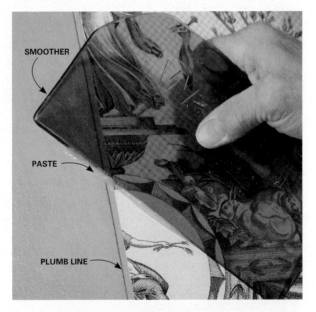

SMOOTHER

PASTE

PLUMB LINE

## Seam inside corners

Corners are rarely perfectly straight. You'll need to create a seam at every inside corner to make the next panel plumb. The first panel installed in a corner should be overlapped onto the adjacent wall at least 1/8 in. When working your way into a corner, measure over from the last panel to the corner at the top, middle and bottom. Then cut the corner panel 1/8 in. longer than the longest of the three measurements. You can use the leftover piece to start the new wall, but you may need to cut it at a slight angle to accommodate a crooked corner. Some wallpaper won't stick to other wallpaper, so run a small bead of seam adhesive in the corner before overlapping the second piece.

OVERLAP

## Use vinyl paper in high-traffic rooms

Wallpaper made from paper absorbs moisture and can be hard to clean. Vinyl products are better suited for bathrooms and kitchen and hallways, but not all vinyl wallpapers are the same. Some are solid vinyl, others have a vinyl face with a paper backing, and some are mostly paper with a thin vinyl coating. Solid vinyl wallpaper is the most resistant to moisture and the most washable. To avoid confusion, many manufacturers have a "Best Uses" label on each roll.

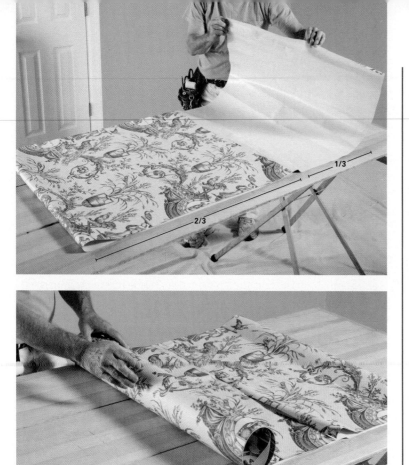

## Wipe down as you go

It's a lot easier to clean up the paste before it has fully cured, so Bob sponges off every panel with warm water as he goes. He uses natural sponges, one in each hand. He swipes with the first and makes a final pass with the other. He uses a few drops of dish soap when he's working with particularly sticky paste. To avoid creating suds, Bob squeezes the sponges out while they're still submerged in water, then he gives them another small squeeze above the water bucket.

NATURAL SPONGE

## Book the paper before hanging

Booking is the process of folding the paper in on itself. It allows time for the paste to activate and the paper to soften. Fold the paper so that when you unfold it, you'll be working with two-thirds of the panel. The longer the paper, the easier it is to get straight. Cut a bunch of pieces of paper at once, and book several at the same time. Set each roll in front of the wall where it's going to be hung. If you're a beginner, set them in a plastic bag to give you more time to work with them.

## Choose the right paste for your paper

There are three basic types of paste: clay, wheat and starch. Each group has several subcategories. Most wallpaper instructions will indicate which paste to use. Avoid the "universal" paste unless the paper you're hanging specifically calls for it.

## Tools of the trade

Hanging wallpaper doesn't require a huge investment. You probably already own many of the tools. Bob's most expensive tools are his beech wood cutting table and his magnesium straightedge. You can substitute an old door slab and a level.

CLAY

WHEAT PASTE

ROMAN
PRO-838
HEAVY DUTY CLEAR
WALLPAPER ADHESIVE

STARCH

WHEAT

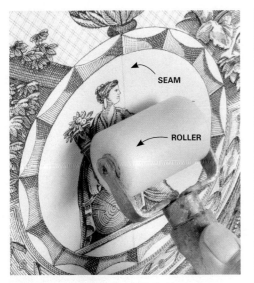

**Roll every seam**

To keep the edges from curling, you need to set them with a roller. But the same rule that applies to the smoother applies to the roller: Don't press too hard or you'll squeeze out too much adhesive.

## Overlap and cut both pieces at once

Sometimes, rather than butting one panel up to another, you'll need to create your own seam. The best way to do this is to lap one panel over the other, and cut down the middle of the overlap. Then peel the two pieces apart, and pull out the small strip that was cut off the underlying piece.

If you don't have a steady hand, you can use a drywall knife as a cutting guide. Try not to penetrate the drywall paper. Angle the knife blade down low so more than just the tip of the blade is doing the cutting. Bob uses a knife with blades that snap off. Blades are a lot cheaper than wallpaper, so he snaps off a section after every cut.

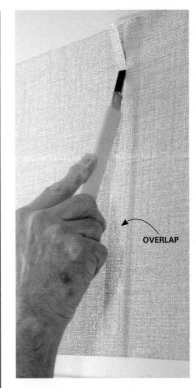

## Make relief cuts before trimming

When you're up against trim or other obstacles, you'll need to make a relief cut before trimming the paper. You could make the cut with a knife, but scissors are better to avoid scratching the trim.

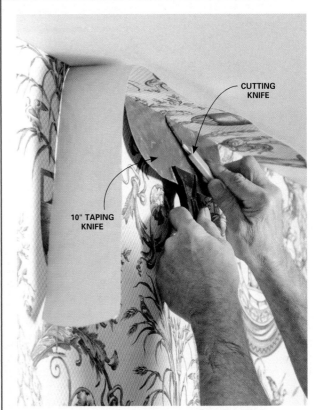

## Use a taping knife as a cutting guide

Leave an extra 2 in. at the top and bottom, and use a drywall knife as a guide to trim it. Bob prefers a 10-in. knife so he doesn't have to move it as often as he would a smaller one. Hold the knife down close to the wall to avoid cutting into the ceiling.

# BASEMENT FINISHING TIPS

*Expert advice for a warm, dry and inviting basement*

by **Jeff Gorton, Associate Editor**

Finishing a basement is a perfect DIY project. For a fraction of the cost of an addition, you can convert basement space to valuable living space.

Advances in waterproofing along with new products mean your basement rooms can be as dry and comfortable as any other room in the house. We talked to basement experts, our Field Editors and manufacturers to find the best tips and products. For more on basement remodeling, search for specific topics at familyhandyman.com

## First, dry it up

If you have a damp or wet basement, you have to fix it before you start any finishing work. The good news is that most water problems can be remedied by two measures: grading the soil to slope away from the foundation and adding or repairing gutters and downspouts.

If these steps don't work, you'll have to take more extreme measures like adding exterior drain tile and waterproofing the walls or adding interior drain tile that empties into a sump basket with a pump. Eliminating water problems is time consuming and expensive, but it's critical to prevent a moldy and ruined finished basement.

## Seal the rim joists

Uninsulated rim joists are huge energy losers. Now's the time to insulate and seal your rim joists. You'll never again have access once you install the basement ceiling. And don't make the mistake of thinking that packed-in fiberglass batts will do the job. Fiberglass batts are simply too porous to create an air seal.

If you have more money than time and want the best job possible, closed-cell spray foam is the way to go. You can buy a DIY kit online or at some home centers that contains enough two-part foam to cover about 100 sq. ft., 2 in. thick, for about $250. Before you go this route, though, get an estimate from a pro. You may find you can have the job done for about the same price.

The second best option is to seal the rim joists with rigid insulation cut to fit (**photo below**). We recommend a minimum of 2-in.-thick extruded polystyrene, but check your local codes to see what's required. If you have a table saw, use it to cut strips equal to the depth of your joists. Then use a fine-tooth handsaw, utility knife or miter saw to cut the strips to length. Fill small gaps with caulk, and larger ones with expanding spray foam from a can.

FINISHED BASEMENT COMPANY

## Install a variety of lighting

For the most interesting space, include several kinds of lighting in your plan. Start with good general illumination for times when you want a brightly lit room. Plan to add a dimmer switch to control the amount of light. Recessed can lights, ceiling fixtures and fluorescent "pillow" lights are a few types of general lighting. If you're worried about noise traveling upstairs, don't use recessed can lights.

In addition to general lighting, you can include indirect sources of light that reflect off the ceiling or walls. Two examples are wall sconces and LED rope lighting built into a cove.

Task lighting is important if you have areas dedicated to hobbies, cooking or reading that can benefit from additional light. Floor and table lamps work well. Or consider adding lights over your sink, countertops or work area.

If you plan to display artwork, sculptures, crystal or pottery, or even a collection of books, special lighting that illuminates these objects can be very dramatic. Small puck lights built into alcoves or bookcases, track lighting and dedicated picture frame lights all work well.

## Hire a pro to design your HVAC system

Don't make the rookie DIY mistake of trying to heat your basement by cutting a hole in your main trunk line and screwing on a heat register. This will only create an imbalance in your entire heating system, and won't provide the heat where you need it. It's important to place heat registers above exterior doors and windows, and provide plenty of cold-air returns in the right locations. In some cases, a new "trunk line," or main rectangular duct, will have to be added to supply enough airflow.

The important point to remember is that money spent on proper design is a good investment. Hire a professional heating contractor to design your ductwork. If you would like to do the work yourself, look for a heating contractor who will provide the plan and possibly even the materials.

## Warm up cold floors with heating cables

Unless you're lucky enough to have in-floor heat already installed, your basement floor will probably be a little chilly, especially in areas that aren't carpeted. You can fix this problem with electric heating cables or mats. And even though this type of heat doesn't warm the room much, it makes floors much more comfortable.

The downside is that heating cables are expensive to install and expensive to run. You can buy a loose cable system or mats with the cable attached. Loose cables are more work to install, but cost less than mats. The more area you cover with cables or mats, the lower the cost per square foot. The cost is roughly between $2 and $10 per square foot just for the materials.

Manufacturers have information on their Web sites for planning the installation. If you're not comfortable with wiring, you can install the cables yourself and hire an electrician to hook them up to the thermostat. Most cables or mats must be covered with a thin layer of thin-set mortar or self-leveling underlayment before you install flooring over them.

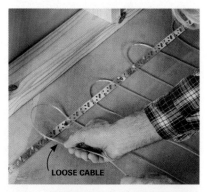

LOOSE CABLE

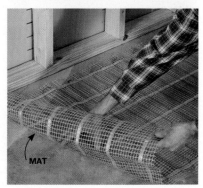

MAT

## Two great basement floor coverings

Choosing material for a basement floor is tricky. Carpet is warm and soft but susceptible to moisture damage. Tile is good for areas that might get wet, but it's hard and cold underfoot. Still, there are a few choices that strike a good compromise.

Interlocking cork flooring is easy to install, sustainably harvested and warm underfoot. Make sure to buy top-quality cork flooring that has a durable, water-resistant core to prevent moisture damage. TORLYS is one brand. In basements, we recommend installing a floating cork floor over a padded underlayment that includes a vapor barrier. This can go directly on dry concrete or over a dimple mat (see p. 49).

The second flooring choice we recommend is luxury vinyl tile or planks. Luxury vinyl is waterproof and virtually indestructible. It's also easy to install and looks great. It's available in a plank form that looks like wood, and squares that look like tile. Floating luxury vinyl floors connect with self-adhesive tabs or interlocking edges. You'll find luxury vinyl at flooring stores, home centers and online ($2 to $5 per sq. ft.).

CORK FLOOR

TORLYS

LUXURY VINYL PLANKS

ARMSTRONG

---

## Buy a powder-actuated fastening tool

I recommend buying a powder-actuated fastener system for attaching plates and other framing materials to concrete floors and walls. Ramset is one brand. For as little as $22, you can buy a tool that accepts .22-caliber loads. You hit the tool with a hammer to fire the hardened nail. Costlier versions look like guns, and you fire them by pulling a trigger. These cost $80 to $350.

Michael Guarraia, Field Editor

## Frame soffits with OSB

Most basements have ducting or plumbing mounted below the joists that needs to be boxed in. The most common method is to build a wooden frame around them that can be covered with drywall. Here's a pro tip for building these soffits. Rather than frame the sides with 2x2s or some other lumber, simply cut strips of plywood or OSB (oriented strand board) for the sides.

Measure the distance from the bottom of the floor joists to the bottom of the duct or plumbing and add 1-3/4 in. Rip the strips to this width. Nail or screw a 2x2 cleat to the joists alongside the ducting or pipes, making sure it's straight. A chalk line or laser works well for this. Then attach a 2x2 to the bottom edge of the OSB and hang the OSB from the ceiling cleat. Finish by running 2x2s between the two sides of the soffit or to the wall, depending on the layout.

DIMPLE MAT

## Install "dimple mats" for a warmer, drier floor

You'll need to fix water problems before you install flooring in your basement. Plastic drainage mats, or dimple mats, aren't a solution for wet floors. But they do allow air to circulate under the flooring and provide a moisture barrier, reducing the potential for moisture damage from condensation or water vapor migrating through the concrete. Dimple mats also provide an insulating layer of air that separates the floor from cold concrete.

The photo shows a type of dimple mat from CertainTeed called Platon. Platon is available in 44-1/2-in. by 49-ft. rolls ($60) as well as several other sizes. After rolling it out and taping or caulking the seams, you can install a pad and floating floor directly over the plastic mat. To prepare for other types of flooring, you can cover it with plywood or oriented strand board (OSB) by screwing through the mat into the concrete below.

## Buy a laser for speedier framing

If you've been looking for an excuse to buy a laser level, this is it. Especially if you plan to stick-frame the walls—that is, build them in place rather than build them on the floor and stand them up. That's because with stick-framing you have to transfer the location of the bottom wall plate to the ceiling. You can do this with a straightedge and a regular level. But a laser is so much faster!

Start by marking the wall locations on the floor with a chalk line. Then simply line up the laser with the chalk line, and the laser beam will show the location of the top plate on the joists. You'll need a laser that projects a vertical line. And we like the self-leveling type for better accuracy and faster setup. Self-leveling lasers cost from $30 to about $400.

LASER LINE ON CEILING

WALL LINE ON FLOOR

## Frame soffits with wood I-joists

In my basement, I have a 32-ft. run of pipes along the ceiling. To create a soffit around the pipes with a perfectly straight bottom edge, I used 14-in. I-joists (I call them TJI floor joists). I held them up to the floor joists and screwed through the flange to hold them in place. I installed two 16-ft.-long I-joists on each side of the pipes to create the sides of the soffit. Then I framed the bottom with 2x2s and covered it with drywall.

The soffit looks great— it's straight as an arrow.

**Ed Stawicki,**
**Field Editor**

## Hire a pro to tape the drywall

When I moved into my new home, the basement was unfinished, so I tried to do it myself to save money. I did OK putting the drywall up, but if

**Dave Switzer, Field Editor**

I could recommend anything, it's if you aren't confident in the taping and mudding, hire someone. My wall has a hump at many seams because I mudded, but it was heavy and I didn't sand it down enough. So when the sun shines in or the light is just right, you can see the "speed bumps" on the wall. That's not a super finishing job!

## Tips for a quieter ceiling

How much time and effort you spend on soundproofing depends on what your goal is. Preventing the deep bass of a home theater from rocking the whole house is complicated and expensive. But if you're just looking to quiet footsteps from the floor above or reduce the impact of your teenager's video game, then there are a few simple steps you can take. If you do nothing else, consider adding fiberglass batts to the joist spaces. Anything will help. You can add a 3-1/2-in. layer, or better yet, fill the joist spaces with fiberglass.

For even more noise reduction, isolate the ceiling drywall from the joists with resilient channels as shown here. Screw the channels to the joists, spacing them 12 or 16 in. apart (ask your building inspector what's required). Then screw the drywall to the channels, being careful not to drive screws into the joists. This creates a "floating ceiling" that reduces sound transmission. You may have to visit a drywall supplier to find resilient channels.

## Add a gas fireplace

You can't go wrong adding a gas fireplace to your basement remodeling plans. Matt Cook, our basement expert, estimates that more than 80 percent of the basement remodeling jobs done by his company include a gas fireplace. In addition to the obvious benefit—everybody loves fireplaces—a fireplace can be a great source of extra heat to warm up a room fast on cold winter days.

One advantage of gas fireplaces is that you may not need to run a chimney through the roof. In some situations, you can run the flue directly through the side wall. A DIY gas fireplace kit starts at about $2,000. For information on how to install a gas fireplace, go to familyhandyman.com and search for "gas fireplace."

FLAME-RESISTANT EXPANDING FOAM

## Seal around pipes and wires

There are several reasons to seal between the basement and upstairs. The first is safety. The openings around pipes and wires act like chimneys for fire. Sealing them will help prevent the spread of fire from the basement to upstairs. The second is energy savings. Warm air will rise through these openings, creating a chimney effect that sucks heat out of the house. And finally, sealing the openings helps prevent sound transfer from the basement to the upstairs.

Seal small cracks around pipes and wires with special "red" high-temperature silicone caulk. Fill larger openings with flame-resistant expanding foam as shown here. Close openings around chimney flues or other large openings by nailing sheet metal over them and sealing the edges with caulk.

# GreatGoofs®

### NO-SLIP BATH RUG

Before the new ceiling drywall went up in our kitchen, I decided to fix the terrible squeak in the master bathroom floor above the kitchen. I easily located the areas where the plywood subfloor was moving up and down on the joists. Aha, another great little project for my newly acquired pocket screw jig. I used construction adhesive and 12 pocket screws to fix the squeak.

However, due to a miscalculation on my part, seven of the 12 screws went through both layers of subfloor, the vinyl tile and the bathroom rug! After my wife got done laughing, I went back downstairs and relocated the screws. Now the bathroom floor is nice and quiet, and I have a brand new project: new vinyl tile.

—Dave Paegelow

### JUST LIKE THE PROS DO IT

My wife and I were excited about installing a new laminate floor in our living room. We moved out all the furniture and removed the old carpeting and baseboards. Then we put down an underlayment. Things were going so well that I bragged to my wife that I should quit my job and become a flooring professional!

The next morning I got up early while the day was still cool and started laying the floor. By midafternoon, the floor was in and I started installing the baseboards. It was getting really hot by then, so I asked my wife to turn on the air conditioning. After about 30 minutes, I noticed the room wasn't getting any cooler. I suddenly realized why. In all my excitement, I'd forgotten to cut out the underlayment over the floor registers, and they were buried under the flooring!

—Gary Fisher

### THIS IS NOT A STEP. REPEAT...AND REPEAT

You know the warning label that's on the top of every stepladder: "Do not sit or stand here. This is not a step"? Turns out that's right. I've "learned" this lesson three times already! The first time I fell and broke my wrist and was in a cast for a month. The second time I was lucky and only ended up with huge, painful bruises. The third time, I knocked my ladder down while I was getting on the roof to clear snow. No one else was home, so to get down, I had to shovel down a big pile of snow and jump into it. It sounds like more fun than it was.

—Bruce Fox, Field Editor

# GreatGoofs®

## HASTE MAKES...A BIG MESS

My father-in-law, J.C., was a great DIYer since he was a carpenter by trade. After years of nagging by his wife, Lucille, he finally decided to fix the cabinet door in the laundry room by installing an external latch. In a hurry as usual, he started drilling the holes for the latch without first emptying the cabinet. That's when he heard a hissing sound coming from inside the cabinet. He opened the door and was immediately sprayed with black paint from the paint can he'd punctured. Not only did the paint hit him, but it hit the floor, the walls, and the washer and dryer. Lucille was not pleased.

— Larry Darnell

## A SCREW (DRIVER) LOOSE

I was using a screwdriver to pry off a large rusted bolt. It slipped and I stabbed myself between my index and middle fingers about 1/2 in. deep. I rushed upstairs with blood gushing to tell my wife to drive me to the hospital. Instead of being sympathetic, she yelled at me for getting blood all over the floor!

—Matthew Karl, Field Editor

## A BIT OF A STRETCH

We had just bought our home, and I decided to replace the ratty carpet in the mudroom with vinyl sheet flooring. I tore out the carpet and unrolled it in the garage on top of the vinyl with the brilliant idea of using the carpet as a template. This project was going to be a piece of cake. I traced the carpet dimensions onto the vinyl, trimmed it up, took it into the mudroom and laid it out. It was short all the way around! Then I realized what a bonehead I was. Of course it didn't fit right. Carpet is stretched!

—James Boschetto

## READY...AIM....OUCH!

My father, John Williams, was a great carpenter and all-around handyman. He was roofing a house using an old roofing staple gun. He rested the staple gun on his knee to reach for a shingle, and when he grabbed the staple gun... Yeah. Right in the knee. On a roof. By himself.

—Scott Williams, Field Editor

# Painting, Staining & Finishing

## PLASTIC-BAG PAINT CONTAINERS

We recently painted our cottage using many colors, and we found ourselves constantly cleaning brushes and containers whenever we switched colors. We finally got the smart idea of putting the paint in zipper lock bags. When it was time to change colors, all we had to do was change the bag in the paint bucket. It's a great way to save time and cleanup when you're using a lot of colors for a small paint job.

Dawn Schmoekel

## PERFECT PAINT SHIELD

Aluminum roof flashing makes a great paint shield. It comes in 10-ft. lengths ($5 at home centers), and you can cut it to any length you want. It's rigid, so you can actually get it up under the baseboard and completely isolate the carpet from the baseboard. Plus, it's bendable, keeps its shape and is reusable. Tape the sharp edges for safety.

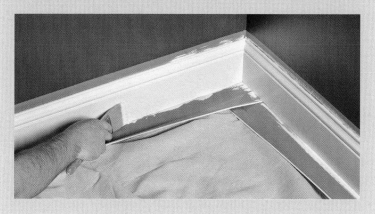

## REMOVING PAINT DRIPS

Thought you could cut in around wood trim without taping it off, huh? Nice try. Now the paint's dry and you have to remove it. Scraping removes the big blotches but leaves paint in the wood grain. So it's really a two-step process. Start by taping off the wall and removing the largest blotches (**Photo 1**). Next, scrub off the remaining paint (**Photo 2**).

**1 Tape and scrape.** Apply painter's tape on the wall to protect the paint. Then apply light pressure to a putty knife and scrape off the surface paint blobs.

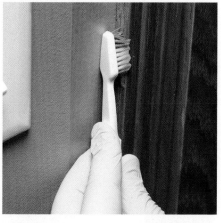

**2 Apply paint remover.** Squirt a few drops of paint remover onto an old toothbrush and brush in the direction of the wood grain.

# Painting, Staining & Finishing

## SIMPLE PAINTBRUSH DRYING RACK

This rack is a great place to let paintbrushes drip dry after washing. Just notch a couple of pieces of 1-by material and attach them to a cross support. Pound in some nails and set the rack on top of your sink edge.

## PERFECT PAINT TOUCH-UPS

After painting my kitchen cabinets, I was constantly touching up the paint here and there. Having to open a can of paint and clean brushes each time was a pain, so I came up with a slick solution. I cleaned out a bottle of nail polish using nail polish remover, filled it with the cabinet paint and put it in a kitchen drawer. Now these small, quick touch-ups are a breeze.

—Mike Kennedy

## GREAT USE FOR LEFTOVER PAINT

We had a lot of leftover latex paint, and we found the perfect way to use it up and save money at the same time. We poured all the paint into one large bucket—tan, peach, red, yellow, blue—a bunch of different colors. We stirred them all together, and the mixture turned out to be a bluish gray/tan. We had enough to paint the walls of our three-car garage! You could also use this type of mixture as a primer coat in any room where you'll be painting over it with a darker color.

Karen Merkel

# FASTER & NEATER PAINTING

*16 tidy tips from a picky painter*

by **Mark Petersen, Contributing Editor**

**Y**ou can always tell a good paint job because the new wall paint is only on the wall—not on the doors, windows, ceiling, carpet or trim. Painting, by its very nature, is a messy operation, and keeping the paint where it belongs requires solid taping techniques and well-planned surface protection. Maintaining your tools for the next job is just as important. We asked a painting pro how he goes about keeping it all neat and clean.

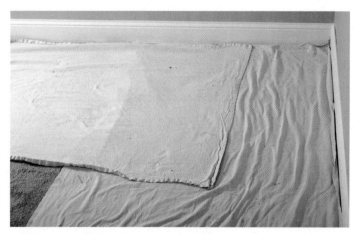

## Narrow drop cloths are better

Large drop cloths work great if you're painting a ceiling, but they're overkill if you're only painting walls and trim. Drop cloth runners are usually 3 to 4 ft. wide and are much easier and safer to work with because you don't have to fold them several times. Folded drop cloths are easy to trip on, and nothing good results from tripping with an open paint can in your hand.

Steve paints a lot of bedrooms and prefers runners no longer than 10 or 12 ft. A 3-ft. 9-in. x 11-ft. 9-in. drop cloth costs $16 at home centers. And when they get dirty, Steve washes his at a laundromat that has oversize washers and dryers.

## Tape off the carpet

When painting baseboard, some painters slip masking tape under the baseboard. But this is time-consuming and doesn't create a seep-proof seal between the baseboard and the carpet. So Steve presses the tape against the baseboard, covering about 1/4 in. of the bottom edge. Press down hard on the carpet while you apply the tape. That way, the tape will hold the carpet down while you paint. Later, when you remove the tape, the carpet will rise and cover the unpainted edge of the baseboard.

Steve prefers a high-quality tape for this job because it grabs and holds the baseboard better. He adds a strip of cheap tape to create a wider shield over the carpet. Finally, he spreads a drop cloth over the tape. This technique won't work if your carpet has a very low pile or if you have no padding under the carpet.

## Set your tape

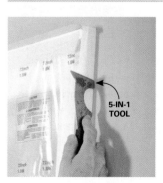

**5-IN-1 TOOL**

After you apply masking tape, run a putty knife, or a 5-in-1 tool, over it to "set" the tape to the trim. This bonds the tape to the surface and helps stop paint from seeping under the tape and up onto the trim.

# Painting, Staining & Finishing

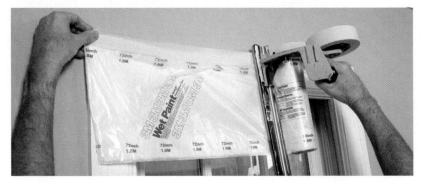

## Completely cover windows and doors

The masking tape you installed to protect the outside edge of the trim won't necessarily protect windows or doors. So it's important to cover them completely, especially if you're painting the ceiling. Here's how Steve does it: He hangs plastic with a Hand-Masker M3000 tool, which dispenses the tape and a folded piece of plastic in one pass. Before unfolding the plastic, he tapes off the perimeter of the trim. Then he unfolds the plastic so it completely covers the door or window and sticks it to the trim tape. Buy the M3000 for about $36 from an online retailer or your local paint store.

## Cut the paint before pulling the tape off

When you remove masking tape that has been left on too long, the tape can pull chunks of paint off with it. Steve usually pulls off his masking tape while the paint is relatively wet; rarely does he leave it on overnight. But when it has stayed on too long, he gently cuts the tape along the line where the paint meets the trim. This prevents the paint from sticking to the tape and coming off the wall.

## Create a smooth path along the ceiling

It's hard to create a straight line when you're painting the wall along a textured ceiling. As you move your paintbrush along, the bristles get hung up on the texture, which creates noticeable paint globs. Use your 5-in-1 tool or a screwdriver to remove about 1/8 in. to 1/4 in. of texture, creating a clear path for the brush.

## Don't flood the masking tape

Masking tape is a precaution, not a guarantee. No matter how careful you are, there may still be a void or two between the tape and the trim. If you expose the tape to a bunch of

paint, some is bound to get through. The trick is to pretend the tape isn't there. Don't force a lot of paint into the corner at an angle. Instead, lightly load the paintbrush and run it down parallel to the trim.

## Wear a rag

Steve never worries about looking presentable when he meets someone for lunch. That's because he seldom gets paint on himself.

Before the first can of paint is cracked open, he attaches a rag to his belt. So when he subconsciously wipes his hand on his pant leg, he's protected. He uses a large rag and unfolds it a bit, so the messy side stays facing out.

## Comb the brush

A paintbrush comb is the best tool for cleaning a brush. Unlike other brush cleaning tools, a comb penetrates and cleans deep between the bristles. It also prevents the bristles from sticking together, which helps your brush stay soft and retain its shape longer.

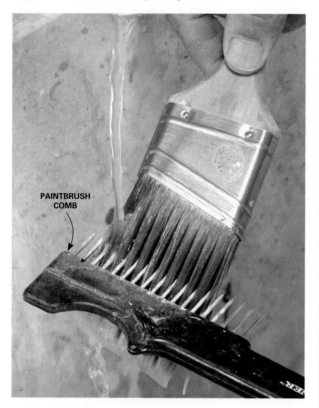

PAINTBRUSH COMB

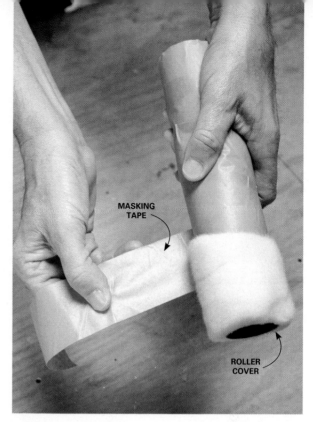

MASKING TAPE

ROLLER COVER

## Remove the fuzz

Some tools need cleaning even when they're brand new. Some new roller covers (usually the cheaper ones) have a layer of fuzz that detaches from the cover. The first time you load up a fuzzy roller, the paint mixes with the fuzz and creates small bumps on the wall. One way to remove the fuzz is to wrap masking tape all the way around the roller cover. When you pull the tape off, the excess fuzz will be pulled off along with it.

## Clean up with old brushes

Even though you diligently clean your brushes, they will eventually wear out. Consider saving a couple of different sizes to repurpose as cleaning brushes. An old paintbrush is an excellent tool for dusting off window trim or whatever else needs a light touch.

## Run water down into the bristles

After a few hours of painting, paint can work its way up into the bristles covered by the steel ferrule. If you don't clean the paint out of there, it will build up and cause your brush to get stiff and misshapen. After you comb all the paint out of the bristles, run water down into the brush. Finally, straighten out the bristles with a comb before you put the brush away. Protect the bristles by storing the brush in the package it came in.

# Painting, Staining & Finishing

POT SCRUBBER

### Scrub your roller

Don't neglect your roller. If you don't rinse off the roller, you'll end up with hardened paint inside the bushings or bearings, and that will ultimately result in a paint roller that doesn't roll. Keeping your tools clean doesn't have to be expensive. Steve swears by the $2 pot scrubber he purchased at a discount store.

### Lube the roller

Metal rusts, and the metal bushings or bearings in your paint roller are no exception. Do yourself a favor, and spray a little lubricant on your paint roller before you store it. A rusty paint roller can squeak. Pushing a roller back and forth for several hours is monotonous enough; adding a few thousand squeaks might drive you completely insane.

### Clean up your mistakes

No matter how careful you are, you're bound to get paint on something you didn't mean to. Keep a can of paint remover on hand. Steve uses Goof Off, one of several brands available.

Paint remover works great for removing dried latex paint from trim, countertops, door hinges, vinyl floors or whatever it is you spilled on. A 16-oz. can costs $6 at a home center. And yes, even Steve won't leave home without it.

PROFESSIONAL STRENGTH

GOOF OFF

THE MIRACLE REMOVER!

REMOVES THE TOUGH STUFF

ADHESIVE & GLUE

ASPHALT & TAR

DRIED LATEX PAINT

EXTREMELY FLAMMABLE. HARMFUL OR FATAL IF SWALLOWED. HARMFUL. EYE IRRITANT. Read other cautions on side panel.
CONTENIDO INFLAMABLE. NOCIVO O MORTAL SI SE INGIERE. IRRITA LOS OJOS. Lea las precauciones en el panel lateral.

1 Pint (16 FL. OZ.) 473mL

### Keep a garbage bag close at hand

Never underestimate how much trash a painting job creates. And running around the house with big wads of plastic and tape covered in wet paint is not a good idea. Steve brings along his garbage bags on the first trip into the house. He either hangs a bag on a doorknob or sets one in a portable bag holder (garbage barrels take up too much room in his van). You can buy the Bag Buddy shown here for $21 at uline.com.

BAG BUDDY

# WATER-BASED FINISHES

*Top Ten tips from an expert*

by **Dave Munkittrick**

**If** you used water-based wood finishes years ago and gave up in frustration, give them another try. Newer versions have many advantages over solvent-based finishes: They dry much faster, so less dust can settle into the wet coat, and there's less waiting between coats. Cleanup takes soap and water, not chemicals. They're low odor, pose no fire hazard and are better for the environment.

But water-based finishes aren't perfect. They raise the grain and are very sensitive to temperature and humidity. They're nonyellowing, which is good, but they can produce a bland appearance on darker woods.

To help you achieve a great finish every time and avoid the pitfalls, here are my top 10 tips for using water-based finishes.

---

## MEET AN EXPERT

**David Munkittrick** has 30 years' experience in woodworking. He is an active freelance journalist, furniture designer and builder. He lives and works on an old farmstead in western Wisconsin where the pig barn has been repurposed as his wood shop.

### 1 Raise the grain first

I always raise the grain on raw wood before applying a water-based finish. Simply brush, sponge or spray on some distilled water and let it dry thoroughly (overnight is best). Then, resand with your final grit paper to break off the whiskers. Now when you apply the finish, the grain will stay down.

BEFORE ADDING WATER

AFTER WATER DRIES

# Painting, Staining & Finishing

## 2 Seal oil-based stain

Oil and water don't mix. Water-based poly can have adhesion problems when applied over an oil-based stain that's not thoroughly cured. That's why I always apply a barrier coat of dewaxed shellac to seal oil-based stain. After the shellac dries, a light scuff-sand will leave an excellent surface for the poly to grip.

The instructions on the can will indicate that you can apply a water-based clear coat right over an oil-based stain *if* the stain has thoroughly cured. However, the curing time can be several days, especially with an open-grain wood such as oak where the stain can sit uncured deep in the pores. Play it safe and seal the stain with shellac. Zinsser SealCoat is a dewaxed shellac available at most home centers and hardware stores.

WET FINISH

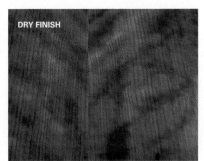

DRY FINISH

## 3 Lay it down and leave it

Water-based poly should be laid down with a couple of quick strokes. Don't worry too much about the appearance of the wet finish. It will look awful at first, but water-based poly has an amazing ability to pull tight as it cures, like shrink wrap. The brush marks will disappear—I promise. If you go back and try to rework the film, you're likely to cause a big mess. Resist the urge. If you see a dust speck, just leave it alone and fix the problem later with sandpaper and another coat.

## 4 Choose the right applicator

Buy a top-quality, fine-bristle nylon brush for spindle work, inside corners and narrow edges. The nylon bristles won't absorb water from the finish and become mushy like natural bristles will. I use a Golden Taklon brush, although I'm sure there are other ones available. Each fiber is extruded to a point to resemble a natural bristle. The brush is very soft, and the variable fiber diameters create more space for holding material, meaning fewer dips in the can. You can get a Taklon bristle brush for $15 to $30 at various online sources. (And for that kind of money, plan on taking care of it!)

GOLDEN TAKLON BRUSH

For large, flat surfaces like tabletops, I turn to a paint pad. It allows me to lay down an even coat in seconds and maintain a wet edge, even over a big area.

PAINT PAD

## 5 Use synthetic abrasives

Synthetic wool is a must-have product with water-based finishes. Traditional steel wool will leave behind bits of steel, which will react with the water and leave rust stains in the clear coat. Synthetic wool comes in various grades and is readily available where water-based finishes are sold. I use coarse to medium synthetic wool between coats. To rub out the last coat, I turn to fine and extra fine. Synthetic wool is available at home centers, hardware stores and woodworking stores.

## 6 Refinish kitchen cabinets with water-based poly

The low odor of water-based poly makes it an ideal choice for refinishing your existing kitchen cabinets in place. It doesn't matter what the old finish was, as long as you prep the surface properly before applying the water-based product. First use a degreaser cleaner like Formula 409 or Fantastik to clean away any buildup of grease or cooking oil. Scuff-sand the old finish with fine synthetic wool, then seal with Zinsser SealCoat. Sand the seal coat with fine synthetic wool, then brush on two to three coats of water-based poly to complete the job.

## 7 Use an extender in hot, dry conditions

Water-based finishes are more sensitive to temperature and humidity than their oil cousins. It's best to apply your water-based poly when the air temperature is between 70 and 80 degrees F and the humidity is below 70 percent. If the air is both hot and dry, the poly may set so fast that it will be difficult to maintain a wet edge as you brush, or the film may not level properly before it sets.

The solution is to add an extender to slow the drying time. This is especially useful when you're coating a large piece like a dining table. One choice is General Finishes Dry-Time Extender, No. 21217, about $12 per pint online (one source is rockler.com). Floetrol is another great additive for slowing things down. It's designed for latex paints but works great with satin or semi-gloss water-based poly and is readily available at paint stores.

## 8    Add color for the look of oil-based poly

Water-based poly dries water-clear and can leave wood with a cold look, especially on dark woods like walnut. To get the warm glow of oil-based poly, add a few drops of dye. Transtint Honey Amber is a great product (No. 21979; $21 from rockler.com). Make a weak solution of dye and water, then stain the wood before you apply the poly. Believe it or not, you can also add dye directly to the poly before you brush it on.

A third coloring option is to seal the raw wood with wax-free shellac, then topcoat with water-based poly. Whichever method you choose, experiment on scrap wood to make sure you'll get the look you want.

## 9    Strain your poly first

Unless you're using a brand new can of poly, always strain it with a medium-mesh strainer before applying it. Once the finish is used, it will be polluted with little bits of dried or semi-dried varnish, which will wreck your new finish. Stands and replacement meshes like the ones shown are available at woodworking stores and online.

## 10    Mist your wood before staining

Dry wood can aggressively suck up dye or stain, making it hard to control the color penetration. The result can be a dark, blotchy mess. For added control, try wetting the wood with distilled water right before you apply the dye or stain. (Be sure you've raised the grain first; see Tip 1.) The increased open time makes the color easier to control. A household pump sprayer or sponge works great.

# 2 Electrical & High-Tech

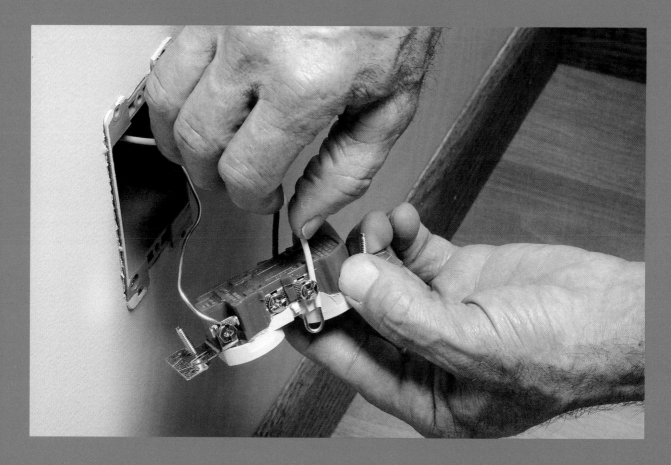

## IN THIS CHAPTER

# HomeCare&Repair

**TIPS, FIXES & GEAR FOR A TROUBLE-FREE HOME**

## STORM TIP

Installing a whole-house surge suppression device is the best way to continuously protect your high-priced electronics. But if you know a storm is coming, you can protect against fried circuit boards by flipping off the breakers to your stove, dishwasher, furnace, A/C and fridge. Just make sure you turn them back on after the storm passes.

## GreatGoofs®

### Adventures with electricity

I asked a friend to help me install extra outlets in my new garage. We ran all the wires and connected everything, and it all looked neat and proper. To see if our wiring job worked, I plugged in an electric drill. When I squeezed the trigger, the drill started humming and the ceiling light went on!

After we stopped laughing, I unplugged the drill and called my brother-in-law, who actually knows something about electricity. He checked out everything and made the proper connections. Now when I squeeze the trigger on the drill, only the drill goes on. I use wall switches to control the lights.

Lester Levinson

## KNOW WHEN YOUR SURGE PROTECTOR BITES THE DUST

It's a good idea to install a surge-suppressing receptacle to protect your refrigerator's electronics. Some surge protectors feature a light to prove they are working. But if you don't clean behind your refrigerator very often (to see the light), look for one with an audible alarm instead (the Leviton No. T7280 is one example; about $40 online).

## REPAIR STRIPPED ELECTRICAL BOX THREADS

If you have an older home with metal electrical boxes, you're bound to encounter a stripped hole sooner or later. Don't think you can get away with ramming a drywall screw into the stripped hole. That doesn't meet code, and it'll loosen up over time. If you have a tap-and-die set, use a No. 6-32 tap and try to reform the existing threads. If that works, you're good to go. If not, consider buying an electrician's tapping tool (one choice is the Klein Tools No. 625-24 Triple-Tap Tool, $15 at home centers). The shaft has tapping threads for the three most common thread sizes you'll find in electrical boxes. Turn off the power and insert the tapping tool as shown.

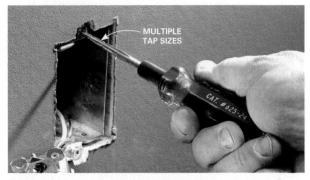

MULTIPLE TAP SIZES

**Reform stripped threads—or tap new ones.** Twist the tapping tool into the stripped threads to reform them. If they're stripped beyond repair, push the tool in farther and twist to tap the cut and tap the next largest size.

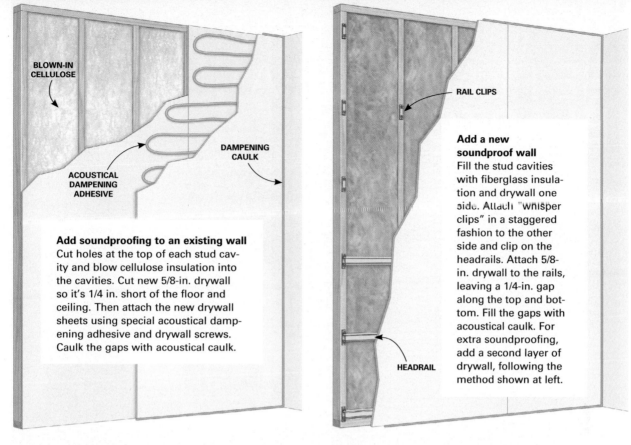

**BLOWN-IN CELLULOSE**

**ACOUSTICAL DAMPENING ADHESIVE**

**DAMPENING CAULK**

**Add soundproofing to an existing wall**
Cut holes at the top of each stud cavity and blow cellulose insulation into the cavities. Cut new 5/8-in. drywall so it's 1/4 in. short of the floor and ceiling. Then attach the new drywall sheets using special acoustical dampening adhesive and drywall screws. Caulk the gaps with acoustical caulk.

**RAIL CLIPS**

**Add a new soundproof wall**
Fill the stud cavities with fiberglass insulation and drywall one side. Attach "whisper clips" in a staggered fashion to the other side and clip on the headrails. Attach 5/8-in. drywall to the rails, leaving a 1/4-in. gap along the top and bottom. Fill the gaps with acoustical caulk. For extra soundproofing, add a second layer of drywall, following the method shown at left.

**HEADRAIL**

## SOUNDPROOF YOUR HOME THEATER (OR ANY OTHER ROOM)

So you've installed a cool home theater and now everyone in the house is complaining that they can't sleep because the sound invades their bedroom. If it's a choice between getting rid of the home theater, turning it down to inaudible levels or installing soundproofing, we know what your next project will be. We talked to the pros at Trademark Soundproofing (tmsoundproofing.com) and got the skinny on how to do the job the right way. Here are their tips for the two most common residential scenarios: where you already have a wall in place, and where you plan to add a new soundproof wall.

For more information and to buy dampening adhesive and acoustical caulk, visit tmsoundproofing.com.

## FIX FOR WOBBLY OUTLETS

If you've got wobbly outlets to deal with, here's a great solution: Use outlet spacers. Buchanan Caterpillar Spacers and Ideal Industries Device Spacers are two choices. You can find them at home centers and hardware stores for about $7 for a pack of 25 strips.

The plastic strips fold accordion-style so you can use one or several, as necessary. And they snap over the screws, so you don't have to remove the screws. One strip of spacers can fix one to four outlets, depending on how much shimming is needed.

## A SMARTER LIGHT TIMER

*I live in northern Michigan where the change in the number of daylight hours from winter to summer is tremendous. How can I hook up a photo sensor with a regular timer so it will turn on at sundown, but turn off after a few hours?*

Rather than reinvent the wheel, check out the "astronomical" timers in the list below ($35 and up). Find the longitude and latitude of your home at worldatlas.com/aatlas/latitude_and_longitude_finder.htm and enter it into the timer. The timer automatically calculates the sundown "turn on" time. Then choose either a set run-time or let the timer turn the lights off at sunup.

- Leviton VPT24-1PZ
- Intermatic EI600WC
- Tork SS721ZA
- Pass & Seymour RT24W

**LEVITON VPT24-1PZ**

# BE READY FOR A
# BLACKOUT

*Don't be left in the dark ... prepare your household with these handy tips*

by **Gary Wentz, Senior Editor**

The experts tell us to expect more outages as the capacity and condition of our power grid go downhill. So we assembled this set of tips to help you survive—and maybe even thrive—without power. Of course, the best preparation is to buy a generator. But whether you own one or not, these tips can provide some comfort and convenience, safety and sanity during the next blackout.

## 1 Fill the grill tank

A blackout limits many of life's little pleasures, but you can still enjoy a hot meal if you have a gas grill and a full tank. During a three-day outage, Field Editor Arthur Barfield fed dozens of friends and neighbors by grilling the contents of his fridge and freezer before anything went bad.

Arthur Barfield, Field Editor

## 2 Get cash!

In a blackout, cash is king. Some stores may stay open, but they probably won't be able to process credit card purchases. And all the cash machines will be on strike. Field Editor Pete Plumer tells us he learned this lesson the hard way during a long power outage: Keep an emergency cash stash on hand.

## 3 Have a backup plan

If a blackout lasts long enough, even a well-prepared family will want to give up and get out. So make just-in-case arrangements with friends or relatives who are willing take you in. If you wait, you might find that phone and Internet communication becomes a lot more difficult.

### 4 Ice saves money

A couple of days without power can cost you a few hundred bucks as food spoils in fridges and freezers. You could try to buy a few bags of ice (along with everyone else) after the power goes out. But Field Editor Shawna Hathaway has a better idea: Fill locking freezer bags with water and keep them in the freezer. During a blackout, they'll help the freezer stay cold longer. Or you can transfer them to the fridge or a cooler. When they thaw, you've got drinking water.

### 5 Fill the tub

When the power grid goes down, your city water system may soon follow. So fill up buckets and bottles for washing, flushing and drinking. Several of our Field Editors pointed out that the biggest reservoir in any home is the bathtub. And Field Editor Tompkin Lee added a critical tip: "Duct tape the bathtub drain. Most drains are not all that tight, and in a day or two, all that precious water will be gone."

Tompkin Lee,
Field Editor

### 6 Turn your car into a generator

A power inverter, which turns DC current from your car into AC current for electric gadgets, is the next best thing to a generator. An inverter to power a tablet or laptop will cost you about $25, but there are much bigger models ($100 and up) that can run power tools and appliances. (To learn more, search for "power inverter" at familyhandyman.com.) Field Editor Cameron LiDestri even used an inverter to get hot water during a recent weeklong outage. His on-demand water heater burns propane but also requires a 75-watt electrical supply. So Cameron plugged the heater into a long extension cord and ran it out to his car. "When anyone wanted a hot shower, I just started the car," Cameron tells us.

### 7 Conserve batteries with LEDs

During a power outage, LED flashlights and lanterns have a huge advantage over incandescent models: They allow batteries to last much longer (typically about six to ten times as long). And LED technology isn't just for flashlights. During a six-day outage, Field Editor Matt Kelly used LED "puck" lights, the type designed for under-cabinet lighting. "I stuck them up in bathrooms, bedrooms and hallways so we didn't have to stumble around in the dark," Matt says.

## 8 Get a radio

If phone and Internet systems go down along with the power grid, a battery-powered radio may be your only source of weather and emergency information. You could listen in your car, but a portable radio lets you listen anywhere. Battery-powered radios cost as little as $20 at discount stores.

## 9 Gas up

Even if you don't plan to go anywhere, your car is a critical part of your survival kit. It's your emergency transport, your charging system for cell phones and maybe even the only heated space you'll have. So don't wait until the blackout hits. As Field Editor (and emergency manager in New York City) Nathan Mandelbaum points out, without power, gas stations can't pump gas from their tanks into yours.

## 10 A CO detector is essential

Blackouts often lead to carbon monoxide deaths. Here's why: To get heat during outages, people crank up fireplaces, gas stoves and all types of heaters—and anything that burns produces carbon monoxide. It's OK to use these heat sources, but take a tip from Field Editor Kevin Yochum. During a recent outage, he fired up his kerosene heater—but first he placed a battery-operated CO detector in the room. You can buy a detector for about $25 at any home center.

### After the power goes out

- Unplug everything. As the grid sputters back to life, it may create power surges that can destroy electronics. Leave one light switched on so you know when power has returned.
- Don't use candles. Flashlights produce more light and won't burn your house down.
- Bring solar landscape lights inside. Don't forget to put them out for recharging during the day.
- Keep the fridge closed. The less you open fridge and freezer doors, the longer your food will stay cold.
- Tap your water heater. It's your built-in emergency water supply. Let the water cool before you open the drain valve.
- Don't take chances. Power outages mean packed emergency rooms and delayed ambulance service; it's a bad time to get injured.

# GreatGoofs®

### That is one mighty fan

I helped my son-in-law install a new ceiling fan and light in their kitchen. The wiring in the house was pretty old, but we'd figured it out—or at least we hoped so. That evening, my son-in-law called to say that when he flipped the switch to show my daughter the new fan, all the power in the house went out! I told him to turn off the switch and reset any breakers. He did as I said, but nothing changed. Anticipating a total project redo, I told him I'd be over shortly. A few minutes later, he called back to say there was a neighborhood power outage. It turned out this was a major outage affecting 42,000 homes. When my daughter put two and two together, she said, "Wow, from one little fan?"

—Louis DeSanzo

# HandyHints®

## A NEW ANGLE ON HDMI CONNECTIONS

What's the point of having a flat-screen TV that hugs the wall if your cables stick straight out? Don't bend the cables and risk breaking the connectors inside your TV. Instead, buy HDMI angle adapters. Choose from 90 degrees up/down, 90 degrees left/right, variable angle or a combination of variable angle and swivel adapter. They're less than $10 each at electronics stores and online (monoprice.com is one online source).

## MAILBOX ALERT SYSTEM

In bad weather or when my arthritis is acting up, walking down our long driveway to see whether the mail has come yet is no fun (especially if it hasn't). My solution was to buy a "driveway wireless alert system" (about $20 at online retailers).

I mounted the sensor module in the back of the mailbox and the receiver module in our living room. When the mailman opens the mailbox door, inserts the mail and closes the door, the chime goes off. No more unnecessary trips.

—Roy T. Stenger

## THERE'S AN APP FOR THAT

### Scan tool for smartphones

If you've ever wanted to know what's going on in your car's engine control computer, this handy tool lets you peek inside. Just plug the sensor (BlueDriver; $100 at lemurmonitors.com) into the onboard diagnostic (OBD-II) port on your vehicle. The unit sends data right to your smartphone via its Bluetooth interface.

Use the free software iPhone app to get generic powertrain (P) trouble codes, ABS codes (for some domestic vehicles), interactive gauges and logs.

Or, buy subscriptions individually (about $10 each) to unlock premium features like these:

- Repair reports (tell you the most likely fix for up to five trouble codes)
- Freeze-frame data (tells you what was going on before and after a trouble code was set)
- Smog readiness check
- Live data (see the data the computer is getting from the sensors).

### More tools for your phone

Smartphones are becoming as important a tool on the job site as a hammer...well, almost. DeWalt has an app for the iPad and iPhone called Mobile Pro. It has stud and drywall estimators, and concrete slab and area conversion calculators, as well as several other helpful tools. All of the features I tried were simple enough for even a non-techie guy like me.

Best of all, it's free, and who's ever offered you a free hammer? For $1 to $10, you can buy add-ons that would come in handy for framers, trimmers and even landscapers. Download Mobile Pro at itunes. apple.com.

—Rick Muscoplat, Contributing Editor

# SMART SWITCHES

*Swap out a switch to cut energy bills and add convenience*

by **Elisa Bernick**

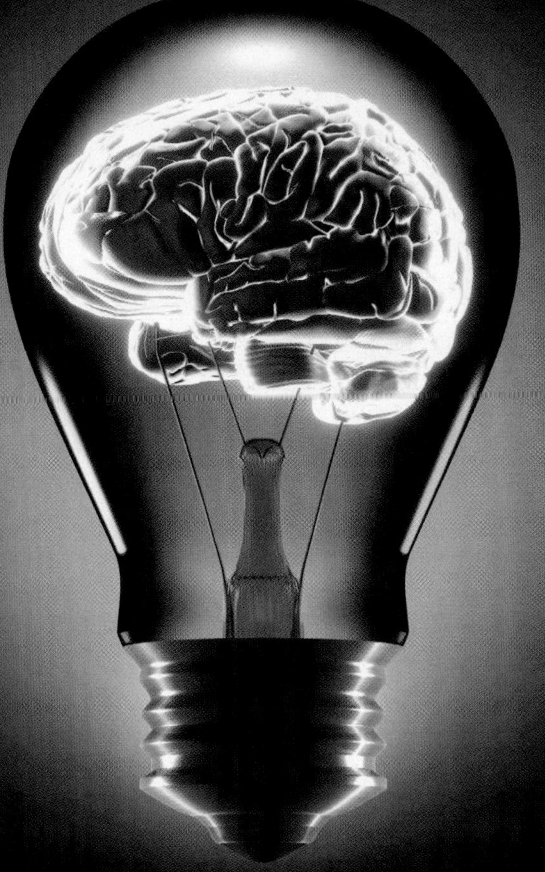

**H**ome control systems continue to evolve. Some require whole-house computer networks or elaborate rewiring. But there are easy to install stand-alone switches that pay back big in money and energy savings, convenience and safety. And best of all, these new smart switches work with CFL and LED bulbs. Check out these simple electronic controls that will help your home work "smarter."

## Check the wiring before you buy

Many of the new, sophisticated smart switches require a neutral wire to run the circuitry inside the switch—particularly those compatible with LED and CFL bulbs. Before you buy a new switch, check the packaging. Most will specifically tell you if a neutral is required, as shown at right.

To see if you have a neutral wire in your switch box:

■ Turn off the power and use a noncontact voltage detector to check that the circuit is off before you remove the cover plate.

■ Remove the cover plate and unscrew and remove the switch. The photo at left shows one common situation without a neutral wire.

**No neutral**
If your switch is wired like this one—connected to a white and a black wire—both wires are hot and neither can serve as a neutral.

**Honeywell**

Programmable
**timer**
Minuterie
programmable

**Neutral wire required**
**Fil neutre requis**

works with
CFL bulbs
Fonctionne avec
les AFC

*Compatible* with
• All types of lighting up to 1800 W
• Ceiling/bath fans & pumps up to

## ILLUMINATED SWITCHES

It sounds like a joke: How do you find a light switch in the dark? Illuminate it, of course. These great little inventions use a tiny bit of electricity from the circuit they're on to light a small LED or neon bulb. They install as easily as regular switches, but be aware that these switches work fine with some CFLs but not so great with others.

Both toggle and rocker switches are available; search online for "illuminated light switch." One source for a broad selection of switches is kyleswitchplates.com. It carries clear, white and red toggles and black, white, ivory and other colors of rocker switches as well as a huge and reasonably priced selection of low-voltage lighting, switchplates and other items.

## OCCUPANCY AND VACANCY SENSORS

Residential occupancy and vacancy sensors have come of age. Most residential sensors use passive infrared (PIR) technology to detect heat and motion and turn lights on and off accordingly. They can cut lighting costs by 50 percent in rooms where lights are frequently left on when no one is in them. Wall-mount sensors install just like a light switch and are available as switches or dimmers. Most require a neutral wire, but there are a few models that don't. The smartest sensors are designed to screen out background interference and detect small movements and natural light. They also work with LED, CFL, incandescent, halogen and other bulb and load types. These specialized switches generally cost $20 to $40. Search online for "occupancy sensor light switch" or "vacancy sensor light switch."

### Occupancy vs. vacancy sensor—What's the difference?

An **occupancy sensor** automatically turns lights ON and OFF. Great for areas where lights are accidentally left on a lot, like in a kid's room, or where your hands are full, like in a laundry area. A **vacancy sensor** has a manual ON and automatic OFF (you can preset different times). Good for bedrooms, so the light doesn't automatically turn on if a spouse enters while you're sleeping, or in the hallway, so your pet doesn't trigger the light.

Lutron's Maestro occupancy/ vacancy sensor switch functions in both modes depending how it's programmed. It's available in two models—one for small rooms (MS-OPS2) and one for larger rooms (MS-OPS5). It includes a push button manual control switch and is available as a dimming sensor as well. It does not require a neutral wire. Learn more at lutron.com.

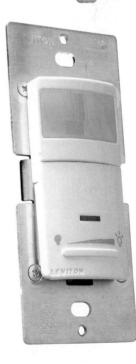

Leviton's Universal Dimming Sensor (IPSD6-1LZ) is an occupancy sensor and dimmer in one unit. It has a 180-degree field of view for up to 900 sq. ft. of coverage and includes manual presets for delayed-off time settings. Compatible with dimmable LED, CFL and incandescent bulbs. It does not require a neutral. Visit leviton.com.

# TIMERS

Timers have a hundred uses, but two stand out. We think every home should have a timer for the bath exhaust fan and one for outside lighting.

## Bath fan timers

Timers for bath fans are important because excess humidity can cause everything from window condensation and mildew to moisture and rot inside walls. Timers connected to exhaust fans must be rated to run electric motors, which makes them more expensive than those running incandescent lamps. Some new wall switch timers have dual controls for turning off both lights and fans after a preset time. Search for "bath fan timer switch." Quality models cost $20 to $35.

For the ultimate in smart bath fan timers, buy a humidity-sensing fan designed to automatically turn on and off as moisture levels at the ceiling rise and fall. Expect to pay several hundred dollars—sometimes quite a lot more—for this high-tech fan.

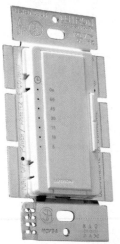

Lutron's Maestro MA-T51 Countdown Timer ($31 at amazon.com) can be set to operate the fan or light for 5 to 60 minutes before turning off automatically. It also has a tap-twice manual override. Orange LEDs indicate the time remaining before the device turns off. This single timer does not require a neutral. It's also available as a dual timer for both light and fan control. Learn more at lutron.com.

Broan's UltraSense bath fans automatically turn on when they detect humidity at the ceiling and turn off when humidity levels fall. These fans are available in single- and multi-speed versions. The latter automatically increase their speed to remove shower steam as quickly as possible. Models with motion sensors increase the fan speed automatically for humidity and odor control when someone enters the room. Visit broanultra.com to learn more and to locate a dealer.

BROAN

## Outside lighting timers

Automated outdoor lighting is convenient, but the smartest timers are astronomic versions that turn lights off and on from a memory of 365 days of sunrise and sunset times based on your home's location. Those with randomized settings can vary on and off times, which adds a heightened level of security by fooling burglars into thinking someone is home when you're away. The newest (and most expensive) astronomic timer switches are compatible with CFL and LED bulbs in addition to incandescent and halogen bulbs. Non-compatible timers can cause CFLs to flicker and shorten their life span. Search online for "outside lighting timer." Prices vary quite a bit; the models shown below average about $40.

Intermatic's EI600 Series In-Wall timers do not require a neutral wire. This timer series is highly recommended by lighting pros, and users report they are easy to install and program. Learn more at intermatic.com.

Leviton's Vizia VPT24-1PZ indoor/outdoor programmable timer comes with three different color faceplates and a five-year warranty. It requires a neutral wire. Learn more at leviton.com.

## DIMMERS FOR CFLs AND LEDs

You can save up to $55 a year by replacing an incandescent bulb with a dimmable LED and using it regularly at low levels. Beyond energy savings, dimmers add comfort and convenience. However, dimming technology has had a hard time keeping pace with advances in CFL and LED bulbs. Problems include:

■ **Reduced dimming range.** Unlike incandescent bulbs, most CFL and LED bulbs will not dim to very low levels. Some dimmable LED bulbs can get close, but it depends on a specific bulb's circuitry.

■ **Lights dropping out.** CFL and LED bulbs will sometimes turn off before the slider reaches the bottom.

■ **Lights not turning on.** After you dim a CFL or LED bulb, it sometimes won't turn on until you move the dimmer slider up. This "pop-on" effect can really be frustrating in a three-way situation where a light can be controlled from several switches, not just using the dimmer.

■ **Lights turn off unexpectedly.** Dimmable CFL and LED bulbs can be affected by line voltage fluctuations and they can turn off (not just dim or flicker, like incandescents) when a hair dryer or vacuum cleaner is used.

The good news is that dimmer switch technology is improving. The newest switches work well and can effectively dim mixed light sources on the same circuit. The bad news is these switches are pricey—the simplest switches start at $15 and those with more functions cost $35 or more—and they require pricey dimmable LED and CFL bulbs (they also work fine with incandescent and halogen bulbs). A list of compatible bulbs can be found on manufacturer Web sites. Some require a neutral and some do not, so check the packaging carefully.

Leviton's SureSlide Universal Dimmer 6674 has an on/off preset function that remembers your preferred setting and is compatible with Decora wiring devices and wallplates. It does require a neutral. Learn more at leviton.com.

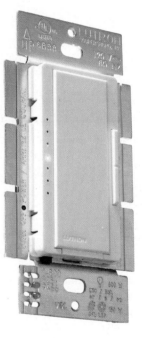

Lutron's C-L Dimmer Collection includes the Skylark Contour and Maestro (shown at right), among other models. These dimmers include adjustable dials that accommodate a broad range of dimmable bulbs. Visit lutron.com for a list of compatible bulbs.

Lutron's Credenza C-L Lamp dimmer plugs into any outlet to dim table and floor lamps with incandescent and halogen as well as dimmable CFL and LED bulbs. The regular Credenza lamp dimmer lets you use a standard halogen or incandescent lightbulb instead of a more expensive three-way bulb and also plugs into standard outlets. Learn more at lutron.com.

# GreatGoofs®

### High-voltage hair tools

My wife and I had just moved into our first home, and it needed a lot of work. I decided to add an electrical receptacle in the bathroom so my wife could plug in her hair dryer and curling iron. Well, the closest electrical source was the water heater, and I wired the receptacle directly to the wires attached to it. I went to work the next morning and received a call from my wife telling me that her curling iron had melted to the vanity top! My father-in-law came over and explained the difference between 240 and 120 volts. That was my first and last electrical "conquest."

—Dan Bixler

# INSTALLING NEW SWITCHES AND OUTLETS

*Brush up on the basics, and learn how to install modern "smart" switches*

by **Jeff Gorton, Associate Editor**

**W**hether you're replacing an existing switch or outlet or adding a new one, here are 10 great tips to help you make sure your installation is safe and long lasting. These tips go beyond the basics, so if you're unsure how to begin installing a switch or an outlet, visit familyhandyman.com and search for articles on wiring switches and outlets.

Before you begin any electrical work, always switch off the circuit breaker in the main panel, and then double-check that you've turned off the correct breaker by testing all the wires in the box with a noncontact voltage detector.

## 1 Use the right tools for safe and fast wiring

Here are four must-have tools if you plan to work on many switches and outlets:

■ **Voltage tester.** You can pick one up for a few bucks and use it to test for hot wires or to find a neutral. Just touch the probes between a hot and a neutral, or between two hot wires. The tester will light up if the wires are "hot." The tester shown also tests for 240 volts.

■ **Combination sheath and wire stripper.** This Klein K1412 (about $25 at home

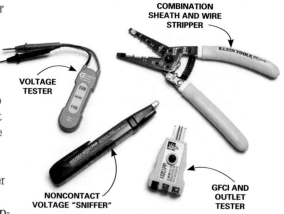

**VOLTAGE TESTER**

**COMBINATION SHEATH AND WIRE STRIPPER**

**NONCONTACT VOLTAGE "SNIFFER"**

**GFCI AND OUTLET TESTER**

centers and hardware stores) is our favorite. In addition to slots for stripping insulation from 14- and 12-gauge wire, it has slots to strip the sheathing from 14- and 12-gauge nonmetallic cable.

■ **Voltage "sniffer."** The beauty of this tool is that you don't have to touch bare wires to see if they're hot. Just hold it near any wire or cable to see if it's energized. We recommend using a noncontact voltage tester like this to double-check that all wires in a box are "dead" after turning off the circuit breaker. Prices range from about $10 to $25.

■ **GFCI receptacle tester.** Just plug it into any GFCI outlet and the lights will indicate whether the outlet is properly wired. Plug it into a GFCI receptacle and press the test button to see if the GFCI is working correctly ($8 to $10).

## Tighten up outlets

In a perfect world, switch and outlet boxes would be flush to the wall surface, but it's not unusual to find them slightly recessed. Switches and outlets mounted to recessed boxes can get wobbly if you rely on device "ears" for support.

To prevent this, slip a coiled-wire shim over the device's mounting screw. The top photo shows how to make a coil from a scrap of insulated wire. Hold the coil against the box to gauge where to cut it to span the gap between the box and the surface of the wall. Slip the coil over the screw and tighten the screw as shown at right. Your shimmed outlet will be solid and secure.

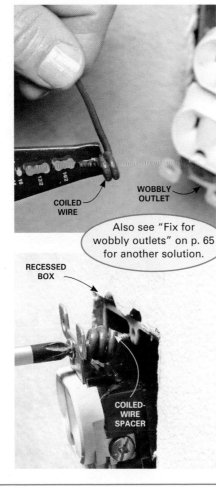

COILED WIRE
WOBBLY OUTLET

Also see "Fix for wobbly outlets" on p. 65 for another solution.

RECESSED BOX
COILED-WIRE SPACER

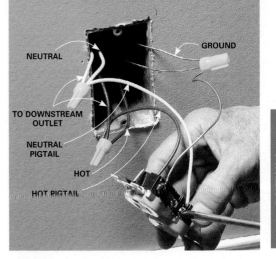

NEUTRAL
GROUND
TO DOWNSTREAM OUTLET
NEUTRAL PIGTAIL
HOT
HOT PIGTAIL

## 4 Use pigtails on outlets

Outlets have pairs of screws on each side that you can use to connect downstream outlets, but it's best not to use them. There are two reasons for this. First, connecting the wires leading to downstream outlets with wire connectors creates a more secure connection. And second, it's easier to press the outlet back into the box if fewer of its screws are connected to wires. Instead, use wire connectors to connect the neutral, hot and ground wires along with 6-in.-long "pigtails." Then connect the pigtails to the outlet.

## 3 Smart switches may need a neutral wire

Switch makers have built all kinds of features including occupancy sensors, timers and programmable dimmers into modern "smart switches" (see pp. 70–73). Unlike an ordinary switch, some of these new switches require a neutral to operate correctly. This is a problem if your old switch is wired as a "switch loop," such that only a hot and a switched hot are available in the box.

Before you shop for a new switch, remove your old one from the box—after making sure the power is off, of course—and look for a neutral white wire. Any wires connected to the existing switch are not neutral wires. If a white wire is connected to the switch, it should be marked as a hot wire with either a piece of black tape or black marker as shown at right. If there's no neutral in the box, shop for a smart switch that doesn't require a neutral. The adjacent photo shows a programmable timer switch that requires a neutral.

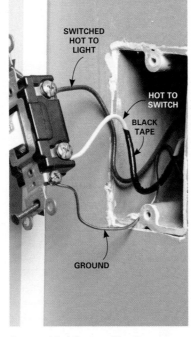

SWITCHED HOT TO LIGHT
HOT TO SWITCH
BLACK TAPE
GROUND

Some switch boxes, like the one shown here, don't contain a neutral wire. Choose a replacement that doesn't require a neutral.

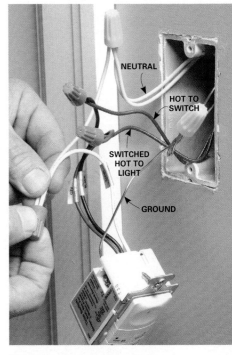

NEUTRAL
HOT TO SWITCH
SWITCHED HOT TO LIGHT
GROUND

Many of today's smart switches, like the one shown above, require a neutral wire to work properly. This switch box contains a neutral wire.

ELECTRICAL & HIGH-TECH

## 5 Choose the right outlet

In an attempt to ~~reduce the risk of~~ electrocution and fires, the National Electrical Code requires specific types of outlets in certain locations. **Tamper-resistant outlets** are required everywhere, **weather-resistant** in certain outdoor locations, and **GFCIs** in areas where dampness or water could contribute to a dangerous shock (kitchens, bathrooms, garages, outdoors). **Arc-fault interrupters** stop arcing that can cause fires and are required in most living areas. Before you install a new outlet, check the code or consult with someone who's familiar with code requirements to see which type of outlet you should use.

**TAMPER-RESISTANT OUTLET**

**TAMPER-RESISTANT, WEATHER-RESISTANT**

**ARC-FAULT CIRCUIT INTERRUPTER**

**GROUND-FAULT CIRCUIT INTERRUPTER**

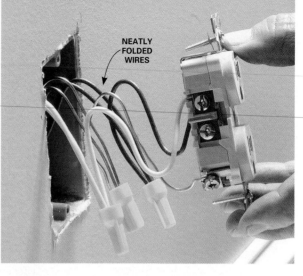

NEATLY FOLDED WIRES

## 6 Fold wires neatly

It's surprising how easily an outlet or switch goes into the box if you fold the wires correctly. The trick is to make an "accordion" out of the wires so you can push the device in without crunching the wires. Another advantage of neat folds like this is that they reduce strain on the wires and keep you from accidentally creating a loose connection as you press the device into the box.

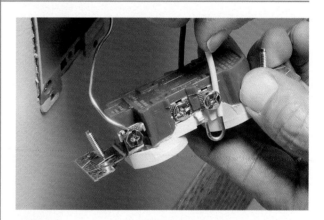

## 7 Make a tight connection

Most outlets and switches have a strip gauge on the back. Use it to determine the correct length of bare wire to leave exposed when you strip the insulation. If there is no strip gauge, expose 3/4 in. of bare wire. Bend a loop in the wire. Most wire strippers have a hole that you can stick the wire through to bend the loop. Otherwise, use the nose of the stripper or needle-nose pliers. Slip the loop over the terminal screw, making sure it's going around in a clockwise direction. Then pinch the open end of the loop with your stripper or pliers so that it encircles the screw. Finally, snug up the screw. Don't use the "stab-in" holes on the back of the device or stack two wires under the screw.

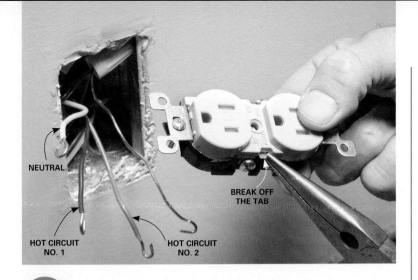

NEUTRAL

HOT CIRCUIT
NO. 1

HOT CIRCUIT
NO. 2

BREAK OFF
THE TAB

## 8 Match the breakaway tab to the original outlet

There are a few different reasons that an outlet breakaway tab may be removed. If one-half of a duplex outlet is controlled by a wall switch, then the hot tab, and possibly the neutral tab, will be broken off. Or if the top and bottom outlets of a duplex receptacle are powered by two different circuits, the hot tab and possibly the neutral tab will be removed. In any case, when you replace an old outlet, check to see whether the tabs are removed, and if so, break off the tabs on your new outlet to match. Grab the tab with the end of a pliers or your stripping tool and wiggle it up and down to break it off.

## 10 Don't scrimp on switches and outlets

Better-quality switches and outlets may cost a dollar or two more, but they're worth it. For starters, the components are better. They feel more substantial and will last longer. And an added benefit is that many include a "back-wire" feature, not to be confused with cheap "stab-in" connections, which we don't recommend using. The back-wire feature still relies on the terminal screw to clamp the wire, but you don't have to bend the wire around the screw. Just strip it, push it in and tighten the screw.

STANDARD-QUALITY
SWITCH

BETTER-QUALITY
SWITCH

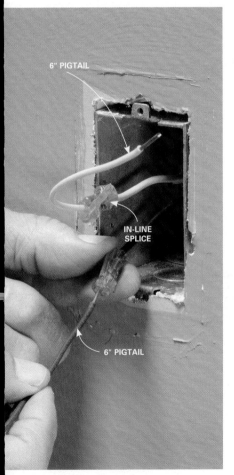

6" PIGTAIL

IN-LINE
SPLICE

6" PIGTAIL

## 9 Extend short wires

Wires that don't extend much beyond the box are a violation of National Electrical Code requirements. And besides, short wires make it very difficult to hook up your new switch or outlet. Luckily, the fix is simple. Just splice 6-in. pigtails to the short wires. You can connect the pigtails with regular wire connectors, or use in-line splice connectors like the ones shown. In either case, check the label on the wire connector package to see how much bare wire to expose when you strip the insulation.

STANDARD-QUALITY
OUTLET

BETTER-QUALITY
OUTLET

# UPGRADE YOUR GARAGE WIRING

*Adding more lights and outlets improves any garage*

by **Jeff Gorton, Associate Editor**

**If** your garage doesn't have enough outlets and you're sick of squinting to see what you're working on, then we've got the solution. Using PVC conduit and metal surface-mount electrical boxes, we'll show you how to connect additional outlets to an existing garage outlet and how to add bright, energy-efficient fluorescent lights to an existing ceiling box without cutting into your walls or fishing wires. Our upgrades cost about $600. Most of that went toward the eight fluorescent light fixtures.

## What it takes

**COST:** Varies. About $100 and up depending on the number of light fixtures.

**TIME:** One weekend

**SKILL LEVEL:** Intermediate to advanced

**TOOLS:** Standard hand tools, a noncontact voltage tester, a wire stripper and a drill.

In our garage, we extended conduit from an outlet to add outlets and a hanging fixture over our workbench area. We also removed a ceiling light fixture and extended wiring from it to install eight new fluorescent fixtures. Remember, though, your existing wiring may not be adequate for large power tools like saws or power-hungry appliances like refrigerators or freezers. For these you may have to add a new circuit, a project we won't cover in this story.

First we'll show you how to prepare for installing PVC conduit by adding an extender to your electrical box. Then we'll show you how easy it is to cut and install PVC conduit and push wire through it. Finally we'll show you how to hook up the outlets and lights and make sure everything is properly grounded.

Installing the PVC is simple, but you'll need a basic understanding of electrical wiring to safely connect the wires. We'll show you how we wired our outlets, switch and lights, but if your wiring is different and you're not sure how to make the connections, consult a wiring manual or get advice from an electrician. You can also find dozens of articles at familyhandyman.com. Just click on the "skills" tab and select "electrical." Whatever you do, pull a permit so an inspector can check your work.

### Plan the system

The first step is to draw up a simple sketch and figure out how many outlets and lights you plan to add. Keep in mind that there is a limit to how many lights you can add to one circuit. The maximum number of fixtures is determined by the capacity of the circuit, assuming there is nothing else on the circuit that would be turned on at the same time. The maximum wattage of electrical load that can be turned on continuously for three or more hours is 1,440 watts on a 15-amp circuit and 1,920 watts on a 20-amp circuit (which includes a 20 percent reduction for safety).

When your plan is complete, make a list of the materials you'll need. On p. 81 we've included a list of the parts we used for this project. Use this as a guide for making your own list. If you need a single-gang to 4-in. square steel box extender like the one we used (Photo 2), you may

## It's easy with PVC conduit

To add lights and outlets, you could spend days crawling around your attic and snaking wire through walls. But running wire through PVC conduit mounted on walls and ceilings makes the job faster and a whole lot less frustrating.

At home centers, you'll find a variety of PVC fittings that let you turn corners and run the conduit exactly where you want it; no need to learn the art of bending conduit as there would be with metal. And unlike metal, PVC plastic is quick and easy to cut. If you goof up, you can cut out your mistake and add new parts using couplings. It couldn't be simpler. And conduit makes your wiring more versatile because you can always add to or reconfigure the wiring later.

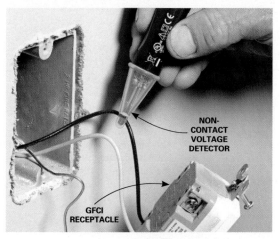

**1 Make sure the power is off.** Hold a noncontact voltage tester near each wire to make sure the power is off before you do any work on the wiring.

NON-CONTACT VOLTAGE DETECTOR

GFCI RECEPTACLE

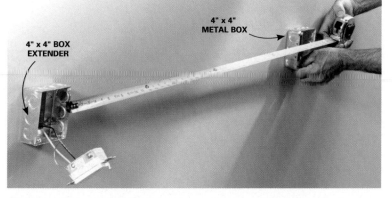

4" x 4" METAL BOX

4" x 4" BOX EXTENDER

**2 Measure for conduit.** Screw a box extender to the existing electrical box. Then hold the next box in position and measure between them. Subtract 1/2 in. for the male adapters to determine the length of conduit needed.

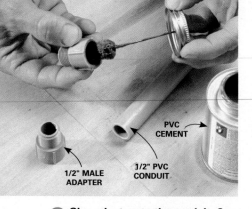

PVC CEMENT

1/2" MALE ADAPTER  1/2" PVC CONDUIT

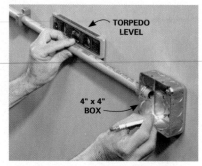

TORPEDO LEVEL

4" x 4" BOX

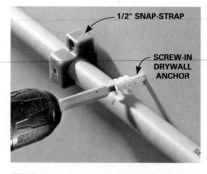

1/2" SNAP-STRAP

SCREW-IN DRYWALL ANCHOR

**3 Glue adapters to the conduit.** Cut the conduit and remove any burrs from the inside of the cut end. Swab PVC cement around the inside of the adapter. Press adapter onto the pipe, twist it about a quarter turn and hold for a few seconds until the glue sets.

**4 Mount the next box.** Extend the piece of conduit between the two boxes. Hold it level and mark two holes in the back of the second box. Remove the box and install drywall anchors so you can mount the box to the wall.

**5 Secure the conduit with a strap.** Position the anchor and drive a screw through it. If you don't hit a stud, move the strap aside and add a screw-in drywall anchor as shown here. Then screw the strap to the anchor.

have to special-order it or pick it up at an electrical supplier. Also, match the wire gauge to your circuit. Buy 14-gauge wire if your circuit is protected by a 15-amp circuit breaker and 12-gauge wire if it's protected by a 20-amp circuit breaker.

## Working with PVC

There are several surface wiring methods, including metal conduit, but we chose PVC conduit because it's inexpensive and easy to work with. You can buy compatible PVC electrical boxes, but at most home centers the selection is limited, so we chose to use metal boxes instead. Combining metal boxes and PVC conduit is fine, but unlike an all-metal system, PVC requires you to run a separate ground wire and bond it to each metal box or light fixture with either a screw or a special grounding clip.

There are a few different techniques for measuring PVC. You can measure between boxes and subtract for the fittings (**Photo 2**). Or you can install a bend or fitting on one end and mark the other end for cutting (**Photos 6 and 12**). Then it's simple to cut the pipe. We bought a PVC Conduit Cutter (about $15 at home centers or hardware stores), but you can also use any fine-tooth saw or even a miter saw. After you cut the conduit, ream the inside of the cut edge with a knife or pliers handle to remove any plastic burrs.

90-DEGREE BEND

MARK FOR LENGTH

**6 Mark the vertical conduit.** Connect a 90-degree bend to the conduit. Hold it against the ceiling and mark the top edge of the electrical box on the conduit. Subtract 1/4 in. and cut the conduit.

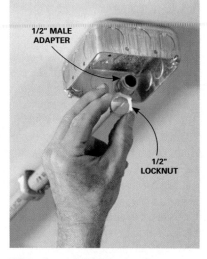

1/2" MALE ADAPTER

1/2" LOCKNUT

**7 Lock conduit to boxes.** Once boxes are screwed in place, the conduit will stay put, so it's tempting to skip or forget the locknuts. Don't. Every male fitting needs a nut.

Join the conduit to fittings with special PVC cement made for electrical PVC conduit (**Photo 3**). Use PVC male adapters and metal locknuts to connect the PVC conduit to metal boxes (**Photo 7**).

You can heat and bend PVC pipe, but we don't show how here. Instead we used 90-degree bend fittings to turn corners. You can also buy offsets that position the PVC flush to the wall surface, but these aren't necessary if you use the type of straps we show in **Photo 5**.

Straps for 1/2-in. PVC must be within 36 in. of electrical boxes and spaced a maximum of 36 in. between straps. There are at least two types of straps. We like the "snap-strap" shown in **Photo 5**. Drive a screw through the hole to hold the strap. If you don't hit a stud or something else solid, back out the screw, move the strap aside and drive in a drywall anchor (**Photo 5**) to secure the strap.

## Figure A
### Existing box wiring

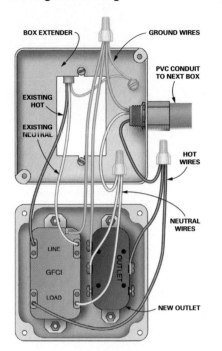

BOX EXTENDER

GROUND WIRES

PVC CONDUIT TO NEXT BOX

EXISTING HOT

EXISTING NEUTRAL

HOT WIRES

NEUTRAL WIRES

LINE

GFCI

LOAD

OUTLET

NEW OUTLET

## Figure B
### Outlet and switch wiring

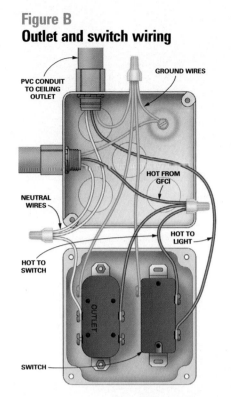

GROUND WIRES

PVC CONDUIT TO CEILING OUTLET

HOT FROM GFCI

NEUTRAL WIRES

HOT TO LIGHT

HOT TO SWITCH

OUTLET

SWITCH

## Figure C
### Ceiling outlet wiring

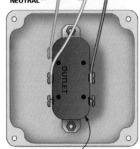

PVC FROM WALL OUTLET

HOT FROM SWITCH

GROUND WIRE

NEUTRAL

OUTLET

CEILING OUTLET

## Figure D  Light fixture wiring

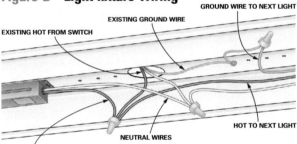

GROUND WIRE TO NEXT LIGHT

EXISTING GROUND WIRE

EXISTING HOT FROM SWITCH

HOT TO NEXT LIGHT

NEUTRAL WIRES

HOT TO BALLAST

---

### MATERIALS YOU MAY NEED

- Box extender (Raco 187 or similar)
- 4-in. square x 1-1/2-in.-deep metal boxes
- 4-in. square raised covers
- 10-ft. lengths of 1/2-in. PVC conduit
- Container of PVC electrical conduit glue
- 1/2-in. PVC male adapters
- 1/2-in. electrical connector locknuts
- 90-degree PVC bend with hub
- 1/2-in. PVC couplings

- Straps for 1/2-in. PVC
- Green ground screws
- White THHN 14-gauge*
- Black THHN 14-gauge*
- Green THHN 14-gauge*
- 1/4-20 x 3-in. two-piece toggle bolts
- Screw-in drywall anchors
- 15-amp receptacles
- 15-amp single-pole switch
- Light fixtures
- Bulbs or tubes
- Wire connectors

*Use 12-gauge wire for 20-amp circuits.*

---

## Add outlets and a light over your workbench

First turn off the circuit breaker to the outlet. Use a voltage tester to make sure the power is off. Then carefully remove the outlet—in our case it's a GFCI outlet—and as a final precaution, test all the wires in the box with a noncontact voltage detector (**Photo 1**).

If you're planning to hang a plug-in ceiling light like the one we used over your workbench, first find the center of your workbench. Then measure the light fixture you plan to use to determine how far apart the hanging chains are. Plan to position the ceiling outlet directly above where the power cord leaves the light fixture. Then position the outlet and switch on the wall directly under the ceiling box location.

## Run the conduit

To get started, screw a metal box extender to the outlet box. We used a single-gang to 4-in. square box extender. You'll run conduit from here to the next box. Hold the next outlet box in position and measure between the boxes. Subtract 1/2 in. to get the length of PVC conduit needed (**Photo 2**). Cut the conduit and glue male adapters to each end (**Photo 3**).

Remove the round knockouts from the metal boxes by bending them out a little, and then grabbing and twisting them with pliers. Remember to remove the smaller knockouts, not the large ones. **Photo 4** shows how to mark for fastening the box. Drive screws at the marks to see if you hit solid wood. If not, remove the screws and install drywall anchors. Connect the two boxes with the

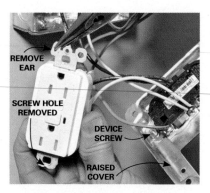

**8** **Push wires into the conduit.** Hang the wire spools on a steel pipe or dowel so they can spin freely. Bend the ends of the wires over so they don't catch on edges inside fittings, and then push them through the conduit.

**9** **Attach the outlets to the raised cover.** Break off the ears and cut off the screw hole to prepare the outlets for mounting. Attach them to the raised cover with the included device screws.

## Ground metal boxes and fixtures

Since PVC conduit doesn't conduct electricity, you'll run a separate ground wire through the conduit. This ground wire must be firmly attached to every metal box and light fixture connected by the conduit with either a grounding screw (shown here) or a special grounding clip.

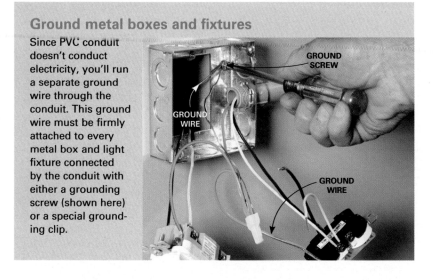

PVC conduit and screw the locknuts onto the male adapters in each box. Then screw the second box to the wall. Finally, add the required clamps (**Photo 5**). If you want to add more outlet boxes, just repeat this process.

Photo 6 shows how to determine the length of the section of vertical PVC conduit running to the ceiling-mounted box. After marking the conduit, cut it, glue on the male adapter, and connect it to the box. Use a level to plumb this section of conduit and secure it to the wall with straps. Finally, add the last section of conduit on the ceiling and anchor the ceiling box to framing or with drywall anchors (**Photo 7**).

### Run wire and make the connections

All of our conduit runs were fairly short, and we used solid copper rather than stranded wire, so we were able to simply push the wire through the conduit (**Photo 8**). If you have longer runs, you may have to first push an electrical fish tape through the conduit and secure the wires to it so you can pull them through.

For a wiring scenario like we show here, you'll need separate hot (black), neutral (white) and ground (green) wires. Leave about a foot of extra wire at each box.

After you've run the wires to each box, you can start making the connections. We're providing ground-fault protection to the outlets and light fixture by connecting them to the "load" side of the GFCI receptacle in the first box.

Double-check to make sure the power is still off. **Figures A, B and C on p. 81** show the wiring diagrams to add outlets and a switched outlet for a hanging light. For more information on making safe wiring connections, go to familyhandyman.com and enter "safe wiring" in the search box.

It's important to make sure all the boxes are grounded. Do this by connecting the new (green) ground wire to the existing ground wire at the first box (see "Ground Metal Boxes and Fixtures" at left). Then connect the new ground wire to every metal box with a grounding screw. **Photo 9** shows how to mount the outlets and switches to the raised cover using the included device screws. Attach the raised covers to the metal boxes with the included machine screws and you're ready to turn on the power and test your work. Use a plug-in GFCI outlet tester at each outlet to make sure your connections are correct. For more information on using electrical testers, go to familyhandyman.com and search for "electrical testers."

**CAUTION:** If you have aluminum wiring, don't work on it yourself. The connections require special techniques. Call in a licensed electrician who is certified to work with it. For more information, go to cpsc.gov and search for "aluminum wiring."

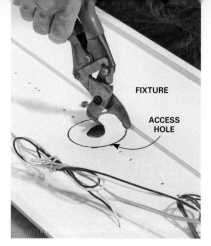

**10** **Cut an access hole.** Start with a hole in the middle to get the snips started. Our fixture had a knockout that we removed. Otherwise, use a small hole saw to drill a starting hole. Snip out to the circle and follow it with the snips.

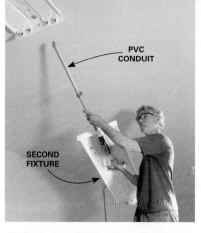

**11** **Connect in-line fixtures.** Hang the second fixture with the conduit already attached. There's no easy way to insert straight runs of conduit between fixtures that are already fastened to the ceiling.

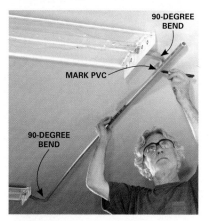

**12** **Connect parallel fixtures.** Connect a 90-degree bend to a length of conduit. Install a 90-degree bend on the second fixture. Hold the conduit with the attached bend in position. Mark the conduit and cut it to length.

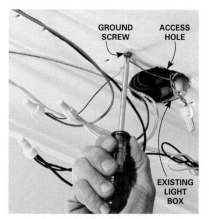

**13** **Ground the light fixture.** Add a ground screw to the light fixture and loop the ground wire around it. Tighten the screw.

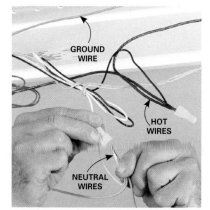

**14** **Connect the fixture wires.** Strip the ends of the new wires and connect them to the wires in the fixture. Connect all neutral white wires together. Connect the colored fixture wire to the black wires.

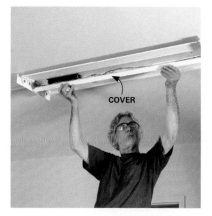

**15** **Install the cover.** Finish the lighting installation by snapping the cover under the tabs. Then add fluorescent lamps. Our fixtures also included a prismatic lens that we snapped on to complete the project.

## Add fluorescent lights

Start by making sure the circuit breaker for the existing light is turned off. Then remove the light fixture and check the wires in the box with a noncontact voltage tester. If the electrical box is in the right location, you can start by adding a fluorescent fixture over the box.

Photo 10 shows how to prepare the fixture. The diameter of the hole you cut can be smaller than the electrical box, but should be large enough to reach through to access the wires in the box. After you cut the hole, smooth the edges with a file to remove sharp edges and burrs.

If your preferred location for the lights is not lined up with the ceiling box, then start by adding a box extender to the existing ceiling light box (Photo 2). Then extend conduit to the first fixture.

You can install ceiling fixtures by screwing them directly to the wood framing above or hanging them from toggle bolts. To use toggle bolts, transfer measurements from the mounting holes in the light fixture to the ceiling and drill 1/2-in. holes in the drywall. Then install toggle bolts on the fixture and simply push them into the holes as you hold the fixture next to the ceiling (Photo 11). Measure, use a laser or snap a chalk line (use erasable chalk) to center a row of fixtures and keep them straight.

Photo 11 shows how to connect fixtures end to end. (We already drilled holes in the ceiling for the toggle bolts, but they don't show in the photo.) Photo 12 shows how to connect two rows of fixtures using 90-degree bend fittings. After all the fixtures are mounted and connected with PVC conduit, push wires through the conduit as shown in Photo 8. Photos 13 and 14 show how to connect the ground wire and make the connections to the fixtures.

Finish up by replacing the covers (Photo 15), installing the fluorescent tubes, and snapping on the lenses if your fixtures include them. Turn on the power, flip the switch, and enjoy your brightly lit garage.

# StormSafety

## BE READY FOR THE **NEXT STORM**

**S**uperstorm Sandy. Hurricane Katrina. Irene. The Joplin tornado. Storms are a fact of life. But part of the DIY life is being ready for household emergencies, small or large. In the following pages, you'll find products, skills and strategies to help you weather the next storm in your neighborhood. (For more tips that might make storm time easier and safer, also see "Be Ready for a Blackout" on pp. 66–68.)

WISE COMPANY

### How about a food cache?

Not everyone who has a stash of food for emergencies is necessarily nutty, you know. Do an online search for "survival food," and you'll be amazed at how many companies are providing survival food packages. Sears, Walmart, Costco and Sam's Club all sell survival food packages online. Typically the kits are freeze-dried packages that are meticulously prepared for storage of up to 25 years. It's basically the same type of food that backpackers and explorers have been eating for years. Not gourmet food, but good fuel.

Prices range from a week's worth of food for one person for $150 to a year's worth of food for a family for a few thousand dollars. How much you buy depends on your budget and how long you think you'll need to hold out.

### Stay tuned in

Batteries are always in short supply right before, during and right after a major weather event. That's where this hand-cranked radio, LED flashlight and phone charger comes in handy. The Eton FRX3 ($60 at home centers and electronics stores) radio keeps you in contact with all seven NOAA weather band stations and the weather ALERT system, as well as local AM/FM stations.

The built-in LED flashlight helps you navigate in the dark. Just charge up the internal battery before the storm, and then keep it charged by spinning the handle on the hand-cranked generator. Or, put it in the sun and use the solar cell to help recharge the internal battery.

According to the manufacturer, you can also charge your cell phone with the generator. It's true. But I'll be honest with you—it takes a LOT of cranking to fully recharge a smartphone (think carpal tunnel). Buy it for the radio, not its phone recharging capabilities.

—Rick Muscoplat,
Contributing Editor

## Emergency cell phone

When the power goes out and your cell phone battery eventually dies, what then? Here's another important item to add to your emergency preparedness kit: a SpareOne Plus Emergency Phone.

This cell phone is built to last for 15 years on a single "AA" battery (included). It can place emergency calls even without a SIM card and has 10 hours of talk time and a built-in flashlight. It doesn't have a display, you can't e-mail or surf the Web, and the call quality is just so-so. But in an emergency, you're looking for fast help, not a long chat with your best friend. It's about $80 at online retailers. For more info, visit spareone.com.

SPAREONE

TO OUTSIDE

WATER-POWERED PUMP

CHECK VALVE

TO SUMP

## Off-the-grid sump pump

Sometimes, the storm that brings rain and floods also knocks out the power, so your sump pump is useless just when you need it the most. There are a couple of safeguards against this double trouble.

For about $300 (including battery), you can install a battery back-up pump. The weak spot in this system is the battery itself; it may not pack enough power to keep pumping through a long outage. A better option for many people is a water-powered pump ($160 and up). With these systems, pressure from your home's water supply pumps seepage outside. That wastes water, of course, so these pumps are for backup only.

Running a supply line to power the pump is standard plumbing work; it could be easy or difficult, depending on access to an existing supply pipe. If your water source is your own well, this option isn't for you—your well won't pump if the power is out. Water-powered sump pumps aren't stocked in most home centers, but several models are available online. One brand is Basepump. Go to basepump.com to figure out what size you need.

## Light up the joint for a long, long time

A battery-powered lantern is your best friend in the aftermath of a power outage. Most of them put out lots of light, but some suck your batteries dry faster than others.

Of all the battery-powered lanterns on the market, the Rayovac Sportsman LED Lantern (SE3DLNCOM) gets excellent marks. The 4-watt LED light pumps out 240 lumens on high mode with three "D" batteries. To conserve battery power, dial it down to energy-saver mode and you'll get 90 hours of continuous light. The lantern also has a "find me" feature that blinks a green LED light every five seconds so you can locate the lantern in the dark even when it's off. Find it at most home centers for about $30.

SPORTSMAN

## Power your phone with sunlight

Lots of companies make solar-powered chargers for mobile electronics, but I had to dig around to find a unit that will charge a cell phone reliably and for a reasonable price. The JOOS Orange does the job. It's built with a large mono-crystalline silicon solar panel that's 20 percent more efficient than most other solar chargers.

Add the optional reflector kit ($25) and you boost charging efficiency to 40 percent. Place the JOOS Orange in direct sunlight for one hour to get two hours of 3G talk time. Or, leave it in the sun to fully charge the internal 5,400 mAh LiPoly battery. That'll give you enough power to recharge your smartphone a few times.

The unit is rugged and waterproof, and the electronics are smart enough to prevent battery overcharging. Find the JOOS Orange for $150 at solarjoos.com or rei.com.

—Rick Muscoplat, Contributing Editor

# StormSafety

## No toilet? No problem!

If you don't have running water, your toilet won't work. But with a GO Anywhere toilet kit, you'll be all set, even if you have a family of 10. The heart of each GO Anywhere kit is a waste bag with powder to absorb liquid, start a composting reaction and control odor. Each kit also has toilet paper, hand sanitizer and an odor-proof zip-close disposal bag.

The bag is enormous, big enough to place on the bowl of a regular toilet. When I tested the GO Anywhere kit, I used it on a 5-gallon plastic pail, which was less comfortable but worked perfectly well (yet another use for the DIYer's friend!). The beautiful thing about the GO Anywhere kit is that after use, it's completely biodegradable, and you can safely and legally toss it in your household trash.

The GO Anywhere bags are a useful addition to your storm readiness kit if your water supply is subject to disruption. They cost about $3 each at outdoor supply stores like REI and many online retailers. Check out the manufacturer's Web site: cleanwaste.com.

—Ken Collier, Editor in Chief

## Cheap emergency heat

What are you going to do for heat if the juice goes out during an unseasonable cold snap—or in the dead of winter? Even gas furnaces need electricity to run the motors and electronics. If you have a woodstove, fine, but otherwise you might consider having a kerosene heater on hand. It won't heat the whole house, but it will keep one or more rooms comfortable. You can spend under $100 to set up a small unit. Just remember the bigger the unit, the more kerosene you'll need to have on hand.

A good Web site to check out is endtimesreport.com/kerosene.html, which sells wicks. They also have a lot of serious information on choosing and using kerosene heaters. But read the instruction manual for any heater carefully: Kerosene heaters can be very dangerous. Windows should be cracked open in rooms, or doors opened to the rest of the house. Carbon monoxide detectors are crucial in rooms where the heaters will be operated. Fuel tanks should always be taken outside to be refilled.

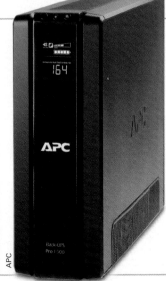

## Battery backup for Internet and home telephone

You can't count on cell phone reception in the wake of a storm. And, if your power is out, you'll automatically lose your Internet and VoIP phone service. That's where an uninterruptible power supply (UPS) system can step in to save the day.

A UPS system does double-duty by protecting your computer system during everyday use and powering your communications devices during a power outage. Buy the largest UPS system you can afford, and add a piggyback battery to extend the reserve power even further (the APC BR1500G UPS system and APC BR24BPG battery pack combination is one example; about $350 from amazon.com).

Plug your cable/DSL modem/router, VoIP and portable phone base station into the UPS, and they'll keep running the instant you lose power. Make your phone calls and send your e-mail, but shut down the UPS when you're not communicating. That'll extend battery power for days. Find UPS systems at any local computer store or online computer supply stores.

# BUYING A **GENERATOR**

According to statistics gathered by one generator manufacturer, 97,000 utility customers, on average, are without power on any given day. That's a lot of spoiled hamburger! A backup generator can really save the day when the power goes out. But buying a generator can be difficult because of the wide range of choices and confusing jargon. Here are 10 tips to get you on the right track.

## A good size for emergency backup is 5,500 watts

If you're shopping for a portable generator—that is, one on wheels that's not permanently connected to your home's electrical system—a generator that supplies 5,500 watts is about the right size. This is enough to power a few critical appliances like a refrigerator, furnace, microwave, TV and some lights.

Of course, you can't run a whole-house air conditioner and an electric water heater at the same time with 5,500 watts, but a generator this size will get you by until the power comes back on. You can buy a good-quality 5,500-watt generator for about $700.

## Buy a standby generator if you can afford it

Portable generators are great in a pinch, but they're often noisy and they require frequent refueling. They also have to be stored when not in use, and connected and started when the power goes out.

A standby generator is permanently connected to your home's electrical system and goes on automatically when the power goes out, providing seamless power. Standby generators can run on propane or natural gas, eliminating the need to monitor the fuel. And they're quieter.

You can buy one large enough to power everything in your house, or you can buy a smaller unit and choose the most critical circuits to power. Standby generators start at about $1,000, plus installation. (And they do need to be installed by a pro.)

The difference in cost between a portable generator and a standby unit may not be as great as you think. Remember, a portable unit requires either expensive extension cords or a transfer switch. Standby units can run on less expensive natural gas, which will save you money in the long run.

# StormSafety

### Buy a generator you can get serviced locally

You may look online and find a great deal on a generator. But what will you do if you can't get it serviced locally? Sometimes it's worth spending a little extra to buy from a local dealer. Parts will be available, and the dealer will be familiar with maintenance and repair procedures for your model. So before you buy a generator, make sure there's someone nearby who can provide parts and service.

### Propane is easier than gas

When it comes to portable generators and ease of use, liquid propane (LP) sure beats gasoline. Gasoline is a handy fuel, but it's not without problems. Storing enough gasoline to get you through a several-day power outage requires constant vigilance. First you have to buy several 5-gallon gas containers and find a safe place to store them. Then you have to add stabilizer and ideally replace the gas after several months to make sure it's still fresh when you need it.

Propane-powered portable generators solve these problems and more. You can store and use liquid propane (LP) indefinitely (it doesn't go bad). Refueling is simple and safe; just replace the propane tank with a full one. And you don't have to worry about the carburetor on your generator getting gummed up with old gasoline. Search online for "propane generators" to research various options, then buy it locally as noted above.

### You can buy a quiet generator—but it'll cost more

One problem with portable generators is the noise that you—and your neighbors—have to put up with. You can compare decibel ratings to find quieter models, but keep in mind that there's no industry standard, so you may be comparing apples and oranges. Standby generators are quieter, and for a stiff premium you can buy a really quiet portable generator like the 6,500-watt Honda shown here. It costs about $4,500.

HONDA

### You'll need heavy-duty extension cords

Remember, if you decide not to install a manual transfer switch, you'll need a lot of expensive, heavy-duty extension cords. Using undersize cords presents a fire hazard and can damage motors as well as stress your generator. To run a refrigerator, depending on how energy efficient it is and how far from the generator, you'll need at least a 12-gauge cord. A 50-ft. 12-gauge cord will set you back about $50. Multiply that by five or six and you can see that a transfer switch starts to sound like a better deal.

### Don't wreck your TV (or computer) with a cheap generator

Computers, TVs and many modern appliances contain sensitive electronics that can be damaged by the "dirty" power produced by less-expensive generators. Inverter-type generators provide the cleanest power but are very expensive, especially in sizes large enough to power a house. But for a little extra money, you can buy generators with power conditioning that provides cleaner power. Total Harmonic Distortion (THD) is a way to measure the quality of electricity from a generator. Look for a generator with a THD of less than 5 percent to safely operate most electronics.

LG

GENERAC

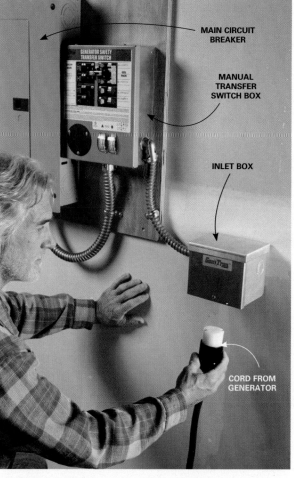

MAIN CIRCUIT BREAKER

MANUAL TRANSFER SWITCH BOX

INLET BOX

CORD FROM GENERATOR

## Furnaces, well pumps and electric water heaters require a transfer switch

You can use extension cords from your portable generator to power any device with a plug, but anything that's directly connected to your home's wiring, including essentials like your well pump, furnace and electric water heater, requires a transfer switch.

A manual transfer switch is essentially a small circuit breaker box that you mount next to your main electrical panel. You match the capacity of the transfer switch to the wattage of your generator. Then you choose which circuits to connect to the transfer switch. The Gen Tran manual transfer switch ($250) shown here came prewired for six circuits and included the inlet box (generator connection) and the cord to connect the generator.

A transfer switch is the only safe way to connect your generator to house wiring because it requires you to disconnect the house wiring from the incoming power lines at the same time you switch to generator power. This prevents the possibility of "backfeeding" generated power into the power lines, which creates a potentially lethal hazard for power line workers.

Connecting a manual transfer switch is an advanced electrical project. An electrician should be able to complete an installation similar to the one shown here in about three hours.

## Add up your watts—then add extra for motor start-up

If you're the adventurous type, you can just go with our recommendation of a 5,500-watt generator and make the best of it. But if you really want to know what size generator you need to power everything you want, then the only way is to add up the wattage of all the lights, appliances and motors that you intend to run simultaneously.

Generator manufacturers and resellers have charts you can refer to that list the average wattage used for various appliances and motors. Or you can check the nameplates on the appliances you want to power. If wattage isn't listed, you can derive it by multiplying volts by amps. For example, if the plate lists 2.5 amps at 120 volts, multiply the two to get 300 watts.

There's one caveat, though. Motors require an extra surge of electricity to get started, and you have to factor this into the equation. Add up the wattage of everything you want to run. Then determine the largest motor you need to run (the furnace, for example), multiply the wattage requirement by 2 to get the approximate start-up wattage required, and add this number to the total.

## Buy gas cans when you buy the generator

A 5,500-watt generator will run about eight hours on 5 gallons of gasoline, so gas management is critical if you want to be prepared for an extended power outage. That may mean running your generator for shorter periods and coasting on things like refrigeration.

Having several filled 5-gallon gas cans available is prudent, but you'll need to add stabilizer to extend the shelf life. Even then, after six months or so you should pour it into your car's gas tank and refill the cans with fresh fuel. The generator itself should be run dry for storage or filled with stabilized fuel. That fuel should be replaced every six months as well.

# STAY SAFE IN A STORM

*Surprising ways a natural disaster can kill you*

You already know the obvious dangers of a natural disaster: collapsing buildings, downed power lines, flying or floating debris.... But in most disasters, more people are injured or killed by things that don't seem all that dangerous, things they weren't expecting or things most of us would never even think of. Here are some of those unexpected dangers.

## Lightning: Don't get struck indoors

Your home is probably the safest place to be in an electrical storm. But lightning can still get to you through the conductive paths in your house; that means your wiring, your plumbing and water. Talking on a corded phone, taking a shower or bath, working on your desktop computer or handling power tools during an electrical storm isn't much safer than standing outside. It's best to stay away from all water and appliances until the storm passes.

## Don't get shocked in a flooded basement

The water in a flooded basement probably isn't electrified by your home's electrical lines. But it could be. So instead of finding out the hard way, just consider it an energized pool of instant death until you call your utility company to disconnect your power. Then you can dive in. And after the water is gone, remember that anything electrical in the basement may still be wet, damaged and dangerous. So it's best to leave the basement power off until your utility company or an electrician gives you the OK.

## Keep your wheels on dry land

Driving through a few inches of water seems safe enough, but it kills people every year. Floodwater hides washouts and the road itself, and you can suddenly find yourself in deep water. In just 6 in. of water, some cars partially float and become hard to control. And any passenger vehicle, even a monster SUV, will become a rudderless barge in 2 ft. of rushing water. When you find a flooded road, better to turn around than risk drowning.

More than half of flood-related drownings involve a vehicle.

## Keep your generator away from the house

A generator is the best thing to have in a blackout. But it can make you black out (or die). Like any internal combustion engine, a generator engine exhausts carbon monoxide gas, which can give you a headache, knock you out or even kill you. This is easy to avoid, though: Don't run a generator in your garage or porch, and keep it at least 10 ft. away from your house.

Hurricane Katrina led to more than 50 cases of carbon monoxide poisoning.

# StormSafety

## Stay out of gushing floodwater

Six inches of floodwater doesn't look dangerous. But if it's moving fast enough, it's enough to sweep you off your feet and carry you into the hereafter. Rushing water also erodes roads and walkways, creating drop-offs that you can't see under the torrent. A long pole, stick or pipe lets you probe for drop-offs and might help you stay on your feet. Still, the smartest move is to stay out of flowing water.

Flooding is the No. 1 cause of weather-related deaths in the United States.

Candles cause about 15,000 house fires in the United States every year.

## Don't burn down your house

When the power goes out, lots of people light lots of candles. And lots of people burn down their home. There's no good reason for this: Today's LED flashlights and lanterns burn brighter and last longer than candles, without the fire risk.

## Flooded basement? Turn off the gas

Floodwater and floating junk can lead to damaged gas lines and malfunctioning gas controls. Leaked gas then bubbles up through the water, giving your basement an explosive atmosphere on top of the flood. And the smell of gas may be masked by other floodwater odors. So call the utility company to shut off your gas even if you don't smell it. If you do smell gas, get out of the house before you make the call.

## Stay dry in a flooded basement

Furniture isn't the only stuff floating in your basement. Chances are, the water contains chemicals stored downstairs and a dose of sewage that backed up through basement drains. That's not just disgusting, but also a toxic soup that can make you sick. Before you go down there, gear up with rubber boots and gloves to prevent skin contact. Also wear gloves when cleaning up the polluted sludge left by the flood.

PHOTO TOM FENENGA

# 3 Plumbing, Heating & Appliances

## IN THIS CHAPTER

## REPLACE A BROKEN OR CORRODED TOILET FLUSH HANDLE

A few readers have written to us asking if there's a trick to replacing a toilet flush handle. What's throwing them for a loop is the retaining nut inside the tank—it's a reverse thread. So, if you're in front of the toilet, turn the nut to the left (**Photo 1**). Remove the old handle and lever and install the new one (**Photo 2**).

**1 Loosen the retaining nut.** Grab the nut with pliers and turn to the left to loosen.

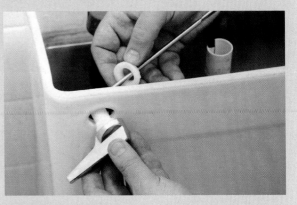

**2 Install the new handle.** Slide the new handle into place. Then thread on the retaining nut. Tighten by turning to the right.

## REMOVE METAL SCRATCHES FROM PORCELAIN

You're supposed to use a closet auger to remove toilet clogs. But many DIYers don't have one and use a regular snake. Sure, it works, but it can also leave metal scratches on the bowl. If that happens to you, don't freak out. Just pick up a pumice stone from any home center. Wet the stone and keep it wet while you gently scrub the marks. Don't scrub too hard or you'll scratch the porcelain. And don't be surprised if the stone wears away quickly— that's normal.

PUMICE STONE

METAL MARKS

## "BETTER" FILTERS CAN DAMAGE HVAC SYSTEMS

Many homeowners believe they're doing themselves, their air and their equipment a good turn by using expensive high-efficiency "allergy" type filters. These have a minimum efficiency reporting value (MERV) of 11 or higher. But these filters are so dense that they can cause equipment damage, high utility usage, poor airflow (particularly to rooms farthest from the furnace) and long run cycles. If your HVAC system uses a standard 1-in. filter, a cheaper MERV 7 or 8 furnace filter is better for most homes.

## EXTEND THE LIFE OF YOUR FRIDGE

If you're like most other homeowners, cleaning the refrigerator condenser coil is at the bottom of even your "low-priority" list. You know that a dirty coil wastes electricity, but the $6 annual electrical savings probably isn't enough to motivate you. Need a better reason? You're killing your fridge. A dirty condenser coil makes the compressor run longer and hotter, and that dramatically reduces its life span. With some refrigerators costing $1,000 or more, it's time to get with the program and clean the beast. Here you'll learn you how to do the job in half the time by blowing the coil clean, rather than brushing it.

You'll need an air compressor, a wand-style compressed air gun, a vacuum cleaner with a hose, a box fan, a pleated furnace filter (not the cheap fiberglass kind), nut drivers and a paintbrush.

Start by converting your box fan into a dust collector. Tape the furnace filter onto the intake side of the box fan. Seal off any open grille area on the fan with masking tape so all the air has to get pulled through the filter. Then pull the refrigerator away from the wall and unplug it. Seal the sides of the refrigerator to the floor with masking tape to prevent dust from blowing out sideways. Next, remove the back access panel fasteners and grille with a nut driver and set the grille aside. Unsnap the grille in the front of the fridge to expose the condenser coil.

Set the fan/filter unit behind the fridge and turn it on to its highest speed. Then aim the compressed air gun at a corner of the condenser coil and blow it clean (**Photo 1**). Continue cleaning until no more dust comes out the back of the fridge. Let the box fan run for a while to remove any airborne dust. Then shut it down and toss the filter.

Move to the back of the fridge and clean the condenser fan blades (**Photo 2**). Then suck up any remaining dust and cobwebs from the back side. Reinstall the access panel, plug in the fridge and push it back into place.

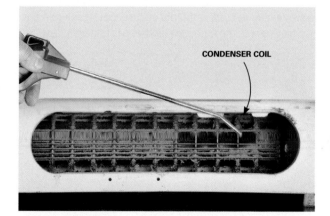

**1** **Blow the dust off the coil.** Tape a furnace filter to the intake side of a box fan and place it close to the rear of the fridge. Then shoot one-second bursts of compressed air into the condenser coil. Allow time between each burst so the fan can collect the dust cloud from the back of the fridge. Then move the wand to the next dirty section and do some more quick bursts.

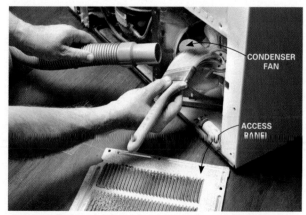

**2** **Brush and vacuum.** Brush the dust off the condenser fan blades with an old paintbrush and suck up all the crud with the vacuum cleaner hose. Then clean the access panel grille and compressor.

## PAINT YELLOWING APPLIANCE HANDLES

The white refrigerator in your kitchen didn't come with yellow handles, but they're yellow now. Even after cleaning, they'll still look pretty grungy against the bright white porcelain cabinet. New handles are pretty pricey, so why not just paint them? It's easy and cheap (less than $15). Buy a can of paint formulated to paint plastic (Rust-Oleum Specialty Paint for Plastic is one choice) at a home center. Then pick up a bottle of degreaser and a scrubbing pad.

Remove the handles (**Photo 1**). Then wash them with degreaser and hot water. Use a scrub pad on textured areas to remove the dirt. Pay particular attention to dirt in crevices. Then wipe the handles with a dry cloth and let them air-dry.

Mask off any emblems or chrome trim and paint the handles (**Photo 2**). Paint the vanity caps at the same time. Then reinstall the handles. You may have to repaint them in a few years, but they'll look a lot better in the meantime.

**1** **Pop the caps and screws.** Pry off the vanity caps that cover the side screws. Then open the fridge door and remove the other screws.

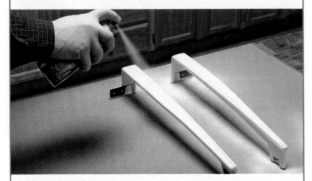

**2** **Apply the paint.** Spray the sides of the handles before doing the flat surfaces. Allow the recommended "flash" time before applying additional coats. Let dry, flip them over and paint the other side.

## SIMPLE DISHWASHER RACK FIX

As dishwashers age, the plastic coating on the rack posts wears off and the exposed metal begins to rust and stain dishes. Here's a simple fix: Get some of the plastic end cap covers that are used for wire shelving and glue them over the posts (polyurethane glue is a good choice). No specialty kits or expensive dish rack replacement necessary. The total cost is under $10, and it will take you all of five minutes.

READER PHOTO

## CLEAR A CLOGGED AIR GAP

An air gap prevents dirty dishwater from backflowing into fresh water lines. But over time, ground-up food and grease can build up inside the air gap and form a clog. If water squirts out the air gap's vent holes or you notice a foul smell coming from it, it's time to clean it. All you need is a bottle brush and some household disinfecting cleaner.

Yank the cover off the air gap and remove the snap-in or screw-on diverter. Remove any loose food particles, then clean with the bottle brush as shown. If you still have a water leak after cleaning the air gap, clean the drain line where it meets the garbage disposer or drain wye (aka "Y").

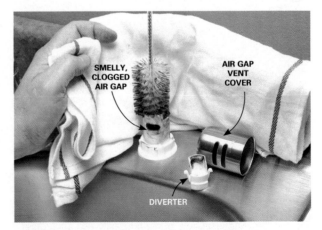

SMELLY, CLOGGED AIR GAP

AIR GAP VENT COVER

DIVERTER

**Clean the air gap with a brush.** Soak the bottle brush in household cleaner and plunge it up and down into the air gap.

READER PHOTO

## DEFROST FREEZERS FASTER

David Hawkins, Field Editor

I wish I could take credit for this one: My wife suggested I try using my dual halogen stand light to defrost the freezer. It was completely defrosted and dry in three hours! Where was she the last time, when I used pots of hot water, a spatula and six hours? Make sure you turn off the freezer and keep the lights at least 12 in. away so you don't melt the plastic or start a fire.

## QUICK FIX FOR A DRYER DOOR

If your dryer door won't stay closed, chances are the latch is either bent or missing, or the strike is worn. The fix is cheap (about $7 for parts) and easy. Buy the parts from any appliance parts store. Then grab pliers, a couple of small, straight-slot screwdrivers and a roll of masking tape.

Grab the bent or broken latch and yank it out. Then install the new one (Photo 1). Next, protect the door's finish with tape and remove the old strike (Photo 2). Snap in the new strike and you're back in the laundry business.

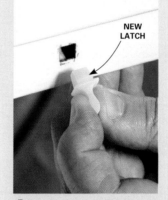

NEW LATCH

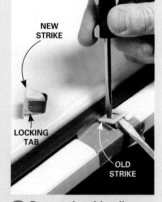

NEW STRIKE

LOCKING TAB

OLD STRIKE

**1 Pop in the new latch.** Line up the replacement latch with the hole and push in firmly until the locking tabs seat.

**2 Pry out the old strike.** Jam a small screwdriver into the strike and bend the metal locking tab inward. Pry upward with a second screwdriver to pop it out.

## INSTALL A MORE RELIABLE VALVE FOR YOUR ICEMAKER OR FILTER

If you're installing an icemaker or a reverse osmosis filtration system, forget about using a traditional saddle tee valve. They clog and leak, and they're almost impossible to shut off completely after several years of use.

Instead, try a Sioux Chief "full-slip" valve tee (601-20cv valve tee; $25 at amazon.com). The unit comes with compression fittings and a ball valve for trouble-free operation.

Shut off the water and cut the copper tubing (Photo 1). Assemble the compression nuts and ferrules on the tee. Angle the tubing out to install the unit (Photo 2). Then connect the icemaker or filter. Make an access panel if you enclose the wall.

MARK

**1 Mark and cut.** Mark the pipe at each end of the tee threads. Then cut out a 1-in. section between the lines.

**2 Slip and tighten.** Slide the valve completely onto the bottom section of the tubing. Then move it up to mate with the top section and tighten the compression nuts.

## CLEAN OVEN DOOR GLASS

It's a mystery how baking slop gets deposited between oven door glass panels. But it's clear that you can't remove it without disassembling the door. The job's not that hard and takes less than an hour.

Remove the oven door (consult the manual for how to unlock the hinges and lift the door off). Then remove the exterior trim panel (**Photo 1**) and the glass hold-downs (**Photo 2**). Lift out the glass and handle it care-

fully (it's expensive and breaks easily!).

Clean off the crud with a nylon scrub pad, hot water and degreaser. Rinse and dry, then clean with glass cleaner. Wear gloves to prevent fingerprints as you place the glass back onto the oven door. Be sure the glass sits inside the locating tabs before you reassemble the hold-downs. Then install the hold-down channels and screws and the trim panel. Put the door on the oven.

**1 Remove the panel.** Remove the screws that secure the front panel to the oven door frame. Note their location and store them in a cup. Then carefully lift off the panel and set it aside.

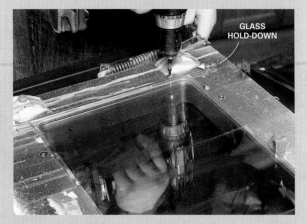

GLASS HOLD-DOWN

**2 Remove the glass.** Remove the screws from the glass hold-downs and set them aside. Note the location of the retaining tabs above and below the glass. Then lift off the glass and clean it.

## DIAGNOSE AND REPLACE A BUM REFRIGERATOR CIRCUIT BOARD

If your refrigerator isn't keeping food cold, the cause could be a burned circuit board or a sticking circuit board relay. Before calling for repair service, try this trick. Unplug the fridge and roll it out. Remove any metal cover plates or cardboard access panels on the back and look for a circuit board. Examine the board for burn marks. Replace it if you see any (**Photo 2**).

If the board looks good, locate the largest relay on the board (look for the largest rectangular plastic box). Then plug in the fridge (don't touch any wires!) and tap the relay (**Photo 1**). If the compressor starts, the circuit board is the problem. Replace it.

If there are no burn marks and the tapping doesn't work, or the compressor makes a humming or clicking sound and then shuts off, the problem may be a relay located on the compressor itself. To learn how to do that fix, go to familyhandyman.com and search for "refrigerator compressor."

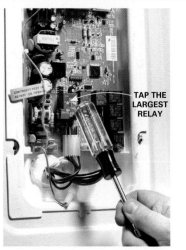

TAP THE LARGEST RELAY

**1 Rattle the relay.** Tap lightly on the compressor relay to rattle the electrical contacts inside. If the fridge starts, you need a new circuit board.

PUSH-ON CONNECTOR

HEADER PINS

NEW CIRCUIT BOARD

**2 Swap out the circuit board.** Move the press-on connectors to the new board one at a time. Press each connector onto the header pins until it's firmly seated.

# REPLACE AN ANODE ROD

Every tank-style water heater contains a "sacrificial anode rod" to protect the steel tank. Its mission is to corrode so the tank won't. Unfortunately, anode rods don't last forever, and when they're gone, the tank starts corroding. By periodically replacing the anode rod, you can double the life of the tank. Replacement rods run from as little as $15 for a solid rod to about $60 for a flexible style.

Most water heaters have a hex head–style anode rod. Follow these directions to remove and replace that type. However, some manufacturers use a "combo" style, with the anode rod built into a "hot" outlet nipple. That type is a lot harder to remove because you have to disassemble the hot water outlet piping. We don't cover that here.

Drain some water from the tank to check for rust. It's time for a new water heater if you see rusty flakes (not just orange water, which can come from corroded pipes or well water). If the water is clean, remove the rod to check its condition.

To loosen the rod, you'll need an air compressor, a 1/2-in.-drive impact wrench and a 1-1/16-in. socket. If you don't have an impact wrench, go buy a cheap one for about $30. Even with a breaker bar, it can be nearly impossible to break the anode rod free.

Turn off the power or gas. Then close the cold-water valve at the top of the tank and drain off several gal-lons. Loosen the hex head with the impact wrench, but unscrew it the rest of the way by hand. Hint: The hex head may be under a plastic cap. Uncover it, then pull it up and out to check its condition (**Photo 1**).

Buy a new anode rod at a home center or online (search for "anode rods" to locate suppliers). Install a flexible rod if you have less than 44 in. of clearance above your heater (**Photo 2**). Turn on the water, the power or gas, and burp the air from the system. Check the condition of your anode rod every three years.

## Tips for buying an anode rod

- A magnesium anode rod protects your tank better but doesn't last as long as an aluminum/zinc rod.
- Aluminum/zinc rods are cheaper and are recommended if you have smelly water. But consult a water treatment specialist before switching to an aluminum rod.

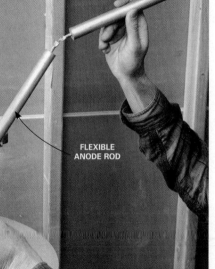

FLEXIBLE MAGNESIUM ROD

DETERIORATED ROD

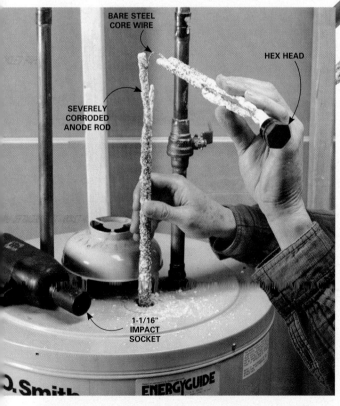

BARE STEEL CORE WIRE

HEX HEAD

SEVERELY CORRODED ANODE ROD

1-1/16" IMPACT SOCKET

**1 Remove the old anode rod.** Loosen the hex head with a short burst from your impact wrench. Unscrew it by hand once it's loose.

FLEXIBLE ANODE ROD

**2 Install the new anode.** Coat the threads with pipe dope or Teflon tape and slide the new rod into the tank. Tighten with a socket and ratchet by hand.

# HOW TO JOIN
# DISSIMILAR PIPES

*Learn what to do when working with various types of pipes*

by **Mark Petersen, Contributing Editor**

**W**hen you go to add or replace plumbing lines in a house that's more than 10 years old, chances are you won't find new pipes that are the same kind as the old ones. That's no big deal—hardware stores and home centers carry hundreds of different kinds of transitional fittings to help you make the connections. What is a big deal is that those hundreds of different kinds of fittings don't all install the same way.

Some fittings need to be soldered; others take just a wrench or pliers. Several require specific crimping tools, and there are newer styles that simply push together. We asked a master plumber how he deals with the ones he encounters the most, but don't run all over town trying to find the exact fittings we show here. There are usually several suitable solutions using parts available at a local hardware store or home center.

## MEET AN EXPERT

**Les Zell has been a plumber for 30 years. Many of his customers have several different types of pipes in their homes, and the number of different kinds of fittings he carries in his van has tripled. Knowing how to join dissimilar pipes has been essential.**

## Buy approved products

Exceptionally fastidious inspectors will want you to show them that you're using approved building materials. If you have to choose between two similar products, buy the one that is clearly labeled as being approved by nationally recognized organizations. ANSI and ASTM are examples of widely accepted product certification organizations. And save your labels until after the inspection is completed. For more information on what these markings mean, check out safe-plumbing.org/product-markings.

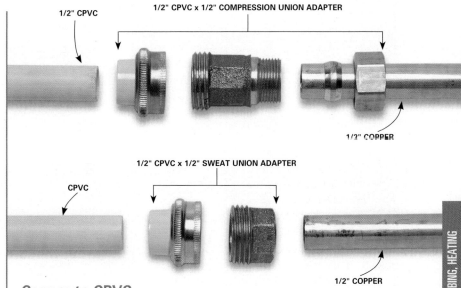

1/2" CPVC

1/2" CPVC x 1/2" COMPRESSION UNION ADAPTER

1/2" COPPER

1/2" CPVC x 1/2" SWEAT UNION ADAPTER

CPVC

1/2" COPPER

www.elkhartproducts.com
khart, Indiana 46515
GB #1
EPC #
NSF. CSA ASTM UPC

## Copper to CPVC

Plastic and metal expand and contract at different rates. This can be a problem when joining CPVC to copper, especially when using threaded connections. One option is to use union adapters. The rubber washer should flex enough to keep the connection sealed. If you choose to solder the copper side, make sure you do that first or you'll melt the plastic side.

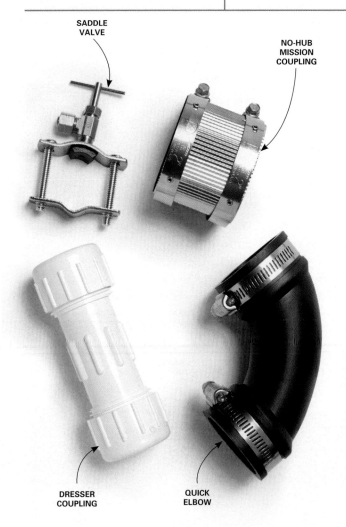

SADDLE VALVE

NO-HUB MISSION COUPLING

DRESSER COUPLING

QUICK ELBOW

## Don't guess

Just because a fitting is the right size or configuration doesn't mean it can be used in any situation. Some can be used above ground but not below. Others work perfectly fine in the open but can't be buried behind drywall. When in doubt, ask your inspector. Here are a few examples of connectors that may seem like the perfect solution but could be rejected by your inspector, or worse, fail to work and cause thousands of dollars in water damage:

**Dresser couplings:** These will pull apart on pipes that aren't completely immobile.

**Quick elbows:** Drain snakes can poke right through them.

**Saddle valves:** These valves are not always allowed. They clog easily and don't always shut off reliably.

**No-hub mission couplings:** These couplings are for cast iron to cast iron connections only.

### Take them to the store

Save yourself repeated trips to the home center or hardware store by taking a small chunk of each pipe you plan on using to the store.

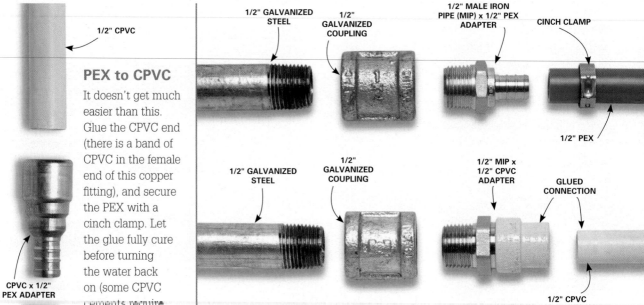

**1/2" CPVC**

## PEX to CPVC

It doesn't get much easier than this. Glue the CPVC end (there is a band of CPVC in the female end of this copper fitting), and secure the PEX with a cinch clamp. Let the glue fully cure before turning the water back on (some CPVC cements require several hours to cure).

**CPVC x 1/2" PEX ADAPTER**

**1/2" PEX**

**CINCH CLAMP**

**1/2" GALVANIZED STEEL**

**1/2" GALVANIZED COUPLING**

**1/2" MALE IRON PIPE (MIP) x 1/2" PEX ADAPTER**

**CINCH CLAMP**

**1/2" PEX**

**1/2" GALVANIZED STEEL**

**1/2" GALVANIZED COUPLING**

**1/2" MIP x 1/2" CPVC ADAPTER**

**GLUED CONNECTION**

**1/2" CPVC**

## Plastic to galvanized steel

The inside of galvanized pipes gets thinner over the years. And the male ends, where the threads were cut into, can become so thin that they leak when you try to screw on a new female fitting over the end of them. So try to make the transition at an existing female fitting. When working with galvanized pipes, Les wraps pipe thread tape on the threads and dabs on a little pipe dope as added insurance against leaks.

## ABS to PVC

One inexpensive method of connecting ABS to PVC drainpipes is to use male and female fittings. Apply pipe thread tape before screwing them together, and then glue the pipes into the fittings using the proper cement. Arrange the fittings so the water flows past the threads on the male fitting, not into them.
This helps solid materials flow by the connection without getting hung up.

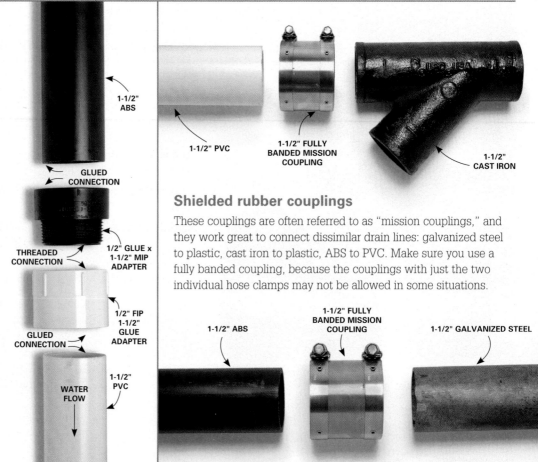

**1-1/2" ABS**

**GLUED CONNECTION**

**GLUED CONNECTION**

**THREADED CONNECTION**

**1/2" GLUE x 1-1/2" MIP ADAPTER**

**1/2" FIP 1-1/2" GLUE ADAPTER**

**GLUED CONNECTION**

**WATER FLOW**

**1-1/2" PVC**

**1-1/2" PVC**

**1-1/2" FULLY BANDED MISSION COUPLING**

**1-1/2" CAST IRON**

## Shielded rubber couplings

These couplings are often referred to as "mission couplings," and they work great to connect dissimilar drain lines: galvanized steel to plastic, cast iron to plastic, ABS to PVC. Make sure you use a fully banded coupling, because the couplings with just the two individual hose clamps may not be allowed in some situations.

**1-1/2" ABS**

**1-1/2" FULLY BANDED MISSION COUPLING**

**1-1/2" GALVANIZED STEEL**

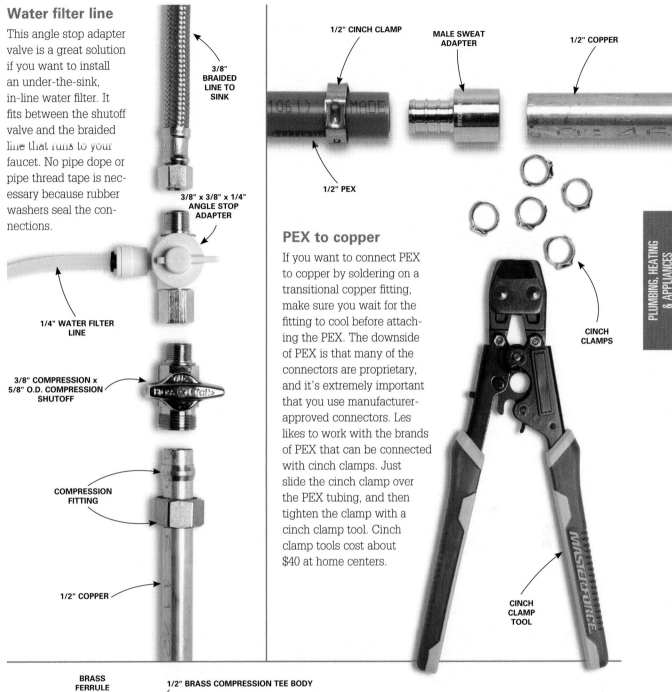

## Water filter line

This angle stop adapter valve is a great solution if you want to install an under-the-sink, in-line water filter. It fits between the shutoff valve and the braided line that runs to your faucet. No pipe dope or pipe thread tape is necessary because rubber washers seal the connections.

**3/8" BRAIDED LINE TO SINK**

**3/8" x 3/8" x 1/4" ANGLE STOP ADAPTER**

**1/4" WATER FILTER LINE**

**3/8" COMPRESSION x 5/8" O.D. COMPRESSION SHUTOFF**

**COMPRESSION FITTING**

**1/2" COPPER**

**1/2" CINCH CLAMP**

**MALE SWEAT ADAPTER**

**1/2" COPPER**

**1/2" PEX**

**CINCH CLAMPS**

**CINCH CLAMP TOOL**

## PEX to copper

If you want to connect PEX to copper by soldering on a transitional copper fitting, make sure you wait for the fitting to cool before attaching the PEX. The downside of PEX is that many of the connectors are proprietary, and it's extremely important that you use manufacturer-approved connectors. Les likes to work with the brands of PEX that can be connected with cinch clamps. Just slide the cinch clamp over the PEX tubing, and then tighten the clamp with a cinch clamp tool. Cinch clamp tools cost about $40 at home centers.

**BRASS FERRULE**

**1/2" BRASS COMPRESSION TEE BODY**

**1/2" COPPER**

**COMPRESSION FITTINGS**

**1/2" COLD COPPER SUPPLY LINE**

**1/4" ICEMAKER LINE**

## Icemaker line

Installing a brass compression tee body is a good way to provide water to your refrigerator's icemaker. Although the brass ferrule seals the copper pipes to the tee, Les still uses a little pipe dope on the ferrule to assist in even compression. Many municipalities don't allow 1/4-in. icemaker lines to be covered by finished walls, floors or ceilings, so you may have to run a 1/2-in. line to the fridge instead.

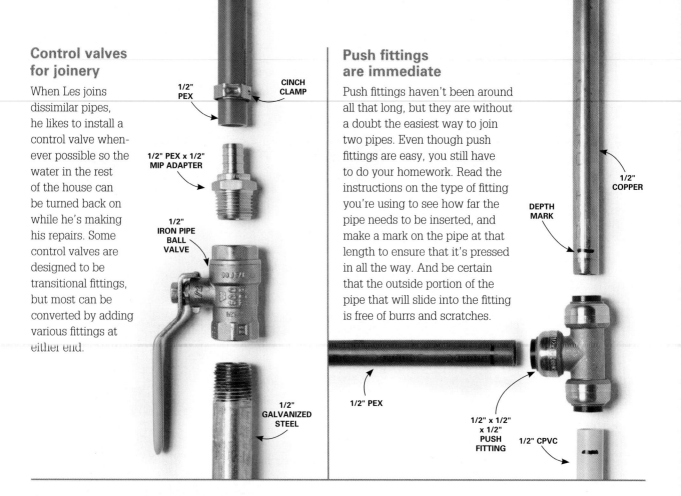

## Control valves for joinery

When Les joins dissimilar pipes, he likes to install a control valve whenever possible so the water in the rest of the house can be turned back on while he's making his repairs. Some control valves are designed to be transitional fittings, but most can be converted by adding various fittings at either end.

1/2" PEX

CINCH CLAMP

1/2" PEX x 1/2" MIP ADAPTER

1/2" IRON PIPE BALL VALVE

1/2" GALVANIZED STEEL

## Push fittings are immediate

Push fittings haven't been around all that long, but they are without a doubt the easiest way to join two pipes. Even though push fittings are easy, you still have to do your homework. Read the instructions on the type of fitting you're using to see how far the pipe needs to be inserted, and make a mark on the pipe at that length to ensure that it's pressed in all the way. And be certain that the outside portion of the pipe that will slide into the fitting is free of burrs and scratches.

1/2" COPPER

DEPTH MARK

1/2" PEX

1/2" x 1/2" x 1/2" PUSH FITTING

1/2" CPVC

## Copper to galvanized steel

Connecting two dissimilar metals can cause galvanic corrosion, which deteriorates metal over time. A dielectric union is a fitting designed to isolate the two metals from each other. There is some controversy as to the effectiveness of dielectric unions, but the bottom line is that if you connect a copper pipe to a galvanized one, some plumbing inspectors are going to require one. Certain municipalities consider a brass fitting a suitable dialectic union, but others do not. Your best bet is to ask your local inspector.

1/2" GALVANIZED STEEL

1/2" DIELECTRIC UNION

1/2" COPPER

---

### PVC PIPES "GROW" DURING ASSEMBLY

*I was cementing some PVC pipes recently and ran into a problem. I had measured all the components, then started gluing up the sections. By the time I got to the last fitting, it didn't match up; the pipes had "grown" in length. How do I avoid this problem in the future?*

PVC fittings have a slightly tapered "interference fit." If you apply cement and press the pipe and fitting together but let go before the weld is complete, the taper will "spit" the pipe out slightly. To get the proper weld, insert the pipe into the fitting after applying the cement. Then immediately push the pipe into the fitting as you twist it a quarter turn until it bottoms out. Hold the two pieces together for a full 30 seconds before you let go. It takes that long for the weld to "set."

# AVOID
# APPLIANCE PROBLEMS

*How to avoid the top 10 appliance repairs*

## by **Rick Muscoplat, Contributing Editor**

**MEET AN EXPERT**

**Costas Stavrou has been fixing appliances for more than 30 years.** He and his wife, Lorrie, run a classic family business. Lorrie handles the appointments, parts ordering and billing, and she keeps Costas on his toes.

Our appliance wizard, Costas Stavrou, spends most of his time solving problems that were avoidable in the first place. "If people would just read the instructions in their owner's manual and then follow a few basic rules, I'd have to find a new line of work," he told us.

We'll show you how to avoid these top 10 repairs. And, we'll go a few steps further and explain exactly what breaks and how much you'll save by following our advice. If you don't follow these rules, Costas wants to thank you for keeping his repair business humming.

## 1 Clean refrigerator coils

On the back or underside of your fridge, there are coils that dissipate the heat that's removed from the fridge (kind of like the radiator on your car). Dust buildup on these coils reduces airflow and wastes energy. Worse, it causes the compressor and condenser fan to run longer and hotter. That causes premature failure. A service call to install a new condenser fan runs $150. And a new compressor runs at least $500. That's quite an incentive to clean the coils. Cleaning the coils takes only a few minutes. See how on p. 95. You can also visit familyhandyman.com and search for "refrigerator coils."

**Don't block air vents**

The freezer and refrigerator compartments require proper airflow to keep foods at the right temperature. So think twice before you buy warehouse-size packs of frozen food. Because if you jam them into the freezer and block the vents, you can cause cooling problems in the refrigerator and force the compressor and fans to run overtime. That'll result in premature fan and compressor failures. Replacing a fan usually runs about $150. But if the compressor fails, you're better off buying a new refrigerator.

 **Don't overload your washer or dryer**

You may think you're saving time, water or energy by cramming more clothes into your washer and dryer. But the manufacturers list a maximum load weight for a good reason. If you overload a top-loading washer, you can fry the drive belts or break the drive coupler ($150 repair bill). And, overloading can also cause socks and underwear to float over the basket. Then they get sucked into the pump and wreck it. That service call will cost you $115.

If you overload a front-loading washer or dryer, you can burn out the rear bearing or motor. That repair is so expensive that you'd be better off buying a new machine. In the dryer, the extra load weight not only takes longer to dry but also wears out drum support rollers and drive belts (up to $250).

Weight limits range from as little as 6 lbs. to as much as 15 lbs. for top loaders and about 18 lbs. for front loaders. So consult your owner's manual and find the load limits for your machine. Then grab an armful of clothes and stand on a scale to get an idea of just how much your machine can handle.

 **Clean fridge gaskets**

If you keep your refrigerator door gaskets clean, they'll seal properly and last the life of the fridge. But if you let sticky foods like syrup and jam build up on the door gasket, they'll glue the gasket to the frame. Pulling harder on a stuck door eventually tears the gasket, and that'll cost you about $150 (up to $300 on some brands). Plus, if the door doesn't seal properly, the fridge has to run longer, and that'll boost your electric bill. Clean the door gasket with warm water and a sponge. Don't use detergents; they can damage the gasket.

**⑤ Clean your dishwasher screen**

If your dishwasher has a filtering screen under the bottom spray arm, clean it regularly. See how at familyhandyman.com. Just search for "dishwasher." If you don't, the stuck food particles degrade into slime that blocks water flow and reduces cleaning performance. So you'll pay a minimum service call (usually about $100) just to have the filter cleaned. And while we're on the subject, cut back on the soap use too. You don't need more than a teaspoon to clean most loads. Excess soap builds up in the entire dishwasher and eventually reduces water flow, requiring another "cleaning" service call. To remove soap buildup, use a product like Dishwasher Magic, available at most hardware stores and home centers.

##  6 Don't slam the door

You can rationalize all you want about why you drop or slam the lid or door to your washer or dryer (your hands are full, you're in a hurry, etc.), but your appliances don't care. So forget the excuse and know this: If you continually drop or slam the lid to your washer or dryer (top or front load), you're going to break the lid/door switch. That'll cost you about $175. That's right—you can avoid this repair by lowering the lid and gently closing the door. Easy, huh?

##  7 Don't drag clothes out of the washer

Nobody likes lifting a heavy bundle of clothes in or out of a front-loading washing machine. But it's a mistake to drag them over the door ledge. That may save your back, but zippers and buttons gradually tear up the rubber door gasket. Replacing that gasket requires a lot of disassembly, and that'll cost you about $250. So lift out the wet clothes.

##  8 Clean the lint filter

With a clogged lint filter, your clothes dry slower, and the machine works harder and wastes energy. But that's just the beginning of your troubles. Because the lint still has to go somewhere, it bypasses the filter, collects in the dryer's vent line, and reduces airflow even further.

At a certain point, the blockage gets so bad that the dryer overheats and the thermal fuse blows. The dryer will still start up, but it won't heat. The service call will run about $200 to replace the thermal fuse and clean the vent line (that charge will most likely include a lecture about cleaning the filter).

Avoid the entire lint and thermal fuse issue simply by cleaning the lint filter after each load. If you've neglected the lint filter and want to avoid a repair bill, clean out the vent line yourself. Find out how at familyhandyman. com. Just enter "lint" in the search box. Also, if you use dryer sheets, wash the lint filter with detergent every six months. Dryer sheets leave behind an invisible film, which blocks airflow.

## 9 Don't spray switches

Most people clean their stove and dishwasher knobs and touch-control panels with spray cleaners. But those liquids can easily work their way into the switches and behind the control panels and short them out. The repair bill for a shorted stove igniter switch can cost $125, and a shorted control panel can easily run about $300. Spray just a little liquid cleaner onto a rag or sponge and then clean the knobs and touch-control panel. That'll prevent shorting.

## 10 Change the furnace filter

A dirty furnace filter can actually damage your furnace. The clogged filter restricts airflow so much that the area around the heat exchanger reaches an unsafe temperature and the burners shut down. Once the furnace cools down, it'll fire up again. But if the overheat/shutdown cycle repeats enough times, the furnace controls will shut it down until it's repaired. Hello, emergency service call (minimum $250 charge for nights and weekends). If you're lucky, the repairperson will just replace the filter and reset the computer. But repeat overheat cycles can also damage the temperature sensor ($75 to replace).

The dirt level in every home is different, so you can't rely on a weekly or monthly schedule for filter changes. Instead of guessing when to replace the filter, install an air filter gauge (General G-99 Air Filter Gauge Kit; around $20 at online sources).

# HandyHints®

## FIX A SHUTOFF VALVE

There's nothing worse than starting a sink or toilet repair only to find that the shutoff valve won't shut off. Some shutoff valves are easy to replace. For those that aren't, turn off the main water valve, remove the packing nut, and then unscrew the stem and take it to the hardware store to find a replacement washer. Clean any grit out of the valve body and pop on the new washer. The valve will work like new.

SHUTOFF VALVE

PACKING NUT
STEM
NEW WASHER
WASHER

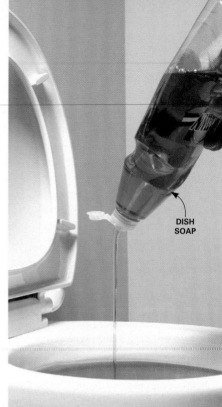

DISH SOAP

## UNCLOG A TOILET WITH DISH SOAP

If your toilet is clogged and the plunger isn't doing the trick, try this simple tip. Pour in about 1/2 cup of liquid dish soap and let it sit for a while, then try to plunge again. The liquid soap reduces friction and allows the contents of the bowl to slide on through.

TRIM RING

## FOAM A LOOSE SHOWERHEAD

Years ago, I bought the cheapest house I could find, a real dump. One of its many problems was a wobbly shower arm. With so many other house troubles, I wasn't willing to tear into the wall and refasten the plumbing. Instead, I shielded the wall with plastic and injected a few shots of expanding foam. The foam encased the pipes in the wall and eliminated the wobble.

Gary Wentz, Senior Editor

## CLEANING WOOD STOVE GLASS

We have a wood stove, and we found the perfect way to clean the glass on the door—use the ashes from the stove! We dip a damp paper towel in the cold ashes and rub them on the glass in a circular motion (much like waxing a car). Before you know it, the glass is clean. If there are any stubborn stains, we wet the glass and carefully scrape them off with a razor scraper.

—David Roller

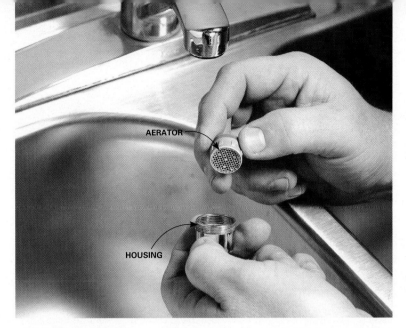

## RESTORE FREE FLOW TO A FAUCET

When our kitchen or bathroom faucet loses pressure because of a dirty aerator screen, I hear about it from my better half. Luckily, cleaning a screen is an easy job. Start by closing the drain plug (so you don't drop parts down the drain). Then remove the aerator using a rag or masking tape so you don't mar the finish with your pliers.

**Kelly Scott,**
**Field Editor**

To remove the sand and other deposits, soak the aerator in vinegar, then scrub it with a toothbrush. This usually solves the problem and puts a smile on my wife's face. If you have to disassemble the aerator to clean it, lay out the parts in the order you removed them so you can reassemble them correctly.

## FLUSH WITHOUT HANG-UPS

Every time I get a new house or toilet, I take 10 minutes and cover the flapper chain with a plastic straw. I remove the chain from the arm attachment, and slide the straw over it, covering about two-thirds of the chain. I then reattach the chain to the arm. It's that simple, and you'll never have a running toilet caused by a kinked chain again.

**Adam Breen,**
**Field Editor**

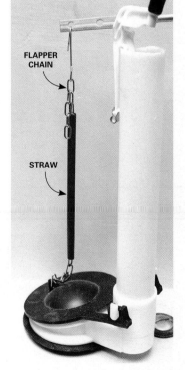

FLAPPER CHAIN

STRAW

## KEEP PAPERWORK ON HAND

After ransacking the house to find paperwork related to our water heater, water softener and other mechanical systems, we decided we needed a better way to store important paperwork. We now use clear magnetic pouches ($12 to $20 depending on size and quantity at craft and office supply stores). They hold manuals, receipts and other paperwork, and we stick them right onto our water heater, fridge, washer and dryer, and furnace. No more digging around for important papers.

**Matt Kelly,**
**Field Editor**

# FLUSH A
# WATER HEATER

*Double the life of your water heater and improve its operating efficiency*

## by **Rick Muscoplat, Contributing Editor**

**H**ave you flushed your water heater lately? This boring but important chore should be done at least once a year to remove sediment that accumulates on the bottom of the tank. That's especially true if you live in a hard-water area. The task is easy to blow off because it's out of sight—but skipping it is costing you a lot. Sediment buildup reduces the heating efficiency of your water heater.

## All about sediment

One sign of excessive sediment buildup is a popping or rumbling sound coming from your water heater. That's the sound of steam bubbles percolating up through the muck. On a gas water heater, the sediment creates hot spots that can damage the tank and cause premature failure. On an electric water heater, sediment buildup can cause the lower heating element to fail. So flushing offers a payback in lower energy bills and extended heater life.

However, if you've never flushed your water heater, or haven't done it in years, you could be in for a nasty surprise. As soon as you open the drain valve, the sediment will likely clog it and prevent you from closing the valve all the way after it's drained. Then you'll have sediment buildup and a leaking water heater. We'll show you the best way to drain the sediment out of even the most neglected heater and save a $200 service call. You'll need about $40 in plumbing parts from a home center, a garden hose, a wet vacuum, pliers and a pipe wrench.

## Buy the parts

Not only will an old drain clog up, but you won't be able to suck debris through its small opening. The key is to build a new drain valve with a 3/4-in. full-port brass ball valve with threaded ends, a 3-in. x 3/4-in. galvanized nipple, and a 3/4-in. MIP x G.H. garden hose adapter (one choice is the BrassCraft/Plumbshop No. HU22-12-12TP). Total cost is about $20.

Then build a shop vacuum adapter. If your shop vacuum has a 2-1/2-in. hose, buy a converter to reduce it to 1-1/4-in. (the Shop Vac No. 9068500, is one option; $10 or less). Then assemble a vacuum hose-to-plumbing adapter (**Photo 1**) with a 1-1/4-in. x 1-1/2-in. female PVC trap adapter, a 3/4-in. MIP x 1/2-in. barb fitting, a second 3/4-in. x 3-in. nipple and a 24-in. piece of 1/2-in. I.D. vinyl tubing (about $10 for these adapter parts).

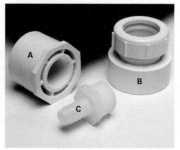

**1** **Build a shop vacuum adapter.** Glue a 1-1/2-in. PVC x 3/4-in. FIP adapter (A) onto a female PVC trap adapter (B). This allows you to attach your vacuum to 3/4-in. pipe (Photo 2). The barbed fitting (C) connects to tubing (Photo 4).

**Yuck!** This is what the sediment looks like.

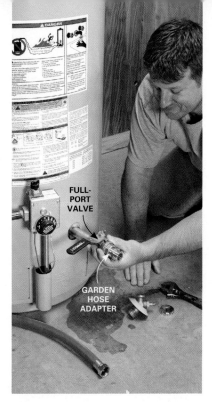

**2** **Apply suction.** Remove the temperature pressure release valve and screw in the vacuum adapter. Attach the shop vacuum hose and fire up the vacuum.

TPR VALVE

VACUUM HOSE 2-1/2" TO 1-1/4" REDUCERS

VACUUM ADAPTER IN TPR PORT

**3** **Swap valves.** Unscrew the old drain valve and install the full-port valve (closed position). Attach one end of the garden hose to the valve and run the other end into a colander and on to the floor drain.

FULL-PORT VALVE

GARDEN HOSE ADAPTER

**4** **Suck out the sediment.** Remove the full-port valve and suck out the remaining sediment with your shop vacuum adapter and vinyl tubing.

## Start the draining process

Shut off the gas or electricity to the water heater and open a hot water faucet and let it run full blast for about 10 minutes to reduce the water temperature in the tank. Then shut off the cold water valve at the top of the tank and attach a garden hose to the existing drain valve and route it to a floor drain. (Use a kitchen colander to catch the sediment so it doesn't clog the floor drain.) Then open a hot water faucet on an upper floor and the water heater drain valve. Let the tank drain until sediment clogs the valve and reduces the flow. Then close the upstairs hot water faucet and water heater drain valve.

Next, remove the clogged drain valve and swap in the new full-port valve. But first, remove the blow-off tube and the temperature pressure release (TPR) valve and apply

suction to the tank so you won't get soaked when you yank the old drain valve (**Photo 2**). Then swap the valves (**Photo 3**). Remove the vacuum hose from the TPR port and finish draining the tank.

Most of the sediment will flush out through the full-port valve. To remove the rest, open the cold water valve at the top of the tank in short bursts to blast it toward the drain. If you still can't get the last bit out, try vacuuming it (**Photo 4**).

When you're done, close the ball valve and leave it in place. But remove the lever handle to prevent accidental opening. Then reinstall the TPR valve and blow-off tube. Refill the water heater and turn on the gas or electricity, and you'll be back in hot water without all the noise.

---

### WHY DOES MY TOILET TAKE SO LONG TO FLUSH?

*I have to hold the toilet flush lever down for 10 to 15 seconds in order to get the toilet to flush. If I let go earlier, it immediately stops flushing. I have replaced the flapper and still have the problem.*

When you operate the flush lever, the chain should lift the flapper flush valve high off its seat and then the flapper should float long enough to allow the tank to empty. However, if the chain between the flush lever and the flapper is too long, the flapper will lift up and immediately close.

Shorten the chain a few links at a time until the flapper stays up when flushed. You may have to tweak the chain length a bit more after you close the lid and try flushing. But once you have the proper length, you should be able to flush and leave.

# GreatGoofs®

## Runaway AC

The old, heavy window air conditioner in our upstairs bedroom had finally died. The window looked out over the roof of the porch below, and because the AC unit was trash anyway, it seemed easiest to remove it from the outside onto the roof, then just drop it off into the grass. Well, I didn't realize the lawn had enough of an incline to allow the unit to roll 6 ft. onto the driveway and smash directly into the side of our car! Luckily the side panels were composite—I got away with buffing out most of the damage.

—Dean Thompson

## The physics of plumbing

I was replacing our shower fixture, and I couldn't budge the large brass nut that was holding the two-way mixing valve in place. Using my expert knowledge of physics, I came up with the perfect solution. I packed the valve in ice to make it shrink in diameter. Then I used my blowtorch on the nut so its diameter would expand, thus freeing it.

I was feeling really clever until I noticed the smoke filling the shower. It turns out two studs were on fire and the flames were moving up inside the wall! Have you ever tried to extinguish a blazing fire through a 6-in. access hole? I didn't worry about the physics at that point—I just ran for the fire extinguisher!

—Dr. Kris Storm

## "Air" on the side of clean

During an unusually long hot spell, I finally decided to install the window air conditioner that had been sitting unused in my garage for five years. I lugged it inside and prepared to put it in the window. My wife suggested I clean it thoroughly before installing it. But since it had been wrapped up in the garage, I figured a light surface cleaning would be enough.

After straining and sweating to install the unit in the window, I turned it on, expecting to receive a delicious blast of cold air. I got the cold air all right. But the mouse droppings, dead bugs and spiderwebs weren't exactly "delicious."

—Harry Kashuck

## Cold commode

Last winter, I brought home a new toilet. I stored the box outside on my porch along with the new wax ring, flange bolts and new water line until I got around to installing it a few days later. I mounted the wax ring and set the toilet over the flange, but the toilet would not sit flush against the floor. I tried everything I could think of, including tightening the floor bolts at the base of the toilet until I nearly cracked the toilet base, but the toilet just would not sit flush. I gave up in frustration and went to bed.

The next morning, I walked outside to get the paper and saw the empty toilet box sitting on my unheated porch. As I shivered in my bare feet, the explanation suddenly hit me. I ran to the bathroom and sure enough, the toilet was sitting flush against the floor and the bolts were completely loose. Turns out the wax ring had been frozen solid.

—Mike Koch

## Washing machine rodeo

My wife and I bought our first high-efficiency washer and dryer set. The instructions said to carefully level the washer, front to back, left to right, and diagonally. After half an hour of adjusting it to perfection, we ran it through a cycle. The thing bucked like an angry bronco! I had to fling my body on top of it and yell for my wife to shut it off.

I rechecked the level and five minutes later, satisfied, we tried it again. Same result—I took another rodeo ride. Two more tries with the same results and I was about to kick the thing. I called a buddy who also had a high-efficiency machine. He said his moved a little but didn't jump around like I described. He then asked if I'd removed the shipping bolts. Once I did that, it washed like a dream.

—Eric Meier

## Doggone bad measuring!

I was installing a new icemaker water line. First I measured from the outside wall of the kitchen to the location of the tubing at the back of the refrigerator. Then I went downstairs to the basement and measured from the outside wall to the same spot. I drilled the hole through the floor and went upstairs to admire my handiwork. But the hole wasn't where I thought it should be.

I suddenly remembered that the house floor cantilevered over the foundation, and I had drilled the hole 18 in. in front of the refrigerator. After a bit of a hunt, I finally found the hole in the hardwood floor—directly under the dog's dish! Without skipping a beat, I cut a piece of 3/8-in. dowel, plugged the hole and slid the dog's dish over it. I figure no one will be the wiser (as long as we have a dog, anyway).

—Laurence Simon

# Beautiful Bathrooms

## HANG A SHELF OVER YOUR TOWEL BAR

For some reason, once the towel bar goes up, we don't consider the wall usable for anything else. Why not hang a shelf for toiletries and decorative items? Just make sure to mount the shelf high enough so it allows easy access to your towels.

## ADD A SECOND MEDICINE CABINET— AND SHELVES!

Here's a way to add more storage and bump up the sophistication of your bathroom. Mount matching medicine cabinets and add shelves between them. To support these shelves, we drilled holes in the sides of the cabinets and inserted adjustable shelf pegs. The shelves are simply boards finished to match the cabinets. This makes the most of the wall space above your toilet and sink. You could also mount something similar over a double sink. The cabinets can be surface mounted or recessed. The shelves give the unit a nice finished quality. Medicine cabinets start at about $80 each.

## REMOVE A TOWEL BAR OR SOAP DISH

Removing a broken or outdated surface-mounted towel bar or soap dish is easy. But removing an "inset" fixture (mounted directly to the tile backer board) is a much bigger job that we won't cover here. To see whether yours is surface mounted or inset, check the fixture edges. If you see grout, it's most likely an inset mount. However, since someone may have applied caulk around the grout, jam a putty knife into a bottom corner of the fixture and tap it with a small hammer. If you hit grout or the edge of the fixture's "inset," stop and recaulk. If the putty knife doesn't hit anything hard, move on to the next step.

Tape off the tile around the fixture to protect it from scratches. Then fit your oscillating tool with a flexible scraper blade and slide it under the fixture as shown. Once the fixture is off, remove heavy caulk buildup with a single-edge razor blade. Apply caulk remover (available at home centers). Let the remover work for three minutes, then scrape the residue with a plastic putty knife. Apply more remover and scrape until it's gone. Wipe the tile with a clean rag wetted with the remover and remove the tape.

FLEXIBLE SCRAPER BLADE

**Use an oscillating tool**
Jam the blade into a corner about 1 in. deep. Then work it all around the fixture. Shove it in deeper and do a second pass around the fixture, cutting through all the adhesive and caulk.

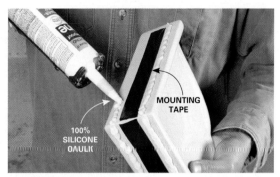

**1** Apply a strip of double-face adhesive mounting tape on each flange, stopping 1 in. short of the outside ends. Then lay a thick bead of silicone caulk around the entire perimeter.

**2** Remove the tape liner and press the shelf into place. (Position the shelf carefully—once the tape sticks, you can't move it easily.) Wipe off the excess caulk and tool the joint with a damp rag or fingertip.

## ADD A CERAMIC SHOWER SHELF

Toss that grungy plastic storage shelf you have hanging over your showerhead and install a classy ceramic corner shelf instead. These are available at tile shops for $20 to $30. Make sure you get a "flat-back" shelf and clean all the soap scum off the tile so the bond will hold well. Tape around the area where the shelf will go (place the shelf in the middle of a tile so grout lines won't run through the caulk). Scuff the tile with 80-grit sandpaper. This gives the silicone caulk something to adhere to other than the slick tile.

## INSTALL A NEW TUB/SHOWER TRIM KIT

Give your shower an instant face-lift by swapping out your existing showerhead, handle and tub spout for new ones. To make this a painless switch, buy a trim kit that uses the existing trim valve—you won't have to touch anything inside the wall.

Before you buy, check the manufacturer's Web site for specs, styles and finishes. Also check your tub spout to see if it slips on or is threaded so you can buy the right replacement. You can buy complete trim kits ($40 and up) or buy each component separately at home centers, plumbing suppliers and online retailers.

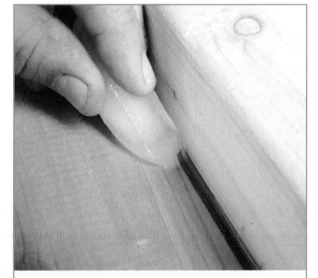

## ICE CUBE CAULK TOOLING

An easy way to tool caulk is to take an ice cube and run it down the caulk line, applying steady pressure. The film of water that forms between the ice cube and the caulk makes a smooth, professional finish, and you can melt the cube in your hand to get any bead shape you want.

# BeautifulBathrooms

## CLEANING
## A BATHROOM

A clean bathroom is a beautiful bathroom. But with all the water, soap, hair products and heavy use, bathrooms get scuzzy fast, and cleaning them can be a real chore. So we've assembled the best cleaning tips to help simplify your job the next time cleaning day rolls around.

 **Vacuum first, then scrub**

Do you ever find yourself chasing strands of wet hair or running into dust balls in the corners with your sponge or cleaning rag? You can eliminate this nuisance by vacuuming the bathroom before you get out your cleaning solutions.

For a really thorough cleaning, start at the top, vacuuming the dust from light fixtures and the top of window casings. Then work your way down. And finally, vacuum the floor methodically so you cover every inch. You don't want to leave any stray hair or dust bunnies to muck up your cleaning water. A soft-bristle upholstery brush works best for this type of vacuuming.

**2 Make your own greener cleaning solution**

Professional housecleaner Maggie Orth likes to make her own cleaning products. Here's her recipe for an all-purpose cleaning solution, modified from one she found in the book *Clean House, Clean Planet* by Karen Logan.

In a 5-quart bucket, mix: 1 cup of distilled vinegar, 3 tablespoons of borax, 1 gallon of hot water and 1/2 cup of soap (Maggie uses Dr. Bronner's Sal Suds). You can add 10 or 15 drops of tea tree, lavender or lemon oil for a nice fragrance. Mix well and pour some of the mixture into a spray bottle. Save the rest in a gallon jug. The ingredients will cost $25 to $30, but you'll have enough to last for years!

Use this mixture to clean tile, countertops and painted woodwork, but not glass. Use club soda to clean glass.

EMPTY SPRAY BOTTLE

LIQUID SOAP

ESSENTIAL OIL

**3 A scrub and a wax**

Field Editor Joe Stiles writes: "Every three months, I use CLR Calcium, Lime and Rust Remover and an old toothbrush to clean all the faucets and lavatories. Then I apply an automotive car wax like Turtle Wax and buff after the wax hazes. Our fixtures look like new."

### 4 Protect your glass shower doors from mineral buildup

When the beads of water left on your glass shower door dry out, they leave minerals behind that are at best unsightly, and at worst can be tough as nails to remove if you let them build up (see Tip 5). You can avoid beading water altogether by coating the glass with an auto-glass treatment.

We're using Aquapel ($5 to $10 for a single pack), but Rain-X will also work. Follow the instructions on the package to apply the treatment to your shower door glass. You can buy Aquapel online or find a local dealer at aquapel.com. You'll find Rain-X at any auto parts store.

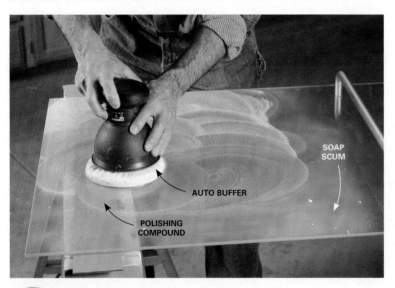

AUTO BUFFER

POLISHING COMPOUND

SOAP SCUM

### 5 Buff off heavy grime on glass shower doors

If you have glass shower doors in your bathroom and don't keep on top of the cleaning as described in Tip 4, above, you can end up with soap scum so tough that it's nearly impossible to remove. That's when you bring out the heavy equipment.

Senior editor Travis Larson came up with this tip, and we think it's pretty ingenious. Pick up some polishing compound at a home center or an auto parts store and use an auto buffer to polish off the offending scum. If you don't own a buffer, you can buy one for as little as $20 or borrow one from a gearhead friend. If possible, remove the doors and take them out to the garage to avoid messing up the bathroom.

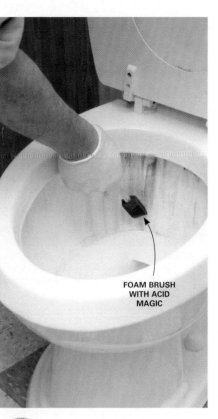

FOAM BRUSH WITH ACID MAGIC

### 6 Remove stubborn rust stains with Acid Magic

If you have a lot of iron in your water and struggle with rust stains in your toilet or bathtub, here's a perfect solution. Acid Magic dissolves rust like, um, magic. It's as powerful as muriatic acid but much safer and more pleasant to use. You should still take all the precautions you would with any strong cleaning solution, like wearing gloves and safety glasses when you're using it. But it's better than regular acid because there are no noxious fumes, and it won't burn your skin.

To clean rust from toilets and other porcelain surfaces, add one part Acid Magic to three parts water. Apply the mixture to the rust stains with a sprayer, brush or foam pad and watch the stain dissolve. Rinse with clear water. You can also use it full strength for stubborn stains. Avoid getting the acid on metal parts because they can discolor. Acid Magic is available online and at Ace and True Value stores for about $10 a quart.

# BeautifulBathrooms

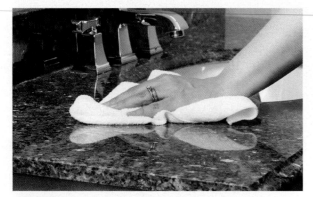

### 7 — Polish with a microfiber cloth

Microfiber cloths excel at putting the finishing touches on mirrors, countertops, and even tile and fixtures. After cleaning surfaces with your favorite cleaning solution and drying them off with a terry cloth rag or a separate microfiber cloth, polish them to a mirror finish with a dry microfiber cloth.

Microfiber cloths are perfect for this because they pick up dust, wipe off smudges and don't shed any fibers. You'll find microfiber cloths wherever cleaning supplies are sold. You can even buy them in bulk at wholesale clubs and use them throughout your house for all kinds of other cleaning chores.

### 8 — Clean grout with a bleach pen

Use a bleach pen to transform your grout from grungy to great. This method is tedious, but the payoff is crisp, clean grout lines. Use the pen to "draw" bleach across the grout lines. The pen allows you to target the grout without getting bleach all over the tile. Wait 10 minutes and then rinse.

For really mildewed grout, you may need a second application, and it can help to gently scrub the bleach into the grout with a toothbrush before allowing it to work

for 10 minutes. Make sure to run the fan in the bathroom and to avoid skin contact. This method is best for light or white grout. If you have colored grout, test a small area first. It might fade.

### 9 — Remove tough grime with less scrubbing

Whether it's built-up soap scum on the shower walls, ground-in dirt on the floor tile, or dried toothpaste on the vanity top, a Magic Eraser sponge will make short work of it. Just dampen it and rub it on the offending mess. In most cases, the mess will come right off. These sponges are especially useful for removing ground-in dirt from porous floor tile and getting those pesky nonslip strips in the bottom of your tub clean.

Magic Eraser sponges are available at grocery stores, hardware stores and wherever cleaning supplies are sold. A pack of two heavy-duty bathroom sponges costs about $3.50. Unlike regular sponges, they wear out pretty fast, so stock up.

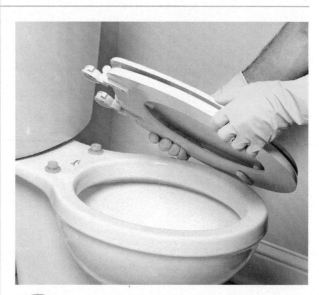

### 10 — Install a detachable toilet seat

It seems like no matter how hard you try, you can never get the hinges on the toilet seat clean. There's always a bit of cleaning solution that seeps underneath and creeps out later. Installing a detachable toilet seat solves the problem. This Bemis brand seat is easy to remove by just twisting two hinge caps about a quarter of a turn. Then you have easy access to clean under the hinges. Detachable seats cost about $20. Installation is straightforward and only requires a wrench.

# 4 Woodworking & Workshop Projects & Tips

## IN THIS CHAPTER

# SPACE-SAVER WORKSTATION

*A big work surface when you need it—compact storage when you don't*

by **Jeff Gorton, Associate Editor**

**M**ost of us don't have space to keep a large worktable set up in the middle of the garage or hobby room. But this cleverly designed cabinet solves that problem. Smooth-rolling locking casters allow you to roll the cabinet out when you need it. And it only takes seconds to flip up the top and swing out the support wings to double the work surface.

We built this project from shop-grade plywood purchased at a home center. At $40 a sheet, it wasn't the least expensive choice, but we liked the smooth surface and almost void-free veneer core. We ordered 3-in. polyurethane-wheeled casters from Amazon, and we used full-extension ball-bearing slides for the drawers. You'll find a full Materials List on p. 126.

Construction-wise, this is closer to a cabinet than to a workbench, and it requires accurate cuts for the best results. You could use a circular saw with a straightedge guide to make the cuts, but a table saw is a better choice. If you don't already have one, now is a good time to make a crosscutting sled for your table saw. It's the perfect tool to cut the wide strips of plywood to length. You'll find instructions for building a crosscutting sled at familyhandy-man.com.

Follow **Figure D** and the Materials List on p. 126 to cut out the parts. Since 3/4-in. plywood is usually a little undersize, and your plywood may not be the same thickness as the plywood we used, we've indicated on the Cutting List which dimensions will need to be adjusted for plywood thickness.

## What it takes

**COST:** $300

**TIME:** One weekend

**SKILL LEVEL:** Intermediate

**TOOLS:** Standard hand tools, saw, drill, self-centering hole punch. A table saw, miter saw and brad nail gun will give you better results and speed up the job.

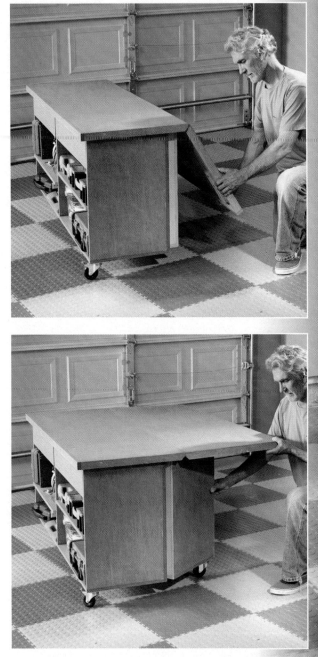

This rolling workstation is designed to set up quickly and pack up small to get out of the way. Just load your stuff into the drawers or onto the shelves, fold in the wings and drop the top, and you're ready to roll it up against the wall. And when it comes time to work again, it's just as quick to roll it out and set it up.

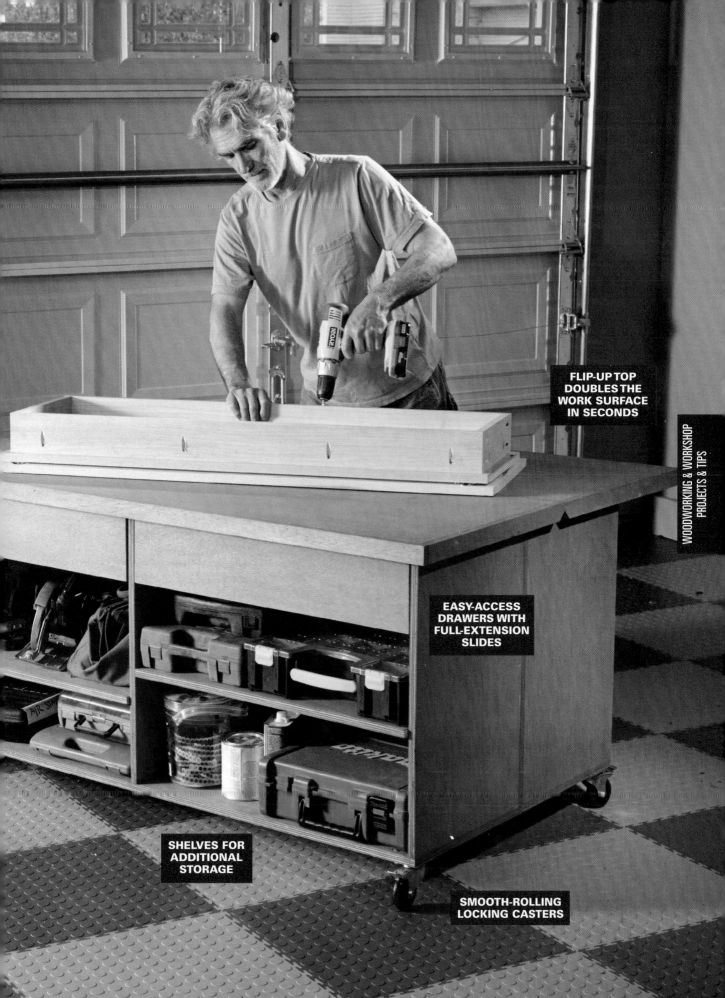

**FLIP-UP TOP
DOUBLES THE
WORK SURFACE
IN SECONDS**

**EASY-ACCESS
DRAWERS WITH
FULL-EXTENSION
SLIDES**

**SHELVES FOR
ADDITIONAL
STORAGE**

**SMOOTH-ROLLING
LOCKING CASTERS**

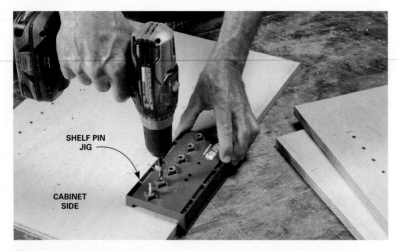

**1** **Drill shelf-support holes.** Drill holes in the cabinet sides and divider for shelf pins. It's easier to do before the cabinet is assembled.

**2** **Assemble the cabinet.** Glue and nail the cabinet parts together. With brad nails holding the parts in place, drilling pilot holes and driving screws are a lot easier.

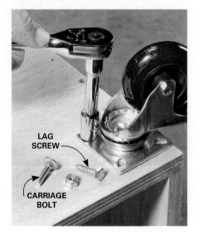

**3** **Attach the casters.** The casters need super-strong connections to the cabinet. Fasten the inside edge of the caster plate with two carriage bolts. At the outside edge, drive two lag screws through the bottom and into the cabinet sides.

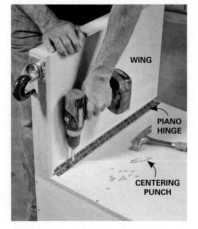

**4** **Mount the wing with a piano hinge.** Align the wing with the cabinet side, making sure the top is 1/4 in. below the cabinet top. A center punch creates divots at the center of each screw hole and makes positioning all those screws a lot easier.

## Build the cabinet box

It's easier to drill the shelf pin holes in the sides and divider before you assemble the cabinet box. In **Photo 1** we show using a Kreg Shelf Pin Jig ($30 to $34 at some home centers or online) to drill the shelf-pin holes, but you can use a scrap of pegboard for a jig or simply mark and drill the holes.

Since there is no caster in the center to support the weight, it's important to glue and screw all the parts. The combination of the screws and the strong 3/4-in. plywood back creates a box-beam effect for a rigid box. It's easier to tack the parts together first with a nail gun and 1-1/2-in. brads (**Photo 2**). Then drill pilot holes and drive the 1-1/2-in. screws. We like GRK or Spax brand screws with a torx-drive head. They reduce splitting and are easy to drive in.

When the cabinet box is done, attach the two front casters (**Photo 3**). To avoid splitting the plywood, move the casters back about 1/2 in. from the front. Use 1/4 x 1-in. lag screws on the outside edges and 1/4 x 1-in. carriage bolts through the cabinet bottom on the inside edges. Drill 5/32-in. pilot holes for the lag screws and 1/4-in. holes for the carriage bolts. Insert the carriage bolts from inside the cabinet and tap the head to seat them in the plywood before tightening the nuts.

## Assemble and mount the wings

Follow **Figure A** to assemble the wings. Glue and nail all the parts. The wings are 1/4 in. shorter than the cabinet box so they can swing open without hitting the hinges. Nail a 1/4-in.-thick plastic furniture glide to the top side of each wing, opposite the hinge side. The plastic glides make up for the 1/4-in. height difference and slide easily across the flipped-up top.

Mount the casters to the wing bottoms with 1/4 x 1-in. lag screws. Hold them back from the front edge about 1/2 in. **Photo 4** shows how to mount the wings with piano hinges. Lining up and driving all those little screws is much easier if you make starter holes with either a self-centering punch or a self-centering drill bit. Line up the hinge and anchor both ends with a screw. Then make the starter holes and drive in the remaining screws.

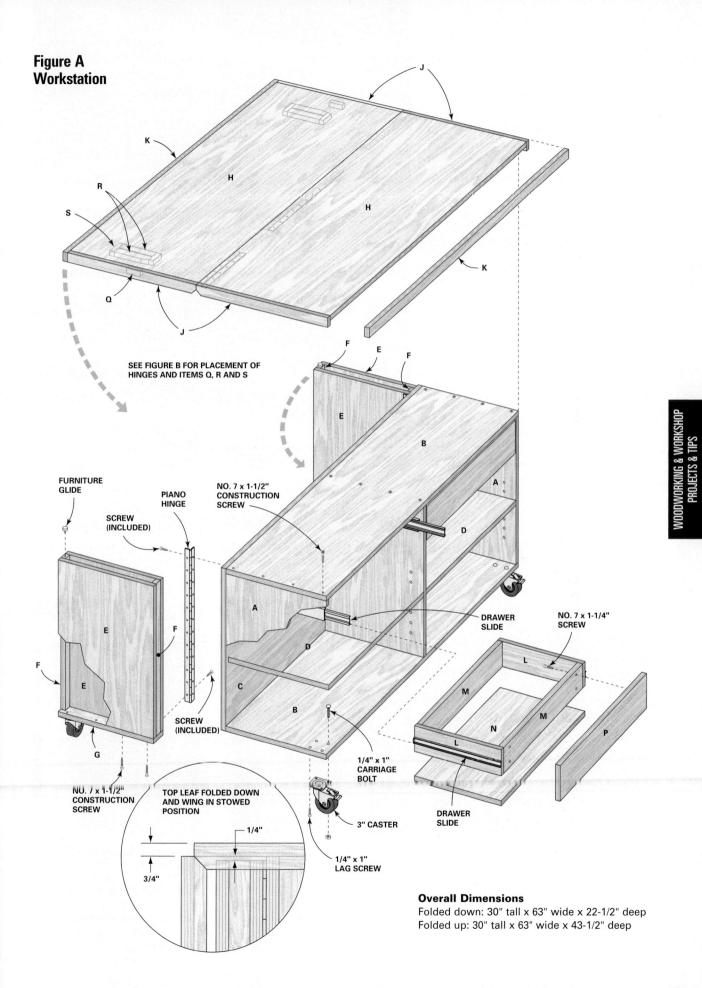

## Figure A
## Workstation

J

K

R

S

H

H

Q

J

K

SEE FIGURE B FOR PLACEMENT OF
HINGES AND ITEMS Q, R AND S

F

E

F

E

B

A

FURNITURE
GLIDE

SCREW
(INCLUDED)

PIANO
HINGE

NO. 7 x 1-1/2"
CONSTRUCTION
SCREW

A

D

E

F

SCREW
(INCLUDED)

A

C

D

B

DRAWER
SLIDE

NO. 7 x 1-1/4"
SCREW

L

M

M

N

L

P

DRAWER
SLIDE

E

F

G

NO. 7 x 1-1/2"
CONSTRUCTION
SCREW

TOP LEAF FOLDED DOWN
AND WING IN STOWED
POSITION

1/4"

3/4"

1/4" x 1"
CARRIAGE
BOLT

3" CASTER

1/4" x 1"
LAG SCREW

### Overall Dimensions
Folded down: 30" tall x 63" wide x 22-1/2" deep
Folded up: 30" tall x 63" wide x 43-1/2" deep

## Build the drawers

Ball-bearing slides like the ones we're using require a close tolerance to operate smoothly. The drawer must be between 1 in. and 1-1/16 in. smaller than the space between the cabinet side and the divider. Photo 5 shows an accurate method to measure for the front and back parts of the drawer that compensates for the thickness of the plywood you're using. Subtract exactly 1-1/16 in. from this measurement and cut the drawer fronts and backs to this length. Nail and glue the sides to the front and back. Then measure for the bottom and cut it to the correct length. Finish the drawer boxes by nailing on the bottom (Photo 6).

The full-extension slides we're using have two parts. One part mounts to the drawer (Photo 7). The other part mounts to the cabinet (Photo 8). There is a release catch on the slides that allows you to separate the parts.

Draw a line parallel to the top edge and 2-3/8 in. down on each side of both drawers. Align the center of the slide mounting holes with this line and screw them on (Photo 7). On the cabinet, draw horizontal lines 3 in. down from the top. Center the slides on these lines when you mount them (Photo 8). To install the drawers, line up the slide parts and push the drawers in.

Finish the drawers by installing the fronts. Measure the distance between the cabinet side and the divider and subtract 1/4 in. to determine the length of the drawer fronts. Cut the fronts to this length. Photo 9 shows how to line up the fronts perfectly before attaching them with 1-1/4-in. screws (Photo 10).

## Assemble and mount the top

The top consists of two equal-size pieces of plywood joined by piano hinges and edged with 1-1/2-in. plywood strips. Photo 11 shows how to attach the piano hinges. The gaps between hinges allow the plastic furniture glides on the top of the wings to pass unobstructed. After you connect the top with hinges, flip it over onto the cabinet. Measure to align the top so that it overhangs 3/4 in. on the sides and front. Then drive 1-1/4-in. screws up through the cabinet top to secure the top. Finish the top by gluing and nailing on the plywood edging (Photo 12).

**5** **Measure for the drawer.** Hold two scraps of the plywood against the cabinet side to represent the thickness of the drawer sides. Measure the exact distance to the center divider. Subtract exactly 1-1/16 in. from this measurement to determine the lengths of the fronts and backs of the drawers.

TWO PLYWOOD SCRAPS

DRAWER BOTTOM

DRAWER BOX

**6** **Build the drawer box.** Glue and nail the drawer sides to the front and back. Then square the drawer and glue and nail the bottom to the sides, front and back.

DRAWER SLIDE

**7** **Mount the drawer slides.** Draw a line on the drawer side to indicate the center of the slide. Take the slide apart and screw the drawer part of the slide to the drawer side, making sure to align the screws with the centerline.

**8** **Mount the drawer slides in the cabinet.** Draw a centerline for the cabinet part of the drawer slides. Hold the slide 3/4 in. back from the cabinet front. Line up the holes in the slides with the centerline and screw the slides to the cabinet sides.

With the cabinet built and top mounted, there's just one final detail to take care of. To prevent the wings from moving around when the top is folded up, mount stop blocks and wing latches to the underside of the flip-up side of the top (**Photo 13**). Build the latches by gluing and nailing strips of plywood, leaving a 3/16-in. space between them. Trim a slight bevel on the wing side of each latch to allow it to slide by without catching. **Figure B** (p. 126) shows details.

Finish the project by filling any voids in the plywood with wood filler and sanding all the plywood edges. Then apply your choice of paint, stain or a clear finish.

**9 Position the drawer fronts.** From inside the drawer box, drive four screws until the tips protrude slightly. Then position the drawer front and tap it against the screws with a soft mallet. The screws will bite into the drawer front and hold it in place.

**10 Screw on the drawer fronts.** Finish driving the screws through the drawer box and into the drawer front.

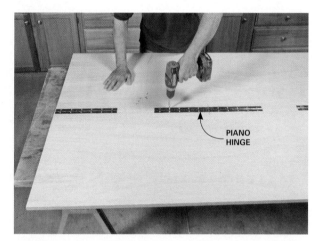

**11 Hinge the tops.** Lay the two halves tightly together on a flat surface with the best-looking sides facing down. Cut one 2-ft. piano hinge in half and the other one to 22 in. long. Install the piano hinges and then mount the top on the cabinet.

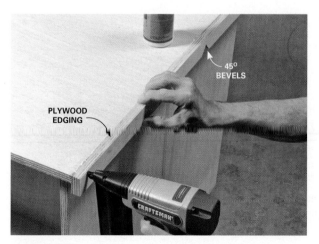

**12 Trim the top.** Glue and nail on the end trim. Cut the 45-degree bevels that allow the top to fold down without binding. Then mark and cut the front and back trim and nail it on.

**13 Mount the wing stops and latches.** Glue and nail the stop blocks against the top trim. Then mount the sliding wing latches. Together these parts lock the wings in place when the tabletop is up.

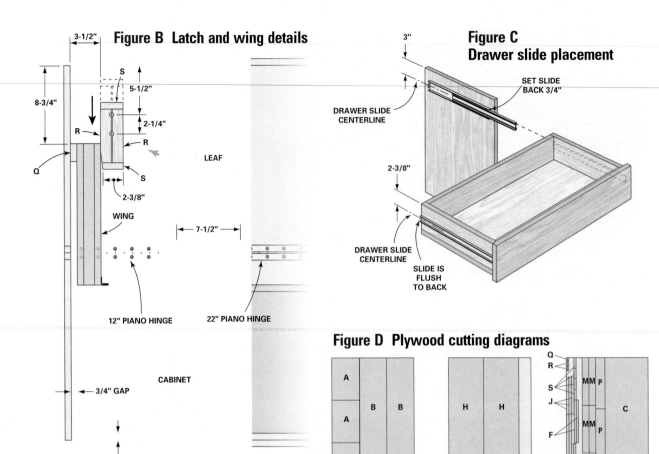

**Figure B  Latch and wing details**

3-1/2"

8-3/4"

S
5-1/2"
2-1/4"
R
R
Q
LEAF
S
2-3/8"
WING
7-1/2"
12" PIANO HINGE
22" PIANO HINGE
CABINET
3/4" GAP
3/4" GAP

**Figure C
Drawer slide placement**

3"

SET SLIDE
BACK 3/4"

DRAWER SLIDE
CENTERLINE

2-3/8"

DRAWER SLIDE
CENTERLINE

SLIDE IS
FLUSH
TO BACK

**Figure D  Plywood cutting diagrams**

A
A
A
B   B
E   E   E

H   H
E   D   D

Q
R
S
J
F
F
K
G
J
MM  P
MM  P
C
L L
L L
N   N

## MATERIALS LIST

| ITEM | QTY. |
|---|---|
| 4' x 8' x 3/4" plywood | 3 |
| Steelex D2608 3" Double Lock Caster | 4 |
| 24" x 1" piano hinges | 5 |
| 14" full-extension drawer slides | 2 pair |
| 1/4" x 1" lag screws | 12 |
| 1/4" x 1" carriage bolts | 4 |
| 1/4" locking nuts | 4 |
| 1-1/2" screws | 60 |
| 1-1/4" screws | 20 |
| 1-1/2" brad nails | 1 lb. |
| Bottle of wood glue | 1 |
| 1/4" shelf pins | 8 |
| 1/4"-thick plastic furniture glides | 2 |

### My version of Jeff's workstation

I've done a lot of writing for the magazine in my shop, using my table saw as a desk. It's a bad height, there's a lot of sawdust—and twice my laptop has been swept overboard by the fence onto the concrete floor. And one of those falls destroyed the hard drive. I needed a better solution.

When I saw Jeff's plan, I knew it was just the ticket. Plus, it could serve double duty as a nice, low assembly table. I jazzed it up a bit with oak trim, door and drawer fronts, and a plastic laminate top. I use one of the little wing pockets for storing my laptop and keep a monitor in the cabinet, away from all the dust. All my office supplies go in the drawers. I love it! It's a fun project and a real problem-solver for me.

—Travis Larson, Senior Editor

## CUTTING LIST (3/4" plywood)

| KEY | QTY. | SIZE & DESCRIPTION |
|---|---|---|
| A | 3 | 15-7/8" x 23-3/4" (sides and divider) |
| B | 2 | 15-7/8" x 60" (cabinet top and bottom) |
| C | 1 | 25-1/4" x 60" (cabinet back)* |
| D | 2 | 15-7/8" x 28-7/8" (shelves)* |
| E | 4 | 15-7/8" x 24-1/4" (wing sides) |
| F | 4 | 1-1/4" x 24-1/4" (wing spacers) |
| G | 2 | 2-3/4" x 15-7/8" (wing bottoms) |
| H | 2 | 21" x 61-1/2" (tops) |
| J | 4 | 1-1/2" x 21" (side trim; bevel one end) |
| K | 2 | 1-1/2" x 64" (front and back trim; cut length to fit) |
| L | 4 | 4" x 14" (drawer box sides) |
| M | 4 | 4" x 27" (drawer box fronts and backs; cut length to fit) |
| N | 2 | 14" x 28" (drawer bottom; cut length to fit) |
| P | 2 | 5-1/2" x 29" (drawer fronts; cut length to fit) |
| Q | 2 | 3/4" x 2" (wing stops) |
| R | 4 | 3/4" x 2-11/16" (latch fronts and backs) |
| S | 4 | 1-1/4" x 6" (latch sides) |

* Adjust for plywood thickness.

# WORKSHOP TIPS
## FROM THE EDITORS
by **Mark Petersen, Contributing Editor**

**T**he *Family Handyman* is the world's biggest DIY idea exchange. And the only thing better than discovering a new trick is passing one along. So we asked our staff editors and Field Editors to share some of their favorite workshop tips. You're sure to find one or two you can add to your workshop routine.

TEMPORARY BLOCK

PAPER BAG

PLASTIC WATER BOTTLE

## Removable clamping blocks

When there's nothing for clamps to grab on to, glue on temporary blocks wherever you need them. Dab on some glue and slap on a scrap of grocery bag paper. Then add more glue and stick the block in place. The block will hold pretty solid but will break off without damaging the wood when you're done with it.

Andrew Pitonyak, Field Editor

## Keep those pencils handy

I used to waste a lot of time looking for pencils in my shop. It seems that I never put them down in the same place twice. I finally cut the tops off several water bottles and screwed the bottles to the walls throughout my shop. It works great and costs nothing.

Bruce Fox, Field Editor

## Big, cheap clamps

When I was a young DIYer, spending a lot of money on clamps wasn't an option, so I came up with homemade clamps that cost only a few bucks. All you need are 2x4s, blocks and lag screws. To apply pressure, just back out the lag screws. To adjust the opening of the clamps, just unscrew and move the blocks. Ingenious, if I do say so myself.

Gary Wentz,
Senior Editor

LAG BOLT

## T-stands for everything

I've made a bunch of these T-stands for my shop over the years. I use them on both my workbench and sawhorses for all sorts of things: I set my projects on them when I'm painting and staining, I use them as drying racks when I'm finishing trim boards, I rest cabinets on them when I'm clamping on a face frame, and I lay planks on them for gluing and clamping. They stack together neatly and don't take up a lot of precious shop space.

Ken Collier,
Editor in Chief

T-STAND

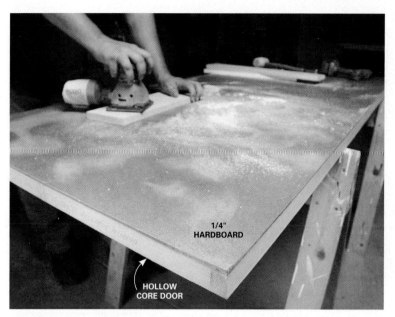

HOLLOW
CORE DOOR

1/4"
HARDBOARD

## Portable workbench

Need more work space? Just lay a door across sawhorses for an instant workbench. A solid-core door makes for a stiff, flat work surface. Hollow-core doors are lightweight but not as strong. To make a hollow-core door tougher and stiffer, glue on a layer of 1/4-in. hardboard.

—David Kurczi, Field Editor

5-GALLON
BUCKET LID

1/4"
CARRIAGE
BOLT

## Bucket-lid blade holder

I got tired of my extra saw blades banging around in the drawer every time I opened it, so I attached them to a 5-gallon bucket lid with a bolt and a thumbscrew. Now they stay put, and the lid protects my hands when I'm digging around for other stuff.

Mark
Petersen,
Contributing
Editor

PANEL
BOARD

## Write on your walls

If you have the wall space, get a 4 x 8-ft.

sheet of panel board and hang it on your wall. It's cheap ($13 at home centers) and makes a great dry-erase board. We use ours for shopping lists, tool wish lists, phone numbers, cutting lists and whatever else comes to mind. Our 5-year-old drew a design of his first birdhouse on it!

Jordan Van
Moorleghem,
Field Editor

### Repurpose a foam brush

Don't throw out a foam brush when you're done with it. Cut away the foam and you'll be left with a great flexible glue applicator!

—Randy Weisner, Field Editor

**FOAM BRUSH STICK**

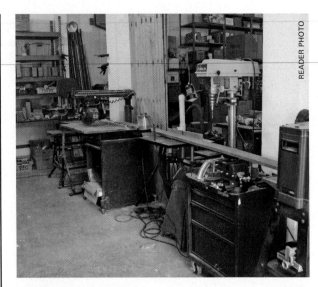

### In-line workshop

I placed my planer, router table and radial arm saw all in a line and at the same height with roller stands on each end. This allows me to take a long piece of stock and cut, rout or plane it all on one worktable.

—Richard Gerhart, Field Editor

### A picture is worth a thousand paint cans

Instead of dragging your paint can to the store to match the color, use a digital camera or your phone to snap a photo of it. If you're really organized, you can snap a photo of all your paint can labels and keep a complete digital record of all your paint colors.

Kraig Sass,
Field Editor

### The right blade for the job

As a former tool salesman and pro woodworker, I can tell you that the type of blade used on your circular saw really matters. A blade designed specifically for the job—whether it's ripping or crosscutting—will give you much better cuts. "Combination" blades are OK, but they can't match the performance of dedicated ripping or crosscut blades.

—Greg Scholl, Field Editor

**RIPPING BLADE**

**CROSSCUTTING BLADE**

**COMBINATION BLADE**

## Save money on casters

If you want some heavy-duty casters, buy a furniture dolly and remove the casters. You'll probably get better casters for less money.  My local home center, for example, sells a furniture dolly with four 250-lb. casters for less than $20. Four individual casters rated for only 170 lbs. cost nearly $30.

Jason Nailen, Field Editor

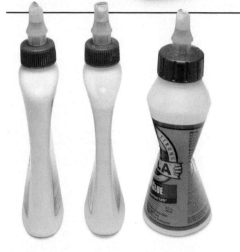

## Keep adhesives from hardening

I found an easy solution for the problem of air and moisture spoiling or hardening adhesives. You can significantly lengthen the shelf life by squeezing out all the air (headspace in the tube or bottle) before you cap it. To date I have not had any adhesives harden or go bad using this technique. As a bonus, the glue is at the tip of the bottle as soon as you squeeze it.

—George Fencik, Field Editor

## A safe chuck key holder

I used to hang the chuck key for my drill press on a string taped to the press. That worked well until the day I bumped it and the string caught the moving chuck and sent it flying. Luckily, it left an indentation in the wall instead of in me. Now I use a magnet to keep the chuck key handy—lesson learned.

Travis Larson, Senior Editor

MAGNET

## Save your containers

I save almost every glass and plastic container we use. Glass jars work well for liquids. I clean my brushes in an old tin can. I brush on glue from small containers of all kinds. Sour cream/cottage cheese containers work for just about everything. I like clear plastic ones for miscellaneous storage so I can see what it is I'm after. I label them all with a permanent marker.

Mark Ripplinger, Field Editor

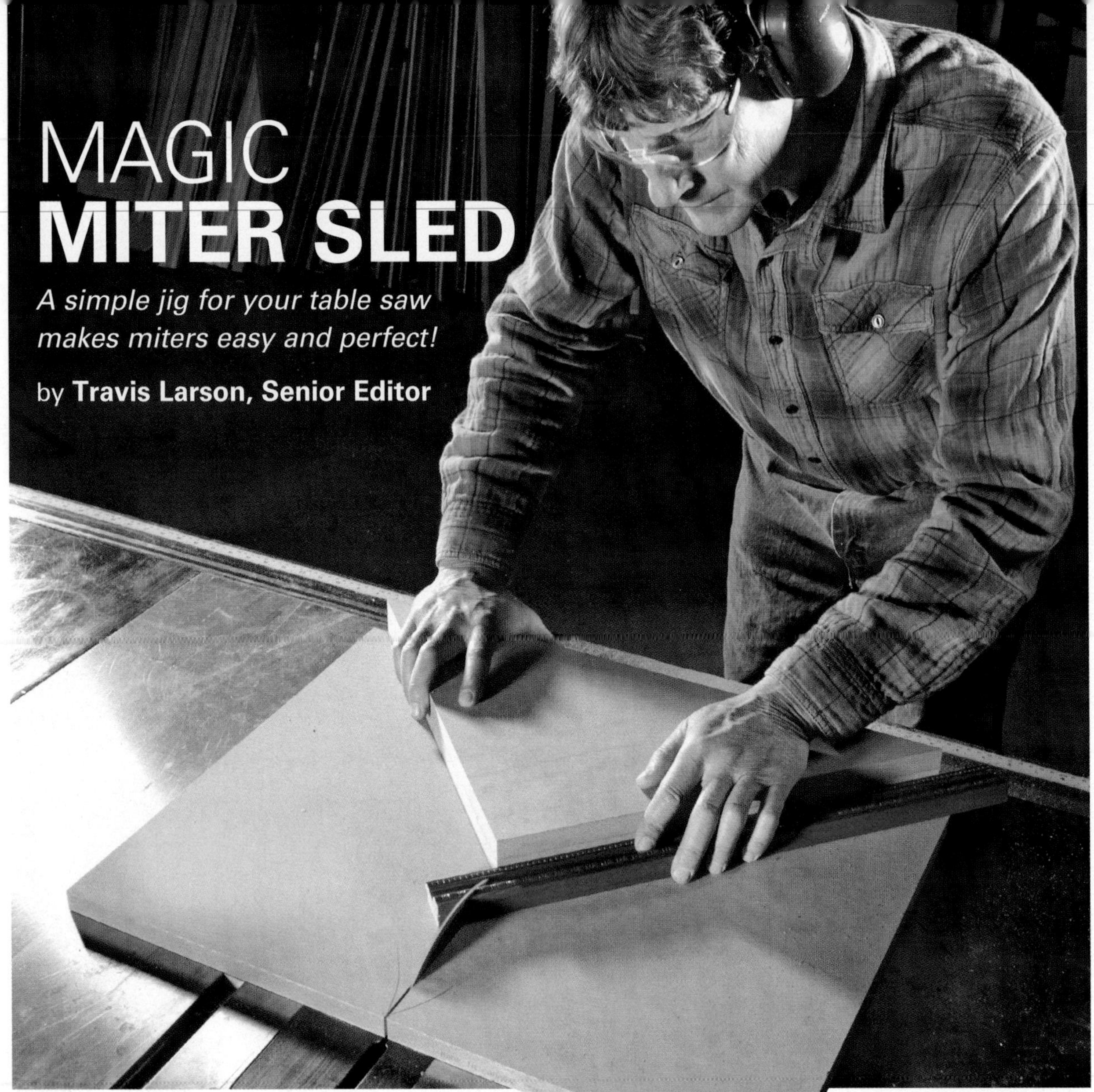

# MAGIC
# MITER SLED

*A simple jig for your table saw
makes miters easy and perfect!*

by **Travis Larson, Senior Editor**

**A**nybody can cut a 45-degree miter by using a miter saw. But how about cutting *eight* precise 45-degree miters to create a perfect picture frame? If you've ever tried it, you know that task can be ticklish, frustrating and difficult.

One way to accomplish this seemingly impossible feat is to build a miter sled for your table saw. You can build the simple sled shown here using nothing more than a half sheet of 3/4-in. plywood, particleboard or MDF, a few squirts of wood glue and a couple of full paint cans for glue-up weights. After you throw it together, you'll be cutting perfectly matched miters for frames, furniture or trim in no time, without muss or fuss.

---

### What it takes

**COST:** Free (if you have a 4 x 4-ft. scrap of 3/4-in. material on hand)

**TIME:** Two hours, including time standing around waiting for glue to set

**SKILL LEVEL:** Rudimentary table saw prowess

**TOOLS:** A table saw to build it—the same table saw to use it

---

### How it works

Here's the beauty of the system. We show you how to position the fence so it's very close to perfect. But if it's a little off, the jig is self-correcting. That's because you cut one miter on one side of the jig and its matching miter on the other side. So if your jig cuts at 46 degrees on the first side, it'll cut at 44 degrees on the other. Even though one of the miters will be a little longer than the other, it's easy to sand off the excess so the difference will be imperceptible. But try to build the jig as accurately as you can. This self-correcting business only goes so far!

The sled base is nothing more than a slab of MDF cut into a 24 x 18-in. rectangle as shown at right; instructions for building it are given on p. 134. The fence is just a 16 x 16-in. square of MDF. Since the factory corner is 90 degrees, mounting it diagonally gives you accurate 45-degree angles for cutting the miters. After the square is glued on top (**Photo 4**), cut it in half (**Photo 5**) and stack the waste on top (**Photo 6**) so the edge of the fence becomes 1-1/2 in. thick and more suitable for cutting thicker material.

The only tricky part is cutting the runners to a width such that they don't wiggle or bind in the slots, and to a thickness so they project about 1/8 in. above the table (**Photo 1**). Rip them so they glide smoothly in the slots without binding or slop. Spend time on them. They're one of the main ingredients of an accurate sled.

## Picture-perfect picture frames

I credit myself with being a fairly accomplished woodworker. But picture frames always drove me nuts! I found that they required more fuss and more precision than any other miter work I ever had to do. I tried miter saws and table saws, even using expensive aftermarket miter gauges. Nothing seemed to work without my messing with shims, recuts, etc. Then I built this miter sled. The frame I'm holding here took me all of 15 minutes to cut and assemble, and it's the first time I've built a frame without recutting a single miter.

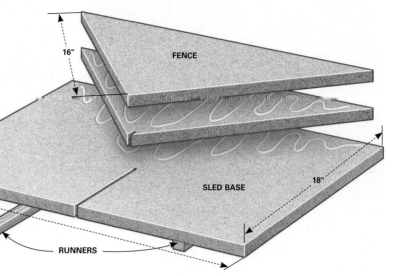

FENCE

16"

SLED BASE

18"

24"

RUNNERS

**Safety tip**

Try to use your fence whenever you can. We left ours off, mostly for photo clarity. If you simply can't use your fence, the next best thing is to take advantage of the 1-1/2-in.-thick fence by keeping the blade below the top. That way it's impossible to catch your fingers on an exposed blade.

# Six steps to a magic miter sled

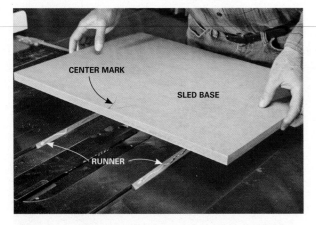

**1** **Mount the base on the runners.** Mark the center of the base. Add a thin line of glue to the runners and rest the base on the strips, aligning the center mark with the saw blade. Keep the runners and the miter base flush with the back of the saw table.

**2** **Square the base.** Rest two paint cans on the table and use a rafter square and the miter gauge slots to square the miter table to the table saw. Let the glue set up for 20 minutes or so. Then give the sled a test slide. If it binds at all, flip it over, clean off any glue squeeze-out and use a sanding block to knock down the edges of the runners.

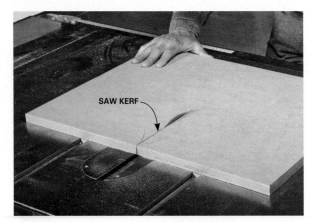

**3** **Cut a centerline.** Cut a saw kerf about one-third of the way through the miter table. Turn off the saw and let the blade come to a stop. You'll use the kerf to line up the fence for the next step.

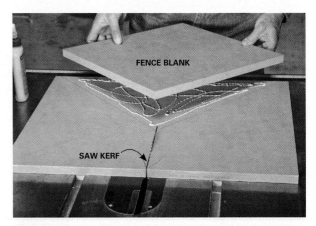

**4** **Glue on the first fence layer.** Apply some glue to the fence blank and sled base. Line up the tip of the blank with the saw kerf and the two other corners with the back edges of the table. Clamp it in place with a paint can for 15 minutes.

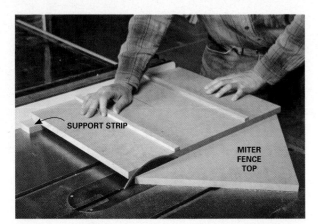

**5** **Cut off the fence.** Lift the sled out of the miter slots and turn it 90 degrees. Adjust the fence so it cuts off the overhanging fence. Use a strip of waste to support the edge of the sled, and cut off the overhanging triangle.

**6** **Top off the fence.** Spread some glue on the fence and square up the edges, holding it down with another gallon can of paint until it sets up. After 15 minutes, you'll be ready to cut a perfect picture frame!

## Identical cuts every time

If you're cutting miters for windows or other house trim, you can get close enough just by careful measuring and cutting. But if you're building a picture frame or any other frame that calls for maximum precision, attach an auxiliary fence to the right or left side of the triangle fence. Screws or hot glue works well. The fence should be long enough so there's room for a stop block behind the longest piece you're cutting.

For the first piece, cut the first miter. Mark the length and cut the miter at the other end, from the opposite side of the sled. When you're satisfied with the length, use the piece as a guide to place a stop block on the auxiliary fence. Now when you cut the matching, opposite side of the frame, the lengths will be identical.

## Crown molding cutting guides

Installing crown molding? Here's an easy way to lock it into position on your miter saw using self-stick vinyl bumpers ($3 at home centers). Position the molding and stick bumpers to each side of the table and you're ready to go! The bumpers will last all weekend with amazing sticking power. When the project is finished, pull off the bumpers and the saw is ready for your next handyman task.

—Rick Grisham, Field Editor

# THE RIGHT **LUBE**

*Everything you need to know about the slippery stuff*

## by **Rick Muscoplat, Contributing Editor**

**Y**our local home center probably carries at least a dozen kinds of lubricant. Ever wonder why so many? I did. So I interrogated the guys in white lab coats and learned this: A lube formulated for a specific job usually provides far better results and wear protection than a general-purpose product or a product designed for a different job. And a specialty product usually lasts much lon-

ger. So by using the right lube, you'll lubricate less often, avoid frustrations, and save time and money.

I'll walk you through all the different specialty lubes and explain where to use each one. But don't worry about memorizing it all: There's a handy chart on p. 139. Refer to it any time you have a question about lubrication.

### DRY PTFE LUBRICANT

"Dry" lubricant actually goes on wet. But once the solvent dries, the product leaves a thin film of dry polytetra-fluoroethylene (PTFE)—the same product used to make nonstick frying pans. The main advantage of dry PTFE is that dust doesn't stick to it. That makes it a great lube for dirty environments like your garage or shop. PTFE bonds to metal, wood, rubber and plastic—so it stays put. It's a light-load lubricant, so it's not the best lube for equipment that carries a heavy load or transmits high torque. And it doesn't have any anticorrosive properties (although some manufacturers spike theirs with an antirust additive), so don't use it on outdoor metal.
Dry PTFE lube is available in both aerosols and squeeze bottles. Check the label to make sure the solvent won't harm the material you're lubricating. Note: Not all "dry" lubes are PTFE. Some are silicone, which is a different ball game.

### SYNTHETIC GREASE

Synthetic grease is the best choice for gears, axles and bearings that carry heavy loads, transmit high torque, operate at high temperatures or are subject to shear stress. Synthetic grease has less rolling friction than the petroleum-based grease you'll see next to it on store shelves. It resists thermal breakdown and shear, too, so it lasts much longer than other types of grease.

### SILICONE LUBRICANT

Silicone is the slipperiest of all lubricants, so it's a great choice for items that slide against one another. Silicone repels water, but not water vapor, so you can use it to dry out electrical connectors. But don't rely on it as a sealant in humid conditions. Use silicone to lubricate metal, wood, rubber and plastic. However, dust and dirt stick to silicone, so use it sparingly or use a "dry" version in dirty environments.
The biggest downside to silicone lubricant is that once you apply it to an object, you can never paint or stain it. And, since the spray drifts, it can contaminate nearby walls and floors. If you ever plan to paint anything in the surrounding area, mask off the spray zone before you spray.

### MARINE GREASE

Like lithium grease, marine grease is formulated to lubricate high-load items. But it's thicker and far more water resistant than lithium grease, so it does a fantastic job of inhibiting rust and preventing metal parts from "welding" themselves together with rust. Use marine grease to lubricate items that are directly immersed in water or constantly exposed to the elements. Like any grease, it's a tacky magnet for dust and dirt.

## USE THE RIGHT LUBRICANT EVERY TIME

### RUST-PENETRATING OIL

Other products will free up stubborn nuts and bolts— eventually. But they won't do it nearly as fast or as well as oil formulated just for that job. Rust-penetrating oil contains an aggressive solvent to penetrate the rust. And it contains a special low-viscosity, low-surface-tension lubricating oil that flows into micro-cracks in the rust to get lube deep into the threads. But don't use it for purposes other than stuck stuff; it does a poor job of keeping things slippery.

### WHITE LITHIUM GREASE

Grease is the lube of choice for higher-load items like bearings and axles because it cushions parts. And unlike oil, which tends to seep away, grease stays in place and lasts much longer. White lithium is a great all-around grease for lubricating light- to medium-load items like tools and garden equipment. It comes in aerosol cans and in tubes. Aerosols are easier to use because the solvent helps the grease seep into tight spaces. That can save you the trouble of disassembling components to grease them.

### CHAIN LUBE

Chain lube penetrates deep into roller chain links and doesn't fly off when the chain is in motion. To use it, clean off the old lube with spray solvent and a brush. Apply the chain lube and slowly rotate the chain to allow it to work into the links. Then leave it alone until the solvent evaporates. Chain lube resists water, dust and dirt better than ordinary oil. Use it for chains on bicycles, motorcycles, scooters, garage door openers and outdoor power equipment. But never use aerosol chain lube in place of a bar chain oil on chain saws.

### GARAGE DOOR LUBE

Garage door hardware operates in an environment that's often dirty and damp, sometimes hot and sometimes cold. That's why there's a special lube for it. Garage door lubes are formulated to penetrate deep into hinges, rollers and springs but dry to a fairly tack-free finish to resist dust and dirt buildup. Many brands also contain anticorrosive additives to protect against rust.

# Lubrication tips

### Avoid the off-brands

Cheap brands cost less for a reason—they contain less of what matters. These two beakers show how much silicone was left after the solvents and propellants evaporated from a name-brand product and a cheaper "no-name" brand. The cheaper stuff cost 79¢ less—and contained far less lubricant.

### Clean out the old lube

Adding fresh lube to old, degraded oil and grease is a prescription for equipment failure. To get the full advantage of fresh lube, always clean out the old lube with spray solvent and a rag (aerosol brake cleaner works well).

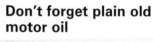

SOLVENT          PTFE
                 LUBRICANT

### Shake before using

All spray and squeeze bottle lubes contain solvents along with the actual lubricant. If you don't shake the product before application, you'll get a lot of solvent and very little lube.

### Prevent seizing

Apply a thin coat of marine grease to a trailer hitch ball mount to prevent it from rusting and "welding" itself to the receiver.

### Don't forget plain old motor oil

That leftover can of 30-weight motor oil isn't the very best lube for all jobs, but it's a handy and acceptable friction fighter for most. Heavyweight motor oil is thicker than most spray oils, so it provides a stronger film cushion. And motor oil has built-in anticorrosive additives to resist rust. Since it doesn't have any solvents, a full drop is really a full drop of lube. And it's cheap—a quart should last a lifetime.

### Choose dry lube for dusty situations

Dusty and dirty conditions call for a lube that isn't tacky. Dry PTFE is a good choice for this vacuum cleaner. It dries tack-free and bonds well to surfaces, so the spinning parts won't throw off lubricant.

DRY PTFE
SPRAY

### Lithium grease for garden equipment

Lubricate heavy garden equipment wheels with spray lithium grease. It'll stand up to the load better than oil, silicone or PTFE. Take the wheel off and spread grease on by hand or shoot it with aerosol white lithium grease. Spin the wheel to work the lube into the axle before the solvent evaporates.

### Grease, not oil, for high loads

Reduce wear on gears and bearings with a heavy-duty synthetic grease. Spread it on all surfaces and rotate the parts by hand to distribute the grease. Never pack the gear case completely full unless directed by the manufacturer.

# LUBRICANTS

| LUBE TYPE | BEST USES | ADVANTAGES | DISADVANTAGES |
|---|---|---|---|
| **All-purpose lube** | Frees up lightly rusted tools and dissolves light rust. Lubricates light-duty mechanisms like drawer slides and hinges. Dissolves some adhesives and removes scuff marks from floors. Removes pressure-sensitive adhesive labels. | Safe for wood, metal and plastic. Works fast. Dissolves gummed-up old lube and relubricates. Flows quickly and penetrates deep into tight spaces. Protects against corrosion. | Lubrication and rust protection don't last long  you may have to reapply frequently. Not for use on rubber products. Not for heavy loads or high-torque applications. Attracts and retains dust and dirt. Works very slowly to free up nuts and bolts. |
| **Dry PTFE lube** | Light-load lubrication for drawer slides, rollers, hinges, hand tools, window tracks/mechanisms, latches and lock cylinders. | Won't gather dust or dirt. Once solvent evaporates, product stays in place (won't drip). Safe for wood, metal, most types of plastic and rubber. | No corrosion protection. Not for heavy loads or high-torque applications. |
| **Spray silicone** | Light-load lubrication for things that slide or roll—drawer slides, hinges, hand tools, window tracks/mechanisms, electrical connectors, weather stripping, etc. Prevents sticking on mower decks and snow blower chutes. | Slipperiest of all lubes. Repels liquid water (not water vapor). Stays wet and continues to spread with every sliding movement. | Remains tacky and holds dust and dirt. No corrosion protection. Once applied, the surface is unpaintable. Overspray makes floors dangerously slippery. |
| **Lithium grease** | Medium- to high-load applications like axles, rollers, bearings, spinning shafts on shop and garden equipment, and hinges that carry a heavy load. Any lubrication job where the lube must stay in place. | Lasts far longer than oil. Stays in place and doesn't drip. Aerosol versions allow grease to seep into tight places so you don't have to disassemble items to apply grease. Protects against corrosion. | Remains tacky and holds dust and dirt. Washes off in heavy rain. |
| **Marine grease** | Trailer wheel bearings, shafts, rollers and gears immersed in water and continually exposed to the elements. Prevents rust and seizing of metal parts. | Handles high loads and torque. Stays in place. Most water-resistant of any grease. | Remains tacky and holds dust and dirt. |
| **Synthetic grease** | High-load, high-torque lubricant for axles, bearings, gears or spinning shafts in power tools and equipment. | Lowest friction of all greases. Most resistant to breakdown under high heat. Stays in place. Dissipates heat well. | Remains tacky and holds dust and dirt. Most expensive of all consumer-type greases. |
| **Chain lube** | Bicycle, motorcycle and [illegible] door opener chain and outdoor power equipment chains. | Penetrates deep into roller links when first applied. Becomes tack-free and sling-free once dry, so it holds far less dust and dirt than other lubes. | Doesn't spread once dry. May harm plastic or rubber (check the label before spraying chains that contain nonmetal parts). |
| **Garage door lube** | Garage door hinges, rollers, cables, reels and springs. | Penetrates, lubricates and protects against corrosion. Less tacky, so less likely to hold dirt. | May harm plastic or rubber parts. |
| **Penetrating oil** | Frees up rusty tools, tracks, slides, nuts and bolts. | Fastest option to break up rust and free fasteners. Dissolves grease and old, gummy lubricant. | Not a good permanent lubricant. Some formulas may dissolve paint or damage finishes. |

# NO-EXCUSES **BOOKCASE**

*Think you can't build it? Think again*

by **Dave Munkittrick, Contributing Editor**

There are lots of reasons why a DIYer might not tackle a project like this one. So before building this bookcase, I made a list of them and eliminated each one as I streamlined, simplified and economized the design. The result is a bookcase with the look of a masterpiece, but without the complications. If you've done smaller woodworking projects, you're ready to tackle this one.

## Build the cabinets

First, cut all your 3/4-in. plywood parts (A – K) to size. If shop space doesn't allow you to slice up plywood on a table saw, you can do a fine job with a circular saw and a straightedge (**Photo 1**). Cut rabbets along the back edges of the sides (A and B). These rabbets create a recess so the edges of the backs aren't visible from the sides. I cut the rabbets using a router and a rabbeting bit that makes a 1/4-in. cut. Set the bit to a depth of 3/8 in. Next, drill holes in the bookcase sides (A and B) for the adjustable shelves (**Photo 2**).

### What it takes

**COST:** $500
**TIME:** Two weekends
**SKILL LEVEL:** Intermediate
**TOOLS:** Table saw or circular saw, drill, miter saw, router or router table

## Excuses eliminated

### Don't have the skills?

The hardest parts of furniture making have been eliminated from this bookcase. There are no miter cuts and no complicated joinery.

### Don't have the money?

The total materials bill is about $500. That's about one-third of what you would pay for a store-bought bookcase of similar size and quality.

### Don't have the time?

Depending on how fast you work, you can build it in a weekend or two. Add a few hours of finishing work and you're done.

### Don't have the tools?

If you have basic woodworking tools, you're ready to build this bookcase. You don't need any exotic or pro-grade equipment.

### Don't have the shop space?

This big bookcase consists of three smaller sections that can be assembled in even the smallest shop. You'll need an 8 x 8-ft. area of open floor space to preassemble the sections, but you can do that anywhere (even on your driveway) and then disassemble them to complete the project.

Crown molding

Bun feet

Adjustable shelves

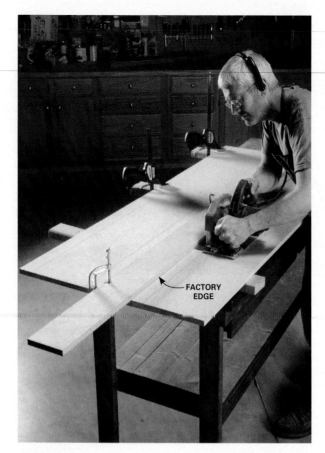

FACTORY EDGE

**1** **Slice up the plywood.** A circular saw guided by a straightedge works almost as well as a table saw. For a straightedge, use the factory-cut edge from a sheet of plywood. For clean cuts, use a fresh blade with a tooth count of at least 40.

ROUTER BITS

**2** **Drill shelf support holes.** Bore the holes using pegboard as a guide. A stop block—simply a wood scrap with a hole drilled through it—prevents drilling too deep. If your pegboard is short, reposition it using a pair of router bits to align and lock the pegboard into holes you've already drilled. For a different approach to drilling shelf holes, see p. 153.

With the plywood parts cut and drilled, it's time to assemble the bookcase. All you need is a drill to drive screws. There's no glue to mess around with. Most of the screw holes in this bookcase are covered by adjoining pieces. The exposed screws are in the tops and invisible from floor level. If the top of your bookcase will be seen from above (from a balcony or staircase, for example), fill the screw holes after final assembly and paint the filler black to match.

Make a couple of I-beam spacers to hold the sides in position while you attach the subtops and subbases (E and J). Build the spacers out of scrap. Be sure the final length of the I-beam holds the sides at the correct outside dimension.

Simply screw the subtops and subbases to the sides

SUBTOP

I-BEAM SPACER

SIDE

**3** **Assemble the shelf boxes.** Screw the subtops and subbases to the sides. A plywood beam spacer takes only a few minutes to make and holds the sides in perfect alignment.

**MEET AN EXPERT**

David Munkittrick is a Field Editor and an airline pilot turned professional woodworker.

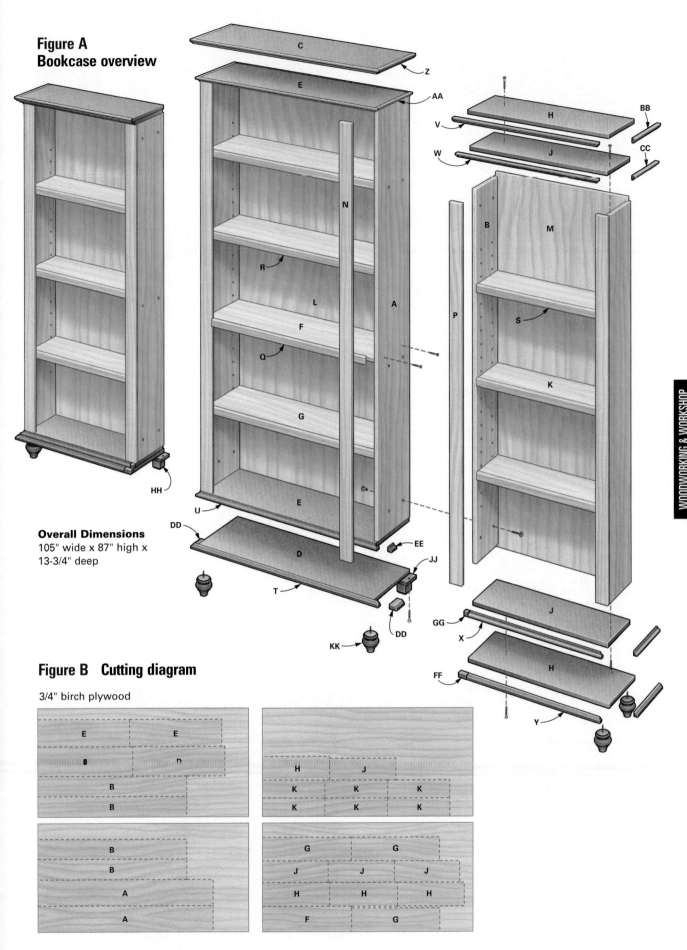

# Figure A
## Bookcase overview

C
Z
E
AA
V
H
BB
W
J
CC
N
B
M
A
R
P
S
L
F
Q
K
E
U
DD
D
EE
T
JJ
DD
HH
GG
X
KK
FF
H
Y

**Overall Dimensions**
105" wide x 87" high x
13-3/4" deep

# Figure B   Cutting diagram

3/4" birch plywood

E    E
D
B
B

H    J
K    K    K
K    K    K

B
B
A
A

G    G
J    J    J
H    H    H
F    G

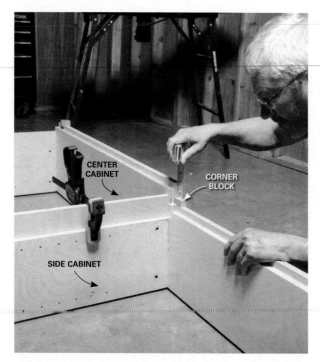

**4** **Position the corner blocks.** Lay the shelf units on their backs and clamp them together. Place the corner blocks where the side cabinets meet the center cabinet. The blocks allow the trim to meet at inside corners without miters.

**5** **Edge the plywood, then rout.** Glue square trim to the plywood, then shape it with a router or router table. This creates perfect outside corners without cutting miters. A backer board prevents splintering at the end of the cut.

(**Photo 3**). The tops and bases (C, D and H) are then positioned and screwed into place. On the smaller side cabinets, remember to keep the tops and bases flush with the cabinet sides where they butt up against the larger center cabinet. The tops and bases overhang the subtops and subbases by 1/4 in. at the back. This creates a rabbet to house the back. Next, cut and fit the backs (L and M).

## Trim the tops and bases

I trimmed the parts C, D, E, H and J using one of my favorite tricks: Glue on the raw, square trim first, then shape it with a router. This approach has two advantages: Square stock is easier to cut and clamp than a fancy trim profile, and you don't have to miter the corners.

There are a few steps to take before you glue on and rout the trim. First, fire up your table saw and cut 3/4 x 3/4-in. stock (you'll need about 50 linear ft.). Lay the cabinets on their backs and clamp them together. Fit the corner blocks where the side cabinets meet the center cabinet (see **Photo 4**). These corner blocks allow you to butt the trim into the blocks at inside corners and eliminate the need for miters. For a closeup of the blocks, see the center photo at the bottom of p. 140.

Here's the process: Start with the bases. Cut and fit the corner blocks (FF and GG) on the bottom of the side cabinets first. Lay them in position. No glue yet. Measure and cut your center cabinet side trim (DD and EE) so it butts up tight to the corner blocks and is flush with the front edge of the plywood (**Photo 4**).

Disassemble the bookcase and attach the trim. Go slow here. Rather than take everything apart at once, take one of the side bookcase tops off and glue and add the trim. Do the same with the other side top, then the subtops and base assemblies. Note that the side trim on parts E and J runs past the back edges by 1/4 in. to hide the backs (L and M).

With the molding stock square, it's easy to lose track of which side is up and what router profile gets put on which piece. I recommend making two piles: one for the ogee profile (subtops and subbases) and one for the simple chamfer (tops and bases). Also, clearly mark which side of the trim gets routed. The underside of the top parts and the top side of the base parts are routed. When you're sure you know which trim gets what cut on which face, go ahead and rout your profiles (**Photo 5**). Use any 45-degree chamfer bit that will cut at least 5/8 in. deep. For the ogee, I used a Bosch No. 85586M. Although you can use a handheld router, a router table makes it all easier. To see how to build an inexpensive table, search for "router table" at familyhandyman.com.

With all the trim attached and routed, reassemble the cabinets. It may seem like a pain, but it's the best way to make sure you've done everything right before you finish. Also, having the tops and bases on the cabinets will automatically position the stiles on the cabinets. This is a good time to drill holes and join the side cabinets to the center cabinets with connector bolts.

Separate the three cabinets and glue on the stiles (N

**6 Drill the feet.** Bore holes for the dowel screws using a guide to steer the drill bit straight into the foot. The guide is simply two wood scraps glued together to form an "L."

## MATERIALS LIST

| ITEM | QTY. |
|---|---|
| 4' x 8' x 3/4" birch plywood | 4 |
| 4' x 8' x 1/4" birch plywood | 3 |
| 1x6 birch boards | 40 ft. |
| *Bun feet | 6 |
| 3/8" x 3" dowel screws | 6 |
| Connector bolts and cap nuts | 12 |
| Adjustable shelf supports, wood glue, 1-5/8" screws, finishing supplies | |

*The bun feet (No. 4045) are available at osbornewood.com for $5 each (plus shipping).

## CUTTING LIST

| KEY | QTY. | DIMENSIONS | NAME |
|---|---|---|---|
| **3/4" plywood (4 sheets)** | | | |
| A | 2 | 11-1/2" x 80" | Center cabinet sides |
| B | 4 | 9" x 68" | Side cabinet sides |
| C | 1 | 12-15/16" x 43-3/8" | Center cabinet top |
| D | 1 | 12-15/16" x 42" | Center cabinet base |
| E | 2 | 12" x 42" | Center cabinet subtop/subbase |
| F | 1 | 11-1/4" x 40-1/2" | Center cabinet fixed shelf |
| G | 3 | 10-7/16" x 40-3/8" | Center cabinet adjustable shelves |
| H | 4 | 10-7/16" x 30-11/16" | Side cabinet tops/bases |
| J | 4 | 9-1/2" x 30" | Side cabinet subtops/subbases |
| K | 6 | 8" x 28-1/2" | Side cabinet adjustable shelves |
| **1/4" birch plywood (3 sheets)** | | | |
| L | 1 | 41-1/4" x 81-1/2" | Center cabinet back |
| M | 2 | 29-1/4" x 69-1/2" | Side cabinet backs |
| **3/4" birch hardwood** | | | |
| N | 2 | 2-1/4" x 80" | Center cabinet stiles |
| P | 4 | 2" x 68" | Side cabinet stiles |
| Q | 1 | 1-1/2" x 37-1/2" | Center cabinet rail |
| R | 3 | 1-1/2" x 40-3/8" | Center cabinet adjustable shelf trim |
| S | 6 | 1-1/4" x 28-1/2" | Side cabinet adjustable shelf trim |
| T | 2 | 3/4" x 45" | Center cabinet top/base front trim |
| U | 2 | 3/4" x 43-1/2" | Center subtop/subbase front trim |
| V | 2 | 3/4" x 31-1/2" | Side cabinet top front trim |
| W | 2 | 3/4" x 30-3/4" | Side cabinet subtop front trim |
| X | 2 | 3/4" x 30" | Side cabinet subbase front trim |
| Y | 2 | 3/4" x 29-7/8" | Side cabinet base front trim |
| Z | 2 | 3/4" x 13-3/4" | Center cabinet top side trim |
| AA | 2 | 3/4" x 13" | Center cabinet subtop side trim |
| BB | 4 | 3/4" x 10-1/2" | Side cabinet top/base side trim |
| CC | 4 | 3/4" x 9-3/4" | Side cabinet subtop/subbase side trim |
| DD | 2 | 1-1/2" x 1-3/4" | Center cabinet base side trim |
| EE | 2 | 3/4" x 1-3/4" | Center cabinet subbase side trim |
| FF | 2 | 3/4" x 1-1/2" | Side cabinet base corner block |
| GG | 2 | 3/4" x 3/4" | Side cabinet subbase corner block |
| **2" birch** | | | |
| HH | 2 | 2-3/4" x 2-3/4" x 3-1/4" | Back feet |
| JJ | 2 | 4" x 6" | Back feet plates |
| **Soft maple** | | | |
| KK | 6 | 3-1/4" x 4" | Bun feet |

## An easy finish for problem woods

Some types of wood—pine, maple, birch and others—absorb stain unevenly, creating an ugly, blotchy finish. To sidestep that problem, I skipped the initial staining step and used a "glaze" finish instead.

Here's how: First, I brushed on two light coats of gloss polyurethane, sanding lightly after each coat. Then I applied a glaze. I used General Finishes Mission Oak gel stain from rockler.com, but other gel stains or products intended specifically for glazing are available. The glazing process is just like staining: Brush it on and wipe off the excess. Then add two more coats of polyurethane over the glaze. This process is no more difficult than staining but avoids blotchiness and gives the wood a deeper, richer glow.

**7** **Assemble it in place.** You can move the bookcase to its new home in three sections. Or you can make moving it even easier by disassembling each section into small, easy-to-handle parts. Join the sections with connector bolts.

**CONNECTOR BOLTS**

and P). While the glue sets, go ahead and drill and mount the feet (**Photo 6**). Be sure the feet are set so the sides bear down directly onto the feet.

## Finish and final assembly

Disassemble the cabinets one last time and sand all parts to 180-grit. Sanding and finishing a collection of flat parts is a breeze compared to working with an assembled bookcase. Prime and paint the upper and lower parts. Satin black spray paint works great. With the finish complete, you're ready to reassemble the bookcase in place. Again, the beauty of this design is that you can take the individual parts to where the bookcase will reside and assemble it there (**Photo 7**).

There, you're done. No excuses.

# GreatGoofs®

### Cloudy with a chance of sawdust

I was building baby furniture in my garage for our first-born's nursery during a stretch of really hot weather. An old box fan kept the garage tolerable and allowed me to make progress on the project.

One sizzling afternoon, I moved the fan closer to keep me cool as I was applying the final coat of paint. As I moved around with the paintbrush, I accidentally bumped the fan, and it fell over right on top of a pile of sawdust. It launched a huge cloud of sawdust, which rained down all over me and my freshly painted project. I spent the next day sanding and repainting everything—and picking sawdust out of my ears and hair.

—Terry Waterworth

# HandyHints®

**FROM OUR READERS**

## DIY DUST COLLECTOR

My shop vacuum hose was a little too big to attach to my miter saw's exhaust port, so I came up with this simple but effective DIY adapter. I cut a 3/4-in.-nap paint roller cover in half and duct-taped it to the saw's exhaust port. The shop vacuum hose fits perfectly over the roller cover, creating a tight seal that allows almost all of the sawdust to be captured. The thicker the nap, the tighter the seal. Works great!

—Martin Weglarz

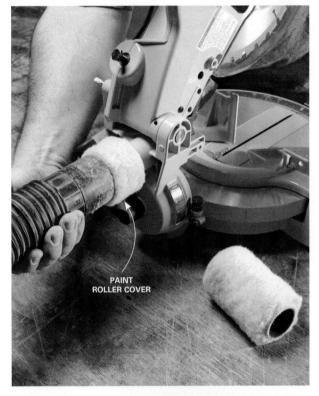

PAINT
ROLLER COVER

## OUTDOOR SANDING STATION

I do a lot of sanding, and to keep the fine dust out of my garage, I came up with an outdoor sanding station. I built a sturdy plywood shelf and attached threaded hooks to the back edge, which clip into eyebolts screwed into the garage wall studs. The front of the shelf is suspended by chains (or cord) attached to eyebolts at the front corners and then snapped into eyebolts placed up high on my garage wall. I position it so the shelf is at a comfortable height for my back. My temporary sanding station goes up and down quickly, and it keeps the dust outside.

—Bill Wells

CAULK

PLUMBER'S
PUTTY

## YET ANOTHER WAY TO SEAL A TUBE OF CAULK

Over the years, I've tried many different ways to seal open tubes of caulk and adhesive. Last year, I began sealing them with a little plug of Plumber's Putty. I remove a little bit of the caulk from the tip of the tube, take a small piece of putty and stuff it in the tip about 1/4 in. I remove the putty by squeezing the gun or digging it out. After more than a year, nothing's dried out yet.

Bill Scott

# 10 TIPS FOR BETTER RIPPING

*Improve your technique—and get better results*

by **Jeff Gorton, Associate Editor**

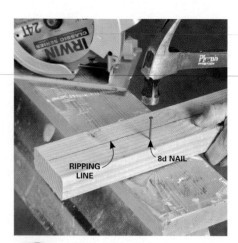

RIPPING LINE

8d NAIL

## 1 Use an 8d nail as a third hand

If you're without a table saw and need to rip boards with a circular saw, here's a tip to make the job a lot easier. Drive an 8d nail through the board and into the sawhorse to prevent the board from slipping while you rip it. When you're done ripping, just pull the board off the sawhorse, flip it over and pound the nail through and pull it out. It only takes a few seconds and eliminates the frustration of a slipping board.

SHOP-MADE PUSH BLOCK

## 2 Build a custom push block

Here's a push block that works great and keeps your hand safely away from the blade. It's just a piece of 1/2-in. plywood with notches to fit 1/4-in., 1/2-in., 3/4-in. and 1-1/2-in. boards or plywood. The notches help hold the board tight to the saw table, and the top handle slides along the top of your fence.

Make the notched plywood 11/16 in. taller than the height of your fence. Then glue it to a 3/4-in.-thick board with a handle attached.

**M**aking long, straight rips in boards or plywood looks easy, but it takes skill and practice to do it safely and accurately. We've assembled a few of the most useful tips from experienced carpenters and cabinetmakers to help make ripping simpler and safer.

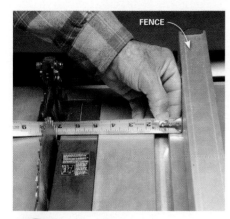

FENCE

## 3 Check the fence alignment

It's critical that the fence be parallel to the saw blade. If it's not, the blade will bind on the wood and cause a burned edge on your board, or worse, a dangerous kickback. If you have a saw with a top-quality fence that locks down squarely, then you should only need to check and adjust the fence the first time you use it. Read your owner's manual for instructions on adjusting your fence. Fences on less expensive saws can be inconsistent, and you'll need to check every time you reposition the fence.

Here's how: Measure the distance between a saw tooth and the fence at the front and back of the blade. Raise the blade fully for the most accurate check. For an accurate reading, make sure to choose two teeth that lean toward the fence. If the measurements are different, either adjust the fence or nudge it into position until the measurements are equal before locking it down.

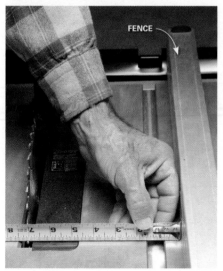

FENCE

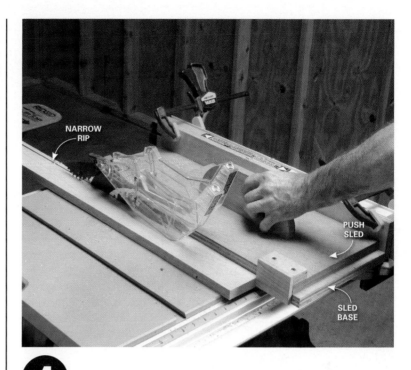

NARROW RIP

PUSH SLED

SLED BASE

## 4 Make narrow rips safely

The problem with making repetitive narrow rips on a table saw is that the blade guard and the fence are too close together to allow a push stick to fit between them. The solution is to move the fence away from the blade and clamp the sled base to the fence. Then build a push sled like the one shown to push the narrow rip through the blade. The sled slides under the blade guard and keeps your hand a safe distance from the blade, allowing you to make thin rips safely and easily.

To use this setup, rip your board as you normally would by sliding it against the fence extension. When you get within reach of your push sled, hook the sled behind the board you're ripping and push it through, just like you would if you were using a regular push stick.

### Figure A Push sled

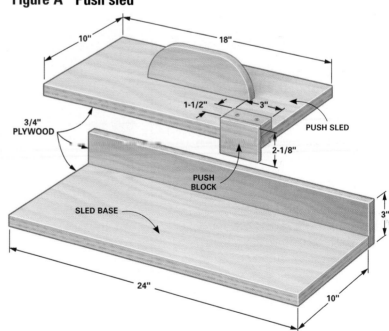

10"

18"

3/4" PLYWOOD

1-1/2"

3"

PUSH SLED

2-1/8"

PUSH BLOCK

SLED BASE

3"

24"

10"

FEATHERBOARD

## 6 Mount a featherboard for accurate rips

There are times when you want your rips to be super accurate, like when you're building face frames, door parts or other cabinet components. The key to accurate rips is to keep the edge of the board in constant, tight contact with the fence. It's easy with a featherboard mounted on your table saw top. This Kreg True-FLEX featherboard (about $20 at home centers and online) has expanding rails that lock into the miter gauge track.

If you have a cast iron bed on your table saw, you could buy a featherboard that attaches with super-strong magnets that make it simple to position and adjust. You can also make your own featherboard out of wood, and clamp it to the saw. Some saw manuals have instructions for this, or you can search online. Adjust the featherboard to apply a small amount of pressure to the board as you feed it through the blade. Make sure the "feathers" are in front of the infeed side of the saw blade to prevent binding. With a featherboard, your rips will be dead-on accurate every time.

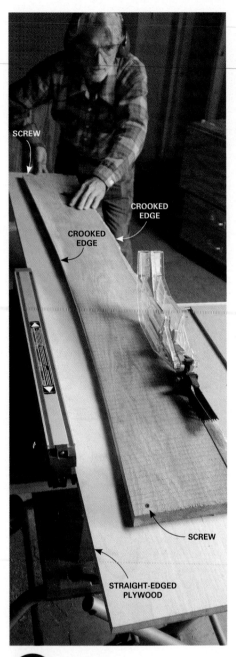

SCREW

CROOKED EDGE

CROOKED EDGE

SCREW

STRAIGHT-EDGED PLYWOOD

## 5 Straighten a crooked edge

If you run the crooked edge of a board against the table saw fence, you'll still have a crooked board when you're done. Or worse, the board will get bound between the fence and the blade during the cut.

Here's a handy, low-tech way to straighten the edge of any board. Just fasten the crooked-edge board to a straight strip of plywood, letting it overhang the edge. Then run the straight edge of the plywood against your table saw fence to make a perfectly straight edge on your crooked board.

Bonus tip! Also see "The right blade for the job" on p. 130.

STRAIGHTEDGE SAW GUIDE

## 7 Make table saw–quality rips with a circular saw

Even if you own a table saw, sometimes it's easier to rip large sheets of plywood with a circular saw. The trick to a perfectly straight cut is to clamp a straightedge to the plywood and use it as a guide for your saw. On most circular saws, the distance between the edge of the saw's base and the blade is 1-1/2 in., so you can simply position the straightedge 1-1/2 in. from your cutting line. But measure this distance on your saw to be sure.

You can buy a straightedge or use the factory edge of a plywood sheet. If your straightedge only has one straight edge, be sure to mark it to avoid using the crooked side.

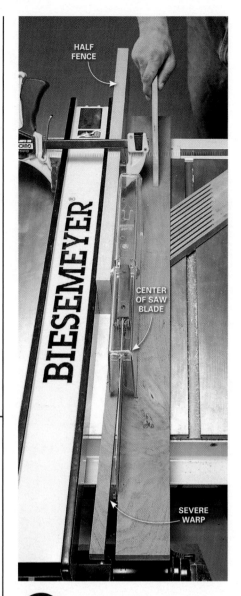

 **Support long boards**

Table saws excel at ripping long boards, but it's dangerous to do it without supporting the board as it leaves the saw.

There are all kinds of ways to provide support. We're using a Ridgid Flip Top work support. The top surface swivels to allow the board to ride onto the support without catching. You can buy a support like this for about $30 at Home Depot.

There are several other types of outfeed supports you can buy, or just build your own. What's important is that you use a support every time you make long rips on a table saw.

 **To rip large sheets, you need well-trained help**

Sometimes you need assistance to rip large sheets. The trouble is, most helpers try to be too helpful. They naturally want to grab the plywood and pull it or push it or steer it. Before you start, take time to teach your helper the right way. Instruct your helper to simply support the plywood, flat palms up, level with the saw bed, and let you do all the work. The helper should move along with the wood, but never grab the board or try to direct it. These simple rules will keep you both safe, and allow you to make a straight rip with no danger of binding or kickback.

**Use a half fence for unruly boards**

Wood with knots or wavy grain and wood that has been dried unevenly will often warp badly as you rip it. If the halves bend outward, one will push against the fence and could cause burn marks or a dangerous kickback. If this begins to happen, shut off the saw and remove the board. You can rip the board safely by clamping a smooth, straight length of 3/4-in. wood against the fence, ending at the center of the saw blade. This half fence gives the trapped piece (the section between the blade and the fence) room to bend without pushing back against the blade. Keep push sticks handy so you can work around the clamps and complete the cut smoothly.

# SHORTCUT BOOKSHELF

*A traditional look, without the usual time and effort*

by **Gary Wentz, Senior Editor**

**What it takes**

**COST:** $130

**TIME:** One weekend

**SKILL LEVEL:** Intermediate

**TOOLS:** Table saw, miter saw, drill, router, sander

There's nothing I like better than spending weeks on a complicated woodworking project. But I rarely have time for that. So instead, I take shortcuts that produce handsome results but simplify the whole project. This little bookcase showcases some of my favorite shortcuts: Some save time, some minimize mistakes and others are low-effort paths to high style. It all adds up to a project you can build in a day, though finishing will add a few hours after that. You'll find all the materials in stock at most home centers.

## Build the box and shelves

To get started, cut the 3/4-in. plywood box parts as shown in the cutting diagram on p. 155. The grain on the box lid (B) runs the "wrong" way, but it's well below eye level and only your pets will see it. To avoid splitting the plywood, drill pilot holes before you screw the box together (**Photo 1**). No need for glue; three screws at each joint will make the box plenty strong, and you won't have to deal with glue squeeze-out.

Drill holes for adjustable shelf supports (**Photo 2**). For another approach to positioning the holes, see p. 142. I made two shelves, used only one and tucked the other away in a nearby closet—better to have a second shelf than to wish for it later. When you edge the shelves (**Photo 3**), cut the strips of screen molding a bit longer than the shelves and trim off the excess after the glue sets. To complete the box, add the back (D). Make sure to cut the back perfectly square so you can use it to square the box. After cutting the back from a half sheet of 1/4-in. plywood, you'll have more than enough left over to cut the spacers you'll need later (see **Photos 5 and 7**).

**1** **Nail the box first, then screw.** Holding corners together while driving screws is clumsy. So tack the corners together with a brad nailer first. The nails will hold the parts in position while you add screws for strength.

PEGBOARD

**2** **Adjustable shelves keep it simple.** Adjustable shelves are easier to make and finish than stationary shelves. A scrap of pegboard is a perfect template to position the support holes. Mark the pegboard holes you want to use and label the end of the template that goes against the bottom shelf.

*A brad point bit reduces splintering when drilling shelf holes. Wrap the bit with a masking tape "flag" to mark the depth of the hole.*

BRAD POINT BIT

DEPTH FLAG

SCREEN MOLDING

**3** **Easy shelf edging.** Spread a light bead of glue over the front edges of the shelves. Set the screen molding in place and "clamp" it with masking tape. Pull the tape tight as you apply it.

**4** **Assemble corner stiles, then cut to length.** Start with corner stile parts (E and F) that are about an inch longer than their final length. That way, you don't have to worry about aligning the ends as you join them. Then trim the ends to length.

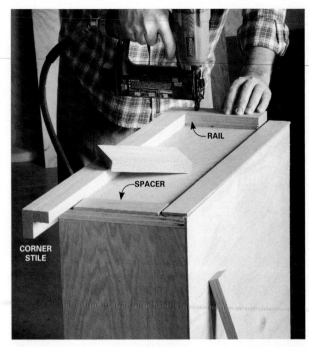

**5** **Attach rails and stiles instantly.** Traditional rails and stiles require clamps and time-consuming joinery. A brad nailer eliminates that whole process. Just glue and tack the spacers into place, then glue and nail on the rails and stiles. Use only enough nails to hold the parts in place while the glue sets.

**6** **Classic style, the simple way.** Common cove molding gives the sides a classic frame-and-panel look. Miter one end of each piece and hold it in place to mark it. Cut the piece a hair long and test the fit. If it's too long, take it back to the miter saw and shave off a smidgen.

## Add rails, stiles and trim

"Rails" are the horizontal parts that frame the outside of the shelf box; "stiles" are the vertical parts. Cut solid wood boards to the widths given in the Cutting List (p. 155). Nail the corner stile parts (E and F) together with 1-1/2-in. brads (**Photo 4**). Next, cut the spacers that go behind the side rails and stiles. I made all my spacers 1/8 in. smaller than the parts that go over them. The purpose of the spacers is to make the rails and stiles protrude an extra 1/4 in. from the sides of the shelf box. Without them, the 3/4-in. cove molding (see **Photo 6**) would be flush with the faces of the rails and stiles—and that would look bad.

**7** **Use basic boards for the base.** The base of the shelf unit is just boards topped off with cove molding. Glue and tack on spacers, then add the baseboards. Sand the joints flush and add the cove molding.

Glue and nail the spacers with 1/2-in. brads, then switch to 1-1/2-in. brads for the rails and stiles (**Photo 5**). Trying to fit a rail between stiles that are already fastened is difficult, and you won't get tight joints. Here's how to avoid that: Nail on one of the corner stiles, followed by the side rails (H and J) and then the rear side stile (G). Note that the lower rail overhangs the box by 1 in. Next, lay the box on its back, set the front rails (K and L) in place and check the fit of the other corner stile. Shorten the front stiles if necessary and nail them into place. Then

nail on the second corner stile, followed by the side rails and stiles.

With all the rails and stiles in place, you're ready to install the cove molding (**Photo 6**). To avoid tedious work later, sand all the molding before you start cutting it. Installing the molding is the slowest phase of the project because cutting it to the right length on the first try is almost impossible. Instead, you'll cut each piece, test-fit it and shave it shorter until it fits. Don't nail any of the moldings until they're all in place. Then attach the baseboards (**Photo 7**) and add cove molding above them.

# Figure A  Shortcut bookshelf

**Overall Dimensions**
32-1/4" tall x 37-3/4" wide
x 11-1/8" deep

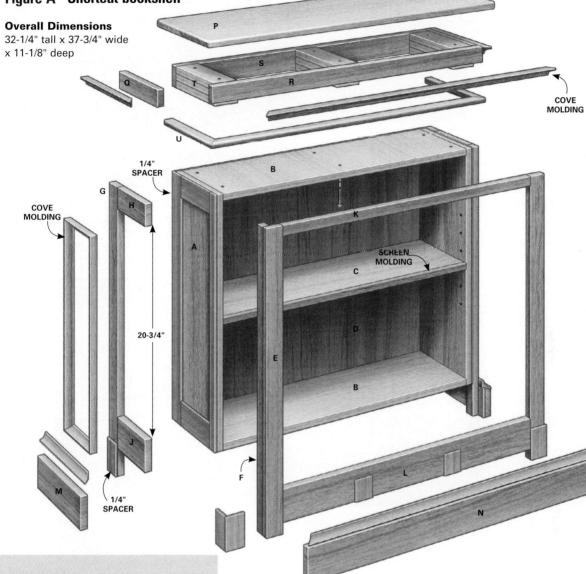

COVE
MOLDING

1/4"
SPACER

COVE
MOLDING

G

H

A

SCREEN
MOLDING

C

K

D

E

B

20-3/4"

J

1/4"
SPACER

F

M

L

N

## CUTTING LIST

| KEY | QTY. | SIZE & DESCRIPTION |
|-----|------|--------------------|
| A* | 2 | 3/4" x 9" x 25-1/4" sides |
| B* | 2 | 3/4" x 9" x 32" box bottom and lid |
| C* | 2 | 3/4" x 8-3/4" x 31-7/8" shelves |
| D* | 1 | 1/4" x 25-1/4" x 33-1/2" back panel |
| E | 2 | 3/4" x 1-7/8" x 29-1/4" front stiles |
| F | 2 | 3/4" x 1-1/8" x 29-1/4" front side stiles |
| G | 2 | 3/4" x 1-7/8" x 29-1/4" rear side stiles |
| H | 2 | 3/4" x 2-1/4" x 6-1/4" upper side rails |
| J | 2 | 3/4" x 3-1/4" x 6-1/4" lower side rails |
| K | 1 | 3/4" x 1" x 31-3/4" upper front rail |
| L | 1 | 3/4" x 3-1/4" x 31-3/4" lower front rail |
| M | 2 | 3/4" x 3-1/4" x 10-1/4" side baseboards |
| N | 1 | 3/4" x 3-1/4" x 37-1/2" front baseboard |
| P | 1 | 3/4" x 11-1/8" x 37-3/4" top |
| Q | 2 | 3/4" x 1-3/4" x 9-1/4" frame sides |
| R | 1 | 3/4" x 1-3/4" x 35-1/2" frame front |
| S* | 1 | 3/4" x 2-1/4" x 34" frame back |
| T | 9 | 3/4" x 2-3/4" x 8-1/2" filler blocks |
| U | 3 | 1/2" x 1" (cut to fit) bead molding |

*Plywood parts. All other parts are solid wood.

## MATERIALS LIST

| ITEM | QTY. |
|------|------|
| 4' x 4' x 3/4" oak plywood | 1 |
| 4 x 4' x 1/4" oak plywood | 1 |
| 1x6 oak boards | 16' |
| 1x12 oak board | 4' |
| 1/2" x 3-1/2" oak board | 3' |
| 3/4" oak cove molding | 20' |
| 3/16" x 3/4" oak screen molding | 6' |

Wood glue, 1-1/4" screws,
2" screws, 1/2" brads,
1-1/2" brads, adjustable shelf
supports, finishing supplies.

## Figure B
## Plywood cutting diagram
(3/4-in. plywood)

## Crown the box with a fancy top

Don't be fooled by the large number of small parts that make up the top assembly—it's showy but not difficult. Start by rounding the edges of the top (P) with a 1/4-in. round-over bit (**Photo 8**). Then assemble plywood and solid wood parts of the frame with nails and glue. When you drill pilot holes to screw the frame to the top (**Photo 9**), mark the depth with masking tape on your drill bit so you don't poke through the top.

Shape the bead molding with a 1/8-in. round-over bit (**Photo 10**). Keep in mind that the 3-ft. length of molding is just barely enough for the front piece; there's no room for error. To complete the top assembly, add the cove molding and the filler blocks (**Photo 11**). Fasten on the top with 2-in. screws (**Photo 12**) and you're ready for finishing. I used General Finishes Mission Oak stain (rockler.com) followed by three coats of Minwax Wipe-On Poly (satin).

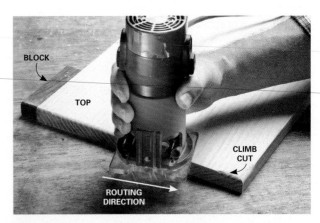

**8 Shape the top—without wrecking it.** A wide slab of solid wood is expensive, so take extra steps to avoid mistakes. To prevent splintering at the front corner, make a reverse-direction "climb cut." Screw blocks to the back corners to prevent gouging as you begin and end routing.

**9 No need to miter the frame.** The square-cut butt joints at the corners of the frame make cutting and joining the parts a lot easier. (The same goes for the baseboards shown in Photo 7.) Assemble the frame with glue and nails, then center the assembly and screw it to the underside of the top.

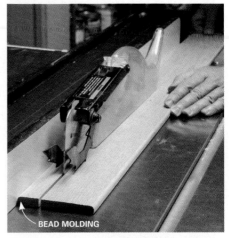

**10 Make bead molding in five minutes.** Round over both edges of a 1/2-in.-thick board, sand the edges and then cut the completed moldings off the board.

**11 Simple moldings for a fancy top.** Trim the frame with cove molding and homemade bead molding. Then glue in two layers of plywood filler blocks. The blocks allow the top to be screwed to the shelf box.

**12 A screwed-on top is better.** Mount the top with screws only—no glue. That way, you can remove it for easier sanding and finishing. Center the top and drive screws through the box lid and into the filler blocks.

# HOW TO MAKE
# BISCUIT JOINTS

*Four simple joints—a world of possibilities*

## by **Ken Collier, Editor in Chief**

I t's easy to fall in love with biscuit joints—they're so fast and easy. At least they are when you get the hang of them. If you're new to biscuits, you can learn here how to do the four basic woodworking joints. Even if you already own a biscuit joiner (or plate joiner—same animal), I'm sure you'll pick up a tip or two that'll take your woodworking up a notch. Either way, be sure to check out familyhandyman.com for related articles and a couple of projects built with this simple joinery technique. Just search for "biscuits."

Ken Collier,
Editor in
Chief

## Biscuit basics

If you want to get started using biscuits (or "plates," as they're sometimes called), you can pick up an entry-level machine for about $100. Five minutes of fooling around with the machine or a little time with some online videos and you'll have the basic idea: Use the machine to cut slots in both parts, and then add glue to each, insert a biscuit, clamp to hold, and you're done. Your tool manual will show how to adjust the tool.

The cool thing about biscuit joinery is that the biscuit is made from compressed wood. The biscuit fits loosely in its slot, which makes assembly easy, but it expands after the glue has had a few minutes to soak in, so it fits extremely tight. You have a little window of time when the two pieces you're joining can be slid sideways into perfect alignment. Biscuit joinery may not be for the DIYer who's just building one cabinet, but if you have a lot of cabinets in your future, a biscuit joiner is a great tool to own.

## Making cabinet boxes: T-joints

This is where joinery shines: the T-joint, where a fixed shelf meets the sides of a cabinet (Photos 1 – 3). The sideways wiggle room that biscuits give you allows you to get the edges of the shelf and the sides perfectly flush, and the case looks good, with or without a face frame, both inside and out. And since the glue is all on the biscuits, there's rarely any squeeze-out to clean up.

The process for making a T-joint begins with marking on the edge of the sides where the top of the shelf should be. Stand the shelf in position and mark the biscuit locations. Then lay the shelf on its side, lined up with its location mark. Clamp the side and shelf together and to your bench, with the edges flush to each other. Now cut your biscuit slots, first in one piece, then in the other. Do the other side of the cabinet the same way, making sure the shelf is oriented the right way: front to front, bottom to the bottom.

**MAKE A T-JOINT**
First, mark the height of the shelf on the cabinet side, then stand the shelf up and mark the location of the biscuit slots on both pieces (**Photo 1**). Then clamp the pieces together, rest the joiner on the cabinet side and cut the slots in the shelf (**Photo 2**). Now flip the joiner upright and cut the matching slots in the sides (**Photo 3**).

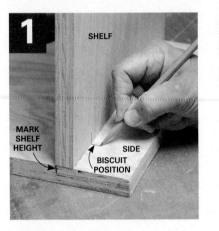

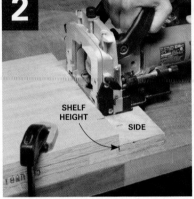

## Making cabinet boxes: L-joints

Biscuits are also a great way to make an L-joint, for example, to join a cabinet top to the sides (Photos 4 – 6). For this kind of joint, you usually want to have the outside edges flush, without a little step. So use the fence to ensure the pieces are flush on the outside. When you're using the fence, be certain your workpiece extends completely off the edge of the workbench. Also, press down firmly on the fence to make sure the slot is cut properly; it's easy for the fence to be tipped.

**MAKE AN L-JOINT**
On the corner of a cabinet, use an L-joint (**Photo 4**). After marking the slot positions, cut the slots, using the fence to register the slot from the top surface of your piece (**Photo 5**). Hold the fence down firmly for accuracy. For the sides, give the joiner more support by clamping both sides of the cabinet together (**Photo 6**).

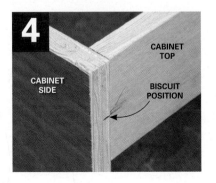

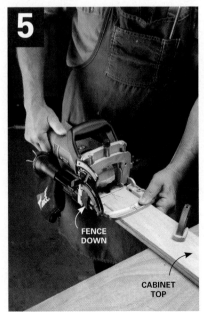

## Making face frames

Plate joinery is a fast way to make face frames. It's also a convenient way if you're already using the joiner for the cabinet boxes. To join face frames with biscuits, you usually need to let the biscuit extend past the outside of the frame and trim it off. Just be sure you've got your face frame pieces supported, since they're usually narrow (**Photo 8**). I like to line up the middle of the biscuit, and the mark on the joiner, with the edge of the face frame so half the biscuit is being glued. Of course, on wide rails you can sometimes use the entire biscuit.

### Fence or no fence?

The joiner is designed to be used two ways: You can have the fence down, which allows you to align the biscuits to a surface that faces up, that the fence rests on (**Photos 5 and 6**). You can also fold the fence in, which allows you to align the biscuits with the bottom of the tool (**Photos 2 and 3**). The trick is to figure out which one to use, then use it consistently.

Imagine you're joining two pieces of different thicknesses edge to edge. Using the fence allows you to get the top surfaces flush; using the bottom of the joiner (no fence) allows you to get the bottom surfaces flush. When you use a joiner without the fence, the slot is centered in 3/4-in. material. For any other spacing, you need to use the fence.

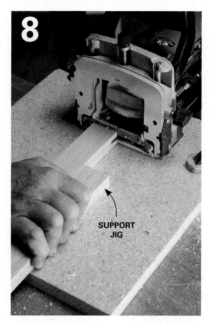

**BUILD FACE FRAMES**
For narrow pieces like a face frame, just let the slot run out the side that doesn't show (**Photo 7**). To support the piece you're cutting, make a simple support jig (**Photo 8**), just a scrap of face frame attached to a base. Keep your hands well away from the joiner, or use clamps.

SUPPORT JIG

---

## Biscuit joints for edging plywood

If you're gluing solid wood edging onto plywood, biscuits can make it a success (**Photos 9 – 11**). If you try to glue the edging on perfectly flush, a small section inevitably ends up lower than the surface of the plywood, which is a disaster. The trick is to leave the solid wood a fraction above the surface of the plywood, then sand it flush. The plate joiner makes it easy.

bottom

**ALIGN SOLID-WOOD EDGING ON PLYWOOD**
First, mark the slot locations with both pieces upside down on the workbench (**Photo 9**). When you cut slots in the edging, put thin cardboard or a few pieces of paper under the joiner (**Photo 10**). The edging will be slightly above the surface of the plywood when you glue it on (**Photo 11**). This gives you a small, safe amount to sand off without damaging the plywood.

CARDBOARD

EDGING SLIGHTLY ABOVE PLYWOOD

# JIGSAW
## ESSENTIALS

*Tips for smoother, cleaner, more accurate cuts*

### by Mark Petersen, Contributing Editor

A jigsaw is one of those DIY necessities. For beginners, it's less intimidating than a circular saw and also very versatile—lots of basic projects require nothing more than a drill and a jigsaw. But DIY veterans need a jigsaw too, no matter how many other tools they own. If you fall in either category, or somewhere between, this article will help you get more from your jigsaw. We'll demonstrate a few practical tips, tell you what you need to know about blades, and point out which features to look for when you buy a jigsaw.

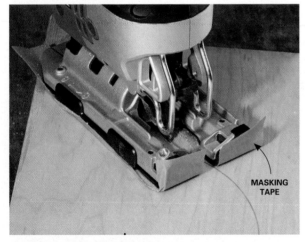

MASKING TAPE

METAL-CUTTING BLADE

### Protect the work surface

When making a cut, you need to firmly hold down the saw to keep the blade from chattering, and even then, it may vibrate a bit. The combination of downward force and vibration is tough on the work surface. Reduce marring by applying a layer or two of masking tape to the base of the jigsaw. Remove the tape when you're done so it doesn't leave a sticky residue on the base.

### Cut anything

The main mission of a jigsaw is to cut curves in wood, and it's easy to overlook its other abilities. Instead of slaving away with your hacksaw, grab your jigsaw to quickly cut steel, copper or any metal. You can also cut plastics and tougher stuff like ceramic tile and fiber cement siding. The key to success is to match the blade to the material (more on that later).

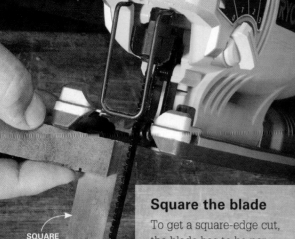

**SQUARE**

## Square the blade

To get a square-edge cut, the blade has to be perfectly perpendicular to the base. So before you make a cut, make sure the blade isn't bent. If it is, just toss it or save it for jobs where a clean, square cut isn't important. With a straight, new blade in the saw, square it up. There's not a lot of surface area on the base, so a smaller square is easier to work with.

## Get the right saw for you

It's helpful to think of jigsaws in three categories: For $50 or less, you'll get a jigsaw that will do its job just fine, but you'll probably sacrifice features and power. For most DIYers, a saw in the $50 to $100 range is a good choice. It will have some special features and adequate power. Saws that cost over $100 will have large motors and all the best features.

**OSCILLATING CONTROL**

**PORTER CABLE.**

**TOOLLESS BLADE CHANGE**

**BASE PLATE BEVEL LEVER**

Our favorite features are toolless blade change, toolless base plate bevel and oscillating control. Bonus features include an LED light, a blower to blow away dust, a larger base plate and a speed control dial.

If you'll be cutting a lot of material that's 1 in. or thicker, look for a saw with a higher amp rating (listed in the specifications). Smaller saws draw 5 amps or less; larger models go up to 7 amps. Larger motors also add a little "heft" to the saw, which helps cut vibration.

Some jigsaws have handles; some don't. Many pros like the no-handle "barrel-grip" style. They feel they have better control with their hands closer to the action. Folks with smaller hands often complain about the barrel being too large to grab.

## Oscillation education

Most jigsaws offer oscillating action: While the blade moves up and down, it also lunges forward with each stroke. Typically, you can turn off the oscillation or select from three levels of oscillation. The higher the setting, the faster you cut.

But faster isn't always better. More oscillation means rougher, less-accurate cuts. So turn the oscillation way down or off when you need clean or precise cuts or when you're working with delicate materials like veneers. Turn the oscillating feature off when you're cutting metal. Practice on a scrap to find the best setting for the material.

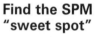

## Find the SPM "sweet spot"

Typically, there's an SPM (strokes per minute) "sweet spot" where the saw cuts the fastest and cleanest and with the least vibration. Try different speeds by changing pressure on the trigger. Once you find the best speed, set the adjustable speed dial so you can pull the trigger all the way while maintaining the desired SPM.

RELIEF CUTS

## Make relief cuts for sharp turns

There's a limit on how sharp a curve a jigsaw can cut, and that depends on the blade—the narrower the blade, the sharper the turns it can make. If you try to force the blade into a turn tighter than it's capable of, you'll either veer off your line or break the blade.

If you're not sure about a particular shape, mark it out on a scrap and practice on that. If you have a curve you know is too tight, make relief cuts. The sharper the curve, the more relief cuts you'll need. And be sure you don't cut past your line. Play it safe and leave at least a blade's width of material between the relief cut and your pencil mark.

## Drill starter holes

If you need to cut out a hole in the center of the work surface—like a hole for a heat register in a sheet of bead board wainscoting—drill a hole slightly bigger than your jigsaw blade in two opposite corners. That way, you can make four neat cuts starting from the two holes.

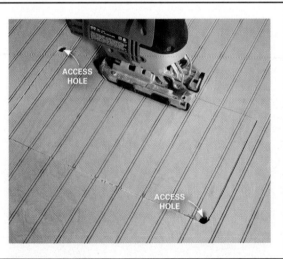

ACCESS HOLE

ACCESS HOLE

## Let the tool do the work

Pushing as hard as you can on the saw doesn't necessarily make it cut faster; sometimes the exact opposite is true. And pushing too hard into a curve can cause you to veer off your line, burn the material or break a blade. Ease off on the pressure until the saw cuts smoothly with little vibration.

## A blade for every occasion

There are a couple of basic things to know about blades: The larger the teeth, the more aggressive and rougher the cut. And the narrower the blade, the tighter the turns it can make. Narrow, double-sided blades are especially well suited for sharp turns because tho tooth on the back side widen the kerf as you turn.

Match the type of blade with the material you're cutting—don't use a wood blade to cut metal. Most manufacturers have taken the guesswork out of blade selection—the description of the blade and what it does is usually written on the blade itself. Buy a combo pack and you'll be ready for most jobs. A 15-pack of quality blades costs less than $20, and you'll avoid making a special trip to the store.

There are also specialty blades designed for very specific jobs: blades for cutting tile and fiber cement, and flush-cut blades that extend the cut right up to the front of the base. Specialty blades are usually sold individually and can cost more than $10 each.

FIBER CEMENT

DOUBLE-SIDED

CERAMIC

FLUSH-CUT

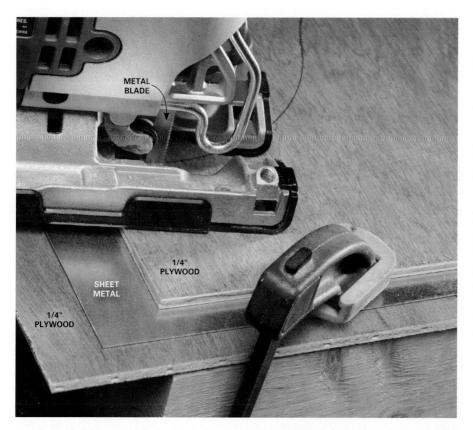

## Make a metal sandwich

Jigsaws are great at cutting sheet metal, but it's difficult to clamp the material down so the saw blade doesn't just rattle the material up and down instead of cutting through it. One way to solve this problem is to sandwich the metal between two sheets of 1/4-in. plywood. Once the plywood is clamped down, the metal has nowhere to go, so you get a fast, easy, clean cut. You don't have to spend a bunch of money on plywood either; 1/4-in. underlayment works fine and costs only $13 for a 4 x 8-ft. sheet.

## Smart starting and stopping

Be sure the blade is up to speed before you start your cut. If you start the saw with the blade touching your material, it can grab hold and rattle the material, possibly damaging it. And let the saw come to a complete stop when you pull it from the material mid-cut. If you don't, you might experience the dreaded "woodpecker effect," when a moving blade bounces off the surface, leaving behind pockmarks and a bent blade.

## Cut with the "good" side down

Most jigsaw blades cut on the upstroke, so chips and splinters occur mostly on the top of the wood. So if you value one side of a board more than the other, make sure you keep the good side face down, and mark and cut the less important side.

You can buy "reverse cut" or "down cut" blades that do cut on the down stroke. These blades are used when you want as little tear-out on the top surface as possible. Cutting out a sink hole in a laminate countertop is one common use for reverse-cut blades.

# COMPACT
# TOOL CABINET

*Build an easy-access pegboard storage unit*

## by **Mark Petersen, Contributing Editor**

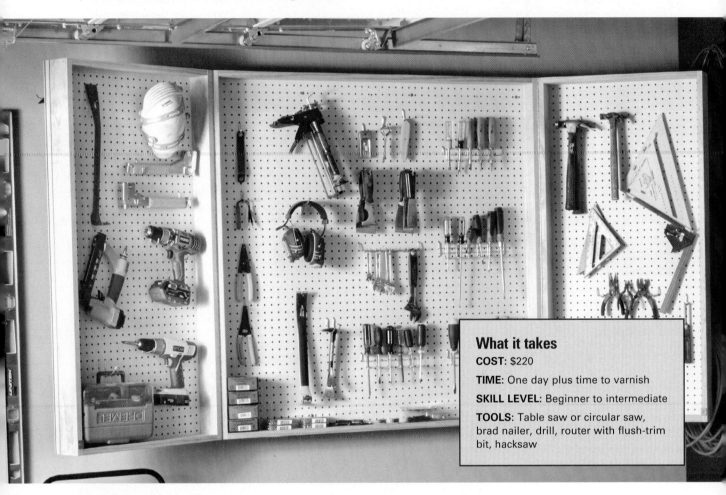

### What it takes

**COST:** $220

**TIME:** One day plus time to varnish

**SKILL LEVEL:** Beginner to intermediate

**TOOLS:** Table saw or circular saw, brad nailer, drill, router with flush-trim bit, hacksaw

**My** brother Curtis is a building maintenance guy, so he knows a thing or two about tools and how to store them. I recently visited his workshop and was instantly drawn to the pegboard cabinet he'd built. He told me that pegboard is his favorite way to store tools. He loves the easy access, and an empty peg always lets him know that a tool has gone AWOL. What he doesn't like about pegboard is that it takes up wall space, which is scarce in any shop. So he built a pegboard cabinet that delivers the best of both worlds. His design provides almost 48 sq. ft. of pegboard while taking up only 16 sq. ft. of wall space. He always was the smart one in the family.

### Build the base frame

Cut your 1x4 frame boards to size. I used a higher-grade pine. It was worth the extra $40 to be able to work with straight, knot-free wood. Sand all the boards with 100-grit sandpaper before assembling the frames. I glued the joints and nailed them with 1-1/2-in. brads, just to hold them together. When the base was fully assembled, I came back and drove in two 2-in. trim head screws. If you don't have a brad nailer, no problem; the screws are plenty strong on their own.

### Attach the pegboard to the base frame

I wanted solid material along all the edges, which meant I couldn't just measure 47-3/4 in. from the end of the sheet and assume the holes wouldn't be exposed. Not all sheets of pegboard are the same size, and sometimes the holes aren't perfectly centered on the sheet. I squared up the frame and held it in place with a couple of temporary cross braces and brads. I laid a half sheet of pegboard on top of the frame so all the rows of holes were inset at least 1/4 in. before fastening it down. Fasten the sheet with 1-in. brads every 8 in. or so (**Photo 1**), and use glue on all the unfinished sides of the pegboard.

Once the pegboard is secure, trim off the excess material with a router equipped with a flush-trim bit (**Photo 2**). If you don't own a flush-trim bit, this is an excellent opportunity to spend $20 on a tool you'll definitely use again. Trimming down pegboard creates clouds of very fine dust, which seems to get into everything. I cut my first edge and then got smart and moved the whole operation outdoors. Don't even think about doing this without wearing a dust mask. If you don't have a router to trim off the excess, just mark the outline of the base frame onto the half sheet of pegboard and trim it with a saw.

## Build the doors

Use the same process to build the door frames and install the pegboard as you did on the base. Again, pay special attention to the spacing of the holes before you attach the pegboard and rout it flush. The only difference this time is that the first layer of pegboard should be facing down.

Once the first layer of pegboard is in place, rip down 3/4-in. strips of wood to act as a spacer between the first and the second layers (**Photo 3**). This will allow clearance

for the peg hardware on both sides of the door. Align the spacers the same way you did with the frame, so the end grain cannot be seen from the sides. Tack them in place with 1-1/2-in. brads.

Tack on the outer layer of pegboard or dry-erase board (white/gloss hardboard panel board) with 1-in. brads, and then drive in 2-in. trim head screws about every 8 in. or so. Pegboard and other hardboard materials tend to pucker when you screw into them, so predrill the holes with a small countersink drill bit. Don't attach the screen mold on the outside of the doors until the doors are hung onto the base.

## Finish the back side of the base

There needs to be space for the peg hardware on the back of the base, so install 3/4-in. strips of pine on the back two sides of the base. Fasten them with glue and 1-1/2-in. brads. Next, install a full pine 1x4 on the top and bottom of the back side of the base. These are the boards you'll screw through when you hang the cabinet on the wall. Glue and tack these boards into place, and then drive 2-in. trim head screws through the boards into the base frame.

Use another 3/4-in. strip of pine to brace up the center of the pegboard. Install this center brace between the holes. Secure it with glue and a few 1-in. brads from the front side of the base. This will prevent the 4 x 4-ft. sheet of pegboard from getting too floppy.

The doors will be thicker than the base once you add the screen molding. This means they'll make contact with

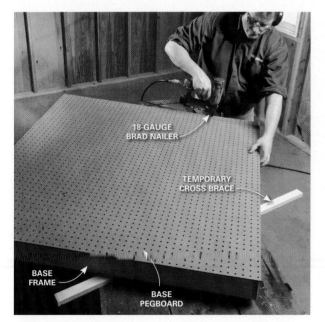

**1 Fasten pegboard to the base frame.** Attach temporary braces to hold the base frame perfectly square. Lay a 4 x 4-ft. sheet of pegboard over the frame. The oversize sheet lets you position the holes so they won't be along the outer edge of the cabinet. Note: If you don't have a router to trim off the excess pegboard (see Photo 2), position the pegboard, mark it with a pencil and cut it to size before nailing it in place.

**2 Trim the pegboard flush.** Install a flush-trim bit in your router and trim off the overhanging pegboard. Routing pegboard whips up a dust storm, so wear a mask.

FLUSH-TRIM BIT

SPACER

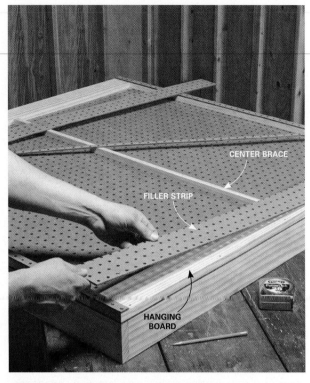

CENTER BRACE

FILLER STRIP

HANGING BOARD

**3** **Complete the doors.** A 3/4-in. spacer between the two layers of pegboard creates space for the hooks.

**4** **Add filler strips.** Installing filler strips on the back of the base will allow the doors to open a little wider.

the walls before they fully open. If you add filler strips of pegboard on the back side of the pine boards you just installed, the doors will open farther, and you'll get another cool-looking dark strip resembling a walnut inlay (**Photo 4**). Even with the filler strips, the cabinet doors will make contact with the wall about 4 in. before they fully open. If you really, really want the doors to open all the way, you can add another 1/4 in. of filler to the back. But if you hang tools on the front of the cabinet or on the walls on either side, it shouldn't matter at all.

### Attach the doors

The cabinet is a little shorter than the hinges; use a hacksaw to trim them down. Install the hinges to the base first. Fold it over the front edge of the base at a 90-degree angle and install the screws. Clamp the doors into place before you screw the other half of the hinge. I used a self-centering screw hole punch to make sure the screws were perfectly aligned (**Photo 5**). The punch costs less than $10 at home centers. Make sure the doors stay shut by installing a magnet catch on the top and bottom.

If the gap between the doors isn't perfectly even, adjust the screen mold on the front of the doors as you install them until it is. Fasten the screen mold with 1-in. brads.

### Finish it up

After filling the holes with putty, I covered the wood

SCREW HOLE PUNCH

PIANO HINGE

**5** **Install the doors.** Clamp the doors to the cabinet and install the piano hinges. A self-centering screw hole punch helps you center the screws in the hinge holes.

with clear polyurethane. It kept the wood color light and really darkened the edges of the pegboard. Don't use an aggressively sticky tape when you tape off the hardboard/dry-erase board or you may pull the finish right off them. Screw the cabinet to the wall with screws that penetrate the studs at least 1-1/4 in., and try to hit at least three studs on the top and three on the bottom. You can install handles on the bottom if you like.

Now that you're done, it's time to shop for the hardware you'll need to hang all your tools. Here's a suggestion for you: Avoid 1/8-in. hooks. They fit in the 1/4-in. holes but tend to pull out when you remove a tool.

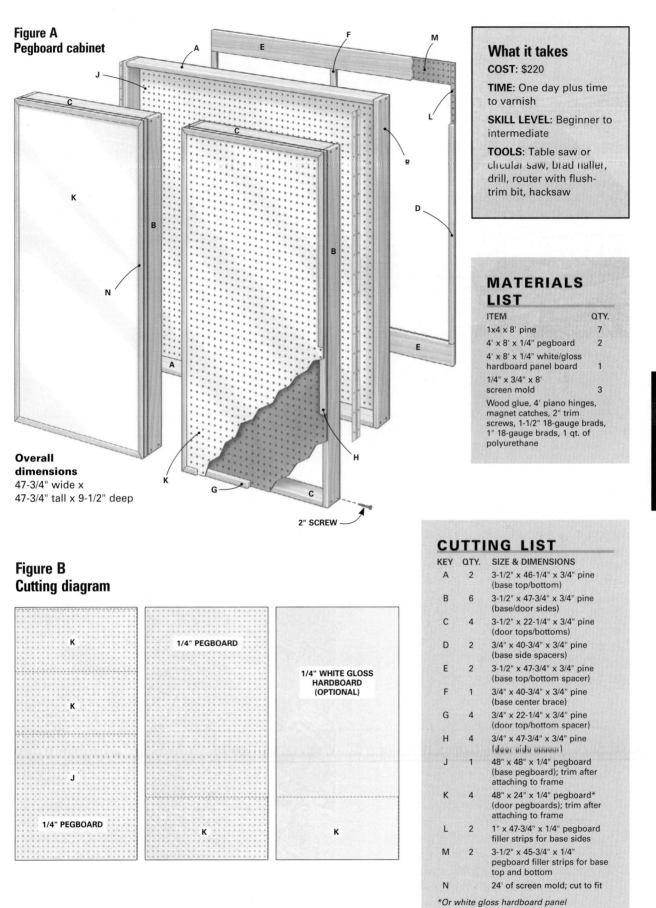

## Figure A
## Pegboard cabinet

A · J · C · K · B · N · A · C · C · B · B · K · G · H · E · F · M · L · R · D · E · C

**2" SCREW**

**Overall dimensions**
47-3/4" wide x
47-3/4" tall x 9-1/2" deep

## Figure B
## Cutting diagram

K

K

J

**1/4" PEGBOARD**

**1/4" PEGBOARD**

**1/4" PEGBOARD**

K

**1/4" WHITE GLOSS HARDBOARD (OPTIONAL)**

K

## What it takes

**COST:** $220

**TIME:** One day plus time to varnish

**SKILL LEVEL:** Beginner to intermediate

**TOOLS:** Table saw or circular saw, brad nailer, drill, router with flush-trim bit, hacksaw

## MATERIALS LIST

| ITEM | QTY. |
|------|------|
| 1x4 x 8' pine | 7 |
| 4' x 8' x 1/4" pegboard | 2 |
| 4' x 8' x 1/4" white/gloss hardboard panel board | 1 |
| 1/4" x 3/4" x 8' screen mold | 3 |

Wood glue, 4' piano hinges, magnet catches, 2" trim screws, 1-1/2" 18-gauge brads, 1" 18-gauge brads, 1 qt. of polyurethane

## CUTTING LIST

| KEY | QTY. | SIZE & DIMENSIONS |
|-----|------|-------------------|
| A | 2 | 3-1/2" x 46-1/4" x 3/4" pine (base top/bottom) |
| B | 6 | 3-1/2" x 47-3/4" x 3/4" pine (base/door sides) |
| C | 4 | 3-1/2" x 22-1/4" x 3/4" pine (door tops/bottoms) |
| D | 2 | 3/4" x 40-3/4" x 3/4" pine (base side spacers) |
| E | 2 | 3-1/2" x 47-3/4" x 3/4" pine (base top/bottom spacer) |
| F | 1 | 3/4" x 40-3/4" x 3/4" pine (base center brace) |
| G | 4 | 3/4" x 22-1/4" x 3/4" pine (door top/bottom spacer) |
| H | 4 | 3/4" x 47-3/4" x 3/4" pine (door side spacers) |
| J | 1 | 48" x 48" x 1/4" pegboard (base pegboard); trim after attaching to frame |
| K | 4 | 48" x 24" x 1/4" pegboard* (door pegboards); trim after attaching to frame |
| L | 2 | 1" x 47-3/4" x 1/4" pegboard filler strips for base sides |
| M | 2 | 3-1/2" x 45-3/4" x 1/4" pegboard filler strips for base top and bottom |
| N | | 24' of screen mold; cut to fit |

*Or white gloss hardboard panel

# ToolTips

## KEEP TOOL CASES DRY AND FRESH

Put four or five sticks of chalk inside a dryer sheet and staple the ends. Then I put these little dryer sheet chalk bundles in all my tool bags, boxes and cases. Chalk is calcium carbonate, which absorbs moisture. So the chalk keeps my tools from rusting while the dryer sheets keep everything smelling fresh. Works great!

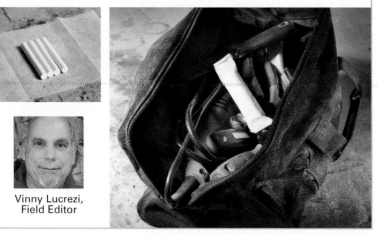

Vinny Lucrezi,
Field Editor

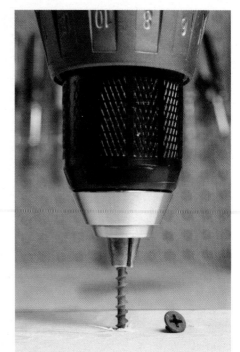

## SOFT SHOE FOR RECIP SAWS

To reduce vibration and protect surfaces while using a reciprocating saw, cut off a 4-in.-long piece of 3/4-in. foam pipe insulation. Open the split side and slide the insulation over the blade to cover the saw shoe. The split will naturally squeeze the shoe, holding it in place. The insulation eliminates scratches and marks on finished surfaces.

## EASY WOOD SCREW REMOVAL

When you're driving a screw into a board and the head breaks off, try this time-saving trick. Don't hunt around for your locking pliers to pull it out. Instead, use the tool that's already in your hand—your drill. Just loosen the chuck and tighten it around the screw shank. Then reverse the drill and out comes the broken screw. Toss the screw and keep on trucking.

## PROBLEM WITH PORTABLE BATTERY CHARGER

*I have a problem with my portable tool battery charger. It starts charging and then flashes red and green lights indicating that the battery is bad. I've tried a new battery and it still happens.*

We have heard this quite often and wondered if there was an easy way to test a battery charger, perhaps with a household voltmeter. So we asked our experts at a factory repair center. It turns out they just insert a known good battery into the suspect charger. If the battery charges, then the charger is good. Unfortunately, there's no way to test a charger because it needs feedback from the battery's "S" terminal. You have to install a battery before the charger will even begin the charge cycle. So it's a conundrum. You'll need to buy a new battery just to find out if the charger is bad.

The latest generation of chargers is much smarter and can let you know if the battery is bad.

## IF I HAD A HAMMER... I WOULD SWING IT PROPERLY

I sometimes see a guy holding his breath while swinging a sledgehammer. I have a Ph.D. in exercise physiology and can tell you that holding your breath during exertion puts a lot of stress on your heart and can be fatal for someone in poor health.

If you watch a guy exerting himself while holding his breath, you can see the strain in his neck muscles, blood vessels and arteries. This is why some people have heart attacks while shoveling heavy snow. They lift a lot of weight while holding their breath and then blood vessels pop.

Barry Cohen,
Field Editor

So whether you're using a sledgehammer, a shovel or another tool, breathing out through your mouth will keep your blood pressure stable and let you exert maximum force.

### BETTER METAL SHAVINGS COLLECTION

Sometimes, folks will collect metal fragments by putting a magnet next to the drill bit. But the shavings can be difficult to remove from the magnet when you're done. Here's an easy way to solve the problem: Put the magnet in a plastic bag. When you've collected all the shavings, stand over a trash can and remove the magnet from the bag. All the shavings will fall into the trash and the magnet will be clean.

### SIMPLE TOOL BED WAXING

I used to coat my metal table saw and planer bed with auto wax because it makes the wood slide nicely across the metal. But then I saw an expert cabinetmaker use wax paper, and now I do the same. I keep a roll in my shop drawer and rub a sheet of it over the metal beds on my table saw, router, planer and disc sander. The wax coating doesn't last as long as a good paste wax, but boy, is it a lot easier and quicker.

—R. J. Hayes

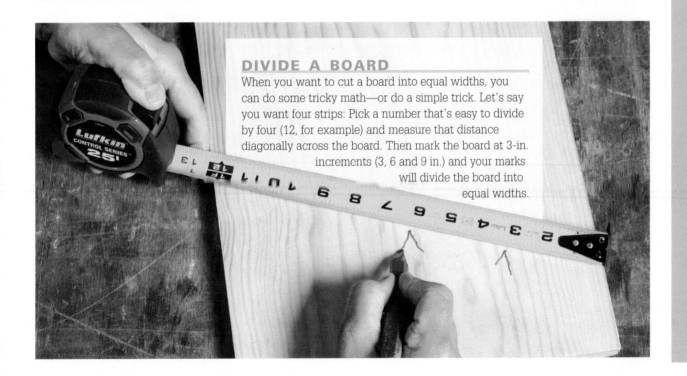

### DIVIDE A BOARD

When you want to cut a board into equal widths, you can do some tricky math—or do a simple trick. Let's say you want four strips: Pick a number that's easy to divide by four (12, for example) and measure that distance diagonally across the board. Then mark the board at 3-in. increments (3, 6 and 9 in.) and your marks will divide the board into equal widths.

# ToolTips

## REPAIR A POWER TOOL CORD

Got a nicked or cut power tool cord? We'll show you how to restore it to "almost new" condition. You'll need heat-shrinkable tubing in both small and large diameters, a soldering gun and rosin-core solder, a utility knife, heat gun and wire strippers.

Start by removing a 6-in. section of the outer jacket (**Photo 1**). Save it for later use. Then cut all the wires and the reinforcement cord. Slide a piece of large-diameter heat-shrinkable tubing onto the cord and push it out of the way for now.

Slide a small piece of heat-shrinkable tubing onto each wire. Stagger the splices and solder (**Photo 2**). Let the solder cool, then slide the tubing over each splice and shrink it with a heat gun.

Finish the job by reinstalling the outer jacket. Then cover the entire patched area with the large tubing and shrink it (**Photo 3**).

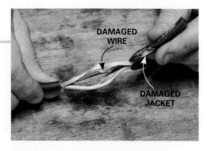

**1 Slit and peel the jacket.** Slice around the outer jacket about 3 in. on both sides of the damage. Then slit the jacket down the center and peel it off.

**2 Strip, twist and solder.** Strip insulation off each wire. Then twist the strands together and solder. Solder each splice.

**3 Cover and shrink.** Slide the shrinkable tubing over the splices and outer jacket. Shrink the tubing with a heat gun.

## 5-GALLON BUCKET TOOL KIT

I worked in the electrical trade for many years, and my 5-gallon bucket tool kit was my constant companion. I used an awl to poke holes around the perimeter for my screwdrivers and stored the rest of my tools in the bucket.

Everything I needed was at my fingertips and easy to carry from job to job. I'm now 89 years old and I retired some time ago, but my tool kit is still on the job. It helps me with the chores that need doing around our house and 56-acre ranch.

Donald F. Bower

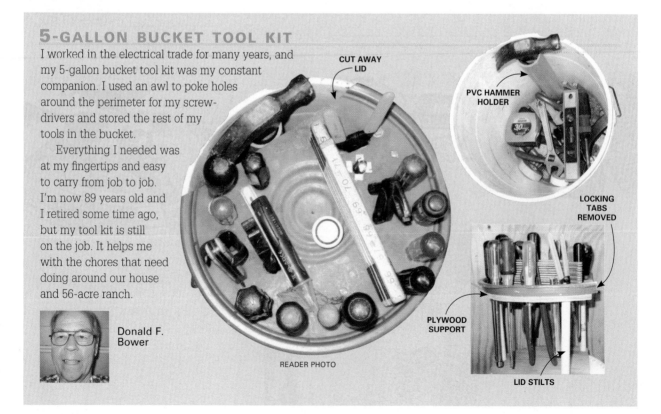

READER PHOTO

# 5 Exterior Repairs & Improvements

## IN THIS CHAPTER

## CLEAN YOUR CHIMNEY

If you use your fireplace or woodstove regularly but can't remember the last time your chimney was cleaned, it's probably overdue. In many cases, you can clean the chimney yourself and save about $200.

Removing ordinary chimney soot is pretty simple. But if you have heavy creosote buildup, you'll have to call in a pro. We'll show you how to inspect yours to see if it qualifies as a DIY job. If it does, just follow these steps. Otherwise, hire a certified chimney sweep.

### Is it a DIY job?

Most chimney fires start in the smoke chamber/smoke shelf area, so it's the most important area to clean (**Figure A**). Since that area is hard to reach in some fireplaces, check yours to see if you can reach into it and still have room to maneuver a brush. If you can't reach it, this isn't a DIY project.

Next, see if you can access the chimney crown. If you have a very steep roof pitch or aren't comfortable working on your roof, then this isn't a job for you. Call a certified chimney sweep. If you decide you can handle the heights, make sure to wear a safety harness.

### Then do an inspection

Strap on goggles and a respirator, clean the ashes out of the firebox and remove the grate. Then open a door or window and wait a few minutes before opening the damper so the pressures equalize. Then open the damper and wait a few more minutes for heat to rise from the house.

Grab your brightest flashlight and a fireplace poker and lean into the firebox. Shine your light into the smoke chamber and flue and use the poker to scratch the surface. If the soot has a matte black finish and the scratch is 1/8 in. deep or less, it's a DIY job. But if the buildup is deeper or has a shiny, tarlike appearance, you have heavy creosote buildup. Stop using your fireplace immediately and call a professional chimney sweep. (See "Chimney Fires Destroy Homes" on p. 173.)

### Get the right cleaning tools

There's no "one-size-fits-all" brush for cleaning the flue. So you'll have to climb up on your roof and measure the size of your flue liner. You'll also need special brushes for the firebox and smoke chamber areas (**Photo 2**). Find the equipment at a home center or at an online store such as efireplacestore.com.

### Minimize the mess

Before you start brushing, protect your home's interior from soot with poly sheeting, a canvas tarp and a shop vacuum (**Photo 3**). Most shop vacuum filters can't trap all the fine soot from a fireplace, and some of it will blow right out the exhaust port. So buy extra lengths of vacuum hose and move the vacuum outside (**Photo 4**). Then close the doors and windows on that side of your house to prevent the soot from reentering your home.

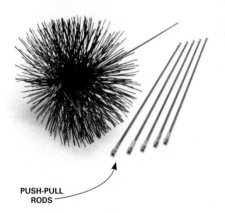

PUSH-PULL RODS

**1** **Match the brush to the flue liner.** Buy a metal bristle brush for a clay flue liner and a brush with plastic bristles for a metal liner. Buy enough rods to handle the entire height of your chimney.

**2** **Get special brushes for the firebox.** Buy a bendable "noodle brush" to clean the smoke shelf and a long-handled brush to clean soot off the sides of the firebox.

**MEET THE PROS**

Jim Smart has owned Smart Sweep Chimney Service for 14 years. He and his son Jesse are certified professional chimney sweeps. Together, this father/son team inspect, clean and repair chimneys in the Minneapolis/St. Paul area. Jim also holds a certificate in forensic chimney fire analysis.

**3** **Protect your interior.** Lay a canvas tarp over the hearth and spread it into the room. Then tape poly sheeting over the fireplace and insert a shop vacuum hose. Seal everything with duct tape.

**4** **Vent to the outdoors.** Add sections to lengthen the vacuum hose, then connect it to your shop vacuum outside. Run the vacuum while you brush, and replace the filter when it clogs.

**5** **Brush the flue.** Ram the cleaning brush up and down several times in a small section of the flue. Use a bright flashlight to check your work before moving on to the next section.

## Chimney fires destroy homes

Creosote buildup may not look dangerous, but it ignites at a mere 451 degrees F, and once it starts burning, it expands like foam sealant. In less than a minute, it builds to more than 2,000 degrees F and can engulf your entire chimney and destroy your home.

Even if you clean your chimney regularly, you should still have it inspected by a qualified chimney sweep once a year. Certified chimney sweeps are trained to recognize chimney deterioration and venting problems and can assess your chimney's condition.

### Figure A
### Chimney diagram

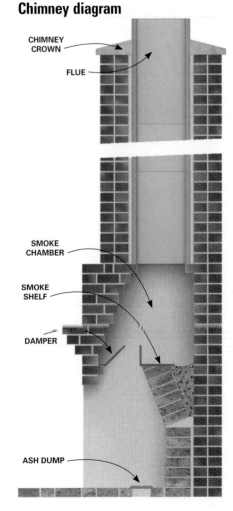

## The cleaning process

Start the vacuum and begin cleaning at the top of the chimney (Photo 5). Continue adding rods and moving down the chimney until you can't feel any more brush resistance. That means you've reached the smoke chamber and it's time to climb down from the roof and work from inside the firebox.

Peel back a small portion of the poly sheeting and use the long-handled brush to clean the smoke chamber. Use the noodle brush to remove all the soot from the smoke shelf. Then switch back to the long-handled brush to clean the sides of the firebox. Finish by vacuuming the entire firebox. Then fold up the poly sheeting and the canvas tarp and move them outside. Shake them out and reuse them the next time you clean the chimney.

# HomeCare&Repair

## REPAIR A CRANKY WINDOW

When a casement (crank-out) window is hard to open or close, people blame the operator (crank mechanism). It may have gone bad, but an operator usually doesn't fail on its own. Operator gears strip out when you crank too hard while trying to open or close a binding or stuck sash. If you just replace the operator without fixing the root cause of the binding, you'll be replacing it again—and soon.

We'll show you how to get to the bottom of most casement window problems and explain how to fix each one. The parts are fairly inexpensive, usually less than $50. But, as with many other home repair projects, you'll spend more time searching for the right parts than you will on making the repairs.

### First, the usual suspects

A sash can sag and bind in the frame from worn, dirty or corroded hinges; loose or stripped screws; or settling. Loose or stripped screws are the easiest to fix, and they're usually the most common cause of binding, so start there. If you have interior hinges (hinges located in the head and sill area and covered by the sash), open the sash all the way to expose the screws. Tighten each one. If the screw holes are stripped, you'll have to remove the sash first to fix them (**Photo 1**). Next, remove the hinge, enlarge the holes and refill them with toothpicks and epoxy filler (**Photo 2**). Then reinstall the hinge screws and sash and see if that solves the problem.

Next, check the condition of the hinges. It's much easier to spot wear if the hinge is clean and lubricated. So clean away dirt and grease buildup with household cleaner and then lubricate the hinges (**Photo 3**). Open and close the window and examine the hinge pivots (top and bottom) as they move. If you see "slop," replace the hinge. Exterior mounted hinges (common on windows from the '50s) are especially prone to corrosion and binding since they're constantly exposed to the elements. You can try lubricating them, but if the binding recurs, you'll have to replace them (see "Find Parts for Old Windows"). Remove the old screws (**Photo 4**). Then, following the hinge profile, slice through the old paint with a utility knife. Pry off the old hinge and install the new one.

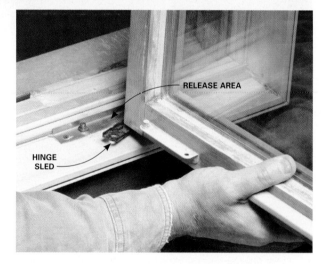

**RELEASE AREA**

**HINGE SLED**

**1** **Remove the sash.** Disconnect the operator arm and hinge arm locks from the sash while holding the window firmly. Then slide plastic hinge sleds toward the release area and lift the sash out of the frame. Tilt the sash sideways and bring it into the room.

If the hinges are in good shape, or you've replaced them and the sash still binds, the window frame has probably settled and is out of square. Resquaring the window frame is a big job. But you can try to fix the problem by relocating the hinges. To learn how to move a hinge, go to familyhandyman.com and search for "repair old windows."

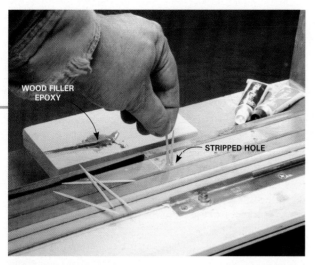

**2 Fill the stripped holes.** Mix a small batch of two-part epoxy wood filler and use a toothpick to spread it inside the enlarged hole. Then dip each of the toothpicks into the filler and jam them into the hole. Slice off the extended portions with a utility knife once the filler sets.

**3 Lubricate the hinges.** Saturate each hinge with silicone or dry Teflon spray lube. Wipe up the excess. Then work in the lube by opening and closing the window several times.

**4 Chip out the paint.** Tilt a flat-blade screwdriver at a 45-degree angle and hammer it along the slotted head to chip out the paint. Then slice through any remaining paint with a utility knife.

**5 Remove the operator trim.** Slide a flat bar under the sill operator trim piece and gently pry it up slightly on one end. Then move the flat bar to the opposite side and pry that up (see top photo, p. 174). Next, remove the operator screws and the operator.

## Finish by checking the operator

Now that the sash is opening and closing smoothly, turn your attention to the condition of the operator. First remove the sill operator cover trim (Photo 5). Then loosen the crank handle setscrew and remove the handle and operator cover. Reinstall the crank handle and rotate it while checking the condition of the gears. Look for gray dust or rough, chipped or missing teeth. Those are all signs the operator needs to be replaced. However, if the operator looks clean and moves smoothly, just tighten the screws, apply a dab of lithium grease to the gears, and reassemble all the trim. Now your window should be in tip-top shape.

### Find parts for old windows

You won't find these 1950s-era hinges (or other window parts) at many hardware stores, but they're available online. The new parts may not be an exact match for your old hardware, but they'll do the job and put your window back in the swing of things. Just measure the old parts, shoot digital photos of the top and bottom pieces (they may be different) and email the info to an online window parts seller (blainewindow.com is one very reputable source).

## WASH OFF UGLY ROOF STAINS

Black streaks on the north- and west-facing and shaded areas of your asphalt-shingled roof can really wreck the appearance of your home. The streaks look like mold, but they're actually algae colonies that form in your shingles and feed on moisture and the limestone filler agents in the shingles.

Using shingles that have been treated with algicide keeps the growth at bay for about 10 years (thus the 10-year algae warranty). But once the algicide wears off, your roof hosts an all-you-can-eat buffet for the neighborhood algae spores. As the algae eat away at the limestone, they dig into the asphalt and dislodge the light-reflecting granules. That's the beginning of the end of your roof. So it pays to clean your shingles as soon as you spot algae growth.

Professional roof cleaners charge $300 to $500, depending on the size of the roof. And they have to repeat the cleaning every few years. If your roof slope isn't too steep and you're comfortable working on it, you can clean it yourself and save the dough.

You'll need a full-body harness, a garden sprayer, a garden hose and a nontoxic, noncorrosive roof-cleaning chemical. Some manufacturers sell a special tool applicator and rinsing tool (about $300 for both). But if the staining isn't severe, you may not need them (see "Tools That Make the Job Easier"). Here's how to do it.

### Choose the right chemicals

If you search online, you'll see hundreds of posts on roof-cleaning methods. In less than 10 minutes, you'll sign off convinced that all you need is a few gallons of household bleach and a power washer set at its lowest setting.

We don't recommend that approach. Even at low pressure, a power washer can seriously damage shingles. Plus, chlorine bleach is a corrosive agent that can damage metal roof flashings, gutters and downspouts. It can lighten the color of your roof and "bleach" anything the overspray contacts. And the runoff harms plants. But here's the kicker. Bleach may kill the top layer of algae and lighten the stains, but it doesn't kill the underlying algae. So the algae colony gets right back to work.

Sodium hydroxide (lye) products, on the other hand, work better than bleach and are less harmful to vegetation. But they're also corrosive, and using them requires you to don full protective gear.

So look for a roof-cleaning product that's noncorrosive and safe for the environment. We chose Defy roof cleaner for this story ($30 per gallon; saversystems.com), but there are other brands.

### Choose the right day and prepare the area

Check the weather forecast and choose a cool or overcast day with little to no wind so the spray hits your shingles, not the neighbors'. Those conditions allow the cleaning solution to soak deep into the algae colonies without evaporating too quickly.

Next, repair any loose shingles or flashings, and clean the gutters and downspouts so they can drain freely.

Then prepare the area by moving lawn furniture and covering vegetation, because you're going to have overspray. Even though the product we chose isn't toxic, the runoff can be pretty ugly. So a little prep work will save you cleanup time later.

### Tools That Make the Job Easier

One manufacturer (saversystems.com) has taken roof cleaning to a new level and developed a special rinsing tool to dislodge dug-in algae colonies. The Roof Rinsing Tool is pricey ($170; find a dealer at saversystems.com) but far more effective than an ordinary garden spray nozzle. If your household water pressure isn't enough to generate the proper nozzle pressure at the jets, the manufacturer recommends boosting it with a supplemental 1/2-hp pump. (One choice is the Wayne PC4 transfer pump shown at right, which is about $130 at homedepot.com.)

If you really want to speed up the cleaning process and are willing to spend $140 more, buy the Defy Roof Cleaner Applicator (shown at left; find a dealer at saversystems.com). Simply pour in the concentrated cleaner. The special sprayer dilutes the cleaner as you spray, eliminating the need to continually pump and refill a traditional garden sprayer.

CLEANER APPLICATOR

PRESSURE-BOOSTING PUMP

**1 Soak the shingles.** Saturate a large area of shingles with the cleaner. Start at the bottom row and work up to the peak. Spray until you see runoff. Respray any areas that dry out.

HARNESS

TIE-DOWN

SPECIALIZED RINSING TOOL

**2 Blast off the crud.** Drag the rinsing tool in a forward-and-back motion as if you're vacuuming. That places the three water jets at the correct angle to blast off the dead algae colonies.

## The cleaning process

Mix the product with water for a 1:7 dilution ratio (a gallon covers about 700 to 900 sq. ft). Pour it into a pump sprayer, strap yourself into a full-body harness, tie it down and climb to the roof.

Before applying the cleaner, spray the roof with water to cool it down. That'll prevent the cleaner from drying out too quickly. Then spray the cleaner onto the shingles (**Photo 1**). Wait about 20 minutes, then rinse.

If the staining is fairly light, you can rinse off the cleaning solution with just a garden hose sprayer. But go slowly and use even strokes. If you don't, you'll wind up with clean patches that were rinsed properly alongside dirty patches that you skipped over too quickly. For severely stained roofs, a garden nozzle won't exert enough pressure to dislodge the stains. In that case, you'll want to invest in a specialized rinsing tool (**Photo 2**; also see "Tools That Make the Job Easier," p. 176).

## Prevent regrowth

Depending on weather conditions, you can expect algae regrowth in as little as one year. There are two ways to slow the regrowth process. One is to install zinc or copper strips along the entire ridge. Theoretically, rainwater picks up algae-killing ions and spreads them over the roof. In reality, the protection falls short because algae can still feed off humidity when it's not raining. But you don't have a lot to lose by trying it.

The second method is to spray on a coating of stain-blocking solution (Defy Stain Blocker for Roofs is one example). A stain-blocking product can buy you up to three years of protection from algae. If you decide to try it, apply it shortly after you've cleaned the roof.

Whether you install the metallic strips or apply the stain-blocking solutions, you're still going to experience algae regrowth sometime down the road. Get back up on your roof and clean it early, so the stains don't set in permanently.

# Home Care & Repair

## OUTSMART WOODPECKERS

Woodpeckers sometimes peck holes in a house to get to insects. But they also peck to attract mates and establish their territory. And once they find a good spot on your home, you'll have to act fast or you'll never get them to leave.

Start by covering all woodpecker holes with metal flashing or tin can lids (fix the actual damage later). Then hang shiny deterrents like Mylar strips, magnifying mirrors or pinwheels all around the repairs. If that doesn't work, cover the entire side of the house with plastic netting from a garden center. Once the woodpeckers leave, you can remove the netting.

**Fence them out**
Drape plastic netting from the gutters and angle it toward the house. Staple it to the siding. Then angle it to the ground, about 3 in. away from the house. Staple it to 2x4s on the ground. Wrap the edges toward the house to seal the entire area.

## FAST WINDOW SCREEN CLEANING

When it's time to switch out the window screens and storms each year, use a power washer to give the screens a thorough cleaning. It makes short work of even the grungiest screens. Just don't stand too close—too much pressure could damage your screens.

## GreatGoofs®

### Mother knows best

I needed help installing a metal roof on my high, steep roof, and my stepson begged to help. He needed the money and wanted the experience. His mother, the worrywart, agreed only after he promised to wear a safety harness. Since no one else was wearing one, I disagreed, thinking it was unnecessary. But she held firm, so I went ahead and bought one for him.

All was going well for a few days until I happened to walk around the corner of the house and saw him dangling off the edge of the roof. When he saw me, he screamed, "Don't tell Mom!" After a touch-and-go rescue, we finally could laugh about the ordeal. But we didn't tell his mother about it until after we finished the roof....

—Charles Oakes

# FAST, FLAWLESS VINYL SIDING

*Learn pro tips to speed up the process—
and get a better job*

by **Mark Petersen, Contributing Editor**

Vinyl has long been a popular choice for both new construction and re-siding projects, and for good reason: It costs much less than metal, brick, fiber cement, stucco or wood. It allows a house to breathe. It doesn't require painting. It's light and easy to work with. And installing vinyl siding doesn't require a whole bunch of expensive specialty tools. Here are some tips to help you keep the siding on your walls and the elements out of your house.

## Buy a vinyl siding blade

Pushing through vinyl siding with a wood blade in your circular saw will cause the siding to shatter, which is both frustrating and dangerous. Buy a blade made to cut vinyl siding. This one from Irwin cost about $10 at a home center. If you're using a sliding miter saw, and the siding is still chipping, try slowly pulling the saw backward through the siding.

## Nailing fundamentals

■ Use 2-in. galvanized roofing nails unless the sheathing has foam on it. Then you'll want longer ones.

■ Don't drive the nails tight: Each panel should be able to move back and forth or the siding will bubble on really hot days.

■ Hit every stud: Expansion and contraction of the siding will loosen nails that are fastened only to the sheathing.

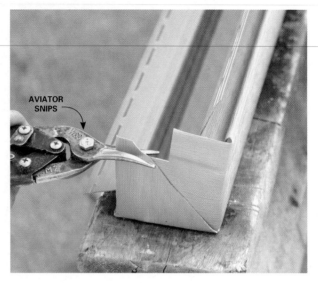

## Cap the corner posts

Mice, bees and all sorts of other critters love making their home inside vinyl corner posts. Keep these pests out by capping each post before you install it. Start by cutting off a few inches of the J-channel portion on the post. Fold back the remaining flaps and gently tap a crease into them with your hammer. Notch the flaps so the post will fit snug up against the wall. The posts will crack if they're not warm, so if it's cold outside, lay them in the sun or bring them into the house before you do this.

## Use the wider starter strip

The bottom of the starter strip (the part the bottom panel hooks on to) should be at least 1 in. below the top of the foundation, but the lower the siding is installed, the better. It protects the sheathing from rain, snow and pests. Most suppliers sell two sizes of starter, 2-1/2 in. and 3-1/2 in. Spend the extra few bucks on the wider stuff and start your siding a bit lower.

## Hide the seams

On the sides of the house, start each row at the back corner so you don't see the seams from the street. If the seams overlap away from the line of sight, they become nearly invisible. Lap them the other way and they'll be a real eyesore.

On the front and back of the house, overlap the seams so you don't see them from the areas where you spend the most time, like front doors, decks and patios. If the visibility of a seam doesn't matter at all, install the siding so the prevailing winds will blow over the seams, not into them.

## Pull up as you nail

Most vinyl siding failures are caused when panels unlock from each other. Once this happens, it's only a matter of time before the wind catches them and sends them flying into the neighbor's yard. I always apply a little upward pressure as I nail each piece; this keeps the panels locked together nice and tight. Don't "power-lift" each piece or you'll put too much pressure on the nailing flange, causing it to break.

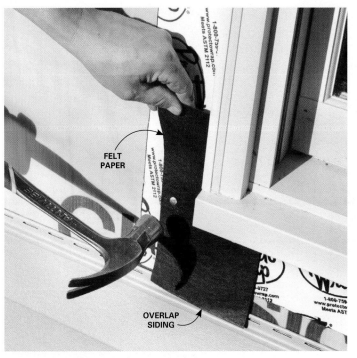

FELT PAPER

OVERLAP SIDING

## Flash the bottom of windows

Cut a piece of flashing out of felt paper and install it at the bottom corners of the windows before you install the side J-channels. Overlap the flashing onto the row of siding just below the window. Now, any water that runs inside the J-channels will come out on top of the siding and out the weep holes designed for this purpose.

## Install longer panels first

When installing siding on each side of a window or door, start on the side that needs the longer panels. Longer siding panels don't stretch as readily as smaller ones, so they're not as easy to adjust if they get out of whack. Before nailing the last couple of pieces on the small side, measure up to the top of the window to make sure both sides are at the same height.

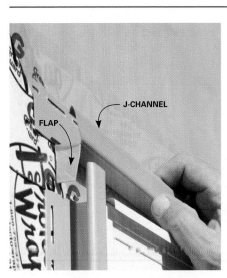

J-CHANNEL

FLAP

## Overlap your top J-channels!

There's no way to stop rainwater from getting into the J-channel that sits on the top of windows and doors. But you can stop that water from getting behind the side J-channels. Create a flap in the top J-channel that overlaps the side channels.

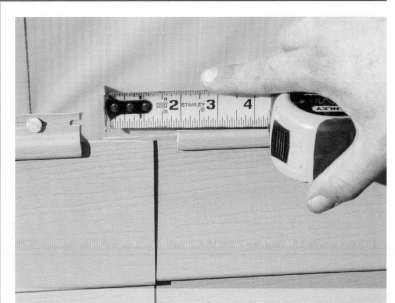

## Mind the overlaps

Always refer to the installation guide on the particular siding that you're installing, but most vinyl siding panels should overlap each other by at least an inch. I add 3/8 in. on hot days because the siding will contract when the temperature drops.

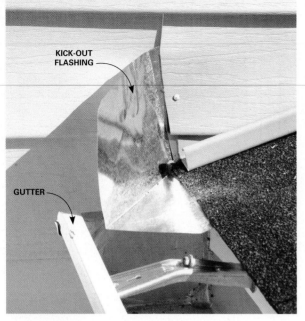

KICK-OUT FLASHING

GUTTER

## Install kick-out flashing

Kick-out flashing prevents water from running down a roof and ending up behind the siding on an adjacent wall. It can be a pain to side around it, but you will fail your inspection if the inspector doesn't see it on your job. Leave the kick-out flashing loose and slide the first panel behind the flashing. Then nail the flashing to the wall and lap the next piece over it. You may need a small trim nail to hold the siding seam tight (a little dab of caulk over the trim nail is a good idea).

## Don't trap water behind corners

Corner posts above the roofline are a notorious source of water infiltration. If a corner post is installed tight to the shingles and the J-channel dead-ends into it, any water that runs down the J-channel will back up at the post and may find its way into the house. Instead, hold the corner post up a bit and run the J-channel beneath it.

J-CHANNEL

CORNER POST

WATER ESCAPE

## Crimp and caulk the top course

Pay close attention to the area where the top row of siding meets the soffits. The most common approach here is to install sill trim at the soffits, rip down the top course of siding, and crimp the siding so the sill trim holds it in place. This works fine most of the time, but I always add a few blobs of caulking inside the bottom lip of the top course for extra security. You can crimp the siding using a Malco Snap Lock Punch, which costs $18 at Home Depot.

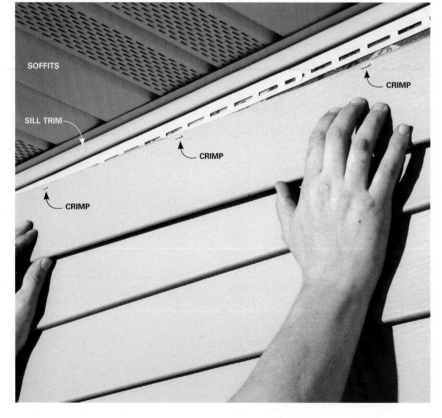

SOFFITS

SILL TRIM

CRIMP

CRIMP

CRIMP

# 9 EASY GUTTER FIXES

*Learn how to identify—and avoid—
the most common problems*

by **Mark Petersen, Contributing Editor**

Gutters can help keep a basement dry, prevent landscaping from washing away and add decades to the life of a foundation. But if they're not working correctly, they can be a major headache. This article is all about DIY solutions to the most common gutter problems. We built a little section of roof with gutters to make it easier to see what's going on.

## 1 Annoying drips
### The fix: Drop in a rope

Is the sound of dripping in your downspouts driving you mad? Eliminate the problem by tying a rope onto one of the gutter hangers and running it down into the downspout. Drops of water will cling to the rope instead of plummeting the whole length of the downspout and causing that loud dripping noise.

Adding a rope does restrict water flow, so this may not be the best option if your gutter is prone to overflowing or if your downspout is easily clogged with twigs and leaves. Buy a rope made of a synthetic like nylon—a rope made from natural fibers will rot away.

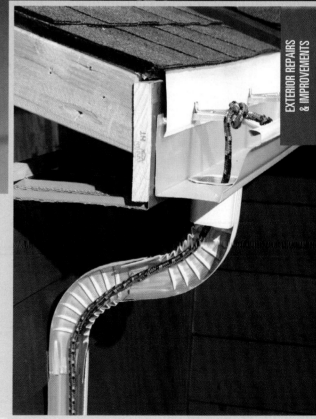

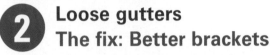
SCREW

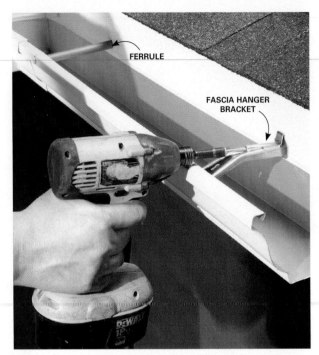
FERRULE

FASCIA HANGER BRACKET

## ② Loose gutters
## The fix: Better brackets

Years ago, spikes and ferrules were a common method for hanging gutters. They do the job all right, but eventually the spikes work themselves loose. Pounding them back in is a temporary fix at best.

One way to make sure your gutter doesn't fall off the house is to install fascia hanger brackets. Installation is simple: Just hook the bracket under the front lip of the gutter, and then screw the other side of the bracket to the fascia. Leave the old spikes in place—a spike head looks better than a hole in the gutter.

If your shingles overhang your fascia by a few inches or you have steel roofing, buy the brackets with the screws built in (the type shown here). They cost more, but the head of the screw remains a couple of inches away from the fascia, making them a lot easier to install.

## ③ Water gets behind the gutters
## The fix: Install new flashing

If water is dripping behind your gutter, it's probably because it was installed without any flashing over the back of the gutter. Gutter apron will prevent the dripping.

Gutter apron is a bent piece of flashing that tucks up under the shingles and over the gutter. Home centers sell 10-ft. sections for about $6. You may have to temporarily remove your hangers as you go, or you can notch out the apron around them. Once the apron's in place, fasten it with sheet metal screws.

If there's a drip edge installed where the fascia meets your shingles and the gutter is hung below the drip edge, get some roll flashing and tuck it up under the drip edge and over the top of the gutter. Home centers sell rolls of 6-in. x 10-ft. aluminum flashing for $6. Use a tin snips to cut the roll in two 3-in. strips. If your gutters are steel, buy steel roll flashing, because galvanized steel corrodes aluminum.

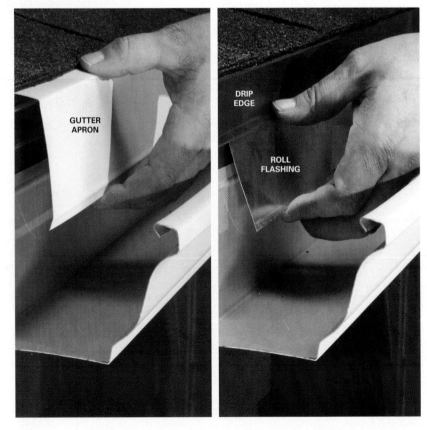
GUTTER APRON

DRIP EDGE

ROLL FLASHING

## 4 Water spills over gutter
## The fix: Add a diverter

Some roofs have long sections of valley that carry a lot of rainwater at high velocity. When that water comes blasting out the end of the valley, it can shoot right over the gutter. A diverter will help direct the water back into the gutter where it belongs. Fasten a diverter with a couple of sheet metal screws to the top of the outside edge of the gutter. A Gusher Guard three-pack sells for $8 at home centers and online.

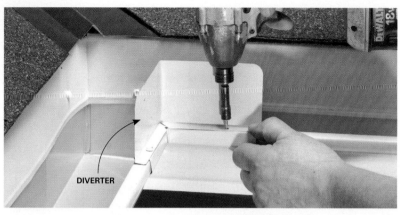

DIVERTER

## 5 Downspout in the way
## The fix: Add some hinges

Are you tired of removing your downspouts every time you mow? Consider installing a hinge where the lowest elbow meets the section of downspout that runs into your yard.

Installation is simple: Just cut the downspout at a 45-degree angle with a tin snips or metal-cutting blade and fasten the two-piece Zip Hinge (about $5) with eight sheet metal screws. The hinges come in white only, so you might have to spray-paint them to match. You can find a dealer at ziphinge.com.

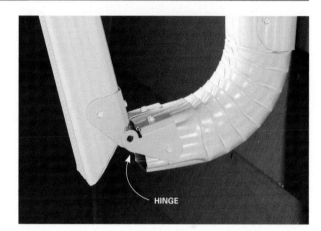

HINGE

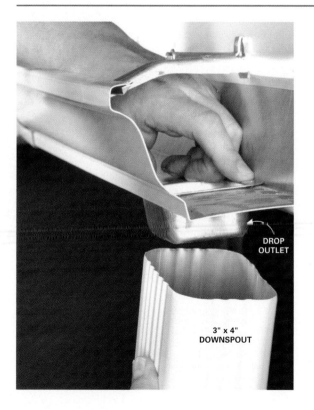

DROP
OUTLET

3" x 4"
DOWNSPOUT

## 6 Gutters overflow
## The fix: A larger downspout

If you have a 50-ft. gutter with one 2 x 3-in. downspout, your gutter probably overflows during heavier rainfalls. When installing an additional downspout isn't an option, install a 3 x 4-in. downspout in place of the smaller one.

Start by removing the old downspout. Use the new 3 x 4-in. drop outlet that you buy with your new downspout as a template to trace an outline for the larger hole. You can cut out the larger hole with a tin snips, or you could use an oscillating multi-tool equipped with a metal-cutting blade. Insert the drop outlet in the hole and fasten the new downspout with sheet metal screws. Make sure to seal the drop outlet to the gutter with seam sealer.

One downspout, one drop outlet, three elbows and two wall clips will cost about $40 at a home center. If you need a color other than white or brown, it will be a special order, but you should be able to get the color you need.

EXTERIOR REPAIRS & IMPROVEMENTS

## 7 No slip joint
## The fix: Make your own!

If a tree branch falls on the last 4 ft. of your 60-ft. seamless gutter, you don't need to replace the whole thing; just replace the damaged section. If your gutters are white or brown, adding a section of gutter to an existing section is easy. Most home centers sell white and brown sections of gutters as well as slip joints to tie them together.

If your gutters are a custom color, a home center can special-order your color but not the slip joint to match. But don't worry; you can make your own from a box miter, and box miters are available in every color gutters are made.

When you buy your new gutter section, make sure you order either an inside or outside box miter at the same time. Cut a 3-in. section from the box miter with a tin snips, and you've got yourself a custom slip joint. Hang the new gutter next to the old one, and then slide the patch under the seam. A box miter will cost about $9.

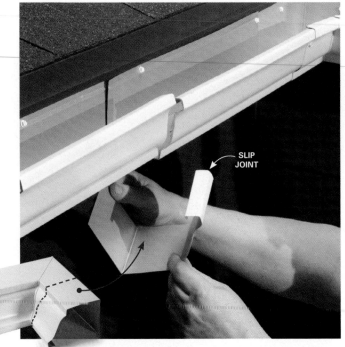

SLIP JOINT

## 8 Sidewalk in the way
## The fix: A rollout spout

There is no perfect way to get water from one side of a sidewalk (or other break in the landscape) to the other, but consider installing a retractable downspout. It rolls out when it rains and then rolls back up when the water stops flowing. Products like these do leak when the water flow is too light to extend the plastic downspout, but they should keep your landscaping from washing away during moderate to heavy rains.

Retractable downspouts are super easy to hook up, and for less than $10, they might be just the solution you're looking for. Pick one up at a home center or order online.

FROST KING

## 9 Leaky gutters
## The fix: Seal the seams

Every connection on a metal gutter needs to be sealed: end caps, splices, drop outlets and miters. Buy a product that's specifically formulated to seal gutter seams. Seam sealer can handle submersion for long periods of time. It's also resistant to light, which it will get plenty of.

Most important, high-quality seam sealer is runny, so it can penetrate down into the seam for a durable, long-lasting connection. Most products refer to this property as "self-leveling." And the runnier the better, so if you're applying it on a cold day, keep the seam sealer somewhere warm so it stays fluid.

Try to remove as much of the old sealer as you can, and make sure the area you're sealing is completely dry. Home centers usually stock seam sealer near the gutter parts. A tube costs about $6.

# Handy Hints®

**FROM OUR READERS**

## HOLIDAY LIGHT HANGERS

Instead of poking nails into aluminum soffits and fascia when you're hanging holiday lights, clip the wires to the bottom lip of the fascia with clothespins.

## HIGH-VISIBILITY BOUNDARY MARKER

Each year I mark the boundaries of my yard so the snowplow driver doesn't damage my lawn. For years I used rebar along the perimeter, but the driver couldn't see it at night. Even with reflectors on the rebar, it would still get hit, bent or broken. Now I've found a better solution. I slip a brightly colored swim noodle over the rebar. You can't miss the markers now.

—Bill Remia

## LIGHT SHROUD MADE OF PVC

My neighbor had a new septic system installed last year. The lift pump inside the tank has a brilliant red light on the top that lets him know the unit is working. But it was so bright that it was like having a harbor navigation buoy in the yard—it drove me crazy! So I got his permission to build a shroud from 3-in. plastic pipe. I cut out a little slot in the shroud, slipped on a cap and caulked it down over the light. Now he can see the beacon from his kitchen window, but the light doesn't bother me.

—Pete Simpson

READER PHOTO

EXTERIOR REPAIRS & IMPROVEMENTS

# HandyHints®

## EASY OUTSIDE LIGHT CONTROL

I love the cheerful glow of outside holiday lights, but going out in the cold to plug them in and unplug them is a pain. I use an outdoor remote control switch so I can control them from inside our home or car. You can buy these devices for about $15 at home centers or online. All you do is plug the switch into any outdoor outlet and use the small transmitter to control it.

—Elisa Bernick

PLUG-IN
RECEIVER

WIRELESS
REMOTE

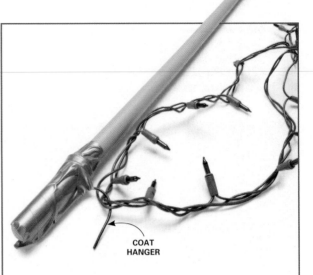

COAT
HANGER

## HOOK FOR TALL TREES

Putting up and taking down holiday lights in a tall outdoor tree can be tricky. The easiest method I've found is to use a paint roller extension pole with a hook on the end. You can use a wire coat hanger or other heavy-gauge wire. Just embed it in the pole threads, bend the wire up into a hook and secure it with duct tape to keep the hook from sliding around the pole.

—Jan Griesenbrock

## DEFUZZ YOUR WINDOW SCREENS

I live around a lot of cottonwood trees, and getting the "fuzz" off my window screens each year isn't a chore I look forward to. Removing it with either a shop vacuum or a power washer is slow-going and hard work.

Here's a faster, easier way: Use a lint roller. Just do a few swipes across the screen surface and the fuzz comes right off. It works on spider webs and other debris, too. To clean high screens without using a ladder, duct-tape the lint roller to a pole. Works great!

—David Lindeman

# TIPS FOR WORKING WITH PVC TRIM

## Treat it right and PVC will look good forever

by **Mark Petersen, Contributing Editor**

Trim made from PVC is even easier to work with than wood trim. No knots, no bowing, no cupping or warping. You can nail and screw right next to the edge without splitting it. And once two boards are glue-welded together, they're never coming apart! Sure, cutting PVC doesn't smell as nice as cutting cedar, but you'll never get a splinter, and you can all but forget about rotting.

Don't worry—there aren't any fancy tools or skills required to install it. If you've worked with wood trim before, you have the moxie to work with PVC. And if you install it correctly, it will still look perfect after decades.

## What's the deal with PVC trim?

The PVC (polyvinyl chloride) trim we're talking about is also referred to as cellular PVC. It's PVC all the way through. Don't confuse it with high-density rigid polyurethane or PVC-coated products. While they too are highly durable and low maintenance, their installation techniques are different. PVC is a form of plastic that's used in a hundred different ways, including for plumbing pipes.

The trim comes in various thicknesses and widths, but it's most often sold in common sizes similar to other wood trim products. Some companies offer material that has an embossed wood grain side and a smooth side. There are dozens of profiles to choose from: bead board, skirt board, tongue and groove, quarter round, brick molding, coves, crowns, just to name a few. You can even get it in sheets like plywood.

The home center near you might stock only 8-ft. boards in a few of the most popular widths, so you'll likely have to special-order longer lengths and the specialty profiles and moldings. The price is the biggest downside to PVC—it's expensive. We paid $23 for an 8-ft. 1x4. AZEK, Trex, Versatex, Fypon and CertainTeed are some of the more well-known brands out there. The profiles shown above are made by AZEK.

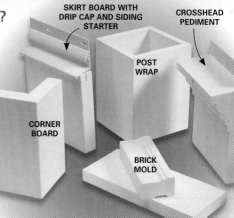

SKIRT BOARD WITH DRIP CAP AND SIDING STARTER

CROSSHEAD PEDIMENT

POST WRAP

CORNER BOARD

BRICK MOLD

### Cement the joints

One advantage of PVC is that you can "weld" joints to keep them tight and prevent water from penetrating behind the trim. Manufacturers recommend a special type of PVC cement that has a longer "open time" than the type of cement that plumbers use on plastic pipes. You can buy this cement wherever you buy the trim.

You'll have about five minutes of working time to clamp and fasten the joints before the cement sets. Smear a little cement on both surfaces and then clamp or screw the joint together. Wipe off any excess right away with a damp rag. Unlike PVC pipe cement, PVC trim cement is water soluble and won't melt finished surfaces if you remove it immediately.

### Work it like wood

You can cut PVC products with the same power tools that you use for wood. But use only carbide-tipped saw blades; plain steel ones dull quickly. In general, the more teeth a blade has, the smoother the cut edges will be. Combination saw blades work well. You can easily rout decorative edges or grooves with routers or shapers, but use carbide-edged bits.

Sawn edges won't have the same shiny finish as factory edges, so if you can, plan your work so that cut edges will be hidden, and let the smoother factory edge show wherever possible.

Sanding isn't always necessary, especially if you plan to paint, but if you have a rough-cut edge near a highly visible area, use a random orbital sander with 100-grit paper. Belt sanding doesn't work well because the friction from the belt melts the plastic rather than smoothing it.

*Moist air and condensation destroyed the window in my bathroom. I replaced the wood window with a vinyl one, and built the interior jambs out of PVC. The jambs still get wet after a long, hot shower, but now I don't have to worry about peeling paint or rotting wood.*

—Mark Petersen, Contributing Editor

Note: There may be some restrictions on the amount of PVC products you can install indoors. Some building codes allow only 10 percent of surfaces to be covered in PVC. PVC isn't a fire hazard, but the smoke it emits when exposed to flames is harmful to inhale.

### "Scarf" the joints

Where ends of trim meet, join them just like wood: Create "scarf joints," that is, overlapping 45-degree joints. Cut the first piece of trim to fall just past the center of a stud so the second, overlapping trim piece can be fastened to the center of the stud. And don't forget to apply cement to both pieces before securing them to the wall.

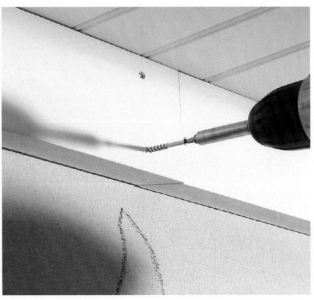

Preassembled trim

## Preassemble window and door trim

Prebuild your PVC trim as shown and then install it as a unit rather than one piece at a time as you would with wood. This will take a little longer but will result in perfectly tight joints. The cement forms super-strong joints. So if you can clamp the parts together, you don't need screws at all. But in most situations, screws are a lot faster and easier than clamping.

Pocket screws are the best method of joining corners when you're cementing window and door trim assemblies. Use the coarse-threaded version of pocket screws. Cut miters to fit and dry-fit your cuts to check the joints and lengths. Measure carefully when applying trim around vinyl- or aluminum-clad windows, and leave a 1/8-in. expansion gap between the trim and the window frame for caulk.

## Bend it to fit

One super-cool property of PVC is that it can be heated and then bent into any shape you can dream of. Once you figure out a system for heating the PVC, you'll find that trimming arched windows is a piece of cake—and kind of fun.

When heated to about 320 degrees F, the stuff turns into a wet noodle. Build a form out of plywood, and you can make consistent parts all day long. The heat blankets used by the guys who do a lot of bending are spendy ($1,000 to $3,000), but you could build your own out of a culvert and a torpedo heater. Azek has plans for heat-forming with this method. Visit azek.com and search "heat forming."

PLYWOOD FORM

PVC TRIM

HEAT BLANKET

## Leave expansion gaps

PVC trim expands when it's hot and contracts when it's cold. As a general rule of thumb, if you're installing trim in temps higher than 80 degrees F, go ahead and fit joints tightly. If it's between 60 and 80 degrees, leave a 1/16-in. gap for every 18 ft. of length. Below 60 degrees, leave a 1/8-in. gap. Some products expand more than others, so follow the instructions with the specific product you're working with to be sure you leave enough room. After installation, cover the gap with paintable acrylic or polyurethane caulk. Avoid silicone-based caulks—they don't adhere well to vinyl.

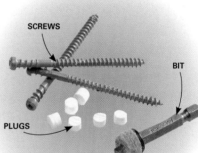

SCREWS

BIT

PLUGS

## Hidden fasteners

Cortex brand fasteners work great for unpainted trim. They come in a kit that includes a bit, plugs and screws. All you have to do is drill the screw through the trim (the bit will stop the screw once the desired depth is reached), and then tap the plug into the hole flush with the trim surface.

Be sure to order the screws that are designed for the type of trim you're working with; that way the plugs will be made of that exact same product. And if you're working with textured trim, align the grain on the screws with the grain on the trim. A kit of 100 costs about $30 at lumberyards and online retailers, and will secure 50 linear ft. of trim that's less than 10 in. wide.

## Use the proper fasteners

Don't scrimp by using fasteners that won't last as long as the trim. Stainless steel trim screws are the best choice because they'll never corrode. You can also use hot-dipped galvanized nails, but they may corrode over time.

PVC expands and contracts with temperature changes, so fasten it well. Fasten to framing, never just into the sheathing. Select fastener lengths that will penetrate the framing by at least 1-1/2 in. No predrilling or countersinking is necessary if the temperature is higher than 40 degrees F. But lower temperatures call for both drilling and countersinking; otherwise the PVC may split. Place fasteners every 16 in. at both edges of the trim, spacing them about 1/2 in. from the edges. If you're using 10-in. or wider trim, add another fastener in the middle; and 16-in.-wide trim needs four screws every 16 in.

> *The wood trim on my basement windows needed a fresh coat of paint every year. So I replaced the wood with PVC and painted it to match the existing trim. Eight years later, they still look good!*
>
> —Gary Wentz, Senior Editor

## If you decide to paint...

Although painting PVC trim isn't necessary, you may want to consider it, especially if you have a bunch of cut ends showing (some brands of PVC are protected from UV sunlight only on the outside). Edges that have been cut or routed could turn yellow over time. Cut edges also collect dust and aren't as easy to clean.

Before you paint, fill small holes with an exterior filler and lightly sand it smooth after it dries. Or use a paintable caulk and smooth it with your finger. Fill larger holes or damaged areas with auto body filler, and again, sand it after it cures. Finally, use mild detergent to clean off grime and oils left over from handling, and make sure the surfaces are dry.

Until recently, you could only use lighter paint colors, because darker colors absorbed more of the sun's heat and increased expansion of the PVC, causing the trim to warp and the paint to peel. Sherwin-Williams is one paint manufacturer that now offers a line of vinyl-safe paints. There are more than 100 color choices, light and dark.

## BIRDS FLYING INTO GLASS

*I've got a major problem with birds crashing into my windows. They're not breaking the glass, but they're killing themselves. I've tried all the usual techniques and nothing has worked. Help!*

Ordinary glass reflects sky and landscape, so birds think they're flying in open air when they hit your windows at full speed. If you're willing to replace the glass in your windows, check out Ornilux bird protection glass. The glass was tested by the American Bird Conservancy and shown to reduce bird strikes. It incorporates a coating that's clear to humans but looks like a patterned area to birds (see photo). For sizing, pricing and shipping information, contact glasswerks.com.

### Special glass reduces bird strikes

What you see · What birds see

# Store Anything

## DISCOVER
## HIDDEN STORAGE

*Look inside your walls for extra space!*

### by **Jeff Gorton, Associate Editor**

**In** almost every room of your house, you can find tons of storage space hidden between the two sheets of drywall. Simple stud-space cabinets like the two we show here are great for capturing some of this wasted space. We'll show you how to build them.

The basic shelf project is simple to build using common carpentry tools and a drill. We used a pocket hole jig, but this is optional. You can get excellent results by simply nailing the parts together. Even if you've never built a cabinet, you'll be able to finish the basic shelf project in a weekend.

The glass door cabinet is a bit more challenging and requires a few more tools. You'll need a table saw and a miter saw to make the precise cuts required. You'll also need a pocket hole kit to assemble the doors and a router with a 3/8-in. rabbeting bit ($14 to $32) to cut the recess for the glass. If you use concealed hinges like we did, you'll need a 35-mm Forstner bit ($13) to drill the hinge recess holes.

Basic version          Glass door version

# BASIC **BUILT-IN SHELVES**

### Cut the hole first

Before you buy materials, choose the location for your built-in cabinet and cut the hole. Then you can adjust the dimensions if your wall studs aren't exactly 14-1/2 in. apart. Remember, your walls are full of pipes, wires and ducts, so you need to do a little detective work to find a good spot. The plumbing wall of a bathroom is probably a bad choice. Look for heat and cold air registers that could indicate ducting, and outlets or switches that mean there's wiring in the stud space.

When you find a spot you like, use a stud finder to make sure the studs are at least 14-1/2 in. apart. Then cut a small access hole to inspect the stud space (**Photo 1**). If there are obstructions, at least you'll only have a small patch to make. If the area is clear, cut the hole (**Photo 2**). Now measure the distance between studs and subtract 1/2 in. to determine the width of the cabinet.

| What it takes |
| --- |
| **COST:** $60 |
| **TIME:** Four hours, not including painting |
| **SKILL LEVEL:** Beginner to intermediate |
| **TOOLS:** Saw, level, tape measure, drill, drill bits |

Measure from the surface of the wall covering—drywall or plaster—to the back of the opening and subtract 1/4 in. to determine the depth of your cabinet. If you have 2x4 walls with 1/2-in. drywall, you can build the cabinet box using standard 1x4 boards.

### Build the box

Cut the sides, top and bottom from 1x4 boards, or from whatever width boards you need. Then drill 1/4-in. holes for the shelf supports (**Photo 3**). Build a simple

**1** **Before you cut the big hole...** Cut a small inspection hole and use a compact mirror and flashlight to peek inside the wall. Look for pipes, wires or other obstructions.

MIRROR

STUD LOCATION

**2** **Cut the hole.** Draw level lines between the studs and use a drywall keyhole saw to cut to the edges of the studs. Then saw along the studs and remove the drywall.

STUD EDGE

**3** **Drill shelf support holes.** Construct a simple hole-boring template from a strip of pegboard with 1/4-in. holes. Center one of the pegboard holes on the line and clamp the template. Tighten a stop collar onto a 1/4-in. drill bit and drill holes for the shelf support pins.

**4** **Screw the sides to the top and bottom.** Drill clearance holes in the sides. Screw the sides to the top and bottom.

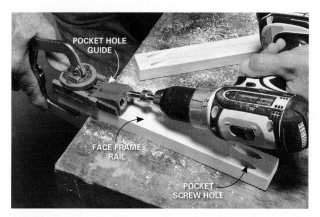

**5** **Drill pocket holes.** Clamp the pocket hole guide to the end of the face frame rail and drill holes with the special stepped drill bit.

**6** **Assemble the face frame.** Clamp the stile to the rail and drive pocket screws to secure the joint.

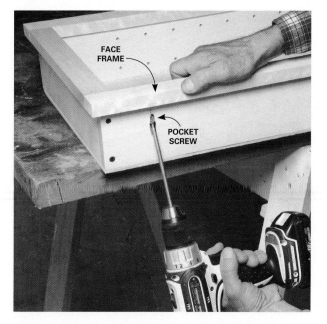

**7** **Attach the face frame to the box.** Drill pocket holes on the outsides of the cabinet box. Align the face frame and clamp it. Attach the face frame with pocket screws.

template from a strip of pegboard screwed to a strip of wood. Locate the center of a row of holes 3/4 in. from the edge of the wood strip. We chose to drill holes every 2 in.

Choose the spacing you prefer, and mark the holes accordingly so you don't get mixed up while you're drilling. Secure a stop collar to a 1/4-in. drill bit so that the shelf support holes are 3/8 in. deep. Set the two sides next to each other, lining up the ends, and draw a square line across the faces, 4-3/4 in. from the bottoms. Make an "X" to indicate the bottom of the sides so you don't get them reversed when you assemble the box. Then align the center of a pegboard hole with the line and clamp the jig before you drill the holes (**Photo 3**).

After you've drilled holes in both sides, assemble the box (**Photo 4**). Cut the plywood back to fit and nail it to the back of the box. Nail one side, then measure diagonally, or use a framing square to make sure the cabinet is square before you nail the remaining ends and side.

Cut the face frame parts, and assemble them with pocket screws (**Photos 5 and 6**). We built the face frame so that it overlaps the inside edge of the cabinet by 1/8 in. on all sides. Drill pocket holes in the cabinet sides

# Store Anything

and attach the face frame with pocket screws (**Photo 7**). If you don't own a pocket hole kit, simply nail the face frame parts to the cabinet with finish nails and fill the holes before you paint.

Cut the shelves to length after you've assembled the cabinet. Measure the distance between the sides and subtract 1/8 in. to determine the shelf length.

## Mount the cabinet

Slide the cabinet into the opening and use a level to make sure it's level and plumb (**Photo 8**). Drive screws through the cabinet sides, or simply drive nails through the face frame to secure the cabinet.

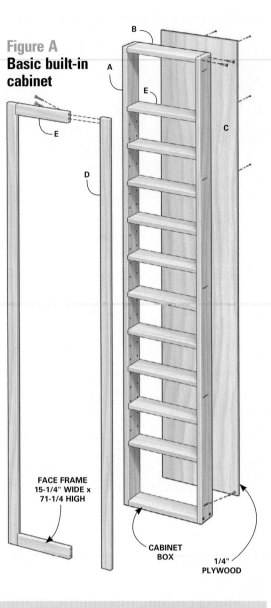

## Figure A
### Basic built-in cabinet

A
B
C
D
E

FACE FRAME
15-1/4" WIDE x
71-1/4 HIGH

CABINET
BOX

1/4"
PLYWOOD

**8** **Install the cabinet.** Level the cabinet and mount it by driving screws into the shelf support holes. Drive a pair of screws at the top and a pair at the bottom. Check for level and adjust by tightening or loosening opposing screws.

## MATERIALS LIST

| ITEM | QTY. |
|---|---|
| 1x2 x 8' paint or stain grade lumber | 2 |
| 1x4 x 8' paint or stain grade lumber | 3 |
| 2' x 8' x 1/4" plywood | 1 |
| **Hardware** | |
| 1/4" shelf supports | 40 |
| 1-1/2" wood screws | 12 |
| 1-1/4" pocket hole screws | 16 |
| Small package No. 16 x 1" wire nails | 1 |

## CUTTING LIST

| KEY | QTY. | SIZE & DESCRIPTION |
|---|---|---|
| A | 2 | 3/4" x 3-1/2" x 70" sides |
| B | 2 | 3/4" x 3-1/2" x 12-1/2" top and bottom |
| C | 1 | 1/4" x 14" x 70" plywood back |
| D | 2 | 3/4" x 1-1/2" x 71-1/4" face frame stiles |
| E | 2 | 3/4" x 1-1/2" x 12-1/4" face frame rails |
| F | 10 | 3/4" x 3-1/2" x 12-3/8" shelves |

# GLASS DOOR
## CABINET

The doors on this cabinet are inset into the face frame and require a precise fit, making this project more challenging than the basic cabinet. You should have some woodworking experience to tackle this project. But because the doors are assembled with simple pocket screw joints and the hinges are fully adjustable, you don't have to be a cabinetmaker. You just have to measure and cut accurately.

Including the glass shelves and frosted glass inserts ($150), hinges and other hardware ($75), and the paintable boards, this project cost us about $300. If you keep at it, you'll be able to complete the cabinet in a weekend. Then you can spend weeknights painting it and install it the next weekend.

This cabinet spans one wall stud to fill two stud spaces. To allow this, we joined two basic cabinets with a mull that's 2 in. wide by 1/2 in. thick. You have to remove the strip of drywall covering the center stud for this cabinet to fit.

### What it takes

**COST:** $300, including frosted glass

**TIME:** Eight to 10 hours, not including painting

**SKILL LEVEL:** Intermediate to advanced

**TOOLS:** Miter saw, table saw, drill, pocket hole kit

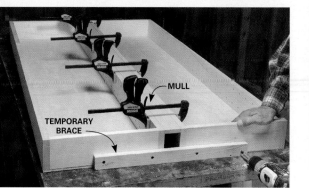

**1 Join the cabinet boxes.** Glue and clamp the 1/2-in.-thick mull between them. Screw temporary braces to the top and bottom to hold the cabinet steady until the face frame is installed.

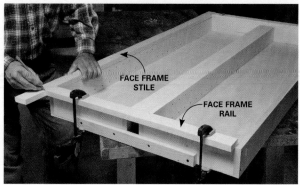

**2 Fit the face frame parts to the cabinet.** Cut the top and bottom rails to fit between the cabinet sides. Clamp them in place temporarily. Then mark the length of the stiles and cut them. Assemble the face frame with pocket screws.

# StoreAnything

DOOR STILES

**3** **Measure for the door rails.** Cut the four door stiles and stack them inside the face frame. Measure the remaining space and subtract 3/8 in. to determine the length of the door rails.

## Start with the basics

Follow the instructions for the basic shelf unit for cutting the holes in the drywall and building the two cabinet boxes. Then join the two boxes by gluing the 1/2-in.-thick mull between them (**Photo 1**). Screw scraps of boards to the top and bottom of the cabinets to hold them steady. Remove these temporary supports after the face frame is installed.

## Add the face frame

Unlike the basic cabinet above, the face frame for this cabinet must fit flush to the cabinet sides to accommodate the concealed hinges we're using. To make sure the face frame fits perfectly, cut the top and bottom rails to fit exactly between the sides of the cabinet. Align them with the inside edge of the box and clamp them temporarily. Then measure and cut the face frame stiles to fit (**Photo 2**). Now you can remove the face frame parts, drill pocket holes and join them with pocket hole screws. Keep the inside pocket holes at least 1/2 in. from the edge to avoid hitting them with the rabbeting bit when you rout the recess for the glass.

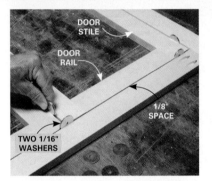

DOOR STILE
DOOR RAIL
1/8" SPACE
TWO 1/16" WASHERS

**4** **Check the fit before you assemble the doors.** Arrange the door parts inside the face frame and wedge them with pairs of 1/16-in.-thick washers. Adjust the lengths if needed. When the fit is good, remove the parts and assemble the doors with pocket screws.

ROUTING DIRECTION
3/8" RABBET

**5** **Rout the glass recess.** Mount a 3/8-in. rabbeting bit in a router. Make two or three passes in a clockwise direction, increasing the depth gradually, to create a 1/4-in.-deep rabbet.

## Build the doors

Inset doors are difficult because they have to be exactly the right size and perfectly flat. The trick to flat doors is to build them with straight and flat boards. Sight down the boards when you choose them at the lumberyard or home center to make sure they're flat and straight. Also, find lumber with straight grain if possible. The fewer knots and curvy grain patterns in the wood, the better it will be for doors.

The Materials List on p. 199 lists 1x6s. Cut 2-in.-wide strips from these on a table saw for the door parts. We cut our boards 1/16 in. oversize, stacked them alongside each other and ran them through our portable

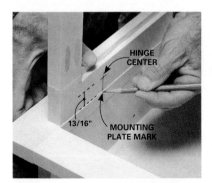

HINGE CENTER
13/16"
MOUNTING PLATE MARK

**6** **Mark for the hinge mounting plates.** Rest the edge of the door on the cabinet and center it. Then transfer the hinge center marks to the cabinet sides to indicate the center of the mounting plates.

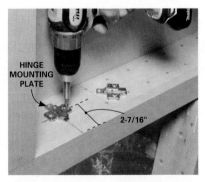

HINGE MOUNTING PLATE
2-7/16"

**7** **Attach the mounting plates.** After marking for the center of the screws, attach the mounting plates to the cabinet sides. Check the fit of the hinges and doors by clipping the hinges to the mounting plates.

planer to remove the saw marks. If you don't have a planer or jointer to dress the edges of the boards, just make sure to use a sharp saw blade when you rip the parts, and then sand off any saw marks after you assemble the doors.

Use the face frame as a guide for building the doors. First cut four door stiles 1/4 in. shorter than the inside dimension of the face frame. Stack them tightly together inside the face frame and measure the remaining width (**Photo 3**). Subtract 3/8 in. from this measurement and divide by two to determine the length of the four door rails. Cut the door rails. Then test-fit all the parts, using 1/8-in. spacer shims between the doors and the cabinet and between the pair of doors (**Photo 4**). Adjust the lengths if needed. Finally, join the rails and stiles with pocket screws.

The next step is to rout the recess for the glass. Mount a 3/8-in. rabbeting bit in your router and adjust the router to cut a rabbet about 3/16 in. deep. Rout the inside perimeter of each door, moving the router clockwise (**Photo 5**). Adjust the router to increase the cutting depth an additional 1/16 in. and make the final pass. Finish the rabbet by

## Figure B
### Glass door cabinet

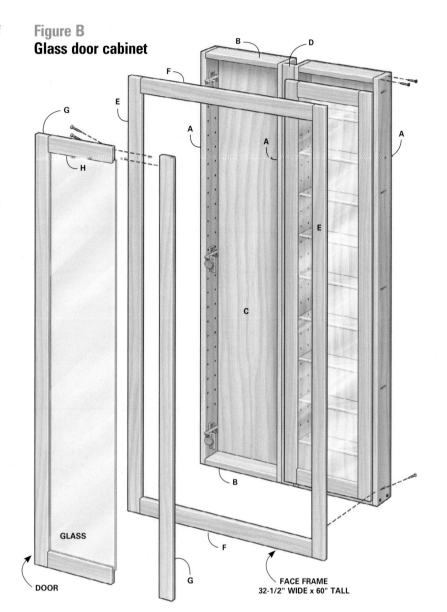

GLASS

DOOR

FACE FRAME
32-1/2" WIDE x 60" TALL

## MATERIALS LIST

| ITEM | QTY. |
|---|---|
| 1x4 x 12' paint- or stain-grade lumber | 2 |
| 1x6 x 10' paint- or stain-grade lumber (rip to 2") | 2 |
| 4' x 8' x 1/4" plywood | 1 |
| **Hardware** | |
| Blum 110-degree clip top hinge (71B3750)* | 6 |
| Blum hinge mounting plates (B175H710)* | 6 |
| 1/4" shelf supports | 72 |
| 5/16" clear door bumpers | 76 |
| 1-1/4" pocket hole screws | 40 |
| 1-1/2" wood screws | 16 |
| Small package No. 16 x 1" wire nails | 1 |

*Online source: Woodworker's Hardware, wwhardware.com*

**Glass**

| | |
|---|---|
| Glass for doors: Measure rabbet recess and subtract 1/8" (check local codes regarding the need for safety glass) | 2 |
| Glass shelves: Measure width and subtract 1/8" | 18 |

## CUTTING LIST

| KEY | QTY. | SIZE & DESCRIPTION |
|---|---|---|
| A | 4 | 3/4" x 3-1/2" x 57-1/2" sides |
| B | 4 | 3/4" x 3-1/2" x 12-1/2" tops and bottoms |
| C | 2 | 1/4" x 14" x 57-1/2" plywood backs |
| D | 1 | 1/2" x 1-1/2" x 57-1/2" mull |
| E | 2 | 3/4" x 2" x 60" face frame stiles* |
| F | 2 | 3/4" x 2" x 28-1/2" face frame rails* |
| G | 4 | 3/4" x 2" x 55-7/8" door stiles* |
| H | 4 | 3/4" x 2" x 10-1/16" door rails* |

*Cut to fit*

*You'll be surprised how much stuff fits in these shallow cabinets.*

# StoreAnything

squaring off the corners with a sharp chisel.

## Mount the doors

We used Blum 110-degree clip top hinges on the doors. These hinges provide three-way adjustments and have a built-in soft-close mechanism. You can save a few dollars by substituting a standard concealed hinge without the soft-close feature. This type of hinge requires a 35-mm recess in the door to accept the hinge, and a mounting plate on the cabinet.

Start by making three marks on the hinge side of each door to indicate the centers of the hinges. Mark the center of the door and 3-1/2 in. from the top and bottom. Then measure in 13/16 in. from the edge to mark the center of the 35-mm hinge bore. Use an awl or sharp nail to make a starting hole for the 35-mm Forstner bit. Before you drill the hinge recess holes, hold the door alongside the cabinet, center it so there's a 1/8-in. gap at each end, and transfer the hinge marks to the cabinet sides (**Photo 6**).

Next attach the hinge mounting plates to the cabinet (**Photo 7**). Draw a line 2-7/16 in. from the face of the cabinet to locate the hinge plate screws. Drill 35-mm x 1/2-in.-deep recesses in the doors with the Forstner bit at each hinge location (**Photo 8**). Practice on a scrap of wood first to gauge how deep to drill. Mount the hinges (**Photo 9**).

Test-fit the doors by clipping the hinges to the plates. You should be able to adjust the hinges until the doors fit perfectly. If not, you may have to plane or sand the door edges a bit. When you're happy with the fit, remove the hinges and plates so that you can paint the cabinet and doors before you install the glass panels and shelves.

**8** **Drill concealed-hinge mounting holes.** Mark the hinge hole locations. Use an awl or nail to make a starting point for the Forstner bit. Drill recesses for the hinges in both doors.

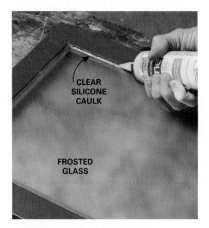

**10** **Install the glass.** After the paint dries, set the glass panels in the rabbet and apply a small, neat bead of clear silicone around the perimeter. Let the silicone cure overnight before mounting the doors.

## Install the glass and mount the cabinet

When the paint or other finish is completely dry, you can install the glass. Set the glass into the recess and apply a neat bead of clear silicone around the perimeter to hold it in place (**Photo 10**). Make sure to cut the tip of the caulk tube carefully to leave an opening about the size of a 6d finish nail. Let the caulk cure before you reinstall the doors. If you need to replace the glass, just slice

**9** **Mount the hinges on the doors.** Press the hinges into the 35-mm recesses and line them up so that the screw holes are parallel to the edge of the door. Attach the hinges with the screws provided.

**11** **Install the cabinet and shelves.** Set the cabinet in the wall and level it. Then attach it with screws driven into the shelf support holes. Finish the project by clipping the doors to the hinge plates and installing the glass shelves. Use the hinge adjusting screws to adjust the doors until the space between them and the cabinet is even.

the silicone bead with a utility knife.

Mount the cabinet in the wall (**Photo 11**). Then install the doors by clipping on the hinges. Finish by adjusting the hinges until the spaces between the doors and the cabinets are equal. Then install the glass shelves. We used nickel "spoon"-type shelf supports. To keep the shelves from slipping, we stuck clear polyurethane door bumpers to the top of each shelf support.

# STORING
# HOLIDAY ITEMS

*Ideas for specialty storage*

## by **TFH Staff and Readers**

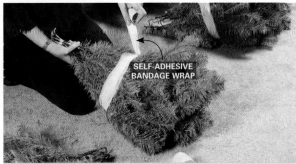

### SOFT TREE BINDING

When dismantling our artificial Christmas tree, we always used the ribbons it was originally packed with to tie up the boughs of each section. Last year, the ribbons finally wore out and we couldn't find a strong enough replacement. Instead, we came up with a terrific substitute—self-adhesive "bandage" wrap. The wrap is strong and reusable, it won't damage the tree and it's not very expensive.

—Ken Pereira

### KEEP YOUR LIGHTS IN BAGS

This has got to be the easiest way to store strings of holiday lights. Just put each string in a separate plastic bag and write where the lights go right on the bag. No wrapping or coiling necessary. It's in the bag!

—Peggy McDermott, Admin. Asst.

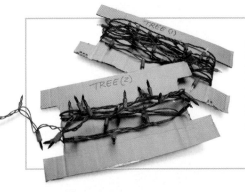

### SIMPLE STORAGE SPOOLS

Here's a great way to recycle cardboard and keep your strings of holiday lights from getting tangled when you store them. Just use strips of cardboard and cut out a slot on each end to make a "spool" to keep the lights from slipping off. Wrap each light string around a cardboard spool, label it and store it in a plastic bin for next year.

—Alice Garrett, Finance Manager

### HOLIDAY LIGHT STORAGE STANDS

We use dozens of holiday light strings each year, and storing that many without wrecking them is tough. But after trying a lot of different methods, I think I've come up with a winner. Just screw a dowel to each end of a wooden base cut to the size of a large plastic bin. Then wrap your lights around the dowels in a figure eight and place the stand in the bin. You'll be amazed how many light strings you can wrap around the stands without tangles or damage.

—Mary Schwender, Production Artist

# StoreAnything

# BIN TOWER

*Tons of easy-access storage—
and more space to hang stuff!*

### by **Mark Petersen, Contributing Editor**

I keep a lot of stuff in plastic storage bins. I had several stacks of them throughout my garage, and it seemed that every time I needed something, it was always in the bin at the bottom. So I decided to build myself a bin storage system to give me easy access to all my bins.

These bin towers are simple to build, don't require expensive tools, and actually add wall space without losing a lot of floor space. I designed the towers to fit 16- to 18-gallon bins with a lid size of about 18 x 24 in.

## Cut up the plywood

I used "BC" sanded pine plywood for this project. The holes and blemishes on the "B" side are filled and make for a good painting surface. It's not furniture grade, but it's priced right and works well for garage projects like this one. Rip all the sheets down to 23-3/4 in. If you don't own a table saw, use a straightedge and make your cuts with a circular saw (for more info, search "cut straight" at family-handyman.com).

Once all the sheets have been ripped down, cut the tops, bottoms and shelves to 18-in. lengths. If you're using a circular saw, save time by clamping two 8-ft. strips together, and cut two at a time. Some home centers will make your cuts for you, so if you don't have a ton of confidence in your cutting skills, ask the staff if they can help.

## Paint the parts before assembly

Finishing the cut components before you assemble them will save you a bunch of time, but before you start slathering on the paint, figure out which edges need to be painted—the back edges of the sides don't, and only the front edges of the shelves do. Configure all the parts so the best edge faces out. I marked an "X" with a pencil on all the edges that needed paint. Some of the edges will have voids in the wood that will need to be filled (**Photo 1**).

I applied a product called MH Ready patch ($6 per quart at home centers). It's easy to work with and dries fast, but it's not stainable, so you may want to find a more traditional wood filler if you plan to stain your project. Make a couple of passes with 100-grit sandpaper before you paint. I covered the wood with a paint/primer in one (**Photo 2**). If you choose a traditional wood primer, have the store tint it close to the final color.

**What it takes** (for three towers)

**COST:** $260 including paint and hardware

**TIME:** One weekend

**SKILL LEVEL:** Beginner to intermediate

**TOOLS:** Table saw/circular saw, drill, 18-gauge brad nailer (optional)

VOID

FRONT EDGE

**1 Fill plywood voids.** Figure out which edge will be exposed on each part, and fill any voids in the plywood. When the filler dries, sand the edge with 100-grit sandpaper.

## Assemble the towers

I used an 18-gauge brad nailer with 1-1/2-in. brads to quickly attach the shelves to the sides, three brads on each side. If you don't have a brad nailer, that's OK; you can assemble everything with screws only. I cut a piece of plywood 18-5/16 in. wide to align the shelves (**Photo 3**). The spacer board may scuff up the paint a little bit,

## Figure A  Bin tower

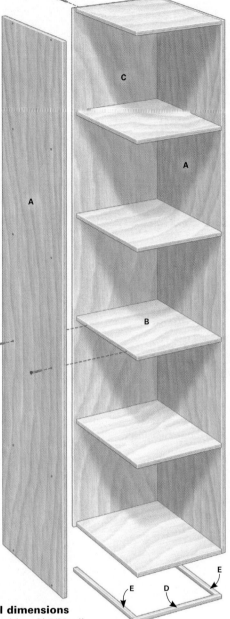

**Overall dimensions**
19-1/2" wide x 8′ 5/8" tall
x 24" deep

## MATERIALS LIST*

| ITEM | QTY. |
|---|---|
| 4' x 8' x 3/4" BC sanded plywood | 5 |
| 4' x 8' x 1/4" underlayment plywood | 2 |
| 4' x 4' x 1/4" underlayment plywood | 1 |
| 1x2 x 8' pressure-treated board | 1 |
| 1" 18-gauge brads | |
| 1-1/2" 18-gauge brads | |
| 2" trim head screws | |
| Can of wood filler or patching compound | |
| Gallon of paint/primer | |

*For three towers

## CUTTING LIST*

| KEY | QTY. | SIZE & DESCRIPTION |
|---|---|---|
| A | 6 | 23-3/4" x 96" x 3/4" BC sanded pine plywood (sides) |
| B | 18 | 18" x 23-3/4" x 3/4" BC sanded pine plywood (shelves) |
| C | 3 | 19-1/2" x 96" x 1/4" sanded pine plywood (backs) |
| D | 3 | 5/8" x 3/4" x 18-3/4" pressure-treated lumber (front bottom strip) |
| E | 6 | 5/8" x 3/4" x 22-7/8" pressure-treated lumber (side bottom strip) |

## Figure B
## Cutting diagrams for 3/4" plywood

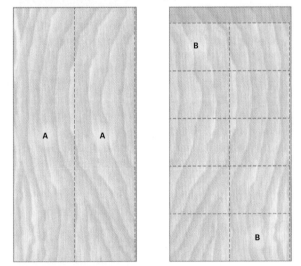

## Install the bottom strips

Plywood will eventually rot if it's sitting directly on a concrete floor. To avoid this, I ripped 5/8-in. strips from a 1x2 pressure-treated board and installed them on the bottom (**Photo 4**). Four square blocks would also keep the plywood off the floor, but I wanted to avoid any space where screws, washers or any other little objects could get lost. I inset the strips about 3/8 in. and nailed them on with 1-1/2-in. brads.

## Fasten the back

Use the 1/4-in. plywood to square up the unit (**Photo 4**). Fasten the two factory-cut edges of the plywood to the back first using 1-in. brads. Nail the short side, and then

but you can touch it up when you paint over your fastener holes after everything is all put together. Arrange the sides so the good surface faces out. The good surface on the bottom four shelves should face up, and the top two should face down. That way, you'll see the nicer finish from almost any angle.

After everything is nailed together, come back and install two 2-in. trim head screws into each shelf (use three if you're not using brads). Wood glue won't hold well because of the painted sides, so I was a bit concerned about the strength of the tower. To ease my mind, I built a small mock-up of one shelf using the same fastening pattern. I was able to jump up and down on it with no failure—and I'm not a little guy.

# StoreAnything

**2** **Finish before you assemble.** Save yourself a ton of time by painting or staining the individual components of this project before you assemble them.

PAINT AND PRIMER IN ONE

18-GAUGE BRAD NAILER

SPACER BOARD

**3** **Shoot, then screw.** Tack the shelves into position with a brad nailer. Then strengthen each connection with 2-in. trim head screws. A plywood spacer lets you position parts perfectly without measuring.

the long side, aligning the edges as you go. Don't install a whole bunch of brads until you know everything is square. Flip the piece over and check for square using a framing square or by measuring from inside corner to inside corner on a couple of different openings—if the measurements are the same, you should be good to go. Finish fastening the back with brads spaced every 8 in. or so, then reinforce it with one 2-in. trim head screw in the center of each shelf and five screws on each side.

## Screw it to the wall

In many garages, the concrete floor slopes toward the overhead door. That means you'll probably have to shim the bottom to get the bin tower to sit straight and tight up against the wall. I'm a big fan of composite shims: they don't compress as much as wood, they break off cleanly, and they won't ever rot. Set the first tower against the wall and shim the front until it sits tight against the wall. Use a level to check for plumb while you shim the low side. Insert at least four shims on the side and three on the front. Go back and snug up the front shims.

Once the tower is plumb, screw it to the wall studs with 2-in. screws. Make sure each tower is fastened to at least one stud. Since tipping is a concern, install a few screws near the top; you'll only need screws down low if you need to draw the tower tight to the wall.

BACK

PRESSURE-TREATED STRIPS

**4** **Use the back as a square.** Use the factory-cut edges of the plywood back to square up your project. Start on the top or bottom, and then work your way up the side. Check for square before finishing it off. Reinforce it all with screws.

Mark all the shims, and pull them out one at a time. Cut them down to size and replace them. I ran a small bead of clear silicone around the bottom of mine to hold the shims in place. If the towers ever get moved, the silicone will be easy to scrape off the floor. Finally, go get all sorts of caddies, hooks and hangers, and start organizing.

# 6 Outdoor Structures, Landscaping & Gardening

## IN THIS CHAPTER

# KILL YOUR CRABGRASS

*Season-long advice to spruce up your lawn*

by **Elisa Bernick**

**No** matter which state you live in, if you have a lawn, chances are you've battled crabgrass. The most effective way to control crabgrass is to use preemergent herbicides, but they work only if you use them right. Follow these tips from a turf pro and you'll be on your way to winning the war on crabgrass in your quest for the perfect lawn.

## 1 Fertilize your lawn and kill crabgrass at the same time

The most cost-effective way to apply a preemergent herbicide is to use a fertilizer with crabgrass preventer added to it. These combination products are readily available in the spring and cost about $20 for a 5,000-sq.-ft. bag at garden centers. Apply it when you would normally apply your first application of fertilizer, and do it just before it rains to work both the fertilizer and the herbicide into the soil. The fertilizer will help thicken the turf. Thicker turf helps to squeeze out crabgrass plants missed by the herbicide. Common brands include Ferti-Lome's Weed-Out, Sta-Green's Crab-Ex Plus and Scotts Turf Builder.

### MEET AN EXPERT

Field Editor Joe Churchill has spent 32 years working in lawn care. He is a store manager for Reinders Inc., a commercial turf distributor.

MIKE KRIVIT

## Check the key ingredient

There are many different trade names for "weed and feed" products on the market. Chemical names can be confusing. Look carefully at the ingredients panel for dithiopyr, prodiamine or pendimethalin. These active ingredients, which are sold under various brand names such as Dimension, Barricade and Scotts Halts, will kill crabgrass in most areas of the country and in many different kinds of turf. However, it's always wise to ask your local extension service which chemicals are best for your area and turf species.

## Don't skip a spring

Killing crabgrass this year doesn't mean you're off the hook next year. Crabgrass seeds can lie dormant in the soil for several years and will germinate once they make their way to the soil surface. Don't be lulled into a false sense of perfect turf. Make a habit every spring of applying a preemergent herbicide to prevent these seeds from getting established. And if your lawn is overtaken by crabgrass right now, applying a preemergent herbicide every spring will eventually wipe it out and prevent those seeds from germinating in the future.

## Time your application by watching your shrubs

Crabgrass germinates when soil temps reach 55 to 60 degrees F, which could be as early as February or as late as May depending on where you live. Applying your preemergent herbicide at the right time is critical because it works by killing germinated crabgrass seeds before they sprout. If you apply it too early, it will lose its potency before the crabgrass sprouts. If you apply it too late, it won't do any good. In the North, a good rule of thumb is to apply preemergent herbicide when lilacs or forsythia is blooming; in the South, when dogwoods are blooming. You can also buy an inexpensive soil thermometer ($15 at garden centers) to monitor soil temperature.

GETTY IMAGES

## Spot-kill crabgrass that comes up

To kill crabgrass that appears later in the summer, spot-spray infested areas with a post-emergent herbicide designed specifically to kill crabgrass and other annual grass weeds—quinclorac is the most common active ingredient. Typical broadleaf herbicides, like the ones that kill dandelions and clover, will not take out crabgrass. The best time to start spot-spraying for crabgrass is when the plants are mature, usually in early to mid-July.

MIKE KRIVIT

## 7 Two applications are better than one

Most preemergent herbicides are designed to provide weed control for about eight to ten weeks. But during unusually hot summers, they don't last that long because warmer soil temperatures degrade them. This makes your lawn vulnerable to crabgrass again by midsummer. To prevent this, use a lawn fertilizer that contains a preemergent herbicide during your second lawn feeding as well as the first. This will extend your crabgrass control into early fall and prevent crabgrass from sneaking back into your lawn during late summer.

## 6 Keep your lawn healthy

A weak, poorly cared-for lawn is an open invitation to crabgrass and other weeds. The best way to stop crabgrass is to shade it out with a dense, healthy lawn. The key to maintaining a healthy lawn is proper watering, mowing, fertilizing, core aerating, top-dressing with compost and reseeding thin spots. For detailed step-by-step instructions on all these topics, visit familyhandyman.com and search for "lawn care."

## 8 Reseed or kill—not both

Herbicides that kill crabgrass will also kill desirable grasses such as bluegrass, ryegrass and fescue. If you treat your lawn with a preemergent, you cannot seed. And if you seed, you cannot use a preemergent herbicide. The solution is to control crabgrass in the spring and do your seeding in late summer or early fall, making sure to keep these two chores at least eight weeks apart. There are a few preemergent herbicides, such as Tupersan, that are compatible with newly established seed, but they're expensive and can be hard to find.

## 9 Apply a double dose near hot spots

Lawn near driveways, sidewalks and curbs or on south-facing banks absorbs a lot of heat during the summer months, which makes it more susceptible to crabgrass. Limit crabgrass growth in these areas by doing a targeted double treatment. After you've treated your entire lawn, go back and make another pass, about 6 to 8 ft. wide, along these areas (and make sure to sweep it off hard surfaces afterward). This will help keep crabgrass from taking hold along these heat absorbers.

**Know when to throw in the towel**

Sometimes a lawn becomes so overrun by crabgrass and other weeds that it makes more sense to start over rather than try to save it. If weeds occupy more than 50 percent of an area, it's best to start over by destroying the entire lawn and reseeding or sodding. Late summer or early fall is the best time of year to take on this project. For step-by-step instructions on how to start a lawn from scratch, visit familyhandyman.com and search for "seed a lawn."

## Consider chemical-free control methods

Preemergent herbicides are the most effective and economical way to control crabgrass. But if you'd rather not use herbicides, you can try hand-weeding individual crabgrass plants in late spring before they get too big. They pull easily in soft ground after a rain.

Corn gluten meal (CGM), a corn byproduct, is another method used to control both crabgrass and broadleaf weeds such as dandelions and clover. It releases a protein that slows the development of weed seedling roots. CGM requires a heavy application rate (20 lbs. per 1,000 sq. ft.), which makes it cumbersome to use and expensive. It costs about $30 for 25 lbs. at garden centers.

# GreatGoofs

## Tree-branch blunder

After a windstorm, I decided to pull down a broken limb hanging from one of our trees. As I pulled on it, I realized it was larger than I'd thought, but I figured I was well away from where it would fall. Unfortunately, as the limb came down it hit another branch, rolled and landed square on the middle of my head. I'm actually amazed that I wasn't knocked unconscious, because it felt like I'd been hit in the head with a baseball bat. The five minutes it would have taken to get my hard hat (yeah, I actually have one) is a lot less than the time it took to get to the emergency room.

—Mike Murdock, Field Editor

OUTDOOR STRUCTURES, LANDSCAPING & GARDENING

# DREAM SHED MADE EASY

*Build this masterpiece designed by a pro*

by **Jeff Gorton, Associate Editor**

**In** the past couple of decades, I've built a lot of garages and sheds, and at least a half dozen have appeared in this magazine. In that time I've learned how to build sheds quicker and better, and how to make a plain shed look great without spending an arm and a leg.

This shed incorporates many of the building methods I've learned. It includes special features like custom brackets and homemade windows and doors, which set the shed apart from kits you'll find at the home center. And the best part is that you can build this shed knowing that I've worked out the kinks.

## What it takes

**COST:** $3,000

**TIME:** Three or four weekends

**SKILL LEVEL:** Intermediate to advanced

**TOOLS:** Standard hand tools, a circular saw and a drill. Nice but not necessary: table saw, miter saw, nail gun and jigsaw.

## Start with a simple shed, then add...

**Frame-and-panel doors**
We made these doors on-site, but they rival expensive factory-made doors in looks and durability.

**Handcrafted brackets**
Building brackets is the easiest part of this project, but they make a huge impact on the look of the shed.

**Lots of trim**
We used LP Smartside trim and siding. The trim costs much less than knot-free wood, so you can add lots of it without blowing your budget.

**Planter boxes**
These planters are just wooden boxes with simple brackets underneath. But they're the perfect finishing touch.

**Custom windows**
Inexpensive barn sashes are the key to making your own windows. Add decorative trim to complete the custom look.

**1** **Level the sleepers.** Set treated 6x6 sleepers on level beds of gravel. Tamp down the sleepers to level them.

TREATED 6x6

6x6 BEAM

TREATED RIM JOIST

**2** **Square the rim joists.** Nail the rim joists together. Make sure diagonal measurements are equal. Then nail or screw the joists to the beams.

## Money, time and tools

You'll find most of the materials to build this shed at home centers or lumberyards. You may have to special-order the LP SmartSide trim. We found the barn sash at a local home center, but if you're not so lucky, go to combinationdoor.com to find a retailer near you. The materials for this shed cost us $3,000.

To build this shed, you'll need standard carpentry tools including a circular saw and drill. A framing nail gun and compressor will speed up the framing. And a power miter saw and table saw would save you time and help you get perfect cuts on the trim pieces. But they aren't necessary. You'll also need a pocket screw jig to build doors like ours.

If you've built a deck or have some carpentry experience, you shouldn't have any trouble building this shed. With a few helpers, you should be able to get the foundation and floor built in a day. The next day you can build the trusses and get a start on the walls. Round up a few strong friends when it's time to stand the walls. If you keep at it, you'll be able to finish building the shed in three or four weekends.

## Getting started

In most areas, sheds 120 sq. ft. or smaller do not require a permit to build, but check with your local building department to be sure. Also ask if there are rules about where your shed can be located on the lot.

Print out the Materials List (you'll find it online at familyhandyman.com/2013shed) and bring it to your favorite lumberyard or home center and go over the list with the salesperson to see what items you may have to order. Then set up a delivery so you'll be ready to build when your help arrives. A few days before you plan to dig, call 811 for instructions on how to locate buried utility lines.

**3** **Complete the floor.** Add the rest of the joists. Then nail treated plywood to the joists, staggering the seams.

TOP OF RAFTERS

**4** **Mark the truss pattern on the shed floor.** Snap chalk lines to make a template for the trusses (see Figure C for details). Screw 2x4 blocks to the floor to complete the pattern.

Here are some of the features that make this shed easy to build, affordable and long lasting:

■ The floor rests on a foundation of treated 6x6s and gravel. It's cheap and simple.

■ Walls are prebuilt on the floor and covered with siding while they're still lying down.

■ The roof is framed with homemade trusses that you also assemble right on the shed floor.

■ The siding and trim are long-lasting composite material that comes pre-primed and ready to paint.

■ Doors and windows are handmade to save money and provide a custom look.

For detailed drawings on framing, siding and trim as well as window and door construction, go to familyhandyman.com/2013shed

**MEET AN EXPERT**

Before starting work at the magazine, Jeff spent more than 15 years as a remodeling contractor building additions and garages and doing whole-house renovations as well as kitchen and bathroom remodeling. He used knowledge gained from this experience to design and build the shed you see here.

## Figure A    Shed

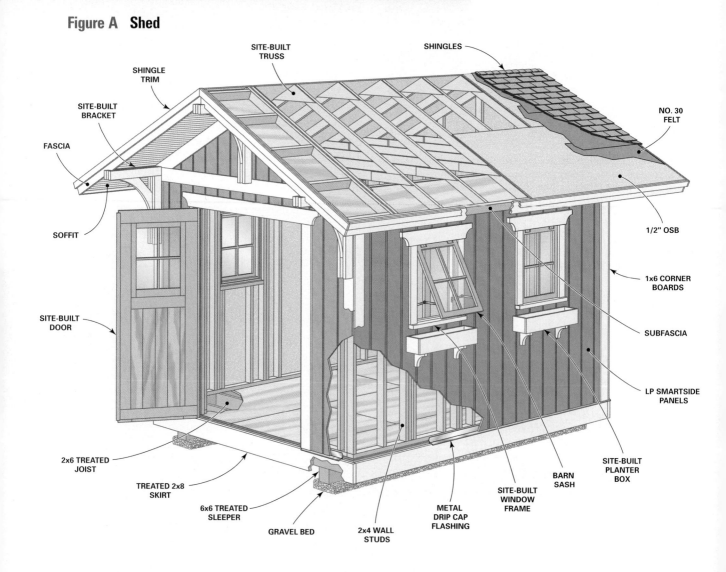

SITE-BUILT TRUSS

SHINGLES

SHINGLE TRIM

SITE-BUILT BRACKET

FASCIA

SOFFIT

NO. 30 FELT

1/2" OSB

1x6 CORNER BOARDS

SUBFASCIA

SITE-BUILT DOOR

LP SMARTSIDE PANELS

2x6 TREATED JOIST

TREATED 2x8 SKIRT

6x6 TREATED SLEEPER

GRAVEL BED

2x4 WALL STUDS

METAL DRIP CAP FLASHING

SITE-BUILT WINDOW FRAME

BARN SASH

SITE-BUILT PLANTER BOX

RAFTER

BOTTOM CHORD

GUSSETS    BLOCK

REGULAR STUD

WINDOW TRIMMER

**5** **Build the trusses.** Join the rafters and chords with gussets cut from plywood or OSB. Fasten the gussets with screws and glue.

**6** **Mark the wall framing.** Cut the 2x4 plates and set them in place on the floor. Mark the position of studs, windows and doors according to the plan.

## Build the floor

We chose to build the shed on a wood floor supported by treated 6x6s, but you could also pour a concrete foundation or choose a different method of supporting the joists.

Start by laying out the perimeter of the shed, either with stakes and a string line, or with a rectangle built with 2x4s to represent the outside edges of the 10 x 12-ft. floor. Now measure in 14-3/4 in. from the long sides and drive stakes to mark the center of the trenches. Dig trenches about 12 in. wide and about 10 in. below where you want the bottom edge of the joists to end up. Pour 4 in. of gravel into the trenches and level it off. Make sure the gravel in both trenches is at the same level. Then cut the 6x6s to 12 ft. long and set them in the trenches. Measure to make sure the 6x6s are parallel. Then measure diagonally from the ends to make sure they're square. The diagonal measurements should be equal. Finally, tamp the 6x6s with a sledge to level them (**Photo 1**).

Now you're ready to build the floor. Start by cutting the 12-ft.-long rim joists for the sides and marking the joist locations 16 in. on center. Assemble the perimeter frame on top of the 6x6s (**Photo 2**, p. 211, and **Figure B** online). Then fill in the remaining joists. When you're done, use a taut string line or sight down the 12-ft. rim joist to make sure it's straight. Then drive toenails through the joists into the 6x6s. Finish up by nailing the 3/4-in. treated plywood to the joists (**Photo 3**).

## Assemble the trusses

The shed floor makes a perfect work surface for building the trusses. Use the dimensions from **Figure C** online to lay out the truss pattern and cut the rafters (**Photo 4**, p. 211). Screw 2x4 blocks to the plywood along the top line to hold

the rafters in place while you connect them with the OSB (oriented strand board) gussets (**Photo 5**). Build five regular trusses and two gable end trusses. Remember to cut eight additional rafters to use for the gable-end overhangs. Take your time building the trusses to make sure they're all identical.

## Stand the walls

Building and siding the walls while they're lying on the floor saves time and ensures that the walls are perfectly square. But it does require you to move heavy walls around. If you don't have help, then leave the siding off until after the walls are standing.

Start by chalking lines on the floor to indicate the inside edges of the walls. These lines provide a reference for straightening the bottom plate of the walls after the walls

ALIGN PLATE WITH CHALK LINE

**7** **Build the walls.** Arrange the studs, trimmers, cripples and headers between the top and bottom plates. Line them up with your layout marks and nail through the plates to assemble the wall.

**8** **Stand and brace the side walls.** Lift the side walls and support them with temporary braces. Align the bottom plates with the chalk lines and nail the plates to the floor joists. Next, lift the front and back walls into place.

**9** **Set the trusses.** Screw a brace to the back wall to support the back truss. Set the front and back trusses. Then stretch a string between the peaks and nail on a truss brace with layout marks to align the remaining trusses. Toenail them to the top plate.

are standing. Cut bottom plates from treated 2x4s and top plates from untreated lumber. Arrange the plates along the chalk lines and mark them (**Photo 6**, and **Figures D and E** online).

Build the front and back walls first. Before you install the siding, align the bottom plate with the chalk line and tack it with a few 8d nails or screws to hold it straight. Then adjust the top plate until diagonal measurements from the corners of the walls are equal and tack the top corners to the floor to hold the wall square. Position the sheets of siding so the bottom edge extends 1 in. beyond the bottom plate and nail it to the studs with 6d galvanized siding nails. Set the front and back walls aside. Then build and stand the side walls (**Photos 7 and 8**).

Finish the wall framing by nailing the corners together and adding a second top plate. Tie the walls together by overlapping the second top plate onto the adjacent wall.

## Set the trusses

There are a few setup steps to take before you're ready to set trusses. Start by marking the truss positions on the top plates of the side walls. Then screw a long 2x4 to the center of the end wall so that it extends high enough to support the end truss (**Photo 9**). Lift the end truss onto the walls and center it so there's an equal amount of overhang on both sides. Then nail it to the plate and screw it to the temporary brace.

Next, mark the truss layout, including the overhangs, on a 16-ft.-long 2x4 to use near the top as a temporary brace. This brace will run parallel to the side walls and close to the ridge. Using this brace as support, set the truss on the other end, once again making sure it's centered. The final setup step is to stretch a string line between the peaks of the end trusses. You'll use this line

as a reference to center the remaining trusses. Elevate the line slightly so it clears the trusses.

Now you're ready to set trusses. Just lift them up, line them up with your marks, and make sure the peak is aligned with the string line. Toenail the trusses to the plates on the bottom, and support the tops temporarily by driving nails or screws through the long 2x4 brace near the peak (**Photo 9**). You can remove the brace after you've installed most of the roof sheathing.

## Add the overhangs

With the trusses done, you can complete the siding on the gable ends. Then finish the roof framing. Start by nailing 2x4 subfascia to the rafter ends. The subfascia should extend 2 ft. on both ends. Sight down the subfascia to make sure it's straight. Correct any waviness by driving shims between the rafter ends and subfascia. Next build the "ladders" that will form the front and back overhangs. **Photo 10** shows how to install them. Then install the roof sheathing (**Photo 11**). Cover the sheathing with roofing paper as soon as you finish the fascia boards. Then if you don't install your shingles right away, you won't have to worry about your shed getting wet.

## Finish the soffits and trim

We used beaded plywood for the soffits to simulate beaded-board soffits. To keep the grooves running the same direction, parallel to the sides, cut the soffit pieces for the front and back overhangs across the 4-ft. dimension of the plywood. Remember, the soffit doesn't have to fit tight to the siding. This edge will be covered by 3/4-in.-thick trim.

After the soffit is complete, install the 1x6 trim boards that fit under the soffit on the sides, and run horizontally across the front and back. Then cut the angled trim pieces

**10** **Add the overhangs.** Build the gable-end overhangs. Line the tops up with the roof framing and nail the overhangs to the wall and subfascia.

"LADDER"

SUBFASCIA

**11** **Sheathe the roof.** Nail OSB to the rafters. Stagger the seams by starting with a half sheet on the second row.

**12** **Install the trim.** Cut trim to fit under the soffits and across the front and back. Then install the corner boards and the trim under the front and back overhangs.

CORNER BOARDS

**13** **Build the brackets.** Screw the parts together, sand-wiching the curved brace between the 2x4s. Sand and paint all the parts before assembly.

for the front and back, and finally install the 1x6 corners. We ripped one of the corner boards down to 4-3/4 in. wide and overlapped the 1x6 for the opposite side onto it. This creates a corner that's 5-1/2 in. wide on both sides.

## Build and install the brackets

The shed has three decorative brackets on the front. They're assembled from a 2x10 sandwiched between 2x4s. Using **Figure L** online as a guide, cut the 2x10 and draw the curve on it. Use a 1x2 with two holes drilled in it as a giant compass to draw the curve. Cut the curve with a jig-saw and sand it. Paint all of the parts before you assemble the brackets to save time and provide better protection.

Connect the L-shaped 2x4 sections with 5-in.-long con-struction screws. Then complete the brackets by screwing the parts together (**Photo 13**). **Photo 14** shows how to mount the brackets.

## Assemble the windows

We used inexpensive barn sash for the windows. You could also use sash salvaged from an old double-hung window. But if you do, plan ahead so you can adjust the size of the rough openings when you build the walls. Start by measuring the sash and building a 1x4 frame that's 1/4 in. wider and taller than the sash. Cut 1x2 stops to fit in the frame and position them to hold the sash flush with one edge of the 1x4 frame. Then attach galvanized screen door hinges to the frame, set the sash in place, and screw the hinges to it (**Photo 15**).

Start the window trim by cutting curves on the ends of the 1-in.-thick top casing (**Figure M**, online) and nailing it to the top of the window. Leave 1/4 in. of the 1x4 frame exposed. Next cut the 1x4 side casings with 10-degree bevels on the bottoms. Nail them to the frame. Finish by cutting out the sill with 10-degree bevels on the front

**14** **Mount the brackets.** Screw 2x2 cleats to the shed wall. Then slip the brackets over the cleats and drive screws through the brackets into the cleats to secure them.

**15** **Mount the sash in the frame.** Build a 1x4 frame and mount the barn sash to it with galvanized screen door hinges.

**16** **Install the windows.** Set the window into the opening. Center it and nail the top corners of the trim. Adjust the frame until there's an even gap around the barn sash and nail the bottom corners. Add a few more nails on the side and top.

**17** **Build the door frames.** Spread waterproof wood glue. Then drive screws though the back frame into the front frame.

and back and screwing it to the side casings. We added Stanley Storm Window Adjuster hardware to the windows to hold them open and as locks.

Installing the windows is simple. Just set them in the opening, making sure they're centered, and nail through the trim to hold them in place. Start by nailing the two top corners. Then adjust the window frame as necessary to create an even space around the sash before nailing the bottom two corners (**Photo 16**).

## Build and install the doors

These doors look great, and to buy similar factory-made

wood doors would cost a fortune. You can easily make them using the system we show here. Choose the straightest boards you can find for this project. You don't want a warped door!

Start by making the front and back layers (**Figure N**, online). You'll need a pocket hole jig for this. You can buy a pocket hole jig at home centers or online. Go to familyhandyman.com and enter "pocket screw" in the search box for information on how to use the jig.

Glue and screw the two layers together to make the door (**Photo 17**). The front panel should extend 1-1/4 in. beyond the back panel on the bottom. This will create a

**18** **Add the sash and door panel.** Cut 1x6 tongue-and-groove boards to fit the opening below the window. Attach them with one screw in the center of each board. Mount the barn sash with one screw in each corner.

1x6 TONGUE-AND-GROOVE

**19** **Install the doors.** Set the doors on a temporary 2x4 ledger. Wedge shims between the doors and the framing to create equal spacing all around the doors. Screw the hinges to the doors and the trim.

SHIMS

TEMPORARY 2x4 SUPPORT

seal on the bottom when the door is hung. If the edges don't line up perfectly, you can plane or sand them later. Finish the doors by adding the 1x6 tongue-and-groove boards and sash (**Photo 18**). We used 1x6s with a beaded pattern running down the center, but you can choose any material you like to fill the panel. The barn sashes are 1 in. thick, so they'll stick out a little on the back.

Install the door trim before you mount the doors. Cut the 1-in.-thick top trim to length and cut curves on the end to match the window trim. Then nail it to the siding, making sure the edge is flush with the framed opening. Cut the trim pieces for the sides and align them flush to the framed opening before nailing them to the wall. Nail 1x2 door stops on the sides and top of the framed opening, 1-1/2 in. back from the face of the door trim.

The trick to mounting the doors easily is to support them on a temporary 2x4 and wedge them into position with shims (**Photo 19**). Attach the doors with your choice of surface-mount hinges. We used black gate hinges. To seal the gap between the doors, nail a 1x2 astragal to the back of the door you want to remain closed most of the time. Then mount surface bolts inside, to the top and bottom of this "stationary" door, to hold it closed. We installed a standard exterior entry lock on the active door and a matching dummy knob on the stationary side.

**20** **Shingle the roof.** Snap chalk lines to indicate the top of the shingle courses. For details on fastening the shingles, check the packaging.

## Finishing up

Before you shingle, install metal drip edge if you plan to use it, then nail a row of starter shingles along the bottom of the roof. Follow the instructions on the shingle package for installing the shingles (**Photo 20**).

We used top-quality acrylic exterior paint for the trim and siding. We protected the window sash, doors and soffit with a coat of Sikkens Cetol SRD translucent finish.

You can add charm with the simple-to-build flower boxes (**Figure P**, online). Inside, add shelves, hooks or cabinets for storage, or build in a workbench for a nice potting shed.

# DECK
# REVIVAL

*Upgrade the decking and railings to make your old deck better than ever*

by **Mark Petersen, Contributing Editor**

**A**re you tired of looking at your tired-looking deck? If the framing is in good shape, leave it in place and just replace the old decking and railing. Your deck will not only look better than the original, but also last virtually forever with no maintenance except an occasional cleaning. This article will give you 10 tips to help turn your shabby-looking deck into the envy of the neighborhood.

## Here's what we did

We helped one of our neighbors rebuild his deck. The deck was just nine years old, but it looked like it was a hundred. The railing was warped, and the decking was weathered and cracked. We decided to scrap the treated lumber and upgrade both the decking and the railing to maintenance-free products available at home centers.

We consulted the pros at Precision Decks in Minneapolis to give us tips for tackling a "re-deck" project. They forewarned us that we couldn't just tear off the old stuff and replace it with new. We'd have joists to straighten, stairs to reinforce and flashing to improve—and they were right. But we think an intermediate DIYer could successfully take on a job like this.

## 1 Be prepared for stripped screws

If the old decking is held down by screws, you're bound to strip out a few of them, so buy a screw extractor before you get started. The one shown here is a Grabit, but there are other brands. A set of three sizes costs $20 at a home center.

All you need to do is bore out the inside of the screw head with the burnishing end of the bit, then flip the bit around and back the screw out. As the bit turns counterclockwise, it digs down into the screw head, creating a very strong connection.

BURNISHING END

SCREW EXTRACTOR

SCREW EXTRACTOR

STRIPPED SCREW

**Straighten bowed joists**

Wood decking is stiff and tends to flatten out the deck, even if joists are bowed. Manufactured decking isn't nearly as rigid as wood, so before you lay down the new decking, check the joists for flatness. Stretch a string or chalk line across the joists at the middle of the deck. You may need to put a spacer under each end of the string to raise it above the joists. Measure the distance between the string and each joist.

If some joists are bowed way up (more than 1/4 in.), snap a chalk line from the top of one end of the joist to the top of the other, and either plane down to the line or grab your circular saw and cut along it. If a joist is bowed down in the middle, you'll have to pull some nails and remove it from the deck. Straighten the edge (as shown at right) and reinstall it with the straightened edge up. Some of the joists on this project were bowed more than 1 in.

NEW TOP SIDE

CHALK LINE

TOP OF JOIST

## Inspect the support posts

Posts usually start to rot where they come in direct contact with the ground. The posts on this deck were in good shape because they had been installed with a bracket that held them above grade.

If your posts are buried underground, dig down and inspect their condition. If the top of the footing is only a few inches below grade and the post is in good shape, clear away any grass, rock and wood chips around them. If your footings seem solid but your posts are in bad shape, you can raise the outside of the deck with a car jack or bottle jack and replace the posts. If you don't have footings, talk to your local inspector about the best way to proceed. For more information, search for "deck repair tips" at familyhandyman.com.

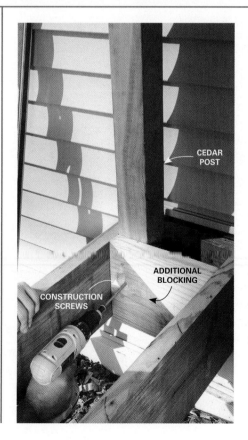
CEDAR POST

ADDITIONAL BLOCKING

CONSTRUCTION SCREWS

 **Brace your railing posts**

If you want super-sturdy posts, install additional blocking. This is especially important if your balusters aren't going to be attached to the deck framing. The 5-in. construction screws we chose are designed to be used with treated lumber and don't require predrilling. LedgerLOK is one brand; a box of 50 costs $38 at home centers. We suggest that you buy cedar posts. Posts made from treated lumber can warp as they dry and wreck your new composite railings.

CONSTRUCTION SCREWS

 **Add joist blocking**

If your joists span more than 8 ft., install blocking between the joists. Blocking holds joists straight and adds stiffness to a bouncy deck. Blocking also allows each joist to share the impact of footsteps with neighboring joists and reduces "deflection," or flexing. Snap a chalk line at the center of the longest span of the deck framing perpendicular to the joists, and install blocks made from the same size material. Stagger the blocks along the chalk line; that way you'll be able to drive the nails or screws straight in from the other side of the joist.

FLASHING TAPE

 **Tape the joists**

Install flashing tape to cover the old joists. If you don't cover the joists, water will get trapped in the nail/screw holes and rot the wood from the inside out. You can use tape designed for doors and windows or one designed for decks. Avoid buying white or shiny silver tape—it may be noticeable in between the deck boards. Flashing tape isn't cheap. We bought a product called Barricade from a local lumberyard, and it cost almost $25 for a 4-in. x 75-ft. roll. If you have more time than money, you could cut the tape in half to double the coverage.

 **Trim off the decking after installation**

Cut the first and the last deck boards to length before you install them, but run the rest of them long. Snap a line between the two trimmed end boards and cut along the line with a circular saw. The fascia board will fit nice and snug against the decking if you let the deck boards run about 1/16 in. past the joist.

CHALK LINE

 **Replace the flashing**

We removed the existing flashing on this deck because it was aluminum, which corrodes when it comes in direct contact with treated lumber. We replaced it with a galvanized steel product designed specifically for deck ledger boards. An 8-ft. flashing costs $7 at home centers.

You'll need to remove a couple of courses of siding to make this happen, but it's a small price to pay to keep water out of your house. Tape the top of the steel flashing with a flashing tape designed to seal windows and doors or a tape designed for decks. If your house wrap ends at the ledger board and isn't installed behind it, install the flashing under the house wrap and tape the house wrap to the flashing.

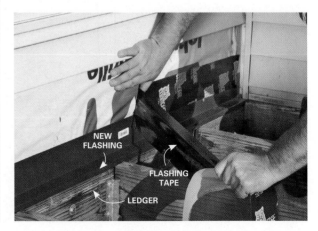

NEW FLASHING

FLASHING TAPE

LEDGER

## 8 Beef up the stairs

When replacing wood decking with maintenance-free decking, you may have to add a stringer to the stair framing (check your manufacturer's specifications). The distance a deck board can span is less on stairs. That's because the force from stepping down onto a stair tread is much greater than the force from just walking around on the deck. Carefully dismantle the stairs, and use one of the old stringers as a pattern for the new one. Space the stringers at equal intervals and reassemble.

BEFORE

NEW STRINGER

AFTER

FASCIA BOARD

## 10 Use plenty of screws on the fascia

Wide PVC and composite fascia boards expand and contract more than regular wood, so they need a lot of fasteners to keep them from becoming distorted. We held the fascia board on with three colored deck screws at the ends and two every 12 in. in the field.

## 9 Use hidden fasteners for a clean look

We ordered boards with a groove on the sides so we could work with the Hideaway Universal Fastener Clips from Trex. A pack of 90 clips costs $25 at home centers and will finish 50 sq. ft. of decking. This system requires you to partially install clips on both sides of the board before permanently tightening the side that butts the installed boards. These clips are self-gapping, and installation is quick and easy.

FASTENING CLIPS

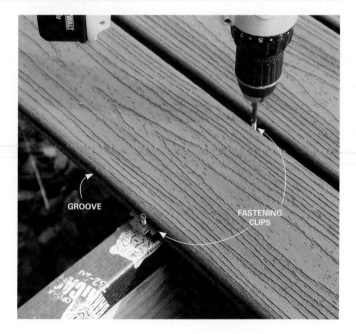
GROOVE

FASTENING CLIPS

# WONDER GARDEN CART

*Better than a wheelbarrow and easy to build*

by **Spike Carlsen**

**What it takes**

**COST:** Less than $150

**TIME:** One weekend

**SKILL LEVEL:** Intermediate

**TOOLS:** Circular saw, drill

## MEET THE BUILDER

A former editor at The Family Handyman, Spike Carlsen now spends his days dreaming up ingenious DIY projects. Find 75 more of his clever creations in The Backyard Homestead Guide to Building Projects (Storey Publishers). Available in spring of 2014.

Wheelbarrows are great for hauling stuff around the yard—unless you're working on a hill ... or trying to negotiate steps and rough terrain ... or moving a lot of bulky material like leaves and branch trimmings ... or trying to load something big into them.

Since I added this garden cart to my outdoor arsenal of tools, life has gotten way easier. Two wheels means it doesn't tip; large pneumatic tires means it's easy to push; a big box lets me haul 10 bags of mulch in one load; and because the front tilts down for loading, my aching back doesn't ache as much. I'll still use my trusty wheelbarrow for mixing concrete and hauling the super-heavy stuff, but these days I "cart" nearly everything else.

I designed this cart to be as rugged and durable as any cart you can buy at any price, yet the materials cost less than $150. It's one of the wisest landscaping investments you can make.

Easy to load

Onboard tool storage

Huge load? No problem

OUTDOOR STRUCTURES, LANDSCAPING & GARDENING

**1 Cut the plywood parts.** A homemade straight-cutting jig turns your circular saw into a precision plywood slicer. To see a video on how to make one, go to familyhandyman.com and search for "straight cuts."

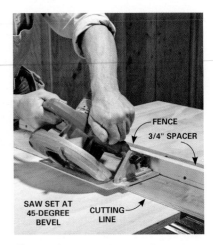

**2 Cut the beveled edges.** Screw a spacer to the fence of your jig and line up the edge with your cutting line just like you would for a standard cut. Then make the long 45-degree cuts.

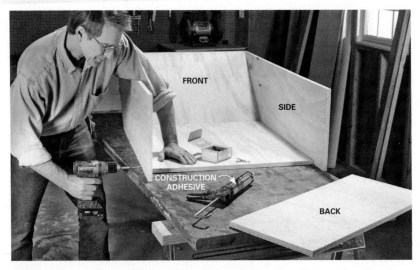

**3 Build the box.** Secure the panels to one another using construction adhesive and 2-in. screws. Drill pilot holes to avoid splintering the edges of the plywood. Flip the cart upside down and install the three bottom braces (E).

**4 Install the wheel assembly.** Install a washer, a wheel, another washer and a locknut on one end of the threaded rod. Measure the overhang required by the wheel assembly, add that length to the other end, then cut the rod to length. Install the axle braces and cover.

## Round up materials

You'll need a straight-cutting jig to cut the plywood. To learn how to make one, go to familyhandyman. com. Search for "straight cuts" to see a video, or "cutting guides" for written instructions. I used exterior plywood and standard pine boards for the structure. You can use treated plywood and lumber, but it may be hard to find treated material that's dry and flat.

I bought wheels at northerntool. com (item No. 145120). The threaded rod, washers and nuts are available at home centers and hardware stores.

## Assemble the box

Lay out the plywood as shown in **Figure B**. Start by cutting the sheet lengthwise into 14-in., 30-in. and 3-1/2-in. strips (**Photo 1**). After positioning the jig for each cut, clamp or screw it into place. Cut the angled sides (A) from the 14-in. strip and the bottom braces (E) from the 3-1/2-in. strip. Cut the front (C), bottom (D) and back (B) from the 30-in. strip.

If you use your straight-cutting jig, as is, for cutting the 45-degree bevels, you'll cut a bevel on the jig itself, making it unusable for future square cuts. Temporarily modify your jig by screwing a 3/4-in. strip of wood to

the jig's fence (**Photo 2**), positioning the edge of the guide on the cutting line (like you would for a square cut), then make your 45-degree cut.

Drill 1/8-in. holes about 3/8 in. away from the edges of the sides (A), spaced about 4 in. apart. Then secure the front with 2-in. exterior screws through the predrilled holes in the sides. **Note:** To ensure maximum sturdiness, use construction adhesive for all the connections—even for the metal corners.

Install the bottom (**Photo 3**) flush with the edges of the sides (A). Make sure the front beveled edge of the bottom makes solid contact with

## Figure A   Garden cart

**Overall Dimensions**
66" long x 24-1/2" tall x 41" wide
(including wheels)

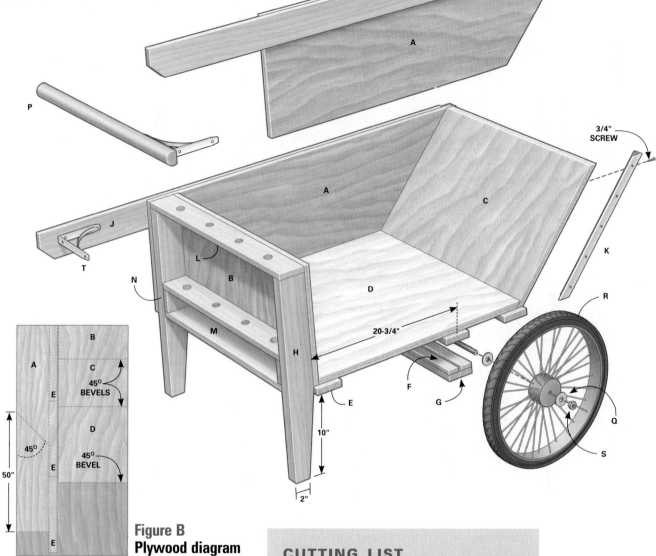

### Figure B
### Plywood diagram

45° BEVELS

45°

45°
BEVEL

45°

50"

3/4" SCREW

20-3/4"

10"

2"

## MATERIALS LIST

| ITEM | QTY. |
|---|---|
| 4' x 8' x 3/4" exterior plywood | 1 |
| 2x4 x 48" pine | 1 |
| 1x4 x 96" pine | 3 |
| 1-1/4" x 30" handrail | 1 |
| 1/2" x 3" x 31-1/2" plywood or solid wood | 1 |
| 20"-diameter wheels | 2 |
| 1/2" x 48" threaded rod | 1 |
| 1/2" washers | 4 |
| 1/2" locknuts | 2 |
| 6" L-shaped shelf brackets | 2 |
| 1" x 1" x 2' aluminum angle | 2 |
| 3/4" exterior screws | 20 |
| 1-1/4" exterior screws | 1 lb. |
| 2" exterior screws | 2 lbs. |
| Heavy-duty construction adhesive (pint tubes) | 2 |

## CUTTING LIST

| PART | QTY. | SIZE & DESCRIPTION |
|---|---|---|
| A - Sides | 2 | 3/4" x 14" x 50" * |
| B - Back | 1 | 3/4" x 14" x 30" |
| C - Front | 1 | 3/4" x 19-3/4" x 30" ‡ |
| D - Bottom | 1 | 3/4" x 31-5/8" x 30" § |
| E - Bottom braces | 3 | 3/4" x 3-1/2" x 31-1/2" |
| F - Axle braces | 2 | 1/2" x 1-1/2" x 31-1/2" |
| G - Axle cover | 1 | 3/4" x 3-1/2" x 31-1/2" pine |
| H - Legs | 2 | 1-1/2" x 3-1/2" x 23-3/4" pine |
| J - Handles | 2 | 3/4" x 3-1/2" x 64-1/2" pine # |
| K - Corner braces | 2 | Cut to fit # |
| L - Long tool rack slat | 1 | 3/4" x 3-1/2" x 30" |
| M - Short tool rack slats | 2 | 3/4" x 3-1/2" x 27" |
| N - Tool rack blocks | 2 | 3/4" x 3-1/2" x 3" |
| P - Handle bar | 1 | 1-1/4" handrail |
| Q - Washers | 4 | 1/2" fender washer |
| R - Wheels | 2 | 20" w/pneumatic tire |
| S - Locknut | 2 | 1/2" locknut |
| T - L-brackets | 2 | 6" shelf brackets (or similar) |

NOTES:
* Angled cut
‡ 45-degree bevel cut, both ends
§ 45-degree bevel cut, one end
# 45-degree cuts, both ends

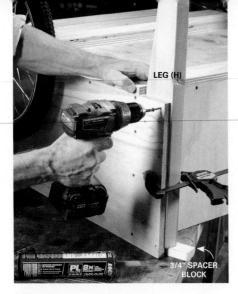

LEG (H)

**5** **Install the legs.** Apply two beads of construction adhesive, clamp the legs into place and secure them with screws. The spacer block positions the leg, leaving room for the tool rack.

3/4" SPACER BLOCK

the bottom edge of the front (C). To complete the box, add the back (B). If you've cut and assembled everything correctly, there will be a 3-1/2-in. cavity at the back of the box to accommodate the tool rack. If it's a little larger or smaller, no big deal.

## Install the wheels

Turn the cart box upside down. Secure the bottom braces (E). Secure the middle bottom brace so the center of it is exactly 20-3/4 in. away from the back of the back bottom brace (E). If you don't get this positioned right, it will affect the balance of the cart.

Position this assembly (**Photo 4**) snugly against one side of the cart and measure the amount of space it takes up. Transfer that measurement to the other end of the rod and mark the rod. Cut the rod and install the other wheel assembly. Tip: Before cutting the rod to length, twist a regular nut onto it beyond the cut mark. After making the cut, twist the nut off; it will "recut" any damaged threads so the locknut will go on easier.

Apply glue to the axle braces (F), snug them tightly against the axle, then secure them to the middle bottom brace (E) with 2-in. screws. Finally, install the axle cover (G). **Note:** If you want to strengthen the wheel assembly for hauling heavier loads, use oak for the middle bottom brace, two axle braces and cover.

## Install the legs, handles and tool rack

Cut the legs and screw them to the protruding sides (**Photo 5**). Use the spacer block as shown so the legs can accommodate the upper tool rack slat. Cut and install the handles (J), leaving space at the front for the aluminum angle.

Cut two lengths of aluminum angle. Don't try to measure them; just hold them in place and mark them for cutting. Drill holes and drill countersink "dimples" for the heads of the screws to nest into. Install the aluminum using adhesive and 3/4-in. screws (**Photo 6**).

Position the handle bar (P) and add the L-brackets (**Photo 7**) to reinforce the handle. Finally, install the three tool rack slats (**Photo 8**).

Remove the wheels and apply a coat of high-quality exterior primer, followed by two coats of exterior paint. To keep your cart in good condition, store it inside; if it will be outside, flip it upside down on a couple of scrap 4x4s.

HANDLE (J)

3/4" SCREW

CORNER BRACE (K)

**6** **Strengthen the corners.** Cut aluminum angle stock to length, then drill holes and countersink "dimples" for the screw heads. Install the corner braces using construction adhesive and screws.

HANDLE BAR (P)

L-BRACKET (T)

**7** **Install the handle bar.** Secure the handle bar by driving screws through each handle into the end of the rail. Add the L-brackets to beef up the connection.

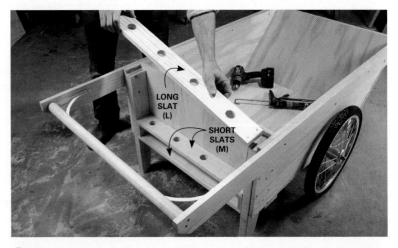

LONG SLAT (L)

SHORT SLATS (M)

**8** **Add a tool rack.** Cut three tool rack slats and drill holes for tool handles. Adjust the size and spacing of the holes to suit your tools. Use adhesive and screws to install the slats.

# REPAIR A **BENT FENCE RAIL**

**W**hen a tree limb falls on your property, you can bet it's going to damage something. And if that "something" happens to be a chain link fence, consider yourself lucky, because fixing a chain link fence is an easy DIY repair. The pros would charge about $150 plus materials for the repair shown here. But you can do it yourself for about $60, including tool rental.

We asked our friends at Premier Fence in St. Paul, MN, to evaluate the damage on this fence and walk us through the repair. Here's how to proceed.

Get a new section of top rail and some wire ties from a home center or fence supplier. The top rail should have one open end and one crimped end. Grab a hacksaw, file and pliers—and a helper.

Start by removing the wire ties that hold the fence fabric to the top rail. Then rest the new rail on top of the

damaged rail and have your helper hold it in place while you mark a cutting line on the old rail as shown in the photo below. Then mark a cut on the opposite end of the new rail where it meets a joint.

Cut the damaged rail at the cutting line (**Figure A**), slide it off the joint and toss it. Then cut the excess off the top rail to mate with the existing joint. Create some maneuvering room by unbolting the top rail from the corner post and sliding it away from the damaged area. Install the larger end of the new rail onto the crimped end of the old rail. Then make the final connection. Reconnect the rail end cap to the corner post.

**Mark a cutting line.** Slide the new rail down so the crimped end is located over a straight section of the damaged rail. Then mark the cutting line.

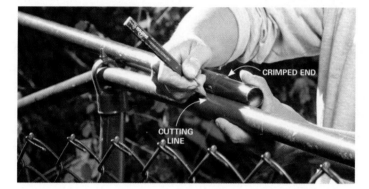

CRIMPED END

CUTTING LINE

## MEET THE PROS

**Chris and Wayne work for Premier Fence in St. Paul, MN. Between the two of them, they have more than 27 years of experience installing and repairing wood, aluminum, iron, chain link and vinyl fencing.**

## Figure A
## Cutting guide

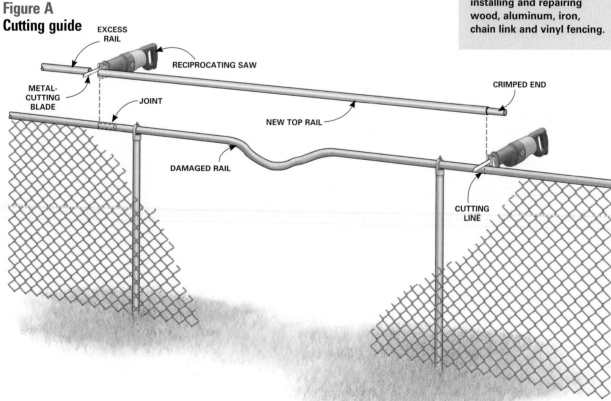

EXCESS RAIL

RECIPROCATING SAW

METAL-CUTTING BLADE

JOINT

NEW TOP RAIL

CRIMPED END

DAMAGED RAIL

CUTTING LINE

OUTDOOR STRUCTURES, LANDSCAPING & GARDENING

# HandyHints®

## SHADY FLOWER SHELF

Here's a beautiful idea for sprucing up the crotch of a tree. Make yourself a shady plant shelf! Just measure the gap and cut your shelving to fit. Cut a notch in each side of your board so that it "hugs" the tree and sits securely. Set your shelf gently inside the crotch of your tree, place your shade-loving plants on it and enjoy your blooms all season long.

READER PHOTO

READER PHOTO

## YARD TOOL HOLDERS

To make it easier to carry yard tools like rakes and shovels around my property, I made tool holders from PVC pipe for my tractor cart. I glued on end caps and attached the holders to the cart with U-brackets. I also drilled a hole in each end cap so water can drain out.

Gary Brigman

## EASIER LAWN MOWER OIL DRAINING

I found a trick to make lawn mower oil changes a lot easier. Older gas mowers had a drain plug to remove used oil. But with many newer mowers, you have to turn the mower on its side to drain the oil, which is awkward. So I came up with the simple idea of clamping plastic tubing to a turkey baster and using it to drain the oil. I stick the end of the tubing into the oil fill hole and suck out the oil. I squirt the used oil into an oil pan and repeat as many times as it takes to empty the oil.

—Neil Greene

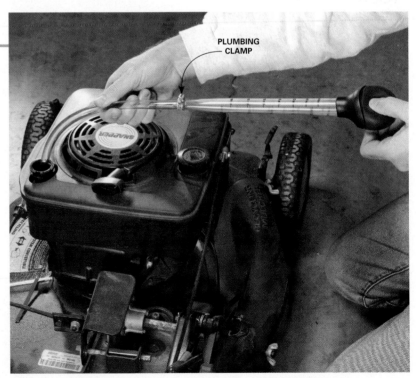

PLUMBING CLAMP

## ROCK DOLLY

Need to move stones, potted trees or bags of soil? Make your own sturdy garden dolly from a two-wheel hand truck and plywood. You can make the box any size you want (a box 31 in. wide will still fit through a doorway) and then attach it to your hand truck with U-bolts. It can handle a lot of weight and is easily removed. It's also low to the ground, so you can just roll stones and other heavy items right into it without lifting.

**U-BOLT**

## SUMP PUMP GARDEN WATERING

I was tired of my sump pump pumping all of its water into our yard and leaving it a swampy mess. So I decided to put the water to good use. I dry fitted some PVC pipe to where the sump exits the house and ran a length of tubing out to our flower bed. Now when the pump comes on, the water is directed to where it will do some good!

—Chad Rood

**Editor's Note:** Be sure to disconnect the setup in the fall to prevent the discharge line from freezing in the winter.

## BIRD-PROOF FENCE

I have a white vinyl fence. The birds love to fly over to my yard for a drink out of my pool and then perch on my fence post caps and do their business. They were leaving many unsightly stripes down the posts. My solution was to make the caps uninviting. I removed each cap and drilled a hole slightly smaller than the shaft of a 1-5/8-in. ring shank nail in the middle of it. Then I tapped the nails through the bottom and replaced the caps. Now the birds see my point, and I don't see any more stripes.

—Paul, via email

## STAND-UP SHOVEL

I like to step out my patio door and have a snow shovel available to shovel off my deck. However, whenever I propped the shovel against the deck, I'd find it face down covered by snow. I solved this problem by buying a broom clip at the hardware store and installing it on the deck railing. No more digging for my shovel after a storm.

Mark Peterson, Field Editor

## SIMPLE SAP REMOVER

We have a lot of trees on our property, and their sap drips all over our garden hoses. Trying to get the sap off my hands every time I watered was a pain until I discovered this easy trick: Use cooking spray. Just a small squirt and a quick wipe with a paper towel are all it takes. I now keep a can of cooking spray out in my garage. It removes most oil-base paints and primers too.

—Jon Swanick

**COOKING SPRAY**

OUTDOOR STRUCTURES, LANDSCAPING & GARDENING

# HandyHints

## FAST ROUTE TO THE ROOTS

**James S. Tira**

To get liquid fertilizer down to the plant roots where it will do the most good, I created my own watering device. I drilled holes into the sides of a long plastic transmission funnel (available at any auto parts store). Then I sharpened a dowel to a fine point and stuck it through the hole of the funnel to make it easier to drive in. When it's time to fertilize, I push the funnel into the soil near the plant and pour in water and fertilizer. The mixture runs out through the holes and down to the roots.

**TRANSMISSION FUNNEL**

**DOWEL**

## FLUORESCENT PAINT YARD MARKERS

I always think I'll remember where the caps to my drain field are, but I never do until I chop them off with my riding mower! This year, I found the solution. I sprayed the caps with fluorescent paint. I did the same thing with lanyards and attached them to my mole traps. Now I can see all of them easily.

—Erik Hass

## WATER BREAK ON THE GO

I don't want to stop mowing the lawn just to run into the house for a drink of water, so I attached a bicycle water bottle holder to the mower arm. Now I fill up the bottle at the start and take my water breaks without breaking my stride.

**Bill Magazzina**

**Editor's Note:** This is an oldie, but it's also one of our favorites.

## EASIER POSTHOLE DIGGING

People get awfully sore and tired trying to dig a hole with a posthole digger. To make it easier, break up the ground first using a 2- or 3-in. "earth" or "garden" auger bit (the kind that's often used for planting flower bulbs). I've found that a 2-ft.-long auger bit attached to a corded drill works great to loosen the soil. (Most cordless drills aren't up to this task.) Then use the posthole digger to scoop up the loose soil. Instead of an hour of backbreaking work, you'll be able to dig the same hole in 15 minutes with very little effort.

—Larry Price, Field Editor

## EASIER MULCH UNLOADING

At least twice a year, I buy mulch in bulk at the nursery. It gets dumped into the bed of my pickup truck with a front-end loader. I used to shovel the mulch out onto my driveway and haul it from there to where I needed

it. But I found a much easier method. I load my pickup bed with 5-gallon plastic buckets and have the mulch dumped into the truck as usual. Then I use a rake to even out the load so every container is filled up. When it's time to unload, I do it one bucket at a time and dump the mulch exactly where I want it. The buckets store nicely in the garage, and I reuse them throughout the year.

Ed Gibson

## EASY-ON-THE-HANDS BUCKET HANDLES

I had some old buckets with broken plastic handles. Whenever I carried heavy bucket loads, the wire cut into my hands. So I cut short lengths of old garden hose, slit each one with a utility knife and slid them over the handles. If you can remove one side of the wire handle, you can just slide the hose grip on without slitting it. The handles work great and keep those buckets working hard!

Jacob Kendrick

## TEMPORARY EXTENSION CORD PROTECTION

If you're having a graduation party or some other occasional event out in the yard, you may require extra electricity. Here's a great way to keep extension cord plugs dry. Cut notches in the opposite sides of a reusable plastic container and snap on the lid. Your plugs will stay dry if it happens to rain or the ground is moist.

## STAY-PUT SOLAR LIGHTS

I love using solar lights along my driveway, but most of them come with flimsy plastic stakes that are impossible to pound into gravel or clay-packed areas. I replaced the stakes with sections of 3/4-in. copper tubing. By coincidence, the diameter matched the bottom of the light heads. The tubes are much easier to pound into hard-packed soil, and they're less likely to be kicked over in high-traffic areas.

—Conrad Garelik

# TOP 10 TIPS FOR PLANTING A TREE

*The key to a thriving, beautiful, mature tree is knowing what you're doing on planting day.*

By **Elisa Bernick**

## MEET AN EXPERT

**Jeff Gillman is a true tree nerd. He has a Ph.D. in horticultural science, is an associate professor at the University of Minnesota and is the author of five books on gardening. Check out his Facebook page, The Garden Professors, for lots of helpful tips on landscaping.**

### 1 Don't choose a problem tree

You'll be living with this tree for a long time, so make sure you plant one you won't grow to detest in a few years. Trees to avoid include cottonwoods, which have invasive root systems (as shown), messy mulberries and stinky female ginkgoes. Before you buy a tree, research its benefits and potential negatives so you won't resent it later on. Contact your local extension service for a list of recommended trees for your area.

## 2 Don't plant too close to a building

Plant a tree with its mature size in mind. Many arborists suggest planting a tree no closer to a structure than one half of its expected mature canopy spread. "I actually like to provide even more room," says Jeff. "Tree roots and branches need space. Pruning a tree planted too close to a structure to keep it from damaging your roof, foundation or siding can damage or disfigure the tree."

Also, some trees develop large surface roots that can crack or lift driveways, patios and sidewalks. If that's a concern, plant well away from these surfaces or choose a tree less likely to produce above-ground roots. Also, watch out for overhead power lines—most shade trees will grow at least to the height of residential power lines. Choose shorter, ornamental trees for these areas.

ELLEN THOMSON

## 3 Match the tree to the planting site

Plant a tree that will grow well given your hardiness zone, existing soil conditions (test if you're not sure), sun exposure and available moisture. "Tree species that are native to the place where you live are probably well adapted to the climate in your part of the country," says Jeff. "If you're planting a nonnative species, research its site requirements carefully." One of the best ways to check how trees will do on your land is to observe species growing naturally in the vicinity with the same conditions.

## 4 Don't add soil amendments

For years, experts recommended adding compost, peat moss or fertilizer to the planting hole. However, most now agree that you shouldn't backfill with anything other than the original soil from the planting hole (despite what the plant tag says—see Tip 3). Soil amendments in the planting hole can discourage the tree roots from spreading into the surrounding soil and can cause poor water drainage. Also, in some instances, fertilizers can kill young roots.

## **5** Don't plant too deep

"If you plant the root-ball of a tree too deep," says Jeff, "new roots can girdle the trunk and may also suffer from a lack of oxygen." He suggests planting a tree so the root collar—where the uppermost roots attach to the trunk—is about an inch *above* the soil level.

"In many cases, containerized trees from nurseries are planted too deep," he says. "Don't go by the soil level in the container. Dig down into the planting medium to find the root collar so you know how deep to plant the tree."

If you're planting a bare-root tree, leave a cone of soil at the bottom of the planting hole and set the root system on top. Place the handle of your shovel flat across the hole from one side to the other to make sure the crown is level with the surrounding soil. You should be able to partially see the root collar, or trunk flare, after the tree is planted.

CAUTION: A few days before you dig, call 811 to have your underground utilities marked. Learn more at call811.com.

## **6** Dig a shallow, broad hole

Dig a saucer-shape hole three to five times the diameter of the root-ball (or the spread of the roots for a bare-root tree). This allows the roots to easily penetrate the softened backfill and properly anchor the tree.

If you're planting in clay or wet soil, Jeff suggests using a garden fork or your spade to roughen the bottom and sides of the planting hole to avoid "glazing." "Glazing happens when the sides and bottom of a hole become so smooth and compacted that water can't pass easily through the soil," says Jeff. "In extreme situations, it could block roots from penetrating the sides of the planting hole."

## **7** Plant in fall or early spring

The ideal time to plant a tree is in early spring before "bud break" or in the fall before the tree goes dormant. Cool weather allows the tree to establish roots in its new location before new top growth puts too much demand on it. Some trees establish better if planted in early spring. These include oaks, pines, dogwoods, American holly, willows and black gum. Avoid planting trees during the summer when they're in full leaf and susceptible to heat stress.

MIKE HABERMANN

## 8 Mulch wide, but not deep

Mulch holds moisture, moderates soil temperatures, reduces competition from grass and weeds, and prevents lawn mowers and trimmers from nicking the trunk. Make a 3-ft. (or larger) circle of mulch 2 to 4 in. deep around the trunk. But don't mulch too deep. This can create surface drainage problems and deprive roots of oxygen. Keep the mulch 3 or 4 in. from the trunk to avoid disease, rot and pest problems.

Some good mulch choices are shredded bark or composted wood chips. "Don't use woven or plastic landscape fabric or other weed barriers underneath the mulch," cautions Jeff. "These can cause major problems later on as seeds grow roots down through these materials and anchor themselves into the barriers."

JEFF GILLMAN

BILL ZUEHLKE

## 9 Set the roots free

Cut away all rope, twine, wire, staples and burlap before backfilling (you can leave natural burlap underneath the root-ball if you can't cut it all away). "If the roots circle the root-ball, but none are thicker than a pencil, use your fingers to tease the root-ball apart," says Jeff. But if the tree is severely root-bound and has circling roots larger than a pencil in diameter, Jeff recommends using a newer method called box cutting. "To box-cut a root-ball, use a pruning saw to shave off all four sides, creating a square root-ball."

## 10 Water carefully

You'll need to water your new tree until the root system is well established. Don't rely on a "rule of thumb" for watering. The right amount of water depends on the weather conditions, your soil and the planting site. The most reliable method for knowing when to water is to stick your finger 2 to 3 in. into the ground. You want to keep the soil at the level of the root-ball moist but not wet. Allow the soil's surface to begin to dry out between waterings.

For the first few weeks, you may have to water every few days depending on the weather. After that, longer (deeper), less frequent watering is much better than shorter (quicker), frequent watering. To help the tree create deep roots to resist drought and wind, Jeff suggests encircling it with a soaker hose a few feet out from the trunk and running it a trickle for an hour.

"Overwatering can be as bad or worse than underwatering," says Jeff. "If you're watering more than twice a week, there's a good chance you're overwatering."

OUTDOOR STRUCTURES, LANDSCAPING & GARDENING

# ELEGANT AND EASY GARDEN ARBOR

*Surprisingly easy, and delightfully elegant*

by **Gary Wentz, Senior Editor**

**T**his combination arbor and swing may look like a challenging, weeks-long project, but it's not. If you can drive screws and handle a saw, you can build it in a weekend. The swing itself is store-bought, and the arbor that supports it requires only basic skills. Don't be afraid of those curves and coves; the following pages will show you goof-proof ways to cut them.

**COVE**

## Perfect coves

To kick off this project, cut the beams (B) to length and cove the ends. You don't need skill or experience to cut perfect coves, just a 7-1/4-in. circular saw. Here's how.

**First, position the saw.** Align the blade's arbor at the end of the beam and mark at the front of the saw's shoe. This mark tells you where to place the stop block.

**STOP BLOCK**

**SUPPORT BLOCK**

**Then make lots of plunge cuts.** Pivot the saw downward while holding the shoe against the stop block. A support block behind the saw prevents you from plunging too deep.

**Finally, bust out the cove.** Break away the flakes, then sand the cove smooth. The more cuts you made, the easier this will be.

## Time and money

Building and installing the arbor are about two days of work, but you're best off spreading it over a three-day weekend. You can build it in a day, add a coat of finish the next morning, let it dry overnight and set up the arbor the following day.

The cedar lumber we used cost about $300. Pressure-treated lumber would cost about half that. You can spend $150 on a porch swing or three times that much. We spent $250. Hardware, concrete mix and finish will cost $50.

## Build the sides

Each side is made from just nine simple parts. Cut them to length following the Cutting List on p. 238. If you don't have a miter saw to cut the thick 4x4 beams (B), cut from one side with your circular saw, roll the 4x4 over and cut from the other side. Your cuts won't line up perfectly, but they'll be close enough to clean up with a belt sander. The posts (A) don't need to be cut, as long as they're approximately 8 ft. long.

Cutting coves in the ends of the beams (B) is easy with a 7-1/4-in. circular saw. Remember to set your saw to full cutting depth before you position the saw. Eyeball the saw blade to center it on the end of the beam; if you're off by 1/8 in. or so, the cove will still look fine.

Measure from the end of the beam to the mark and make identical marks at each end of both beams. Trace along a square to complete the marks. Clamp down hard on the stop block so it can't move, and begin cutting. Take your time and make lots of cuts close together. I try to leave only 1/16 in. between cuts. After you break out the remaining wood, sand the cove smooth. The front end of a belt sander is perfect for this, but you can also drag the edge of an orbital sander along the curve or even hand-sand it.

To assemble the sides, start with the rungs (C) and side slats (D). My slats were only about 1-3/8 in. square, so I cut a 2-1/2-in. spacer block to get equal spacing between them. Your slats may be a bit fatter and require a slightly smaller spacer. With the slats/rungs assembled, "toe screw" the rungs to the posts (**Photo 1**). Driving screws at an angle is a lot easier if you drill pilot holes first to guide the screws. When you screw the beams to the posts, make sure the screw heads sink in flush with the surface so they're not in the way when you set the arches on them. Bore countersink holes if you have to.

## Build the top

The arches (E) are the biggest part of the arbor, but they won't take any longer to make than the beams. Cut the arch material to length and screw oversize blocks to the ends. Then cut a spring stick to a length of 107-1/2 in. and bend it between the blocks (**Photo 2**). Almost any flexible material will work as a spring stick. I used a strip of PVC "lumber." If you use real wood, eyeball the curve—inconsistencies in wood grain can form an arch that's lopsided or wavy. The

### MEET THE BUILDER

**Gary Wentz is a Senior Editor at The Family Handyman.** He's built three arbors over the past 10 years and says this is his best design—easy but beautiful.

**What it takes**
**Time:** Two days
**Cost:** $350 to $600
**Skill level:** Intermediate
**Tools:** Circular saw, jigsaw, drill, orbital or belt sander

OUTDOOR STRUCTURES, LANDSCAPING & GARDENING

## Figure A  Swing arbor

Overall dimensions: 107"
wide x 87" tall x 40" deep

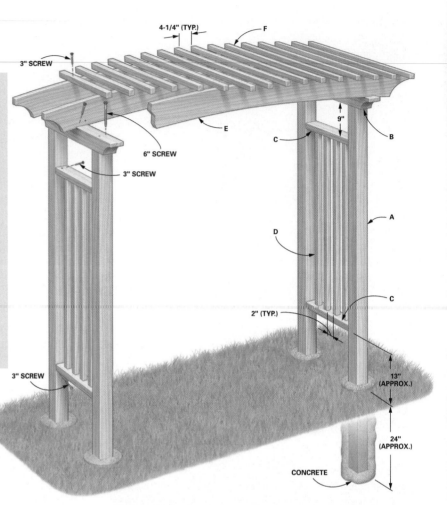

### MATERIALS LIST

| ITEM | QTY. |
| --- | --- |
| 4x4 x 8' | 5 |
| 2x4 x 8' | 1 |
| 2x2 x 8' | 14 |
| 2x12 x 10' | 3 |
| 2x4 x 10' (for bracing) | 3 |
| Concrete mix (80-lb. bags) | 4 |

Eight 6" screws, 2 lbs. of 3" screws,
two 4" screw hooks, exterior stain,
5' porch swing

### CUTTING LIST

| KEY | QTY. | SIZE & DESCRIPTION |
| --- | --- | --- |
| A | 4 | 3-1/2" x 3-1/2" x 8' posts |
| B | 2 | 3-1/2" x 3-1/2" x 36" beams |
| C | 4 | 1 1/2" x 3 1/2" x 18" rungs |
| D | 8 | 1-3/8" x 1-3/8" x 47" side slats |
| E | 3 | 1-1/2" x 10" x 107" arches |
| F | 19 | 1-3/8" x 1-3/8" x 40" top slats |

## Figure B  Arch details

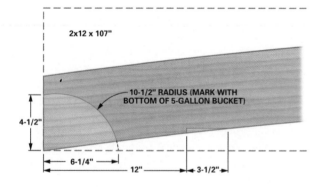

2x12 x 107"

10-1/2" RADIUS (MARK WITH
BOTTOM OF 5-GALLON BUCKET)

4-1/2"

6-1/4"    12"    3-1/2"

SLAT

RUNG

POST

BEAM

**1** **Assemble the sides**. Screw
the slats between the
rungs, then drive screws at an
angle through the rungs and
into the posts. Finally, fasten
the beam to the posts with
long construction screws.

**2 Mark the arches.** Screw on end blocks and bend a spring stick between them. Trace an arch along the stick, move the stick up 6 in., then trace again. Mark the bird's-mouths and coves as shown in Figure B before cutting out the arch. Use the first arch as a pattern for the other two.

**3 Cut arches with a circular saw.** On a gentle curve like this one, a circular saw is faster and easier to control than a jigsaw. Take your time and cut along the outer edge of the mark. Then clean up the cut with a sander.

width of material needed for the arch is about 10 in., and a 2x12 is 11-1/4 in. wide. That gives you a little leeway to experiment with the positioning of your arch marks to avoid knots.

It's critical that you make the marks shown in **Figure B** before you cut out the arches; you'll need the straight edge of the board to mark the coves and bird's-mouths (the notches that fit over the beams). The bottom of a 5-gallon bucket is perfect for marking the cove. When all your marks are made, set your circular saw blade depth to 1-3/4 in. and cut the curves (**Photo 3**). Then cut the coves and bird's-mouths with a jigsaw.

With the arches cut and sanded, you're ready to install the top slats (F). As you install the center slat and the cleats, check and double-check to make sure you have the arches spaced correctly. Then make sure the center slat and arches are perpendicular to each other using a square. You may have to nudge the whole assembly to adjust it for squareness. To position the slats quickly—and prevent mistakes—I made a 4-1/4-in.-wide spacer from scrap plywood (**Photo 4**).

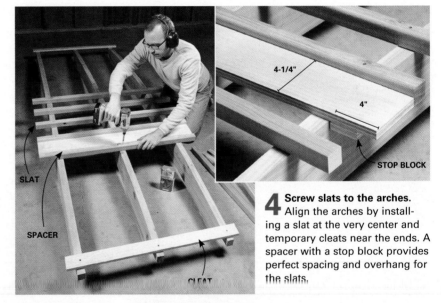

**4 Screw slats to the arches.** Align the arches by installing a slat at the very center and temporary cleats near the ends. A spacer with a stop block provides perfect spacing and overhang for the slats.

## Final assembly and setup

After the sides and top were assembled, I put a coat of exterior stain on them. Staining the top slats was slow and tedious—if I had it to do over again, I'd stain the arches and slats before assembly.

You'll need a helper to assemble and set up the arbor. Take your time as you brace and square the arbor (**Photo 5**). Place the horizontal braces 72 in. from the tops of the beams. Then fasten the top by driving screws diagonally

through the arches and into the beams. Stand up the arbor exactly where you want it and mark the locations of the postholes. For tips on digging postholes, go to familyhandyman.com and search for "dig a hole."

Lower the posts into the holes and level the arbor side-to-side and front-to-back. If you built the arbor with surgical precision, making one post perfectly plumb will mean that they're all plumb. But for me (and all the other carpenters I've ever worked with), leveling is a compromise. Check all four posts and make adjustments until they're all almost plumb (**Photo 6**). Then pour concrete mix into the holes. No need to mix it up; just dump it in dry and soak it with a garden hose.

To hang the swing, drive screw hooks into the center arch right next to the beams. That way, the chains will splay outward rather than run straight up. That helps prevent the swing from swaying sideways and crashing into the posts. To extend the life of a wooden swing, unhook the chains and store it inside in winter.

**5** **Assemble it, square it, brace it.** Screw braces to the posts to hold them the correct distance apart. Then screw the arches to the beams. Take diagonal measurements to square up the arbor and add a diagonal brace to hold it square.

DIAGONAL BRACE

HORIZONTAL BRACE

**6** **Level the arbor.** Dig postholes and set the arbor into them. Level the posts by stacking blocks and shims under the braces. When the arbor is perfectly positioned, fill the postholes with concrete.

# SCOUT BENCH

*Simple enough for kids, tough enough for camp, perfect for your yard!*

## by **Travis Larson, Senior Editor**

**O**ur photographer, Tom Fenenga (he's the one with the striped shirt and big grin), is very involved with his son Adam's Boy Scout troop. Tom wanted to teach the scouts about construction, and they needed benches around the fire pit at the scout camp they visit each year. So we came up with this design. They're simple enough for teenage boys to build, tough enough to handle their roughhousing and economical enough at less than $100 each. You could build one in a Saturday.

### What it takes

**COST:** Less than $100 per bench

**TIME:** 4 hours for the bench, plus an hour of shovel work

**TOOLS:** Circular saw, screw gun

FLUSH WITH PLYWOOD

SEAT SUPPORT

10° ANGLE

BACK LEG

FRONT LEG

BASE PIECE

GUIDELINE

GUIDELINE

90°

10° ANGLE

23-1/2"

6-3/4"

**1** **Screw together the leg units.** Screw the parts together with two 3-in. deck screws at each joint. Draw guidelines alongside the 4x4s to use for the other set of legs. Center the base piece and make the seat support flush with the top of the front 4x4 and square to the back one. Flip the assembly over and screw the second base piece and seat support onto the other side of the legs.

**2** **Bolt the seat supports to the 4x4s.** Bore through both seat supports and the 4x4s with a 3/8-in. spade bit. Connect the parts with 8-in. carriage bolts.

8" x 1/2" CARRIAGE BOLT

SEAT SUPPORT

We decided treated wood was a must—along with exterior 3-in. deck screws rated for treated wood. And the benches had to be embedded in concrete in the ground to keep them from being "relocated."

## Assemble the legs

Start by cutting all the parts to length, following **Figure A** and **Photos 1 and 2**. Then preassemble the legs with screws. You can do this in your shop or garage where you have a flat surface. Place a plywood scrap under the first set of legs and position the 4x4s following the measurements in **Photo 1**. Outline those positions so you can use them as a pattern for the other set of legs to be sure they match perfectly. Keep the screws away from the center of the 4x4 so you don't hit them when you drill holes for the carriage bolts. Drill and bolt together the seat supports and 4x4s. You can buy a special 1/2-in.-dia. x 12-in.-long spade bit or extend a standard-length spade bit with a magnetic bit holder (**Photo 2**).

## Brace it temporarily

Set the legs on a level surface, spacing them 4 ft. apart, and temporarily brace both ends of the base pieces and the front of the seat supports with 2x4s (**Photo 3**). That'll hold everything together with the proper spacing while you attach the seat and back boards. Once they're screwed on, remove the braces.

## Attach the seat and back

Evenly space the seat boards from the edges of the seat supports and screw them to both seat supports with 3-in. deck screws: two screws into each support for the 2x4s and three for the 2x10s. Place a carpen-

## Figure A  Scout bench

45° BEVEL

20-1/2"
2x4 BACK
SUPPORT

45° BEVEL

6' 2x4 (SEAT
AND BACK)

6' 2x10
(SEAT AND
BACK)

12" 4x4 LEG

10° BEVEL

1/2" x 8" CARRIAGE
BOLT

17-1/2"
2x4 SEAT
SUPPORT

45° BEVEL

20-3/4"
2x4 SEAT
SUPPORT

26-1/2" 4x4 LEG

24" 2x4
BASE PIECE

3" DECK
SCREWS
(ALL)

### MATERIALS LIST

For each bench you'll need:

- Two 8' treated 4x4s (legs)
- Two 10' treated 2x4s
  (base pieces, seat, seat
  supports and back support)
- Two 6' treated 2x10s
  (seat and backrest)
- Four 6' treated 2x4s
  (seat and backrest)
- Three 4' untreated 2x4s
  (temporary spacer boards)
- Four 1/2" x 8" carriage bolts
  with nuts and washers
- Seventy-four 3" deck screws
- Three 60-lb. bags of
  concrete mix

TEMPORARY
BRACE

PENCIL

**3 Brace the legs.** Cut the three untreated 2x4s to 4 ft. and screw them to both ends of the feet and the front of the seat supports. They'll serve as temporary braces while you attach the bench seat and backrest boards.

**4 Add the seat and back.** Cut the seat boards to 72 in. Evenly space the ends of the seat boards from the edges of the legs. Screw the boards to the seat supports with 3-in. deck screws: two in each 2x4 and three in each 2x10. Space the boards with a carpenter's pencil.

ter's pencil between the boards to space them (**Photo 4**). Flip the bench upside down, center the back supports and attach them with 3-in. screws (**Photo 5**). Run those in at an angle so the tips won't penetrate the seat and back (or your seat or back).

## Dig the trenches and add the concrete

Set the bench exactly where you want it and outline the trenches around each base. Then set the bench aside and start digging (**Photo 6**). Your goal is to have a level bench with the seat about 15 in. above the ground at the front—the typical height for benches. But once you achieve that, just sit on the bench. You might want it lower, higher or reclined a bit more. Get it just the way you like it. Then mix up three bags of concrete mix and pour half over each base, filling the space between and alongside. Throw any extra over the top. Then backfill the holes, wait a few hours, start the campfire and roast some hot dogs and marshmallows.

**5** **Screw on the seat supports.** Screw the seat supports to the middle of the seat and back, then remove the temporary braces.

BACK SUPPORT

BEVELED ENDS

**6** **Dig the trenches and install your bench.** Position and mark the trenches and dig them about 8 in. deep. Rest the bench in the trenches. Check the bench for level and height, then remove it and adjust the soil levels as necessary. Pour 1-1/2 bags of concrete mix beside, between and over each base and cover with soil. Pour a couple of gallons of water over the dry mix and backfill the trenches.

# GreatGoofs®

## Hot-weather hijinks

Peter Karpf,
Field Editor

I was working alone on a large outdoor deck in 100-degree weather. I had to lop off a 3-ft. piece of a rim joist. To envision what happened next, it helps to think about Wile E. Coyote sitting on a limb of a tree and sawing it off! I stood on the rim joist without realizing I was standing on the very piece of wood I intended to cut off. The joist split when I was about two-thirds through it with my circular saw, and I fell with it. Fortunately, I dropped the saw on the way down, and I didn't land on any of the many objects that could have caused serious injury. But I did end up in the hospital with dehydration and sunstroke.

# HOW TO BUY A
# RIDING LAWN MOWER

*Real-world advice to help you buy the machine that's right for you*

by **Rick Muscoplat, Contributing Editor**

CL B CADET

**S**hopping for a riding mower can be as confusing as buying a new car. First, you have to choose the basic style you need, then compare deck and engine sizes, transmission choices, and power and accessory options. And, since even the stripped-down models can cost more than a thousand dollars, you can't afford to make a mistake and buy the wrong machine for your yard.

We'll help you navigate the various styles and options to find which machines are right for your particular lawn and budget. And we'll give you some buying tips so you can get the most bang for your buck.

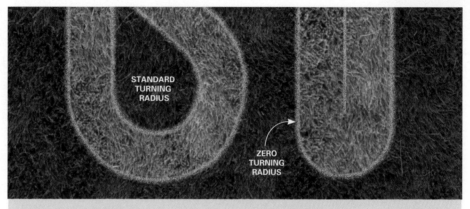

STANDARD TURNING RADIUS

ZERO TURNING RADIUS

TORO

## What Is a ZTR?

Zero turn radius (ZTR) mowers are the newest class of riding mowers. They're growing in popularity simply because they cut grass much faster than other styles. And because they have caster wheels in the front, they can make a 180-degree turn and start cutting the next lap without doing a "turn-around" maneuver. It's like turning a grocery cart around in the middle of the aisle.

You operate the machine using two joysticks to turn and control ground speed. There's a slight learning curve to get the feel of the joysticks. But once you get the hang of it, you can mow at a top speed of 7 mph. One manufacturer, Cub Cadet, has eliminated the joystick approach and gone to a traditional steering wheel and gas pedal arrangement.

## Basic vs. loaded

Two mowers that look alike can have very different price tags. The model on the left, for example, costs $2,300 more than the one on the right. So what do you get when you spend more on a tractor? Count on a larger cutting deck with "gauge wheels" that reduce "scalping" when the tractor hits a low spot. And the loaded models have a power deck lift (as opposed to a manual lever lift). Most high-end models come with power steering, and some even include a tilt-wheel feature for added comfort.

The hydrostatic transmissions on some expensive models are "input sensitive." So you get much better pedal control and fewer "jerky movements" when operating at very low speeds around garden edges and trees.

Many high-end models are equipped with more powerful V-twin engines that produce more torque at lower rpm and reduce vibration and noise. These models usually have larger gas tanks, so you refill less often. And they have more comfortable seats.

$4,000

$1,700

# FOUR BASIC DESIGNS

All riding mowers fall into one of four classes. Step one in the buying process is to decide which type best suits your needs and budget.

## REAR ENGINE

**Rear engine riding (RER) mowers** are designed to do only one job—cut grass. They usually cost less than a comparable-size lawn tractor. So they're popular with homeowners who just want to cut grass and spend less on the machine. RER machines have declined in popularity over the past few years as homeowners have migrated to ZTR mowers.

Starting price: $1,100

### PROS:

- Lowest cost of all the styles.
- Engine heat and noise are behind you, not between your legs.
- Better visibility—no engine in front of you.
- Needs less storage space.
- Fits through gates.

### CONS:

- Slow mowing speeds—1.5 to 4.5 mph.
- Narrower cutting width (28 in.).
- Lever-operated transmission means taking your hand off the wheel to adjust speed.
- Accessory options are very limited.

SNAPPER

## LAWN TRACTOR

**Lawn tractors** are the most popular of all riding mowers. They're great for cutting large lawns and for light-duty gardening jobs. Most entry-level models are equipped with a 38-in. cutting deck, while the more expensive versions can cut up to 54 in. Most are powerful enough to run an optional grass collection system or tow a garden cart loaded with supplies. However, lawn tractors aren't designed to accept large attachments or do heavy-duty work.

Starting price: $1,500

### PROS:

- More deck options—cutting widths 38 in. and up.
- A hydrostatic transmission, which allows you to control the speed by pedal, comes standard on many models. This is also the smoothest type of transmission.
- Cuts faster with mowing speeds of about 5.2 mph.
- Most have larger engines with pressurized lubrication systems, which keep oil flowing on steeper slopes.
- Accepts some accessories.

### CONS:

- Needs larger storage space.
- Larger decks may not fit through your gates.
- Less visibility because the engine is in front.
- Can't handle ground-engaging attachments such as tillers and cultivators.

HUSQVARNA

# GARDEN TRACTOR

**Garden tractors** are built on heavy steel frames and have larger engines. So they can accept wider cutting decks (up to 60 in.) than a lawn tractor. And, they're powerful enough to handle attachments like tillers, cultivators, plow blades and snowblowers. Many are equipped with power takeoff (PTO) to run a pump or even a generator. But be prepared to dig deep—they're expensive.

Starting price: $4,000

## PROS:

- Heavy-duty construction can handle any job.
- Power takeoff (PTO) available on some models.
- Largest cutting widths of all four styles: up to 60 in.
- Powerful enough to run a snow blower or tiller.
- Hydrostatic transmission, power steering and power deck lift are usually standard.

## CONS:

- Needs the most storage space.
- More limited visibility because of the large engine in front.
- They're heavy and harder to maneuver in small spaces.

CRAFTSMAN

# ZERO TURN RADIUS

**ZTR mowers** are designed to cut mowing time in half. They move faster (up to 7 mph). And because they can turn on a dime, they save the time otherwise required to circle around to cut the next row. Because they're more maneuverable, you can cut right up to trees and garden edging. That almost eliminates the need to trim with a weed trimmer. If you just want to cut grass, and do it in the shortest time possible, check out a ZTR mower.

Starting price: $3,000

## PROS:

- Fastest mowing speed of all the styles.
- Most maneuverable; gets closer to trees and gardens.
- Most fun to drive!

## CONS:

- Can't use on steep hills because the casters on the deck dig into the slope.
- Only a few attachments available such as a cart or vacuum grass catcher.
- Learning to drive requires some practice.
- More expensive than comparable-size tractors.

KUBOTA

# BEFORE YOU **BUY**

## Measure twice, buy once

Every homeowner wants the largest machine possible to be able to finish mowing faster. Great. But you have to store the beast somewhere, so don't start shopping until you figure out how much storage space you have. And, if you have to pass through a gate or use a pathway, measure those widths at the same time. Finally, measure the total area you plan to mow, and use an angle gauge to measure the slope angle of your steepest hills. Those measurements will determine the style and size of machine you can buy.

## Accessories

Most riding mowers accept optional grass catchers, vacuum systems and carts. But if you're buying a larger tractor and live in snow country, consider adding a snow-blower or plow blade. They're expensive, but they move snow a lot faster than a stand-alone snow blower.

JOHN DEERE

## Dealers vs. big-box stores

When it comes time to shop, don't assume big-box store clerks don't know their stuff. They're often very knowledgeable about the features of the models they carry. And prices at big-box stores are often the lowest, especially when they have a sale. If you have a truck and don't mind hauling the unit home and assembling it yourself, you can save money by buying at a large retailer.

On the flip side, dealers usually have more in-depth knowledge, and they carry an extensive selection. So you may find a different model that fits your needs better. Plus, many dealers offer test drives, and they usually deliver the machines to your home and pick them up when they need service. Some dealers even take trade-ins. And many will match other retailers' prices.

## Prioritize the tasks

Some machines can do it all. But do you really need all those capabilities? If mowing grass is your primary objective, buy a machine dedicated to cutting grass. For example, a less expensive RER mower may be all you need. However, if you'd rather spend your weekends golfing and you've got the extra cash, check out a fast-moving ZTR machine.

The same holds true for tractors. If you're an avid gardener, don't automatically assume you need a garden tractor. The implements for garden tractors are pricey. In many cases, you'll save money by buying a lawn tractor and a freestanding tiller. On the other hand, if you have a large driveway and get a lot of snow, a garden tractor fitted with a snow-blower or plow blade may be worth the cost.

## Buying tips

- Buy a name-brand machine with a name-brand engine. Your machine is going to need service, and if you can't get parts, you're out of luck.
- More horsepower doesn't get you faster mowing speed. It only gets you more power. That's important if you plan to mulch.
- Comfort is critical. If the seat isn't comfortable or doesn't have enough adjustments, or the pedal locations don't fit your build, you'll hate the machine.
- To make life a lot easier, get a unit with power steering and a power deck lift.

# 7 Vehicles & Garages

## IN THIS CHAPTER

# HandyHints®

## SAVE YOUR BACK AND KNEES WITH A ROLLING SEAT

A rolling creeper seat doesn't need much explanation. You sit on it. You store tools and parts under it. And you roll around to reach the tools and parts you forgot.

Find creeper seats at any auto parts store, home center or online tool site. The model shown here (the Sunex Padded Creeper Seat, at globalindustrial.com) costs about $36. A unit with a pneumatic lift and a contoured seat (for you Ferrari owners) could set you back $150 or more.

## A DRIP PAN SAVES TIME

Car repair is a messy business, and if you don't use a drip pan or a large piece of cardboard, you'll wind up with an oily mess on your garage floor. If you're the kind of cheapskate who saves appliance boxes just for this purpose, more power to you. But the rest of you can easily afford to buy a real drip pan with a lip all around the edge ($10). When you're done, just pour the oil into your recycling bottle and put the pan back under your car to catch any remaining drips.

## GET A BEEFY BENCH VISE

A wimpy $30 vise may satisfy your wallet, but you'll regret buying one the first time you have to crank the bolts off a really big part. So skip the cheapies and invest in a heavy-duty vise. You want a vise with at least 5-1/2-in. jaws, a pipe clamping area, dual swivel locks and a large anvil area. I found this Masterforce model at a home center for $100. But you can find great deals on good used vises on Craigslist or at neighborhood garage sales.

## BLOW OUT THE DIRT BEFORE CHANGING SPARK PLUGS

Before you slap your socket onto the spark plug, use your compressed air gun to blow out all the crud at the base of the plug. Otherwise, it'll all go inside the cylinder once you unscrew the plug. A two-second blast is all you need to protect your engine.

## SAVE YOUR KNUCKLES WITH AIR POWER

An electric impact wrench is a heckuva lot better than a hand wrench. But seriously, nothing beats raw air power and air tools when you want to make quick work of just about any auto or small-engine repair. For recommendations on types of tools, search for "air tools" at familyhandyman.com.

To take advantage of the power of air tools, you need a real air compressor like the one shown, not a weak $99 2-gallon unit designed to run a nail gun. And don't get suckered by horsepower ratings; they don't mean anything. Instead, look for a compressor with at least a 15- to 20-gallon tank and a minimum output of 5 cfm at 90 psi. That'll power just about any air tool you want, except a sandblaster. For that, you need at least 10 cfm, and a rich uncle.

## FAST TIRE CHANGES WITH AN ELECTRIC IMPACT WRENCH

In less time than it takes your air compressor to pump up to full pressure, you could remove the lug nuts from two wheels using an electric impact wrench. Sure, the electric models don't pack the same torque as an air-powered wrench, but you don't need that much torque just to remove lug nuts. If all you're doing is tire rotation and an occasional heavy-duty repair, an electric impact wrench is just the ticket (one choice is the DeWalt No. DW292 1/2-in. 345-ft.-lb. electric impact wrench; about $160 at homedepot.com). Just make sure you use a handheld torque wrench to tighten the lug nuts.

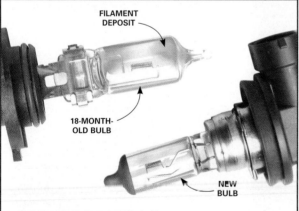

FILAMENT DEPOSIT

18-MONTH-OLD BULB

NEW BULB

## SEE MORE ROAD

As headlight filaments age, they deposit a gray/brown film on the inside of the bulb. Over time, that coating can reduce visibility by almost 300 ft.

If your headlights aren't as bright as they used to be, yank one of the bulbs and look for gray or brown residue on the glass. If you find any, replace both bulbs now and get back to seeing more of the road.

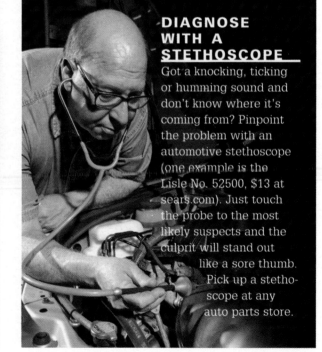

## DIAGNOSE WITH A STETHOSCOPE

Got a knocking, ticking or humming sound and don't know where it's coming from? Pinpoint the problem with an automotive stethoscope (one example is the Lisle No. 52500, $13 at sears.com). Just touch the probe to the most likely suspects and the culprit will stand out like a sore thumb. Pick up a stethoscope at any auto parts store.

VEHICLES & GARAGES

# HandyHints

LOCKING
NUT

LOCKING
NUT KEY

## BURGLARPROOF YOUR ALLOY WHEELS

Many late-model vehicles come with alloy wheels and low-profile tires (there's a shorter distance between the rim and the tread). Because the rim rides so close to the pavement, shops are seeing a dramatic increase in the number of bent alloy wheels. Since new factory wheels cost upward of $300 each, vehicle owners usually opt for a used wheel from a recycling yard. And that's creating a shortage of used alloy wheels.

And the result is ... you guessed it. Alloy wheel theft is on the rise. Police reports show that thieves can strip all four wheels from a vehicle in about five minutes.

If you have alloy wheels, install locking lug nuts to deter the crooks. Locking lug nuts aren't foolproof, but it takes a special socket to remove them, and that slows down the thieves.

A set of four locking nuts costs about $40 from any auto parts store. Remove one lug nut from each wheel and install a locking nut in its place. Want more security? Add two per wheel.

## ZIP THROUGH METAL WITH AN ELECTRIC CUTOFF TOOL

Sometimes it's just not worth the time and effort to save a rusted fastener or clamp. A cutoff tool is the perfect solution in these situations. They allow you to slice through the rusted part and install a new one. You can buy an air-powered cutoff tool at any home center for about $30, but it consumes a lot of air (10 cfm). If you don't have a huge two-stage compressor, an electric version may be a better option (one example is the Chicago Electric No. 68523, about $35 at harborfreight.com).

Cutoff tools aren't just for cutting rusted parts. They're great for cutting angle, shelf brackets and threaded rod.

## BURP AIR OUT OF A GREASE GUN

Loading a new grease cartridge is easy. But removing an air lock can be frustrating. You can prevent air locks by filling the grease gun head before adding the new cartridge (**Photo 1**). Insert the new cartridge and screw on the barrel until it seats against the head. Then back it off two turns and release the spring tension. The remaining air should bleed out through the loose threads. Finish tightening the barrel.

If you've done that but still have an air lock, remove the plug (**Photo 2**).

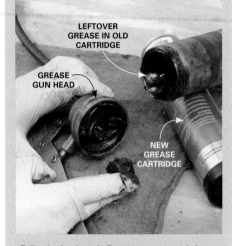

LEFTOVER
GREASE IN OLD
CARTRIDGE

GREASE
GUN HEAD

NEW
GREASE
CARTRIDGE

**1** **Pack the head.** Scoop any remaining grease out of the old cartridge and pack it into the head.

BLEED
PLUG

**2** **Burp from the top.** Unscrew the plug on the head of the gun, but keep it positioned directly over the hole. Screw it back in as soon as the air bubble clears.

# WHAT TO DO IF...

*Learn what those lights mean, and other tips to keep your car running*

### by Rick Muscoplat, Contributing Editor

**In** a quick survey of coworkers and friends, I discovered that many people really don't know what to do when a warning light appears on their dash. And they're just as confused when it comes to which maintenance services are really important. So I've put together these tip lists for warning lights, maintenance services, driving advice and emergency kits. I guarantee you'll find something here to help you be a safer, smarter driver and car owner.

GETTY IMAGES/ CARLOS GAWRONSKI

## WHAT TO DO WHEN
# WARNING LIGHTS COME ON

You're driving down the road and your "HOT" light comes on. If your first thought is, "You're hot? I'm sweatin' bullets in here," you've failed to understand the seriousness of the situation. Those warning lights aren't a joke. If you ignore them and keep driving, you're setting yourself up for major repair bills. Here's what the lights mean and what you should do if any of them come on when you're driving.

**TPS (TIRE PRESSURE SENSOR).** At least one tire is low on air pressure. Fill it as soon as possible. Driving on an underinflated tire can cause a blowout, possibly resulting in an "at-fault" accident. Air is free (or cheap). But a new tire is about $125, and an accident will cost you your deductible and increased premiums in the future.

**OIL.** The oil pressure is too low to keep driving. Pull over to a safe spot immediately. Check the oil level. If it's low and you have oil on hand, add it and see if the light goes out. If you don't have oil, call a tow truck or ask someone to make a roadside delivery. It's better to spend $150 on a tow than $4,000 to replace a seized engine.

**HOT.** The engine is overheated. Pull over to a safe spot immediately. Open the hood, then call a tow truck ($150 average tow to the nearest shop). If you keep driving, you can warp the cylinder head (minimum $1,000 repair bill) or completely destroy your engine.

**BATTERY LIGHT.** Something is wrong with the battery or charging system. Turn off all high-load electrical accessories such as the air conditioning, heater fan and rear window defogger, and drive to the nearest shop.

**FLASHING "CHECK ENGINE" LIGHT.** The computer has detected a misfire serious enough to damage your catalytic converter. Pull over to a safe place or drive to the nearest exit and call a tow truck. Get the underlying misfire problem fixed right away—a new catalytic converter can cost $1,500.

**STEADY-ON "CHECK ENGINE" LIGHT.** The computer has detected a problem with the engine or the emissions system. If the vehicle is running fine, you don't have to rush in for service. But if it's running rough, stalls, hesitates on acceleration or gets poor gas mileage, make an appointment to get it checked out sooner rather than later.

VEHICLES & GARAGES

# WHAT TO DO TO
# KEEP YOUR ENGINE RUNNING

Shops recommend 30,000-, 60,000- and 90,000-mile services that can easily cost $400. The majority of the items on those lists are inspections. Sure, they're important, but the "replace" items are the most important. Here are the top five items you must replace in order to avoid major repair bills later.

**TRANSMISSION FLUID.** If you put on 200,000 miles during the life of the car, you'll spend about $800 on fluid changes. If you skip the fluid changes, you'll only have $800 to put toward the $2,000 cost for a transmission rebuild. Did you buy an extended warranty? Well, you just voided that, too. It never pays to skip this service.

**COOLANT.** If you change the newer long-life coolants twice over a 200,000-mile period, you'll spend $300. If you don't change it, plan on spending about $1,800 on a new radiator, heater core and water pump. Kiss the extended warranty good-bye, too. For best results, always use genuine factory coolant.

**OIL FILTER.** You already know how important oil changes and synthetic oil are to the life of your engine. But an extended-life oil filter is just as important. They cost about $10 but are rated to last 7,000 to 10,000 miles. Economy filters start to clog and self-destruct after about 4,000 miles. Once the filter media disintegrates, it can spew debris into critical parts and cause thousands in repair bills.

**SPARK PLUGS.** Newer-style platinum/iridium spark plugs are rated for 100,000 miles. But they start misfiring at about 80,000 miles. Misfires damage spark plug wires, ignition coils, ignition modules and sometimes even your catalytic converter. If you don't change the plugs, you can count on a minimum of $400 in ignition system–related repairs.

**TIMING BELT.** A broken timing belt will leave you stranded (if your engine has one). If you're lucky, you'll just have to pay $150 for a tow and then $600 (parts and labor) for the new belt. But if you have a certain type of engine (called an "interference" engine) and the belt breaks while you're driving, it'll destroy your engine, costing you about $4,000.

NEW COOLANT

OLD, RUSTY COOLANT

FRESH ENGINE OIL

WORN-OUT ENGINE OIL

FRESH TRANSMISSION FLUID

BURNT, SMELLY TRANSMISSION FLUID

WORN-OUT SPARK PLUG

NEW SPARK PLUG

# WHAT TO DO **IN AN EMERGENCY**

Most people don't think clearly in an emergency. So copy this section and stuff it in your glove box. Follow the steps and you'll improve your chances of getting out safely.

## What to pack in an emergency kit

If you follow every expert's advice on what to carry in the event of an emergency, you'd have a trunk full of supplies (especially candy bars). I'm not disputing the value of carrying all those items, but I don't know anyone who does. So I've assembled a list of "must-have" items that take up very little space and can really help you in an emergency.

- **Pad/pencil** for accident information
- **Air compressor** to inflate your spare tire
- **Duct tape** to use as a handyman bandage or to reattach vehicle parts after an accident
- **Cell phone charger** to keep your cell phone running until help arrives
- **LED headlight** so you can use both hands while you fix a flat tire, add oil, etc.
- **Oil** to refill your engine if it's critically low from leaks or excessive consumption
- **Jumper cables** to get you going again and right to a service station
- **A can of Fix-a-Flat** (about $8) to fix a flat tire when the wheel is rusted in place and won't come off

## Cold weather gear

If you've ever changed a tire in winter, you know how quickly your hands get numb from working with subzero tools. And wind can freeze your ears in seconds, making you unable to finish the job. Frostbite is a serious risk. If you pack nothing else in your winter emergency kit, make sure you at least have warm gloves and a hat to cover your ears.

> *"No one taught me how to change a flat tire. So I had to change my first flat on the side of a busy road at dusk. I almost got hit four or five times. Now, I'll make sure all of my kids change a tire BEFORE they get any keys."*
>
> —Tim Boehnen

## An app for young drivers (and parents)

DriveScribe is a free app for iPhone and Android systems (drivescribe.com). It's designed to help young drivers develop safe driving habits. Parents with young drivers can make using the family vehicle contingent on keeping the app on while driving. Some parents offer to pay or subsidize insurance if young drivers use the app. It's also a rewards program: When driving safely, young drivers earn points that are redeemable for products and discounts.

When running, the app blocks all incoming text messages. It warns drivers of upcoming changes in speed limits and curves in the road. The app immediately notifies parents if the young driver runs a stop sign or speeds. And it tracks the car's location in real time so parents can monitor the driver's whereabouts.

## WHY IS MY TIRE PRESSURE LIGHT ON?

*My TPS light is on, and I've checked all four tires. They're at the correct pressure. My friend said I might need new batteries in the sensors. How do I replace the batteries?*

The batteries in a TPS (tire pressure sensor) last five to seven years. But they're not serviceable. When they fail, you have to replace the entire sensor.

But before you run your vehicle into the shop, check the pressure on your spare tire. Some manufacturers install sensors on those tires as well, and they lose air just like your regular tires. Low pressure in that tire could be lighting up your TPS.

# REJUVENATE YOUR
# CAR'S INTERIOR

*Spiff up your ride in a weekend*

### by **Rick Muscoplat, Contributing Editor**

**D**ealers know that spiffing up the interior of a used car is the best way to command a higher price. Whether you're planning to sell your vehicle or just want to freshen up your daily driver, we'll show you how to slap the shabby off your vehicle's interior. It's neither hard nor expensive, and you'll be amazed at just how new your car's interior will look.

You can recondition the plastic/vinyl on your doors, dash, seats and console areas for about $75. Or, spend about $150 and do it all, including the carpet, velour and upholstery. You can recolor just about everything in the interior. If you vacuum and shampoo your vehicle ahead of time, you can complete the whole rejuvenation process in a single weekend (allowing for drying time between steps).

Several companies make reconditioning products, but we chose SEM because it's the brand most professional shops use. Plus, it's available at many auto parts stores

### MEET AN EXPERT

**Larry Trexler is the National Trainer and Technical Service Manager for SEM Products. He's been "hands-on" in the auto body repair and restoration business for 27 years.**

and online sources (such as vinylpro.com). SEM makes products to repair and refurbish plastic, vinyl, velour, leather and carpet. When applied properly, the flexible colored coating won't chip, flake or fade.

We asked SEM's restoration expert, Larry Trexler, to show us how the pros recondition vinyl, plastic, carpet and velour. For instructions on restoring leather, visit semproducts.com.

BEFORE

AFTER

## Get the right materials and prep the vehicle

SEM makes refinishing products in more than 50 colors, so get the color chart from a local dealer and match color chips to your carpet and plastic parts. This process isn't designed for changing colors in your car. You'll get the best results by choosing colors that are as close as possible to the original ones.

It's important to buy the correct "plastic adhesion promoter" with the kit, so take a minute to watch the training video at semproducts.com to determine the type of plastic you have in your car. Adhesion promoter helps the color coating "bite" into the plastic. You'll also need the manufacturer's cleaner and prep materials, scuff pads, a nylon brush, masking materials, nitrile gloves, a respirator, eye protection, and clean, lint-free rags.

# VINYL AND PLASTIC

**1** Apply SEM Soap to vinyl and plastic surfaces and scrub with a scuff pad. Put extra effort into textured and recessed areas. Wipe the surface with a clean, damp, lint-free cloth and let dry.

**2** Spray Vinyl Prep on vinyl areas and wipe off the residue in one direction with a clean, damp, lint-free rag. Then spray Adhesion Promoter on plastic surfaces and let it "flash." Wipe off with a clean cloth. Let dry.

**3** Spray on several light coats of colorant (Color Coat is shown), allowing five to 10 minutes between coats. Let the colorant dry for 24 hours before using.

# CARPET AND VELOUR

Prepare the vehicle by vacuuming and cleaning all surfaces with household cleaners. Shampoo the upholstery and carpet and let everything dry completely. Then move the car outside to a shaded area and roll down the windows (the coatings have a pretty strong solvent smell).

Mask off all areas you don't want to recolor, and cover the seats and carpet with a tarp to protect against overspray. And, if you're coloring the carpet, consider removing the seats rather than masking around them—you'll save time and get better results.

**1** Spray Plastic & Leather Prep on the carpet or velour and scrub lightly with a nylon bristle brush. Let dry and vacuum.

**2** Apply colorant to the carpet or velour and immediately brush in all directions with a nylon bristle brush to keep the fibers separated. Let dry. Then brush again and vacuum.

VEHICLES & GARAGES

# BURGLAR-PROOF
# YOUR GARAGE

*Is your garage an easy entrance?*

## by **Gary Wentz, Senior Editor**

**M**ost homeowners close the overhead garage door and assume they've locked out bad guys. And they're mostly correct; a garage door connected to an opener is pretty secure. But there are a few ways that crooks might get through your door. This article will show you how they do it—and how to stop them.

### Ways to lock out crooks

■ **Beef up the service door.** The walk-through entry door (called the "service door") is the No. 1 security weak spot in most garages. It should be equipped with a dead bolt and a heavy-duty strike plate, just like any other exterior door in your house.

■ **Lock the entry door.** If you have an attached garage, lock the entry door that leads into the house. Too many homeowners rely on the service door and leave the entry door unlocked.

■ **Cover windows.** If crooks can't see the tools and toys in your garage, they won't be motivated to get in. Sheer curtains or translucent window film lets in light but keeps valuables out of sight.

■ **Add lighting.** Bright lighting makes burglars nervous and just might make them go elsewhere. Motion detector lighting is better than on-all-night lighting because it saves energy when it's off and attracts attention when it's on.

■ Get more security tips for your garage and home at familyhandyman.com. Search for "security."

### Don't keep the clicker in your car

A thief who breaks into your car can grab the remote for easy access to your garage. This isn't just a problem when your car is parked in the driveway; the registration card in your glove box gives a crook your address. So get rid of the remote on your visor and buy a keychain remote ($25 and up). You can easily take it with you every time you leave the car. Home centers stock only a small selection of remotes, but you'll find more online. Start your search by typing in the brand of your opener, followed by "remote."

## Prevent fishing

Every garage door opener has an emergency release that disconnects the door from the opener. Without it, you wouldn't be able to open the door when the opener is on the fritz. But some clever crooks have turned this essential feature into a security risk.

"Fishing" a garage door isn't exactly easy, and in some situations it's almost impossible. Some openers, for example, have a release mechanism that must be pulled straight down and won't release if the cord is tugged at an angle toward the door. Others are a bit easier to fish, especially if your garage door has a window that allows the crook to see what he's doing.

## HOW IT'S DONE

WEDGE

RELEASE LEVER

RELEASE CORD

**Push and probe**
By pushing the door inward to create a gap at the top, a crook can insert a wire hook and fish for the release. Some use a wedge to hold the gap open.

**Hook and pull**
Once the cord is hooked, all it takes is a good yank to disconnect the door from the opener. On some models, hooking the release lever works too.

## 2 WAYS TO PREVENT IT

**Make a shield**
A shield makes grabbing the release cord almost impossible. This shield is simply a wood cleat and a scrap of plywood screwed to the opener's arm. The plywood is fastened to the cleat with just two brad nails, so it can break away—rather than do damage—if it runs into something while the door is traveling.

SHIELD

CLEAT

ARM

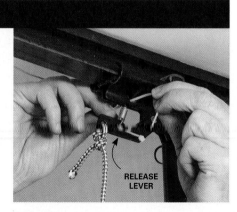

RELEASE LEVER

**Add a tie**
If your trolley has a pair of holes, you can lock the release with a small plastic tie. Use the smallest tie you can find. It will be strong enough to resist the tug of a fishing wire but will break away with a hard pull on the release cord.

VEHICLES & GARAGES

## High-security, high-tech opener

One way to protect your garage is to choose an opener with built-in security features. One example is Chamberlain's MyQ line, which features:

### A monitor
No more getting out of bed to make sure the door is closed. A monitor placed anywhere in your home tells you whether the door is open or closed. Unlike the monitor shown on p. 261, this one has a button that closes the door.

### A self-closing system
When you forget to close the door, this opener does it for you. As with the system shown on p. 261, you can adjust the open time or override the self-closing feature. Unlike that system, this one is built right in.

### Lighting controls
The opener itself has two bulbs, but it can also switch on lamps or fixtures, inside your home or out. The lights can switch on when the opener operates, or you can use the remote to flip them on independently of the opener.

### Smartphone connection
From anywhere on earth, you can make sure the door is closed or open it to let in the plumber. Better yet, the opener can send a notification when the door opens so you know exactly when your teenager got home last night.

MyQ-enabled openers cost about $250; accessories like monitors and lighting controllers cost $30 to $50. The smartphone app and service are free. Find out more at myqhome.com.

## Lock up the overhead door

Some people "lock" the door when they go on vacation by unplugging the opener. That's a good idea, but physically locking the door is even better. An unplugged opener won't prevent fishing, and—if you have an attached garage—it won't stop a burglar who has entered through the house from opening the garage door from inside, backing in a van and using the garage as a loading dock for his plunder. Make a burglar's job more difficult and time-consuming by locking the door itself.

**Lock the track**
If your door doesn't have a lockable latch, drill a hole in the track just above one of the rollers and slip in a padlock.

## Don't forget to close the door

Lots of garages get looted simply because someone forgot to close the door. A **garage door monitor** (about $30) is a good reminder. Just stick the sensor to the door and set the monitor in a conspicuous spot like your nightstand. To find a monitor, search online for "garage door monitor." The brand of your door or opener doesn't matter; any monitor will work.

An **automatic door closer** ($45 and up) provides even more security, since it closes the door whether you're home or not. Installation requires some simple low-voltage wiring and takes less than an hour. To find one, search online for "automatic garage door closer."

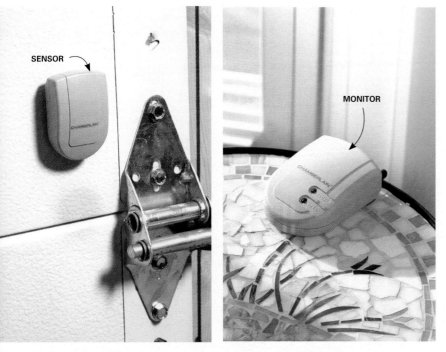

**Garage door monitor**
The sensor sends a signal to the monitor, telling you whether the door is open or closed. Both units are battery-operated—no wiring is required.

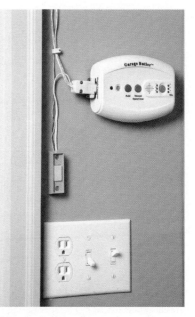

**Automatic door closer**
This device allows the door to stay open for a set amount of time, then closes it. You set the timer and can override it on those summer days when you're working in the garage.

## GreatGoofs®

### Smokin' new man cave

After hours of meticulous, testosterone-enriched planning, I began building my garage "man cave." I installed cabinets with workbenches, storage units, a dust collection system, air filtration and even a heater. Because of the low ceiling, I carefully installed recessed lighting so that my custom hand-carved garage door would roll up unobstructed once it was installed.

On the first warm day of spring, I rolled up my old garage door (the new one hadn't arrived yet) and started working in my new man cave. After about 15 minutes, I smelled smoke and realized my garage door was smoldering! I rolled it down and found three scorched spots where my recessed lights were burning into the door. I'm just glad my custom door hadn't been installed yet!

—Wade Clary

VEHICLES &
GARAGES

# CLEAN UP YOUR GREASY ENGINE

*Roll up your sleeves and find out how easy it is to have a clean engine*

by **Rick Muscoplat, Contributing Editor**

**I**f you're a clean freak, you've probably been degreasing your engine for years. But if you've never done it, here are two good reasons why you should. First, a clean engine is easier to work on. Second, a clean engine brings more at resale. But you can't just spray it with degreaser and hose it down. I'll show you how to prepare the engine to protect critical electrical connections. I'll also give you some tips for doing the job in an environmentally safe way.

## Picking a degreasing product

Degreasing products come in two types: solvent and water-based. Both types work on greasy engines. And

**1 Protect everything electrical.** Wrap ignition wires and coils and all electrical connectors with plastic wrap. Then add a flag of fluorescent surveyor's tape so you don't forget to remove the wrap later.

both require special environmental handling once they're applied—even if the label says "environmentally safe" or "biodegradable." Because once the degreasing solution starts dissolving the grease, it's considered hazardous waste.

I prefer solvent-based degreasers because they work faster and seem to cut through heavy grease buildup better than most water-based products. The downside is their strong solvent smell. If you're sensitive to solvents, choose a concentrated water-based product instead.

To get better "cling" on vertical surfaces, choose either a foam or a gel formula (such as GUNK Heavy Duty Gel Degreaser; about $6 at auto parts stores).

While you're at the auto parts store, pick up a drip pan and three 3-packs of absorbent mat. We used PIG Universal Medium Weight Absorbent Mat, which costs about $5 at NAPA auto parts stores and tooloutfitters.com.

## Warm it up, wrap it up and spray away

Degreasers work best when the grease is warm and soft. So start the engine and let it run for about five minutes. Then shut it off and let it cool down until you can safely touch the exhaust manifold. Never spray cleaners (especially flammable solvent types) on a hot engine.

If you're using a concentrated water-based product, test it on a greasy spot. If it doesn't cut the grease fast enough, add more concentrated degreaser to the brew.

Next, seal all the electrical connections (**Photo 1**). Then set the absorbent mats under the engine to soak up the runoff (**Photo 2**). Prep the worst areas (**Photo 3**). Then apply the degreaser (**Photo 4**). Aim carefully to prevent the overspray from reaching painted areas. Rinse lightly with water and remove the plastic wrap. When you're done, place the wet mats in sunlight to allow the water to evaporate. Then dispose of the mats following local regulations.

For extra protection, spray an engine protectant (GUNK Engine Shine is one brand) onto the dry engine. The spray imparts a slight shine and a protective layer of grease to make cleanup even easier next time.

**2** **Soak up the hazardous waste.** Spread absorbent mats on a drip pan and slide the pan under the engine.

**3** **Scratch the surface on the worst areas.** Break up the baked-on crud with a wire brush before you apply the degreaser. Brush gently or switch to a nylon brush around plastic components.

**4** **Spray, soak and rinse.** Spray the degreaser over the entire engine and let it soak for the recommended time. Apply additional coats (if needed) to really greasy areas. Then rinse with a water mist, using as little water as possible.

# 12 TRAILER UPGRADES

*Add custom features to your utility trailer to increase its usefulness*

by **Rick Muscoplat, Contributing Editor**

**M**ost utility trailers come from the factory with just enough features to satisfy local safety regulations (if any) and your wallet. Sure, they work, but they're not very user-friendly. They rarely have factory tie-downs or loading ramps. Factory taillights usually have incandescent bulbs, which need constant replacement.

Your trailer doesn't have to stay that way. Here are eight upgrades to make your trailer-hauling jobs a lot easier and safer. And the security upgrades prevent trailer theft. You can build and install most of the upgrades with just a socket set, drill, saw and screwdriver. Find the plumbing and hardware components at a home center or hardware store and the security items at any trailer accessories store or online. Choose the upgrades you like. If you tackle them all, you'll drop about $300.

## Can't have too many tie-downs!

Did you know that poorly secured loads are responsible for more than 25,000 crashes and approximately 90 fatalities in this country each year? There's simply no such thing as too many tie-down anchors. Hitching rings work great for this. You can find them at most hardware stores for about $4 each. Buy at least six 3/8 x 5-1/8-in. hitching rings (National Mfg. Co., No. 220-632), and mount two each in the front, middle and near the tailgate. Just drill holes in the frame (not the floorboards), insert the long bolt end and secure the threaded portion with a locknut.

HITCH RING

## The plumber's trick

Ever tried to transport long or fragile items like pipe, drywall corner beads or drip edge? First you have to tie them in a bundle. Then you have to secure the bundle to the trailer. Forget that! Instead, build the same kind of rig a plumber uses. Then just slide in the long items, screw on the cap, secure a red flag and you're good to go. Build the entire unit for about $25.

Buy a 10-ft. length of 4-in. PVC pipe, an end cap, a cleanout adapter, PVC cleaner and adhesive, and four J-hooks. Prime and glue the end cap and cleanout adapter. Take advantage of the wasted space on the side of your trailer and mount the tube there. Secure the four J-hooks to the side of the trailer and snap the tube into place. Tie the rig with rope for added security.

J-HOOK

TIE-DOWN ROPE

## Save your back with ramps

BOTTOM ADAPTER

LOCKDOWN PIN

TOP ADAPTER

Why lift heavy items when you can wheel them up? Build this ramp using an aluminum ramp kit (such as the Highland No. 0700500; $37 at summitracing. com) and a 2x8. Just measure the height of the trailer deck and cut the 2x8 to the recommended length. Mount the aluminum top and bottom pieces to each board. Then space the ramps to fit the equipment you haul most often. Install the locking pins, lock the ramps in place and load 'er up.

## Winch it in

Boat owners use a winch to pull their boat onto the trailer. You can install one on a utility trailer, too. It'll save your back and eliminate the need for a helper. Just wrap the strap around the heavy object and crank it up the ramp toward the front of the trailer. A winch with a 20-ft. pull strap and hook costs about $33. Bolt it to the trailer A-frame or tongue.

WINCH STRAP

WINCH MOUNTED TO TONGUE

## 7 ways to prevent trailer disasters

**1. Tires:** Always replace trailer tires with "Special Trailer" (ST) tires (never passenger-rated tires). ST-rated tires have stronger sidewalls and are built to handle heavier loads. ST tires have a maximum life of five years from the date of manufacture. Replace yours accordingly.

**2. Tire pressure:** Inflate trailer tires to the pressure shown on the tire's sidewall. Or, if the sidewall pressure conflicts with the recommended pressure shown on the trailer manufacturer's nameplate, follow the manufacturer's pressure recommendation. Low tire pressure is the No. 1 cause of trailer tire failure. Overloading the trailer is No. 2.

**3. Lug nut/bolt torque:** Tightening lug nuts or bolts to the proper torque is critical. If you're not using a torque wrench, you'll never get it right. The recommended torque should be listed on the trailer manufacturer's nameplate, and it's usually much higher than for cars and trucks. Never drive a loaded trailer with a missing lug nut or damaged lug bolt.

**4. Safety chains:** Always cross the safety chains when you hook up to the hitch. The crossed chains catch the tongue and prevent it from hitting the pavement if it ever detaches from the receiver. Leave only enough chain slack to allow for turns. If your chain is longer than that, shorten it. Secure the coupler throw latch with a lock or clip to prevent it from popping open.

**5. Wheel bearings:** Failed wheel bearings are the No. 2 cause of all trailer breakdowns. Repack the bearings at least once a year (go to familyhandyman.com and search "trailer" for a step-by-step article on repacking bearings). And don't pack the hub with grease. Extra grease in the hub generates heat that can cause premature bearing failure.

**6. Load placement:** Place 60 percent of the weight toward the front of the trailer to prevent sway and fishtailing.

**7. Lubricate the ball:** If you don't, you're wearing out either the ball or the coupler. And that wear can cause a sudden and dangerous disconnect. Sure, grease is messy. But it's the only way to reduce heat and wear. Grease it or lose it.

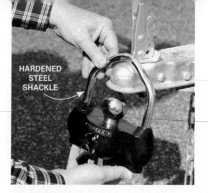

HARDENED STEEL SHACKLE

## Foil trailer thieves

Trailer thieves get quite a laugh out of coupler "latch locks." They can cut them in an instant with even the smallest bolt cutter. Then they're on their way with your trailer. If you want real protection, use a coupler lock that presents thieves with a real challenge. (Shown here is the Trimax UMAX100 Universal Coupler lock; about $50 online.) Just insert the ball into the coupler and slide on the U-bracket. Unless the thief has the time to unbolt the entire coupler and install a new one, you'll be well protected.

## Headache-free trailer lights

Who hasn't had trouble with trailer lights? Even if you're a cheapskate and hate the idea of spending $50 on new taillights, these newer-style LED lights will change your mind. Imagine never having to change a bulb or deal with corroded contacts. Better yet, imagine never getting stopped by the police for a dead trailer light. LED taillights are worth every penny. The Blazer C7280 LED submersible trailer lights shown here are $50 to $60 online.

MOUNTING PLATE

## Light it up

If you've ever loaded a trailer or hooked one to the hitch in the dark, you know it's not fun. These magnetic LED tap lights (the Energizer Hard Case Professional 3-LED Area Light; about $10 online) are removable so they won't get wrecked. Just mount the backing plate where you'll get the best illumination for loading and hitching, then slap the light onto the plate. Those babies are weatherproof, unlike most tap lights. But stow them before you take off. The magnets might not hold them on rough roads.

## Really foil trailer thieves

If you have a really expensive trailer, it pays to get an extra layer of protection by using a "boot"-style lock in addition to the coupler lock. There are many styles to choose from, but I liked this particular model (the Trimax TCL75 Wheel Chock Lock; usually $65 to $70 online) because it doubles as a wheel chock to prevent the trailer from rolling. Just slide it onto the wheel and press in the lock cylinder.

1-1/2" ELECTRICAL CONDUIT STRAP

## The landscaper's trick

Landscapers and lawn care guys always haul around rakes, shovels, brooms and other implements by mounting vertical tubes on the front of their trailers. Here's our version. Cut 36-in. lengths of 1-1/2-in. PVC pipe and glue on an end cap. Then drill a hole in each end cap to provide drainage. Attach the tubes using PVC electrical conduit straps and nuts. If you plan to use the tubes in winter, secure them with metal straps—PVC gets brittle in cold weather and can shatter. For added security, hook a bungee strap to each implement.

TRIMAX

"Chock It & Lock It"

WHEEL CHOCK TEETH

## A cargo net and D-rings are great for "lighty, loosey" items

At highway speeds, light items can fly right out of your trailer. Even if they're tied down, they can break loose and take off. So you need one final mode of protection. We recommend a cargo net. Find one for about $30 in the automotive section of the home center or at any auto parts store. Install D-rings ($1.50 each) every 18 in. along the top rails. You may be tempted to screw them into place. Don't. As the wood rails age, the screws can pull out. Instead, secure the D-rings with nuts and bolts. When you're finished loading, just throw the net over the trailer and clip the snaps to the rings.

## Stow the spare

Flat tires are the No. 1 cause of trailer breakdowns. If you're not carrying a spare tire when you get a flat, you're in a heap of trouble. But where do you keep it? In the trailer bed where it's in the way? This spare tire carrier (Fulton Performance Heavy Duty Spare Tire Carrier; about $40 online) doesn't require assembly and can be mounted easily to the trailer rails. To lock the tire in place, simply run a bicycle locking cable down the tube and snap it shut.

## Vertical storage bins

Here's a great way to store your ratchet straps and bungee cords with the trailer, where they belong. Build vertical storage bins from 6-in. PVC pipe. Glue a cap on the bottom and drill a hole in it to overcome the suction when you pull off the lid. Then mount a handle on the top cap and attach a chain. Perfect dry storage for whatever will fit inside.

CAP AND CHAIN

# HandyHints®
### FROM OUR READERS

## High-visibility trailer

I painted the top of my trailer's loading ramp white so I could see it better. It makes a huge difference when I'm backing up, especially on rainy days. At night, my back-up lights reflect off the white paint, and I can maneuver the trailer much more easily.

—Cody McGee

READER PHOTO

# GARAGE DOOR
# OPENER FIXES

*Don't blow $200 on a new opener. Most repairs are cheap and easy!*

by **Mark Petersen, Contributing Editor**

**N**ot many appliances get as much of a workout as the garage door opener. They usually give us years of hassle-free service, but openers do break down. When that happens, don't assume you need to replace it. There are several repairs you can make that don't require a lot of money, a bunch of special tools or an engineering degree. Here we've assembled advice and repair experiences from a garage door expert and our Field Editors to make the job easy for you.

### MEET AN EXPERT

**Field Editor Dan Mueller has been in the garage door and opener business for more than 20 years. He's worked on everything from small residential openers to commercial models that lift 40 x 30-ft. doors.**

# KNOW YOUR OPENER

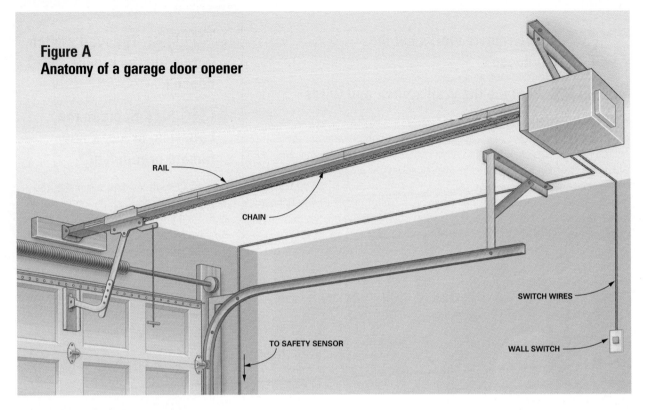

**Figure A**
**Anatomy of a garage door opener**

RAIL

CHAIN

TO SAFETY SENSOR

SWITCH WIRES

WALL SWITCH

**Figure B   Carriage assembly**

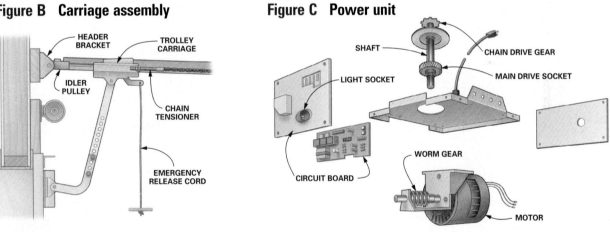

HEADER BRACKET

TROLLEY CARRIAGE

IDLER PULLEY

CHAIN TENSIONER

EMERGENCY RELEASE CORD

**Figure C   Power unit**

SHAFT

LIGHT SOCKET

CHAIN DRIVE GEAR

MAIN DRIVE SOCKET

CIRCUIT BOARD

WORM GEAR

MOTOR

## Check your door first

With the door closed, pull the emergency release cord and lift the door to see if it opens and closes smoothly. If it doesn't, the problem is with your tracks, roll ers or springs rather than your opener. This article covers opener problems only.

## And play it safe

**Work with the door down.** If the problem is a broken door spring and you pull the emergency release cord while the door is in the raised position, the door could come crashing down.

**Unplug the opener.** That way, you won't lose a finger if your unsuspecting spouse hits the remote button while you're working. Even worse, you could electrocute yourself, in which case you wouldn't be able to blame your spouse at all.

## Where to buy your parts

Go to an authorized online parts dealer like prodoorparts.com or stardoorparts.com, or call your local garage door company. Home centers carry some parts, such as photo eye sensors, lubricants and remotes.

# Diagnosis and repair

**The remote works but the wall switch doesn't.**

**Replace the wall switch and wires**

If the remote works but the wall switch doesn't, you may need to replace either the wall switch or the switch wires. To determine whether the switch or the wires are bad, first unscrew the switch from the wall and touch the two wires together (don't worry, the wires are low voltage and won't shock you). If the opener runs, you have a bad switch. If you have an older-model opener, a cheap doorbell button might work. If you have a newer opener that has a light and a locking option on the switch, buy the one designed for your model. A new one should cost you about $15.

If the opener doesn't run when you touch the wires at the opener, use a small wire and jump those same two wires at the opener terminal. If the opener runs, the wire that connects the opener to the switch is bad. Sometimes the staples that hold the wire to the wall pinch the wire, causing a short. Install 18- to 22-gauge wire.

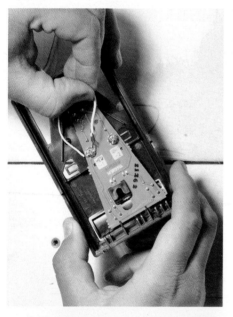

**Test the wall switch**
Unscrew one wire and touch the other terminal with it. If the opener runs, replace the switch.

**Test the wires**
Jump the two terminals on the back of the opener with a short wire. If the opener runs, replace the wiring.

**The wall switch works but the remote doesn't.**

**Replace the batteries, or buy a new remote or receiver**

If the wall switch works but one of the remotes doesn't, check the batteries first—still nothing? You may need a new remote. Home centers carry a few models, and you can find a wide selection online (about $40).

If you can't find one for your opener model, you can try a universal remote or you can install a new receiver. A receiver replaces the radio frequency the opener uses with its own. An added bonus of a new receiver is that it will automatically update older openers to the new rolling code technology, which stops the bad guys from stealing your code. Just plug the new receiver into an outlet close to the opener, and run the two wires provided to the same terminals the wall switch is connected to. A receiver with one remote costs about $60.

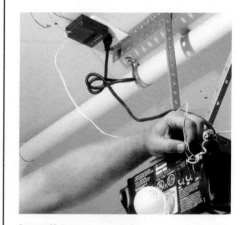

**Install a new receiver**
Plug your new receiver into an outlet and run two wires to the opener.

*"No special training or online course is needed to fix a garage door opener. The only requirements are patience, a DIY aptitude and determination."*

—Dave Pike, Field Editor

## Symptom The door goes up, but it only goes down when you hold down the wall switch.

## The Fix Align or replace the safety sensor

If the door goes up but goes down only when you hold down the wall switch, check to see that the safety sensors are in alignment. The small light on each sensor should be lit up when nothing is between them. Door sensors do go bad, so if no light is showing at all, you may need to replace them. You can save yourself some time by using the existing wires. Also, direct sunlight shining on sensor eyes can make them misbehave. A new pair of sensors sells for about $40.

**When sensors go bad**
Sensors are brand-specific; buy new ones made for your opener.

## Symptom You have power to the outlet, but there's no sound or no lights when you push the wall switch and remotes.

## The Fix Replace the circuit board

If the outlet has power, but there's no sound or no lights when you push the wall switch and remotes, you probably have a bad circuit board. Lightning strikes are the most frequent reason for the demise of a circuit board. The circuit board consists of the entire plastic housing that holds the lightbulb and wire terminals. The part number should be on the board itself.

Replacing a circuit board sounds scary, but it's really quite easy. It will take 10 minutes tops and only requires a 1/4-in. nut driver. Just follow these steps: Remove the light cover, take out the lightbulb, disconnect the switch and safety sensor wires, remove a few screws, unplug the board and you're done. A circuit board will cost about $80, so make sure you protect your new one with a surge protector. You can buy an individual outlet surge protector at a home center for less than $10.

**Remove the circuit board**
Removing the circuit board is as easy as unscrewing a few screws and disconnecting a couple of plugs.

## Symptom Everything works except the lights.

## The Fix Replace the light socket

If the bulbs are OK but don't light up, you probably have a bad light socket. To replace the socket, you'll need to remove the circuit board to get at it. Use the same steps as in "Replace the Circuit Board" to accomplish this.

Once the circuit board has been removed, pop out the old socket by depressing the clip that holds it in place. Remove the two wire connections and install the new socket. Replacement sockets cost less than $15.

Be sure to use a bulb of the correct wattage. Using lightbulbs with a higher wattage than the socket is rated for will cause a socket to fail. Not only is this bad for the socket, but it can also be a fire hazard. If your light cover has turned yellow from heat, you're probably using too strong a bulb.

**Remove the old socket**
Remove the circuit board housing to access the light socket. Then unclip the old socket and snap in the new one.

*"Always use rough-duty bulbs in your opener. You won't have to change them as frequently."*
—Steve Yaeger, Field Editor

# Diagnosis and repair

## Symptom | The trolley carriage moves but the door doesn't open.

### The Fix | Replace the trolley carriage

If the trolley carriage moves but the door doesn't open, the culprit is probably a broken trolley carriage. Before you pull the old one off, clamp down the chain to the rail. This will help maintain the location of the chain on the sprocket and speed up reassembly.

Once the chain is secure, separate it from both sides of the trolley. Disconnect the rail from the header bracket and move the rail off to one side. Slide off the old trolley, and slide on the new one. Reattach the chain and adjust the chain tension. Replacing the trolley on a belt drive and replacing it on a screw drive are similar procedures. A new trolley will cost $25 to $40 depending on your model.

**Slide on the new carriage trolley**
Leave the rail attached to the opener, and install the new trolley from the other side. Clamp down the chain to make reassembly easier.

**Mark the chain and sprocket**
If you have to remove the chain for any reason, mark its location on the sprocket with a marker or wax pencil. The opener will require less adjusting when you put it back together.

## Symptom | The opener makes a grinding noise and the door doesn't move.

### The Fix | Replace the main gear drive

If the opener makes a grinding noise and the door doesn't move, your main drive gear is probably toast. The main drive gear is the plastic gear that comes in direct contact with the worm drive gear on the motor. The main drive gear is the most common component to fail on most openers.

Replacing it is a bit more complicated than the other repairs discussed here but still well within the capabilities of the average DIYer. There are several components that need to be removed before getting at the gear. For a detailed step-by-step description of this procedure, visit familyhandyman.com and search for "rebuild a garage door opener."

Once you get the gear out, you can remove it from the shaft with a punch, or you can buy a kit that comes with a new shaft. Make sure you lube it all up when you're done. The gear alone should cost you less than $20. A complete kit that comes with the shaft will cost closer to $40.

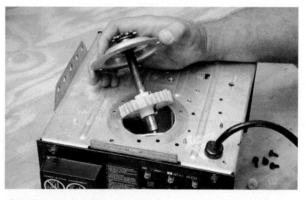

**1** **Pull out the old gear.** The shaft, sprocket and main drive gear should all come out as one piece. This procedure is best performed on a benchtop.

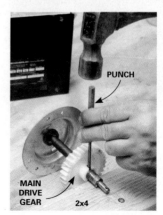

PUNCH

MAIN DRIVE GEAR    2x4

**2** **Remove the gear from the shaft.**
Support the shaft on a 2x4 and use a punch to drive out the pin that holds the gear in place.

# Make your opener last longer

## Lube the rail

No matter what type of garage door opener you have, you should always lube the rail where it comes in contact with the trolley carriage. Use a lubricant that doesn't attract dirt. Silicone spray is a good choice. If you have a screw-drive opener, you'll need to grease several spots along the rail gear at least once or twice a year. In colder climates, use lithium grease, which won't harden when the temperature drops. Many home centers sell specifically formulated products near the openers. And don't use too much or it could drip on your car.

**Grease the screw drive rail**
Once a year, apply 1- to 2-in. dabs at three points along the rail.

## Check the chain tension

Most chain drive openers suggest you tighten the chain so there's about 1/4 in. to 1/2 in. of slack from the rail to the chain (check your manual). Overtightening the chain will put excess wear and tear on the shaft and gears. Too little tension could cause the chain to skip off the sprocket and fall down on your car.

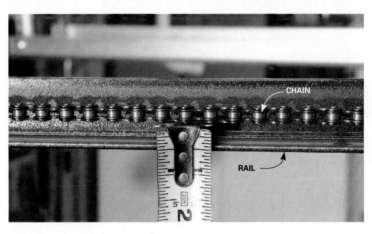

**Measure the slack on the chain**
Check for proper chain tension by measuring the distance between the chain and the rail at a point close to the center of the rail.

## Adjust the travel of the door

There are two knobs on the opener that control how far the door travels up and down. Your door should press snugly against the garage floor so the weather stripping seals the gap. If the door travels too far down, it will cause the rail to bow upward. This also causes excess wear and tear on the shaft and gears.

Your door should travel up far enough so that the bottom of the door is just about the same height as the doorjamb. There is a door stop that prevents the carriage trolley from crashing into the opener. Make sure the trolley stops before hitting this bolt.

**Overtravel causes bow in the rail**
If you notice an upward bow in the rail, reduce the distance the door travels down. A door that travels too far down causes excess wear and tear on the opener.

**Stop the trolley short of the door stop**
The carriage trolley will be damaged if it crashes into the door stop.

VEHICLES & GARAGES

# HOW TO CHANGE YOUR
# SPARK PLUGS

*Learn about the latest spark-plug technology, and how to work with it*

### by **Rick Muscoplat, Contributing Editor**

**If** you've changed your own spark plugs in the past but are intimidated by the newer-style coil-on-plug (COP) ignition systems (pretty much the standard since 2000), it's time to reconsider. COP systems may look complicated, but they're actually easier to work on than the older, distributor-based systems. Sure, you'll have to learn a few new tricks, but the basics are still the same.

Changing your own plugs takes about an hour (for a four-cylinder engine) and will save you at least $125 in labor. You can use the same old tune-up tools (ratchet, spark plug socket and gap gauge). You should use a torque wrench to tighten the plugs. But there's a way to get around that if you don't have one. Just follow these steps and you'll be tuned up in no time.

I talked with Dave Buckshaw, Technical Trainer for Autolite Spark Plugs, to get the skinny on the latest spark plug technologies. Dave's advice was simple: Regardless of which brand you buy, spend the extra money for a fine-wire iridium-tipped spark plug. These plugs cost about $2 more than platinum plugs, but they last longer and provide a much better spark.

For longer spark plug life, buy an iridium plug with a platinum-enhanced side electrode. They're available at all auto parts stores. While you're there, ask the clerk for the spark plug gap and torque specifications for your vehicle. And buy a small packet of dielectric grease.

## Remove the extras and clean your work area

Start by removing the plastic "vanity" cover (if equipped) and the air cleaner assembly from the top of the engine. Be sure to label any vacuum hoses you remove so you get them back in the right place. Then clean the top of a four-cylinder engine, or the banks on a "V" engine, before you remove other parts (**Photo 1**).

## Remove the ignition coil and boot

Disconnect the ignition coil electrical connector by depressing (or pulling up) on the locking tab. Then rock the connector off the coil. Next, remove the coil hold-down bolt and pull out the entire coil and boot assembly (**Photo 2**). Some COP systems have a detachable rubber boot and spring. If they don't come out with the coil, retrieve them with needle-nose pliers and replace them with new parts. Then remove the old spark plug.

## Gap the plug

Always check the spark plug gap before installing it. Buckshaw recommends using a wire-style gap gauge instead of the inexpensive variable-thickness "disc-style" gauge. They can bend the electrode off-center or even break it off.

Slide the correct wire gauge between the electrodes. The wire should drag slightly between them. If the gap is too small, open it with the gap gauge (**Photo 3**). If the gap is too large, tap the side electrode lightly on a solid surface.

## Install the new plug

New spark plugs have an anti-corrosive coating on the threads, so just screw them in and use a torque wrench to tighten to the correct torque.

If you don't have a torque wrench, go to the spark plug manufacturer's Web site to find manual tightening techniques.

## Lube the boot and button it up

Apply a thin coating of dielectric grease around the inside of the spark plug boot before reinstalling the coil (**Photo 4**). The grease prevents misfires and makes it easier to remove the boot in the future. Then reinstall the ignition coil, hold-down bolt and coil electrical connector. Finally, reinstall the air cleaner and vanity cover and fire it up. Enjoy the extra power and gas savings.

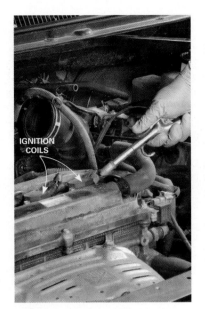

**1** **Blow away the crud.** Blast compressed air around the ignition coils to prevent crud from falling into the cylinders. Then blow any remaining loose dirt off the engine before you set out your tools and new plugs.

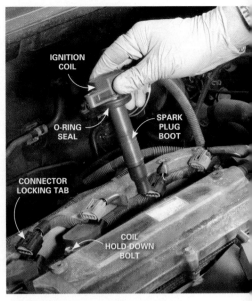

**2** **Pull the coil.** Twist the ignition coil about a quarter turn to break the O-ring seal loose. Then lift it straight up and out.

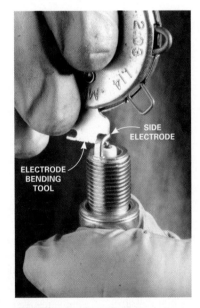

**3** **Open the gap.** Hook the adjusting tool onto the side electrode and pry it up slightly. Then recheck the gap.

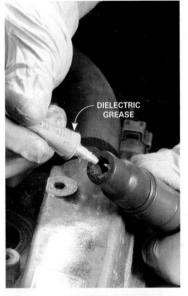

**4** **Lube the spark plug boot.** Squeeze a dollop of dielectric grease into the spark plug boot and spread it around with the tip of the applicator tube.

## When should I change the plugs?

Not all spark plugs are rated for 100,000 miles. In fact, some carmakers recommend replacement at 30,000-mile intervals. So always follow the spark plug service intervals shown in your owner's manual. But if you can't remember when you last changed your spark plugs, you can pull them and check the gap and their condition. Once you've put in the labor to do that, however, you may as well change them and establish a new baseline for the future.

# RESTORE A GARAGE FLOOR

*A fresh new face for ugly concrete in one day!*

## by **David Radtke, Contributing Editor**

**If** your slab is suffering from low self-esteem because of pits, craters or cracks, you can cover up those scars. Concrete "resurfacer" is a cement-based coating that forms a smooth, new surface right over the old concrete. The cost of resurfacer for a two-car garage is typically less than $200. You'll also need to buy or rent some special tools, so expect your total cost to be about $300.

Cleaning and resurfacing the floor usually takes one day (clearing out your garage so you can work may take weeks!). Spreading the resurfacer smoothly is the trickiest part of the project, so it helps to have some experience with concrete or drywall finishing. Cool weather, with temps in the 60s, also helps. Warmer weather makes resurfacer harden faster, reducing the time you have to finish the surface.

## Prep the slab

The cleaner the concrete, the better the resurfacer will stick. Start with a thorough sweeping. If you have oil spots to clean, scrub them with a deck brush and concrete cleaner. Once you've removed the stains, apply cleaner to the whole slab with the brush. Then fire up the pressure washer (**Photo 1**). Start in the back of the garage and work your way to the front, forcing the excess water out the overhead doorway.

**Important:** If you find that the cleaner doesn't soak into the concrete but just beads up into droplets on the surface, you have a sealer over the concrete that you'll need to remove. In that case, apply a stripper first to remove the sealer, then clean.

When the slab is clean, look for any pieces of con-

## Results to expect

As a first-timer, you might achieve a perfectly smooth, flat finish. Or you might end up with a few rough spots and small ridges. But even if your work is far from flawless, you'll still make a bad floor look much better. And remember this: If you make some major mistakes, you can add a second coat—this time with the benefit of experience.

Resurfacer is tough stuff that will withstand decades of traffic. It will permanently fill craters, but with cracks, long-term success is hard to predict. Tight, stable cracks may reappear. Cracks that have shifted slightly with the seasons or gradually widened over the years probably will reappear. That doesn't mean you shouldn't resurface the floor—even a crack that reappears and gradually grows will look a lot better than one that's left alone.

## Gather your materials

Everything you'll need for this project is available at home centers. Aside from basic tools like a hammer and chisel, buckets and a steel trowel, you'll need:

### Resurfacer

We used Quikrete Concrete Resurfacer (about $20 for 40 lbs.). Similar products, such as Sakrete Flo-Coat, are available. To estimate the amount you need, check the label and then buy two or three extra containers. Better to return some than to run out before the job's done.

### Plastic sheeting

Protect walls with a band at least 3 ft. high. We used 6-mil plastic, but lighter stuff will work too.

### Concrete cleaner

We used Quikrete Concrete & Stucco Wash. Other brands are available.

### Brush

A stiff version designed for stripping decks and mounted on a handle will keep you off your knees ($10).

### Pressure washer

For thorough cleaning, you'll need a model with 3,000 psi and a 15-degree spray tip. Rent one for about $40 for four hours.

### Squeegee

Get a beefy version designed for floors, not a lightweight window-cleaning tool. A quality squeegee will give you better results and is worth the price ($30 to $45).

### Mixing equipment

A powerful 1/2-in. drill and a mixing attachment ($12) are the only way to go. Mixing by hand is too slow.

### Protective gear

Rubber boots and gloves protect your skin against the degreaser and resurfacer (which can burn skin). You'll also need eye and hearing protection.

### What it takes

**COST:** $300

**TIME:** One to two days

**SKILL LEVEL:** Intermediate

**TOOLS:** Hammer, chisel, pressure washer, trowel, drill, mixer, squeegee

---

crete that the sprayer may have loosened. Chip these away (**Photo 2**) and collect the debris as you go, sweeping it into a dustpan with an old paintbrush. Now's the time to fill these cracks or divots. Mix some resurfacer to a mashed potato–like consistency and push the mix into the cracks. Smooth it with a cement trowel flush with the surrounding surface (**Photo 3**).

If you have expansion joints cut into the existing slab, push a weather strip into the joint. This will maintain the joint and give you a convenient time to stop and take a break. Apply and smooth no more than 150 sq. ft. of resurfacer at a time for the best results. You can glue a length of weather strip to the slab to define a stopping point if you don't have a control joint and then continue from that edge once you've smoothed the first section.

For a nice-looking finished edge under the overhead door, I applied a heavy-duty vinyl weather strip (**Photo 4**) that I picked up at a local home center. Just be sure to dry the slab along the location with a hair dryer so your adhesive will work properly.

**1** **Start with a clean floor.** Scrub with a concrete degreaser and a stiff brush, then follow up with a pressure washer. Rinse twice to remove all residue.

**2** **Remove the loose stuff.** Chisel away any loose fragments along cracks or craters; there's no need to bust away concrete that's firmly attached.

**3** **Fill cracks and craters.** Mix up a stiff batch of resurfacer, using just enough water for a workable consistency. Scrape off the excess so repairs are flush with the surrounding floor.

GARAGE DOOR
WEATHER STRIP

**4** **Create a dam.** Glue weather strip to the floor exactly where the garage door rests. This will stop resurfacer from flowing onto the driveway.

## Mix and spread the resurfacer

This is the time to recruit a helper. You'll need one person to mix and another to spread resurfacer. Take two minutes to read the directions before mixing. The key to a smooth, lump-free mix is to let the resurfacer "slake," that is, sit in the bucket for a few minutes after the initial mixing. Then mix a bit more (**Photo 5**). It's also good to have a slat of wood on hand to scrape the sides of the bucket as you mix.

The concrete should be damp when you apply the resurfacer, but not wet to the touch. Pour the mix onto the slab and immediately spread it (**Photo 6**). Work quickly and carefully, blending each stroke into the previous one until you get a nice, uniform look. Smooth the resurfacer

along the side walls by pulling the squeegee toward you. As you reach the edge of the door weather strip, use your steel trowel to gently blend the resurfacer against the weather strip. You can remove the excess with the trowel and drop it into a bucket.

With the slab finished, let the mix set up. In hot, dry weather, it's a good idea to mist the hardened surface; keeping it damp longer will allow the resurfacer to fully harden. After several hours, the finish will support foot traffic. Depending on the weather, wait at least 24 hours before driving on your newly finished slab. After a few days of curing, you can apply a sealer if you'd like to protect the slab from oil and other stains.

**5 Mix like mad.** Recruit a helper to mix the resurfacer while you spread it. The material begins to stiffen quickly, so the faster you get it all mixed and applied, the better your results.

**6 Spread it smooth, then let it set.** Push the squeegee forward to work the resurfacer into the concrete, then drag it back to smooth the coating. Aim for a thickness of 1/8 in. When you've covered the whole floor, let it cure for 24 hours before you drive on it.

### Erase your mistakes

If you end up with ridges, shallow craters or squeegee marks, you don't have to live with them forever. Go to a rental store and rent a concrete grinder for about $125 a day. It looks like a floor polisher, but it grinds down the surface, removing about 1/16 in. with each slow pass. It's a dusty job that might take all day, but you'll get a much smoother, flatter surface—perfect if you want to apply a finish like epoxy paint.

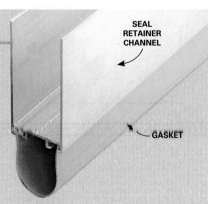

## SEAL A GARAGE DOOR GAP

If your garage floor is uneven under the door, you probably have gaps between the bottom of the door and the concrete. Here are two solutions to improve the seal of the garage door.

The easiest, but least elegant, method is to install several pieces of bottom seal retainer and rubber gasket in the gap areas. Just measure the thickness of your bottom panel and buy sections of seal retainer and gasket from a garage parts supplier (garagedoorpartsusa.com is one online source). Mount the retainer to the bottom panel wherever there's a gap (as shown). Finish the job by sealing the top edge of the retainer with caulk and then paint to match the door. This fix works on wood and metal doors.

If you have a wood door and want a cleaner look, remove the existing bottom seal and scribe/cut the bottom panel to match the contour of the concrete floor. Seal the freshly cut wood with wood sealer. Then remount the bottom seal. For more information on scribing, go to familyhandyman.com and search for "scribe for a perfect fit."

SEAL RETAINER CHANNEL

GASKET

**Install bottom retainer to seal gaps**
Slide a section of retainer and gasket onto the bottom edge of the garage door. Tilt it until the rubber gasket touches the concrete floor. Then screw the retainer in place.

**VEHICLES & GARAGES**

# GreatGoofs®

## Time for a new clock

A friend of mine gave me a Corvette clock for my garage. At the top of each hour, the clock sounded like a particular year of Corvette revving its engine. One day I was fixing the fan shroud on my 1976 Stingray. I had my hands buried deep in the engine near the fan blades and got to wondering how many people injure their hands working so close to the blades.

Suddenly, I heard the engine start up! I threw my arms straight up into the air, sending my wrench sailing. With my arms still up, I realized that the clock was striking the hour with the sound of a Stingray revving its engine. After my heart slowed down, I sheepishly retrieved my wrench. And then I took the battery out of the clock!

—Eric Millward

## Drive-through surprise

At the end of a concrete-pouring job, my friend Ben and his partner packed away their tools, and his partner took off with the Bobcat and trailer. Ben did one final sweep and noticed his 14-ft. ladder lying in the grass. Since the trailer was gone, he strapped the ladder into the back of his pickup and left.

While driving through town, he saw the bank and remembered that he needed to cash a check. So he pulled in and drove up to the drive-through window. Suddenly he heard a loud BAM! Jumping out to check on the damage, he saw that the tailgate had broken off and the building's stucco overhang had a huge scratch. Luckily, the ladder missed the electronic open/closed sign!

—Mitch Schwitters

## Don't toss the installation manual

My neighbor worked all day long on adjusting his garage door so it would operate more smoothly. I eventually walked over to see how he was doing, and he said he was going nuts. After lubricating the chain and cleaning up the garage door, he couldn't get it to close properly. It would go down about 6 in. and then open right back up!

I asked him if he still had the manual for the opener. "You actually read these things?" he said. "Of course," I told him as I flipped to the last page. Then I whipped out my cell phone and called the manufacturer's help line. The technician had one question: "Is the cover on the opener? Because it won't work without the cover back on."

I looked down, and sure enough, the opener cover was sitting on the floor. My neighbor couldn't get over the fact that he'd spent all day trying to fix something, and the solution was a simple phone call and 30 seconds of work. "You just gotta read the manual," I told him. "Especially the 800 number on the last page."

—Dennis Blair

# GreatGoofs®

## Remodeling mishaps

### Watch your step!

We stripped our bathroom down to the bare walls for remodeling. We also tore up the old subfloor so we could shim and level the floor joists. My friend came over to help with the plumbing, and he tacked down plywood strips over the joists to set the height of the toilet flange. The next day I went into the bathroom to get to work.

You probably know what happened next: I stepped on one of the plywood strips, which broke, causing me to fall between the floor joists into the living room below. The entire suspended ceiling in the living room collapsed and I landed on the couch! As I sat there counting my blessings that I didn't have one scratch on me, my wife came in to find me covered in debris and still holding my hammer. This story gets repeated so often that I told my family to put it on my tombstone!

—John M. Nonnemacher

### Let me out—I'm a pro!

I've worked in construction most of my life, and last year I put a bathroom, wet bar, laundry room and rec room in my basement without any problems. Then it came time to install a prehung door on my basement storage room. Piece of cake, right?

I fit the door in the opening, plumbed it, nailed the jamb into the framing and then nailed on the trim. It took all of five minutes. Then I noticed the 1-in. plastic shipping bolt that held the door closed. I couldn't budge the door or extract the bolt. The only tools I had were a nail gun and a level, so I was stuck! The only way out was to kick the door open (and destroy it in the process). I removed all traces of the door before my wife got home. I met her in the driveway and told her I was almost finished. I just needed to get a door for the storage room. I left out the word "again."

—Ralph Boldyga

### A really relaxing soak

I finished remodeling my master bath and decided to refresh the water jets in my whirlpool tub. They were yellowed with age and the paint was peeling off them, and I hoped a good cleaning would make them shine again. I tried sanding and cleaning them without any success, so I decided to soak them in lacquer thinner overnight to get off the remaining paint. The next day when I went to pull them out of the lacquer thinner, all I found was white gelatinous goo. The lacquer thinner had melted all the jets into one big white glob. It cost me $80 to get new ones.

—Richard Helmes

## Use your head, not your hammer

My husband is a novice handyman with a great heart. So when I asked for a new sink in our upstairs bathroom, he got to work. After two weeks of struggle and leaking pipes, it was done. Whew! But when I turned on the hot water, there was water "hammering." He said he must have loosened a pipe and that it was beating against a stud. He spent the next hour knocking holes in our nice drywall trying to trace the hammering. But he still couldn't find the problem. I then asked him if the hot water valve below the sink was fully open—problem solved. The contractor did a beautiful job of repairing our drywall....

—Mari Nelson

## Too tall to fit

Last year I decided to build a full-length broom closet to match our kitchen cabinets. I wrote down measurements, drew up a plan and got to work in my garage shop. The cabinet was large, so I had my neighbor Bob come by to help me carry it to the kitchen. He grabbed one end and I grabbed the other, and we carried the cabinet through the doorway into the kitchen. We tried to stand it up, but it wouldn't fit under the ceiling. It was too tall! I made it the full floor-to-ceiling height, forgetting to leave some space so it could be tipped up. We carried it back into the garage, where I cut the 4-in. built-in kick panel off the bottom. I then made a separate kick panel to install once the cabinet was tipped into place.

—Jon Greeley

## They watch "Oprah" in the ER

It was a Sunday afternoon about an hour before the Super Bowl and I was cutting small blocks of wood on my chop saw. A piece I had just cut was struck by the spinning saw blade and went flying. The blade threw the block so hard that it broke both my thumb and my thumbnail. Instead of watching the Super Bowl in my favorite chair, I sat in the emergency room watching "Oprah" reruns.

—Jerry Hendershot, Field Editor

# INDEX

# ACKNOWLEDGMENTS

## FOR THE FAMILY HANDYMAN

| | |
|---|---|
| Editor in Chief | Ken Collier |
| Senior Editors | Travis Larson |
| | Gary Wentz |
| Associate Editor | Jeff Gorton |
| Senior Copy Editor | Donna Bierbach |
| Art Directors | Vern Johnson |
| | Marcia Roepke |
| Photographer | Tom Fenenga |
| Production Artist | Mary Schwender |
| Office Administrative | |
|    Manager | Alice Garrett |
| Production Manager | Judy Rodriguez |

## CONTRIBUTING EDITORS

| | |
|---|---|
| Elisa Bernick | Rick Muscoplat |
| Spike Carlsen | Mark Petersen |
| Dave Munkittrick | David Radtke |

## CONTRIBUTING ART DIRECTORS

| | |
|---|---|
| Roberta Peters | Ellen Thomson |

## CONTRIBUTING PHOTOGRAPHER

Paul Nelson

## ILLUSTRATORS

| | |
|---|---|
| Steve Björkman | Jeff Gorton |
| Mario Ferro | Frank Rohrbach III |

## OTHER CONSULTANTS

Charles Avoles, plumbing
Myron Ferguson, drywall
Al Hildenbrand, electrical
Joe Jensen, Jon Jensen, carpentry
William Nunn, painting
Dean Sorem, tile
Costas Stavrou, appliance repair
John Williamson, electrical
Les Zell, plumbing

For information about advertising in *The Family Handyman* magazine, call (646) 293-6150

To subscribe to *The Family Handyman* magazine:
- By phone: (800) 285-4961
- By Internet: FHMservice@rd.com
- By mail: The Family Handyman
  Subscriber Service Dept.
  P.O. Box 6099
  Harlan, IA 51593-1599

We welcome your ideas and opinions.
**Write:** The Editor, The Family Handyman
2915 Commers Drive, Suite 700
Eagan, MN 55121
**Fax:** (651) 994-2250
**E-mail:** editors@thefamilyhandyman.com

Photocopies of articles are available for $3.00 each. Call (800) 285-4961 from 8 a.m. to 5 p.m. Central, Monday through Friday for availability and ordering, or send an e-mail to FHMservice@rd.com.